M000007765

☆ ☆

ENDORSEMENTS

— Peter B. Bensinger, DEA Administrator (1976-1981)

"Charles Lutz's story is an extraordinary one that should be of great interest to all Americans, and to all who respect democracy and the rule of law. He was an outstanding Special Agent and leader within the DEA, and his public service prior to and subsequent to the DEA is a reflection of his commitment to the mission, and to our country."

☆ ☆ ☆ ☆ ☆ ☆

—Paul Brown, Assistant Special Agent-in-Charge,
DEA Houston Field Division (Retired).

Welcome to the real world of DEA special agents, criminals, diplomats and politicians. A difficult book to put down, Charles Lutz captures the history of international drug trafficking and terrorism, much of which you will not read about in other books. He takes you back to the mid-sixties through the early 2000s, and brings to life scenes from his past experiences that are more exciting than anything you will see on TV. It is the most authentic narrative of a government agent's career I have ever read.

☆ ☆ ☆ ☆ ☆ ☆

— Thomas V. Cash, Special Agent-in-Charge,
DEA Miami Field Division (Retired)

"I had the right man on my team in Miami. Charles Lutz's leadership helped reduce the amount of cocaine and marijuana coming into our country through the Caribbean. His story is one of his many accomplishments in a career that literally spans the globe. When it comes to international drug law enforcement, Lutz knows what he's talking about."

☆ ☆ ☆ ☆ ☆ ☆

— Gary Fouse, DEA Special Agent (Retired) and author.

"This book is more than just an account of one DEA agent's outstanding and distinguished career. It provides a valuable history of a great law enforcement agency, the Drug Enforcement Administration, and an overview of the evolving drug threat worldwide. It is the best book I have ever read about international drug law enforcement written by a DEA special agent. I am proud to have worked with Charles Lutz and to be his friend."

☆ ☆ ☆ ☆ ☆ ☆

— Stephen H. Greene, DEA Deputy Administrator (Retired)

"Charles Lutz reveals a wealth of knowledge about the complex history and difficult mission of illegal drug suppression efforts. He had a long and distinguished career as a Special Agent in the Drug Enforcement Administration, serving at many of DEA's most challenging posts, both domestically and overseas, and in senior positions at headquarters and in the field."

☆ ☆ ☆ ☆ ☆ ☆

— John H. Kramer, Emeritus Professor of Sociology and Criminology, Pennsylvania State University

"Charles Lutz takes the reader along his career path from Vietnam through his distinguished career in the DEA and to his latest crusade to recognize the contributions of Harry Anslinger, the first head of the Federal Bureau of Narcotics. Readers will be inspired by Charles's dedication at each stage of his career. His story gives us an inside look into the career of one of many unsung heroes who have devoted and risked their lives to strengthen our country."

☆ ☆ ☆ ☆ ☆ ☆

☆ ☆

— John C. McWilliams, Professor of History, Penn State U. (Retired)

"Charles Lutz — whose own thirty-two-year career with the DEA included extensive experience in the United States and abroad with tours in Southeast Asia, the Middle East, and Central and South America overseeing jungle operations — accords Anslinger his place as a formidable figure in shaping federal drug control initiatives. Anyone interested in the history and nature of federal drug enforcement will benefit from Lutz's use of archival documents and his access to other DEA agents as he recognizes Anslinger's extraordinary career and legacy in federal drug enforcement."

☆ ☆ ☆ ☆ ☆ ☆

— Rick Scovel, TSA Assistant Federal Security Director (2002-2005)

"Charles Lutz could have devoted this entire book to those turbulent times for the Transportation Security Administration. What struck me and his staff was his diplomacy and patience with the politicians and their appointees during his years as Federal Security Director. I probably wouldn't have lasted three months in his position."

UNPOPULAR CAUSES

☆ ☆

TABLE OF CONTENTS

"It is not the critic who counts . . . the credit belongs to the man who is actually in the arena . . . who strives valiantly; who errs, who comes short again and again . . . but who does actually strive to do the deeds . . . who at the best knows in the end the triumph of high achievement, and who at the worst, if he fails, at least fails while daring greatly, so that his place shall never be with those cold and timid souls who neither know victory nor defeat."

– Teddy Roosevelt

☆ ☆

INTRODUCTION

During almost forty years in the government arena, I strove for high achievement, dared greatly at times, enjoyed many triumphs, and suffered a few defeats. I faced the war in Vietnam, the war on drugs, and the war on terror, all considered unpopular causes by one group or another. I hadn't been deterred, though. Being unpopular didn't mean they were wrong.

Vietnam was a peace-keeping mission that escalated into a full-blown war, perhaps the most unpopular in our history. I sat on the bench in Saigon for six months, itching to get into the fight, and then blustered my way onto the field only to find I still had to finagle my way into combat. Those wartime experiences built my self-confidence and prepared me for a career in government service in which I was to face many more foes.

When I left Vietnam, it wasn't yet entirely done with me! Several years later, I penetrated anti-Vietnam War protesters on the National Mall in a little known, secret operation of the Nixon Administration to shut down their drug-infused demonstrations. Then twenty years after the war had ended, in an extraordinary turn of events, I traveled to Hanoi to help normalize relations with my former enemy.

For thirty-two years after Vietnam, I waged another unpopular war — the one on drugs – a war that has lasted longer than all our military wars combined. I battled drug traffickers in virtually every region of the world where drugs were produced for or transited to the United States. I conducted criminal investigations on both coasts as well as overseas, twice posted in Southeast Asia, and once in the Middle East. From stateside, I managed

☆ ☆

drug interdiction operations in the Caribbean, and for four years ran DEA's jungle operations in South and Central America — the most unpopular operation in the DEA's history. And I endured more than my fair share of "suit" time in Washington. After run-ins with ruthless drug traffickers, organized crime thugs, and policymakers in Washington, I'm still not certain which of them had been the more formidable adversary!

After the tragedy of 9-11, I fought two battles against international terrorism. In the first one, I was hired by the TSA to help secure America's air transportation system from another terrorist attack. At one of the nation's largest airports, I was trusted to see that passengers were being thoroughly screened, airport authorities and air carriers were acting in compliance with federal security regulations, and appropriate law enforcement responses were being made to security incidents. In those early years, it was an agency unpopular with not only airport authorities, air carriers and local police, but with the flying public.

And then I parlayed my military, law enforcement, and airport security experience into one last hoorah back overseas where my life's adventures had begun. Hired by the State Department to bolster the law enforcement capabilities of the Philippines in their war against international terror, I soon realized that to get the police into the fight a new law would need to be passed and government policies changed — the latter not a particularly popular idea with the host nation's military leadership, or even among some of my American colleagues.

After my full-time working career had ended, I battled in both the government and public arenas to have the record and reputation of the first Commissioner of Narcotics restored. He had been ignored by history, forgotten by his hometown denizens, forsaken by his descendants in drug law enforcement, and disparaged by those who hated the legacy he left behind.

So, my story is about the Vietnam War seen from three sides — that of a Saigon warrior, a combat warrior, and a reconciler of the differences between our two nations. It's an episodic tale about the adventures of a narcotics agent roaming the world of drug law enforcement that takes you into the heart of some legendary, award-winning investigations and interdiction operations; behind the scenes of some little-known historic events; and glimpses the hierarchy of the nation's premier drug agency. Then it dissects some of the struggles in securing the air transportation system after 9-11 and reveals one of the foibles in our nation's fight against international terrorism. My story ends with bringing a forgotten national hero out from the shadows.

It all began in Vietnam.

CHAPTER 1 -

SAIGON WARRIOR

I almost got myself killed. Moments after I jumped off the helicopter, the enemy decided to make Swiss cheese of the runway.

The whooping of the whirlybird's rotor blades had faded away. It was pitch black and deathly silent as I strolled across the airfield toward the base camp. Then I heard a faint thud followed by a popping sound and knew instantly what it was. A round had been dropped down a mortar tube, struck a primer that ignited a charge, and launched a hi-explosive round toward its target. I only hoped the target wasn't me.

I heard the whistle of the round in flight, and then saw a blinding flash at the far end of the runway followed by a thunderous, ear-shattering explosion that shook me to my core. It ripped a huge gouge out of the tarmac, flipped chunks of macadam into the air, and no doubt sprayed shards of lethal shrapnel in every direction. I had nowhere to hide. All I could do was run.

A second explosion immediately followed the first but at the opposite end of the runway. Then two more. There must have been mortar teams bracketing the airstrip, starting at each end and working their deadly rounds toward the middle. The alternating explosions sounded like the footsteps of two mythical giants storming toward each other.

They were trying to pockmark the runway to make it useless for landing aircraft. From what I could see, they were doing a pretty good job of it; I just didn't want to be part of the collateral damage. I continued running across the airstrip with one hand holding down the steel pot on my head and the other gripping the butt of the holstered .45 caliber pistol slapping my side.

They say you never hear the one that kills you. I don't know how anybody knows that. However, I was strangely relieved to hear the whistle of each round in flight.

I was gasping for air. The base camp was just across the road now. The gate guards would be hunkered down, uncertain as to whether it was an attack on the airfield or the prelude to an assault on our compound. I yelled the password as I approached, praying they would hear me over the din. To my immense relief, the barbed-wire-topped gate slowly cracked ajar.

I headed for the nearest bunker and jumped inside. When the bombardment had ceased and the all-clear signal sounded, I gathered up my belongings and headed to the bunkhouse. That was enough excitement for one night, and probably the closest I ever came to earning a Purple Heart — even though that had not been one of my goals. However, getting myself into that situation was on me.

I had been assigned some cushy jobs in Saigon for the first six months in-country. Then my big mouth got me transferred to the boonies. Now I was getting the taste of battle for which I had volunteered. The trick was to survive.

It had been eight months since I boarded an airplane at Philadelphia's International Airport, the first time in my life I had been in one. I was a bundle of emotions. I wasn't crazy about

☆ ☆

the idea of going to Vietnam. I guess I was sensing my mortality. At the same time, I was proud to be a newly minted Army lieutenant, and anxious to test my courage on the battlefield as legions before me had done.

After an overnight at Travis Air Force Base near San Francisco and already feeling like an experienced globetrotter, I boarded a chartered Continental Airways Boeing-707 for the remainder of the trip halfway around the world. The planeload of GIs mostly dozed, played cards and joked around. But once we started circling over rice paddies, the chatter quieted down. The "Fasten Seat Belt" sign came on, signaling no turning back. After having read media accounts in the *Stars and Stripes* of the post-Tet offensive battles on the way over, I fully expected to step off the plane into combat. The previous month, May 1968, had been the bloodiest of the entire war. I braced myself for landing onto Bien Hoa Airfield's runway.

As we taxied to the end, the pilot told us to line up in the aisle and disembark as soon as the door opened. Once the plane stopped, portable stairs were pushed alongside. Bleary-eyed and exhausted from the long flight, we rushed out the door, duffel bags slung over our shoulders, and took cover in a ditch alongside the runway. Workers quickly unloaded our footlockers from the cargo hold. Then the pilot wheeled the plane around, gunned the engines, and took off down the runway like a race car driver at Daytona Motor Speedway. The jet lifted off in an almost vertical climb that I hadn't imagined possible. Obviously, the pilot didn't want to stick around long enough to draw enemy fire.

Once the plane had disappeared, an eerie calm fell over the airfield. We dusted ourselves off and walked under the scorching sun to a wooden barrack in a copse of palm trees where a staff sergeant with a clipboard checked off names. When he got to mine, he mumbled, "Oh no, not another intelligence staff officer." I wasn't expecting to hear that. I had been told they needed guys like me in Vietnam.

It was the Army ROTC cadre at Penn State that had recommended I sign up for the Intelligence Branch. They said it was a natural for a Political Science major. Among the Branch's occupational specialties, two were right in my wheelhouse: Foreign Area Studies that tracked the political, social and economic environments of the countries in which the Army might have to operate, which could be almost anywhere in the world; the other was Counterintelligence that focused on foreign intelligence threats to the Army.

I received the disappointing news that I hadn't gotten either one of them as I was finishing up the Infantry Officer Basic Course at Ft. Benning, Georgia. Instead, I was ordered to a six-week Tactical Intelligence Staff Officer Course at Ft. Holabird, the Army Intelligence School located on a wharf in the Baltimore Harbor, then straight to Vietnam. They said there was a critical need for intelligence staff officers.

I learned later that the critical need had been the result of an ill-fated plan to expand the size of the newly reconstituted Intelligence Branch. The Intel brass had laid claim to all the infantry battalion S-2 slots, intelligence staff officer positions, intending to fill them with their own officers. It made perfectly good sense to have trained intelligence officers in those positions. However, the Intelligence Branch weenies had apparently forgotten to mention it to the infantry that traditionally filled the S-2 positions with their own young officers. Giving up those slots would reduce the total number of infantry officers needed and thereby reduce the total number of general officers needed to command them. Being no fools, the infantry generals refused.

☆ ☆

The Intelligence Branch honchos must not have gotten the word because they kept churning out Tactical Intelligence Officers with nowhere to put them. Now I was part of the excess baggage.

So, I said to the sergeant at Bien Hoa, "Hey, that's okay. If I'm not needed, I'll just wait here and catch the next flight home."

Apparently, he wasn't able to take a joke. "Don't worry, lieutenant. I'm sure they'll find something for you to do."

The relative calm at Bien Hoa was beginning to steady my nerves. But as I boarded the bus for Saigon, I noticed chicken wire covering the windows to prevent hand grenades from being tossed inside. That brought me back to reality. I was in a war zone. However, the bus ride from Bien Hoa into Saigon began to alter my view once again.

I expected to see families cowering in sand-bagged bunkers along the roadsides fearing for their lives. Instead, it was a hive of human activity. Motorbikes buzzed around our bus like swarms of bees, some stacked so high with precariously balanced goods it was a miracle they didn't tip over. Others had entire families straddled on them from handlebar to back fender like in a circus act. Petite young women in traditional *ao dai* pantsuits sat daintily aboard motor scooters winding their way through the traffic, their long black hair and silky tunics flowing gracefully behind them. Three-wheeled motorized tuk-tuks darted around Pedicabs, and mini-bus drivers raced each other from corner to corner to pick up waiting fares.

Old men with wispy white beards, clad in pajamas, sat outside shop-houses playing cards, and women chatted at curbside while keeping watchful eyes on children playing nearby. Peddlers hawked all manner of strange-looking foodstuff from wooden carts, including durians, that awful-smelling green fruit with a prickly rind. It was certainly a different scene from what a kid who grew up in southwest Philadelphia was used to seeing, but no one appeared threatened.

The bus dropped me off at The Ponderosa, headquarters of the 525 Military Intelligence Group that controlled all the Intelligence Branch officers in Vietnam. The Ponderosa's formidable stone walls were topped with embedded shards of broken glass and strands of barbed wire. Cinder block guard posts at each corner provided fields-of-fire in all directions. A Vietnamese soldier rolled aside a triangular barbed-wire barricade to allow our bus to enter.

The Ponderosa, Headquarters of the 525 Military Intelligence Group, Saigon, South Vietnam.

Several white villas with red tiled roofs and dark green doors and shutters sat in the compound with white-washed stones lining the paths between them. A majestic-looking tree spread its arms across the meticulously groomed lawn, and flowering red bougainvillea along the interior walls filled the air with a fragrant scent. It was an oasis in a war-torn country.

☆ ☆

The Saloon, watering hole at the Ponderosa, Saigon, South Vietnam.

I stowed my gear in my room and moseyed down to the saloon for a cold one. With the swinging cafe doors and mirrored oaken bar, it could have been the set for a Wild West movie. A raven-haired waitress sat a Bière 33 down in front of me, Vietnam's national brew, one of the legacies of French colonialism along with baguettes and cognac. I lit up my first Lucky Strike of the day (by the time I left Vietnam, I was smoking two packs a day) and leaned back in my chair to take stock of what I had seen so far. Suddenly gunfire erupted behind the compound.

I dove under the table, cradling a newly issued M-16 in my arms. I was trying to figure out what my next move should be when a fellow lieutenant stooped down and, stifling a laugh, said, "You must be new around here?"

"Just got here," I sheepishly replied. Then I noticed no one else in the room had paid any attention to the noise. A captain tossing darts hadn't missed a throw.

"They've got a couple of Viet Cong trapped in a gas station around the corner," the lieutenant said. "You wanna go watch?"

☆ ☆

"Are you kidding me?" I didn't want to go anywhere near the gunfire. But not wanting to be the wimp, I put on my flak vest and helmet, slung the M-16 over my shoulder, and followed the unarmed, uncovered lieutenant out the front gate.

We rounded the corner and stopped at a police barricade. Two tanks had demolished what had been a gas station, identifiable only by the bullet-riddled Caltex sign left standing. The gunfire was coming from a squad of Vietnamese soldiers taking target practice on the rubble to be certain none of the suspected Viet Cong infiltrators thought to be inside had survived. But it was the onlookers who caught my attention.

Dozens had gathered to gawk, like spectators at a Fourth of July fireworks display, and local entrepreneurs were taking advantage of the crowd. One woman squatted on the sidewalk next to a steaming cauldron of vegetable beef soup, *pho*, the Vietnamese national dish, ladling it into plastic bowls while her customers sat on the curb eating. A peddler sold paper kites and balloons from a wooden pushcart to schoolkids dressed in blue and white uniforms. A bearded, turbaned Indian man in a white gauze vest and pantaloons hawked seeds and nuts from a compartmented wooden tray strapped to his neck. Despite the war, life was carrying on. It wasn't anything like what I had expected to find.

After a day or two of marking time, I got my first assignment. The "Don't worry, lieutenant. I'm sure they'll find something for you to do," turned out to be a job with Capital Military Advisory Team 100, code-named Operation Hurricane. It was a hastily set up operation in an abandoned French boarding school to prepare for the defense of Saigon in the event of another Tet Offensive. I hopped a ride to and from work with an Army major. While we were forbidden to ride in open-air local conveyances, such as trishaws that would make us easy targets for would-be assassins, driving through the bustling, pedestrian-clogged streets of Saigon in the major's topless jeep was apparently okay. Rank had its privileges.

I was charged with reviewing overnight intelligence reports of enemy sightings that might indicate a threat to Saigon. Before I got the job, a very capable specialist fourth-class intelligence analyst had been doing it by himself. Now he was to assist me. I took the job seriously, but we were receiving so few reports of any consequence there wasn't enough to keep the two of us busy, but at least they had found a spot for one of the intel branch's excess bags. Me.

What relieved my monotony was watching the helicopters ferry the "who's who" of the American and Vietnamese governments with each landing and takeoff on the compound's soccer field. They were the ones who were regularly seeking updates on the latest threats to Saigon.

Operation Hurricane, headquartered in a repurposed former French boarding school with soccer field, parade ground, and helicopter landing pad, Saigon, South Vietnam.

☆ ☆

As I became more and more comfortable with my surroundings, I began to explore the nearby neighborhoods. While there was always the risk of enemy sympathizers having infiltrated into the populace, like the VC in that gas station on the day I had arrived, Saigon was pretty peaceful. I wandered around taking in the sights and sounds of daily life in the cosmopolitan, French-influenced city. Its ornate buildings on wide, tree-lined boulevards had earned it the nickname "Paris of the Orient," although it was now teeming with homeless refugees from the hostilities in the countryside.

Life was good for soldiers posted in Saigon. There were separate clubs for officers and enlisted personnel at Ton Son Knut Air Base, each featuring top name entertainment from Hollywood to Motown, and sports celebrities occasionally flown in to sign autographs. The Air Force controlled the air bridge so had first dibs on everything. My favorite hangout, though, was a little O Club not far from the airport that on weekends featured a Filipino band. When I closed my eyes, I couldn't tell them from the singers they mimicked, from Elvis to James Brown to Dusty Springfield.

But I could never seem to win on those damn slot machines. After the war some senior NCO's pleaded guilty to skimming money from the proceeds. They probably walked away with more than a few of my Military Payment Certificates — issued in lieu of U.S. currency so it couldn't get into the hands of the enemy and be used to buy weapons in international markets.

And then there was the main PX in Cholon, Saigon's Chinatown, the soldier's Walmart. It had everything— everything, that is, unless a South Korean unit had gotten there first. Unfettered access to the PX must have been part of the deal to get the Republic of Korea to fight in Vietnam alongside our

☆ ☆

Australia, Philippines and New Zealand allies. And they cleaned it out every chance they got. The irony was that Korean soldiers seldom fought. Having a reputation for ferocity, wherever they were stationed was considered among the safest places in Vietnam because the enemy kept its distance.

There was the Rex Hotel downtown on Lam Son Square, a Bachelor Officer Quarters. Its outdoor rooftop restaurant offered a steak, baked potato and salad for two bucks. There was always a live band, with the nightly fireworks on Saigon's outskirts as the backdrop — flares to illuminate suspected enemy movements and exploding ordnance once their positions were thought to have been detected. The war seemed very distant from atop the Rex, almost in a different universe.

The local bar scene was an indelible part of the city's fabric. For young girls who had fled from rice paddies to Saigon with no education or skills, there were few options other than working in a bar or massage parlor. Barroom companionship could be purchased for the price of a Saigon tea. Their sales pitch wasn't very subtle: "No P (referring to Piaster, the local currency) no tea, no tea no me." Roughly translated, if you don't buy me a glass of tea for the price of a brandy for which I get a cut, then 'Hit the road, Jack.'" The duration of companionship was in direct proportion to the number of Saigon teas purchased. Or a girl could be bought out of the bar for a "date" by paying the Mama-san for the bar's lost revenue. One could also go to any one of dozens of massage parlors for a scrub and a rub by girls of similar circumstance.

Not to excuse prostitution and human trafficking, but it's hard for me to blame lonely GIs stationed halfway around the world from home for whom it may have been their first, and maybe last opportunity to get laid. The temptation was just too great. But it did tarnish the image of American soldiers who had been stationed there, creating a legacy of unwanted children reared without their fathers and banished to the streets by their mothers.

Jungle fatigues were the norm, even in urban Saigon. Rank and branch insignia and the equivalent Vietnamese military rank were sewn on uniforms, their muted colors particularly important for officers who led small units into combat. Lieutenants had the highest casualty rate per capita of the war because the enemy had figured out that the lieutenant was the guy standing next to the soldier with the radio on his back. Wearing shiny gold or silver bars would have made them even easier targets.

During my in-briefing at the 525 MI Group, I'd been told not to wear Intelligence Branch insignia. "If they catch you, you'll go a little further north a little faster," the sergeant had opined. "They won't know that you probably don't know a damn thing that can help them." As a result, most of the intelligence officers I knew wore the crossed rifles of the Infantry Branch, by far the most common insignia. The only insignia we couldn't wear were those afforded special treatment under the Geneva Accords, such as Medical Corps and Chaplain.

I gave it some thought. While crossed rifles would certainly make me more inconspicuous, Saigon had a midnight curfew from which only one group of officers was exempt. So, I became perhaps the only intelligence officer in Vietnam to wear the crossed pistols of the Military Police. While I seldom stayed out past curfew, those crossed pistols did come in handy a few times. Instead of taking down my name, rank and serial number, the White Mice (Saigon police, so called because of the white helmets they wore) would salute before sliding the vehicle barricade out of my way.

☆ ☆

It didn't take long for the top brass to figure out that there wasn't going to be another Tet Offensive, particularly given the beating the enemy had taken during the first one. Consequently, Operation Hurricane was shut down and I was transferred to the 519th Intelligence Battalion at the foot of the Binh Loi Bridge. I hadn't been given a choice of assignments and was disappointed to miss an opportunity to go out to the field. But I figured my new job would have to be a little more interesting than the last one. It only got worse.

I was assigned as the Assistant S-4/Property Book Officer, essentially a quartermaster, a job for which I had no training, no intellect, and no interest. I kept track of the million-dollar inventory of desks, chairs, jeeps and weapons of the 525 MI Group — about as exciting for me as watching lotus blossoms grow. If the VC weren't going to kill me, the boredom would. But it was a responsible job, subject to audits, and had to be taken seriously. If the 519th wasn't going to give me the taste of battle I longed for, at least it had some perks.

Decorating for Christmas at the 519th Support Battalion compound, Bien Loi, South Vietnam, December 1968.

Close to Saigon, I continued to live there and, as Property Book Officer, requisitioned myself a brand-new jeep for the commute. I was reunited with a buddy from Ft. Holabird, Bob Cope, who was the Assistant Operations Officer, S-3. And I got to travel a bit, once taking my sergeant with me to pick up a load of M-16's from an arsenal in the picturesque seaside town of Qui Nhon.

I was coming up on "one-eighty and a wake up" — with half the days of my one-year tour of duty about to end. I was struggling with mixed emotions. I had a safe and comfortable lifestyle in Saigon that would be the envy of many in the field. But I felt I wasn't making any contribution to the war. More troubling, I wouldn't have the chance to prove myself in combat, never knowing how I'd react under fire. While at the 519th, twice I had requested re-assignment to the field, but nothing came of it. Being at the halfway mark, I pretty much had accepted my fate as a Saigon Warrior.

Then one night, near to New Year's Eve, after having a few too many beers in a downtown Saigon bar, I boisterously, half-jokingly, lamented to Bob Cope and another buddy, "You know, if they had me out in the field instead of stuck here in Saigon, this war would've been over a long time ago!"

"Maybe I can help you lieutenant?" piped up some guy sitting at the end of the bar. He turned out to be a personnel sergeant at MACV, Military Assistance Command Vietnam, headquarters for soldiers assigned as advisors to the South Vietnamese military. When he left the bar that night, he took with him my name, rank and serial number scribbled on a cocktail napkin and left with me a promise that he would try to switch me with the next tactical intelligence lieutenant that came through his command. I thought he was just being a wise ass.

☆ ☆

I had enough brews that night to have forgotten the incident until a few weeks later when the orders came through. *What's this all about? Where the hell's Xuan Loc?* Then it came back to me. My big mouth had accomplished what the system had been incapable of doing. I was finally going to the field. However, getting my wish meant I would have to trade my comfort and security for the unknown, and that was a little disconcerting. But it was too late to worry about that now. And I was confident I would be able to handle whatever was thrown my way.

For better or worse, I would be getting a new start with MACV's 87th Advisory Detachment . . . in some God-forsaken place, the name of which I couldn't even pronounce.

☆ ☆

CHAPTER 2

FIREFLIES

It was no Saigon. That's for sure. Although a provincial capital, Xuan Loc was a one water-buffalo town with rutted dirt streets and wooden shanties instead of the boulevards and villas I had become used to seeing. A few meagerly stocked shop-houses lined the main street offering farm equipment, seed and feed to the local rice and mushroom farmers. A tin-roofed open-air food market sat in the middle of the town square with stalls for meat, fish and vegetable vendors.

There was only one restaurant in town. Our Vietnamese counterpart took us there for dinner once. The cuisine turned out to be pretty tasty, although I didn't have a clue as to what I was eating. Our medic had warned us to stay away from anything that wasn't served piping hot, definitely not the salads — the lettuce and other vegetables likely fertilized with night soil. I didn't have to be told that. I learned my lesson after having shared a plate of chateaubriand and fried potatoes with some pals at a French restaurant on Tu Do Street in Saigon. Being the only one who had eaten the side salad I spent the next three days at the 5th Field Army Hospital with a bout of gastroenteritis.

And there was only one bar in town, a rundown cinder block building with a hand-painted sign that read, "Soda Suds Booze Broads / Drop in and Sip a Few," with no explanation as to which

☆ ☆

ones were to be sipped. Each time I rode by there would be a few young girls standing outside beckoning customers. But it looked to be a dark and dank place into which no one in their right mind would venture. I always wondered if they sold Xuan Loc tea.

Xuan Loc was home to the 18th Infantry Division of the Army of the Republic of Vietnam. They had originally been designated the 10th. However, during the war the term "Number 10" came to signify "the worst" in bar maids' Pidgin English — "You, Number 10, GI," they'd say if you didn't buy them a Saigon Tea. So, the South Vietnamese Army changed its designation to the 18th to remove the stigma. But it hadn't done much to improve the morale.

MACV Team 87 Airfield, Xuan Loc, South Vietnam.

MACV's 87th Advisory Detachment was housed in a self-contained, chain link fenced-in compound. There were a few Quonset huts at the rear of the encampment with offices for the base commander and his staff and some storage lockers. We slept in screened-in wooden bunkhouses with built-in canvas

☆ ☆

cots that reminded me of the ones we'd slept on at Boy Scout camp. There were outdoor latrines, and cold showers courtesy of a water tanker truck. The mess tent had a table for officers, and separate areas for the officer's and enlisted men's "happy hours." Even in a small camp like ours, fraternization between the ranks was frowned upon.

The chow wasn't half bad. Every once in a while, we even ate steak — our mess staff having traded captured North Vietnam flags, AK-47's, and other war memorabilia for cases of them with the supply clerks in Bien Hoa who were too far from the action to find their own souvenirs. And booze was cheap. Once, we received a pallet with cases of Ballantine beer. The copper-colored cans apparently hadn't done very well under the relentless sun. It sold for five cents a can but was so bitter they would have had to pay me to drink it.

Local hires from town did all the chores — laundry, yard work, even barbering. It took some getting used to being shaved by a Vietnamese barber with a razor blade in hand, whose loyalty, for all I knew, may have morphed between barber-by-day and Viet Cong-by-night.

An occasional enemy probe of the compound was commonplace, more harassment than anything — a few shadowy figures in the dark, some shots exchanged. Although we lost a few in the field during operations, there hadn't been a serious assault on our compound. The nearby artillery base made a much more attractive target and hadn't been so lucky. It was overrun one night resulting in lives lost and the big guns silenced for quite a while. That kept us from getting complacent.

At one point we received intelligence that as many as four North Vietnamese Infantry Divisions were in our Province with orders to capture Xuan Loc. The base commander ordered our entire detachment to sleep in the bunkers until the threat abated. Sleeping on that hard dirt floor for three weeks in the company of every insect known to tropical Vietnam made those canvas cots in the bunkhouses feel like memory foam mattresses.

MACV Team 87 compound officer's billets, Xuan Loc, South Vietnam.

It was the same routine every day. I would travel in convoy to the 18th ARVN Division Headquarters compound each morning, spend the day working in their Intelligence shop along with a captain, another lieutenant, a sergeant, and a handful of enlisted men, and be back to the base camp before nightfall. We pretty much did the same things I had been doing in Saigon at Operation Hurricane — sorting through reports of overnight firefights and enemy sightings, collating and analyzing the information to figure out where the enemy might be hiding.

If we thought they were in any one of the dozens of Michelin rubber tree plantations, we were out of luck. The plantations were "off limits" to military operations, a concession, I had been told, to both the French and South Vietnamese Governments to protect the precious trees. Ironically, that provided safe haven for the folks who were causing all the problems for the South Vietnamese and had run the French out of the country fifteen years earlier.

Our intelligence assessments would be given to the Vietnamese colonel in charge of the intelligence section who would then pass them along to his counterpart in the operations section, who could use our reports to point his troops in the right direction. They would also be used to develop targets for our allotment of B-52 strikes, Operation Arc Light, and our Firefly missions.

After we called in one of the B-52 strikes, I was anxious to see the results. So back at the base camp, as the hour neared, I climbed the ladder of the camp's water tower to a walkway near its dome and sat down to wait. I couldn't see or hear the planes approach. Then suddenly a hundred bombs exploded across a swath of land a half mile long and a quarter mile wide. Each blast bubbled up a cloud of smoke blanketing the entire strike zone. Our intelligence indicated an enemy encampment had been set up there recently, and had they not gotten dug in quickly enough, not one of them would have likely survived.

After I climbed down from the tower, I realized how stupid I had been. Having silhouetted myself against the tower I made myself a perfect target for an enemy sniper. Worse yet, if I had repeated it, and the enemy caught on, each time I climbed the tower would have signaled to them when, and in which direction the next bombing run was to occur. From then on, I stayed off the water tower.

Firefly missions were more up close and personal than the B-52 strikes, but no less deadly. They were designed to ferret out and destroy the enemy at night when they most often conducted

☆ ☆

their operations and moved their manpower and equipment. Fireflies had a one-two punch of find'em and fix'em.

The find'em was a UH-1H Iroquois "Huey" helicopter jury-rigged with a powerful searchlight, a cluster of landing lights from a C-130 cargo aircraft or a xenon searchlight from an M-60 tank. Upon reaching a target zone, the searchlight would be flipped on and light up the battlefield like Bourbon Street during Mardi Gras. The lamp could illuminate up to an acre of ground depending on the helicopter's altitude.

The fix'em was an AH-1 Apache Cobra gunship that loomed above the Huey ready to strike. Variously equipped with mini-machine guns, grenade launchers, 40 mm cannon and rocket launchers, the "snakes," as they were called, were arguably the meanest flying machines of the war, more vicious than their namesakes implied. And they were as thin as runway models, with armored cockpits only thirty-six inches wide, making them less vulnerable while engaging the enemy.

A few of the lieutenants in the detachment went out on foot patrols, but they were Infantry officers. And although I had gone through the same Infantry Officer Basic Course as they had, there was no way I would be allowed to advise a Vietnamese infantry unit. But one of the Intelligence lieutenants did go out on the Firefly missions, and he had seen plenty of action. Despite the wisdom of never volunteering for anything, when Doug Vance got transferred to a unit in the Mekong River Delta, I jumped at the chance to replace him.

That first night I briefed the pilots on the general area to be searched, and then climbed aboard the Huey helicopter with a map of suspected enemy locations in my hand and a bit of apprehension in my belly. I buckled into my seat and donned the radio headphones to communicate with the crew. We followed a

☆ ☆

meandering river running through the triple canopy jungle to the target area. On cue, the door gunner flipped on the searchlight that illuminated a small wooden boat loaded with crates. They had to be enemy. There was a sundown curfew for the locals who knew anything moving in the jungle at night would be fair game for us.

I watched as four of the crewmen frantically paddled toward shore while a fifth stood on the bow firing what appeared to be an ancient long rifle up toward the only thing he could see, the light. And here I was, sitting in a canvas seat, right next to it. Not wanting anyone to think I was afraid, I nonchalantly slipped the steel helmet off my head and sat on it.

Suddenly the Cobra gunship swooped down below us, its cannons blazing. The boat disintegrated in seconds; plumes of smoke billowed in the air. I couldn't tell if the crew had jumped into the water or had been blown into it. They may have survived. Probably not. But what little was left of the wooden boat and its cargo could have been stuffed into a duffel bag.

We hunted at least once a week, sometimes more often, the number of missions based upon the enemy activity in our area. The results were not always as readily apparent as on that first night. But in all, the missions gave me the excitement I had been longing for and my share of war stories to tell my buddies once I got back home. Finally, I felt as if I was making a contribution.

Over time I got to know the pilots by name, and one night the Cobra pilot invited me to be his gunner. Before we took off, he showed me how the controls for the weapons systems worked. He warned me not to touch anything until he gave the order. I got more excited by the minute.

I buckled into the gunner's armored seat up front in the two-man cockpit. The pilot climbed into the elevated seat directly

☆ ☆

behind me. While the Huey plodded along below us, the pilot showed off the speed and maneuverability of his bird. It could top out at 170 miles per hour and do loop-de-loops better than any ride at a Six Flags amusement park. I think he was trying to see just how much I could stomach. After months of mess hall chow, I found I could stomach just about anything.

Then suddenly the searchlight from the Huey sparked to life lighting up the field below, catching several armed men in the open. They scattered. While the Huey engaged several of them with its M-60 machine gun, one of the enemy, dressed in shorts, t-shirt and sandals, the typical uniform of the farmers-by-day and soldiers-by-night Viet Cong, shimmied up a solitary palm tree to hide among its fronds.

The Cobra pilot swooped down and hovered in front of the tree like a coiled snake ready to strike and then released me to fire. With a burst of adrenalin pumping through my veins, I squeezed the trigger of the 40-millimeter cannon mounted under the forward fuselage. I could barely hear the rounds over the roar of the engine. What I clearly saw, though, were puffs of smoke bursting from the treetop, an AK-47 assault rifle fall to the ground, followed by a lifeless body.

I have no idea how many enemies we killed in those Firefly missions over the four or five months I flew them, but watching the devastation from high above always gave it a bit of detachment. Only that one time had I seen the enemy face-to-face.

I haven't given it a lot of thought over the years. I don't take any pride in it. Given the enormous firepower at my disposal, it hadn't exactly been a fair fight. But I don't have any regrets either. We were at war, and I'm certain that gunman wouldn't have thought twice about turning the tables on me had he been

☆ ☆

given the chance. In fact, he had probably been firing his AK-47 at me from his perch in the tree.

I had just stepped off one of those Firefly missions the night the VC decided to launch mortars across from our base camp at the runway that almost got me killed. During those few terrifying moments, I got to know what it was like to be the hunted instead of the hunter. I was lucky to have survived it. So too had those VC. Had the Firefly team not departed the area minutes before the bombardment began, those mortar teams would have been sitting mongooses for the Cobra gunner.

Viet Cong prisoner, MACV Team 87 airfield, Xuan Loc, South Vietnam.

When I got home, they pinned a Bronze Star Medal to my chest; the buttons almost popped off my shirt. It made me feel like a hero, and my mother thought I was one, but I knew better. I took some chances. So had countless others. The real heroes risked their lives saving others, and many had come home in body bags.

☆ ☆

Army LTC William Hess pinning on the Bronze Star Medal
at Ft. Bragg, North Carolina.

The medal was for meritorious achievement in ground operations against hostile forces during my time at Xuan Loc. In other words, I had done a good job. However, over time it has come to mean much more. It signifies the danger I had faced, and my having coped with it. And the self-confidence that resulted was to serve me well in my next career. It was a blessing. Those without confidence seldom achieve anything.

I spent the last six months of my two-year active-duty obligation at the Continental Tactical Intelligence Command at Ft. Bragg, North Carolina. Before mustering out I was offered a promotion to captain if I signed up for four more years. I was tempted.

I could have easily made a career of the Army. Military service, even Vietnam, had been a positive experience for me. I learned a lot about myself. I matured. In college I was only responsible for myself and hadn't done a very good job of it. In Vietnam, others depended on me. When asked where I grew up, I often said, "Vietnam." In every WWII movie I could recall, the captain was referred to as "the old man." Here I was, barely twenty-four years old. And, it would have been a nice bump in pay. But I turned it down.

It had nothing to do with the unpopularity of the war, the intensity of which had increased after the Tet Offensive. Although we had beaten back the enemy to win a decisive victory, the mounting causalities, and the ability, perhaps the audacity, of the North Vietnamese to conduct such a massive operation startled Americans. The protests had gotten uglier — returning veterans were being disrespected. But no, my reasons for getting out of the Army were much more pragmatic.

By then I had learned that advancement in the Army was much easier for officers well-grounded in a combat arm. I should have started off in the Infantry or Artillery and then specialized in Intelligence. I wasn't about to start over, though. Also, I had read the Sanskrit on the wall! In time, Nixon's "Vietnamization" policy had begun to turn the fight over to the South Vietnamese, and the number of U.S. combat troops was steadily dwindling. Peace talks were underway in Paris. The end to the war was in sight. A RIF (reduction in force) was inevitable. And the first to go would be the reserve officers, like me, not the "ring knockers," the ones who had graduated from West Point. So rather than wait for the bayonet to fall, I decided it best to move on. Once I had made that decision, I pretty much knew what I wanted to do.

The idea of being a cop had always been in the back of my mind. While growing up, whenever the other kids wanted to play cowboys and Indians, I tried to talk them into cops and robbers. Dragnet's Sergeant Joe Friday was my hero, a detective solving crimes with, "Just the facts, Ma'am."

☆ ☆

One of my proudest moments in school had been when Mrs. Cohen, my third-grade teacher, selected me to be a crossing guard. I can still picture myself standing on the corner at 52nd Street and Baltimore Avenue in Southwest Philadelphia with my arms raised, proud as can be to have been entrusted with the safety of my fellow students. I had even given law enforcement some thought when entering college. However, Penn State hadn't offered a Criminal Justice program in that day.

So, there may have been more to my choosing to wear the crossed pistols of the Military Police in Vietnam than just to avoid the Saigon curfew. It may have been an omen of things to come. Certainly, the privileges and courtesies extended to me while wearing the MP insignia hadn't gone unnoticed. But I had no idea which law enforcement agency to shoot for. Then opportunities came like bolts out of the blue . . . the thin blue line, that is.

☆ ☆

CHAPTER 3

THE CARE AND FEEDING OF A NARC

I was getting a haircut in a downtown Philadelphia barbershop and pondering my future. The barber droned on about current events, and then stopped to ask, "Now that you have your college degree, and your military service is behind you, what are you going to do next?"

"I don't know. I'm thinking about getting into law enforcement."

"You might be someone we're looking for," piped up a stranger who had been waiting his turn in the chair.

"Who are you?" I asked, my mind flashing back to that "Good Samaritan" sergeant in that Saigon bar who had gotten me transferred to Xuan Loc.

He introduced himself as Ed Cassidy, a group supervisor with the Bureau of Narcotics and Dangerous Drugs (BNDD), an agency I had never heard of before. He said I might qualify to be a special agent and suggested I stop by the U.S. Customs House to check it out. With nothing to lose, I walked down to 2nd and Chestnut Streets to learn more.

The BNDD was the new kid on the block. Just two years earlier Lyndon Johnson had merged the Food and Drug

Administration's Bureau of Drug Abuse Control into the Treasury's Federal Bureau of Narcotics and settled it into the Department of Justice. The BNDD was charged with enforcing the federal narcotics laws and regulating the pharmaceutical industry. They had offices in almost every state in the union, with nearly ten percent of their agent workforce stationed overseas. Those sent abroad conducted investigations with host nation law enforcement authorities in more than fifty drug source and transit countries around the world. That sounded pretty good to me.

That night I told my mother what I was thinking of doing. She put her foot down. "You can't do anything before talking to Cousin Harry!"

My cousin Harry Fox was the Deputy Police Commissioner of Philadelphia. I didn't know him very well. The last time I saw him was at my father's funeral during my freshman year of college. Fox worked under Commissioner Frank Rizzo who had become nationally renowned during the civil unrest following the assassination of Dr. Martin Luther King. Rizzo was attending a banquet in the ritzy Bellevue Stratford Hotel when the rioting broke out. He was photographed marching out onto Broad Street to take charge of his men dressed in a tuxedo with a nightstick tucked in the cummerbund. He parlayed that tough-guy image into a run for the mayor's job, and soon after was known as "Hizzoner."

"You don't want to get involved in narcotics," Cousin Harry told me from behind his executive desk at the Roundhouse, Philadelphia's Police Headquarters. "There's too much corruption." I wasn't expecting to hear that.

He was likely referring to the Knapp Commission hearings that got some of New York City's finest in trouble . . . or perhaps

☆ ☆

he had in mind some police corruption closer to home. In either case, I didn't know a thing about the Knapp Commission, nothing about drug law enforcement for that matter. In fact, I knew hardly anything about drugs.

Even in college I was oblivious to the drug scene — the amphetamines swallowed by classmates for all-nighters, the marijuana joints passed around in psychedelic-lit rooms — preferring a few beers instead. The first time I saw marijuana up close was when one of my enlisted men tried to sneak some home from Xuan Loc stuffed between the woofers and tweeters in his stereo speaker cabinets.

Harry picked up the phone and got his secret service buddy on the line. After reciting my *curriculum vitae* he said, "He's just the type of guy you're looking for," then hung up, told me his pal was waiting to see me, and wished me luck.

A secretary ushered me into the boss's office where I was told the primary duty of a Secret Service agent was to protect the President. "We do some investigative work as well," he said, "tracking down threats to the President and going after counterfeiters of U.S. currency." He continued further by saying that they had a few agents stationed overseas, primarily to build relationships with counterpart agencies they would have to rely upon for security assistance whenever POTUS traveled abroad. Then he gave me a few forms to fill out. I don't know how much pull he had with his higher ups in Washington, but he pretty much offered me the job.

On my way home I had to laugh. The day before I had only a vague notion of what I wanted to do with my life but not a single job prospect. Now I had two federal law enforcement agencies practically begging me to work for them. I thought maybe if I

☆ ☆

stopped back at the barbershop for a shave, the FBI might make me an offer.

That night I gave it some serious thought. I wanted to be a criminal investigator, and the idea of working overseas really appealed to me. Secret Service agents were primarily bodyguards, and those working overseas did mostly liaison work. FBI agents were investigators, and the bureau had agents stationed abroad as well, doing what I didn't know. But they were looking to hire lawyers and accountants anyway. It wasn't rocket science. The BNDD was the place for me.

President Nixon had doubled the number of BNDD special agent positions in what the media called his "war on drugs," thus the reason they were hiring. The BNDD personnel officer told me I'd first have to pass the Federal Service Entrance Exam, then it would take at least a couple of months to have a background investigation completed. If I passed that, then I'd have to get in line with the other applicants. I thought my chances were pretty good and wasn't happy about the delay. But the wait turned out to be fortuitous.

My mother's next-door neighbor told me the 1970 Census folks were looking to hire crew leaders. Being concerned about how much time I had left until my unemployment checks ran out, I jumped at the chance. To my delight, the bevy of female census enumerators placed under my wing included a cute young brunette named Joy, and her mother Glendora. Joy always said I was attracted to her mother more so than her. Come to think of it, her mother's eye of round roast was to die for. But it was Joy all along who had caught my eye.

Shortly after the Census Bureau job ended, a telegram arrived offering me a slot in a BNDD basic agent training course to begin in June. But by then I had plunked money down with my two best buddies on a cottage for the summer in Margate, New Jersey so asked if I could be rescheduled for a class in the fall. Little did I know it at the time, but there were so many applicants that they were eliminating them for far less than turning down an initial offer. Fortunately for me, I got lucky because they assigned me to a class that would begin in October.

So, I spent the summer drinking seven-for-a-dollar draft beers at Maloney's Tavern and driving to nearby Ocean City where Joy worked that summer. Every Thursday I would drive home in the 1966 Corvette Stingray roadster I had purchased when I got back from Vietnam, pick up one of my renewed unemployment checks, take my golf lesson, and head back down to the shore. Life was very good.

I turned twenty-five the week before I reported to the BNDD National Training Institute, the boot camp for the war on drugs. I didn't expect it to be much of a fight, though. Naively, I thought everyone hated illegal drugs. Over the next thirty-two years I came to learn just how ingrained drug abuse was in our society, of the controversies our actions caused, and how difficult it would be, if not impossible, to actually win a war on drugs.

Fittingly, BNDD headquarters was located on McPherson Square in the heart of Washington's "tenderloin" district. A solemn-looking Civil War General, James Birdseye McPherson, sat on a bronze horse in the building's shadow trying to maintain his dignity in the midst of the drug addicts and hoodlums that surrounded him in the park each evening. Catty corner to the building sat a string of bars and strip joints. DC Mayor Marion Barry had been standing outside one of those bars when the FBI videotaped him from a BNDD headquarters window snorting cocaine, an act that began his slide from political power into

☆ ☆

prison. Maybe the BNDD should have held some of its classes out on that street corner.

I was as qualified as any of the students in the class, the only educational prerequisite being a college degree. It didn't matter in what discipline. Several of my fellow classmates had prior law enforcement experience, but that gave them no advantage. The BNDD actually preferred students with clean slates who could be taught to investigate narcotics crimes "the BNDD way." My having served in the military gave me no advantage either, except for some of the personal attributes it had instilled — like finally learning never to volunteer for anything.

Thirty-six of us started in Class #12, thirty-two finished. Three times during the first several weeks of training, Domestic Training Chief Paul Malherek had summoned a student from the classroom, neither to be seen nor heard from again. We were never told the reason why those students were dropped from the program, but we collectively cringed whenever Malherek stuck his head in the classroom doorway. The fourth student not to graduate quit halfway through the twelve-week course.

The training was designed to teach us the basics of what we would need to know in order to do the job, to be polished off during a year of on-the-job training in the field. We spent a lot of evenings doing vehicular surveillance in the Washington suburbs, mostly following the instructors around. We would trade off the eyeball, the one directly behind the "suspect," and take parallel streets to avoid being discovered. It looked a lot easier in the movies than it was in real life. What they didn't teach us was how to while away the countless hours that were to come, sitting in a G-car watching some mutt's house, drinking coffee from paper cups and eating gag-in-the-bag sandwiches.

46 |

We planned and executed raids. To make one of the raids as true to life as possible, the instructors had rented an apartment in a sleazy tenement building not far from headquarters. A handful of us trainees quietly climbed the rickety stairs with a contrived search warrant in hand and banged on the door yelling, "Federal agents. Open up!" Within seconds we heard toilets flushing throughout the building. There must have been a lot of pissed-off junkies once they learned it had only been a training exercise.

We also spent a lot of time in the gym next door, a former bank building. The ground floor had been turned into a mini-basketball court with a pistol firing range on the top floor. We did some physical training there, mostly improvised, like strengthening our legs by carrying a sandbag up the three flights of stairs every time we went up to practice marksmanship.

Not every lesson was what it had been made out to be. For example, former Philly cop (and amateur boxing champ) John Wilder taught a class in the "sweet science." I'd been in a few fist fights growing up but never learned how to box. Wilder taught us the principles of footwork and balance, how to throw a punch and, most importantly, how to defend ourselves.

I was in pretty good shape in those days, and for the final exam got paired up with a weightlifter, a V-shaped guy with muscles bulging from places I didn't know were supposed to have muscles. I figured I was going to get pounded. Somehow, I would have to survive; backing down wasn't an option. Not only would I flunk the test, but lose face with my classmates.

The match didn't last very long, though. We put on head protectors, touched gloves and, at the bell, swung away. I absorbed my opponent's first few blows then realized I hadn't felt a thing. He couldn't throw a punch — he was muscle bound. That's when I moved in for the kill. His head protector flew off as

☆ ☆

I pummeled him to the floor, and several of my fellow classmates had to pull me off him. Okay, I know I was being a little overly dramatic at the time. But it played well to my buddies, and I hoped with the instructors as well.

It had been my sparring partner who soon quit the course. I realized then that Wilder's class wasn't so much about teaching skills as testing wills. I learned never to take anything for granted, and that regardless of the odds stacked against me, to never back down in a fight. If you're prepared to give or take a beating, you're less likely to have to do either.

The classroom work was important too, but not nearly as exciting. They taught us the history of drug law enforcement and about the BNDD's principal predecessor agency, the Federal Bureau of Narcotics, and its founder Harry Anslinger. Instructors made us aware of our authorities under the Controlled Substances Act that we were about to enforce, and the nuances of its provisions. We learned drug identification and practiced field testing. We studied the recruitment and handling of informants. We learned report writing, being warning that we would have to testify under oath in a court of law to everything we put in writing. No creative writing. We even conducted a mock trial with students as witnesses on the stand.

What surprised me was how little time we spent on undercover work because it was so critical to drug law enforcement. There were just a few practical exercises in which students had the chance to play an undercover role, not nearly enough to give everyone a chance. I guess it was because, for other than a few general principles, like "don't front the money," and "don't lose your surveillance," there really wasn't that much to teach. Like the short game in golf, it's done mostly by feel.

☆ ☆

Undercover was so critical because most other criminal investigations began with a complaint, while drug investigations seldom did. Victims of bank robberies and car thefts complained to the cops, and an investigation was initiated to determine who had done it. Drug crimes were victimless crimes, not that there weren't any victims downstream. However, dealers didn't generally rat on themselves, and users didn't usually have guns stuck to their heads forcing them to indulge, so the cops had to become the victims. The best way to do that was for them to buy dope undercover and then complain to a jury that the guy who sold him the drugs had broken the law.

Undercover work was so important in the BNDD that it had become a rite of passage, a prerequisite to being accepted into the brotherhood of special agents. Every agent was expected to try it, at least once. The bosses liked the case-makers in the office, the guys who were making the arrests and seizures, putting the meat and potatoes on the table; however, it was the successful undercover agents who were the most respected, and envied, by the other agents. I couldn't wait to get my chance.

One afternoon Chief Malherek led two special agents into the classroom who had just received the Attorney General's Award for Distinguished Service, the highest award that could be bestowed upon a special agent within the Department of Justice. Dominic Petrosi and Harry Fullett told us about their investigation that had begun with a wiretap of a telephone in a Chicago tailor shop and ended with the arrests of 135 wholesale cocaine distributors in Chicago, Miami, New York and Los Angeles, and unveiled a network of cocaine producers and smugglers in Latin America. Operation Eagle had been a clarion call of the cocaine epidemic that was about to sweep the nation. I was in awe of those agents!

☆ ☆

We graduated in a downtown government auditorium. Paul Malherek called out our names with his thundering voice, sounding like Michael Buffer announcing a championship fight card. One-by-one we strutted onto the stage to receive our badges and credentials, the symbols of the oath of office we had just taken to support and defend the Constitution of the United States . . . and bear true faith and allegiance to the same. It was the second time I swore that oath, and it gave me the chills to do so once again.

Most of us were sent back to the cities in which we had been hired. That was fine with me. I moved back into my mother's home in the Philadelphia suburb of Drexel Hill where we had moved when I was in high school, not far from Joy's home.

I was assigned to a group of agents supervised by "The Bear," Dick Johnson. We rookie agents were supposed to be tucked under the wing of a senior partner for our first year, someone who could help us take the principles we had learned in class and apply them to real life situations on the street. I actually ended up with ten senior partners, all of whom chipped in to teach me the ropes.

I volunteered to go out on the street as much as I could on the cases the other agents were developing. I tried not to miss an arrest or a raid. It was the best way to learn. On my very first raid, I found the heroin hidden under a bathtub that the other agents had missed. I was the hero that day but knew enough not to gloat.

Most of the work was surveillance. We would follow known drug dealers to try and identify their associates and locate their stash pads. And we would cover agents anytime they worked undercover. I remember many a night sitting in a G-car parked around the corner and down the street from a tavern in the event a distress call was signaled by the undercover agent working inside, all the while wishing I was the one in the bar doing the negotiating.

I would get my turn soon enough. And it would almost get me killed.

☆ ☆

CHAPTER 4

A CLOSE CALL

There was more heroin on the streets of Philadelphia than flour in the Tastykake bakery. It was an epidemic. Not that I was complaining; it was what had gotten me hired. But now that I was part of the effort to clean it up, I wanted to do what I could to sweep it off the streets.

It was not that there weren't other illegal drugs around. Marijuana was prevalent in minority communities and with the younger generation, particularly college aged students. Most of it came across the border from Mexico although a homegrown industry had begun — the cultivation of weed in hot houses with much higher levels of THC, tetrahydrocannabinol, the hallucinogenic ingredient. But no one in the office wanted to work kiddie dope.

There were downers (barbiturates), and uppers (amphetamines), most of them diverted from legitimately produced pharmaceutical supplies and sold out of the back door by sleazy wholesalers and pharmacists. And there were unscrupulous "fat doctors" who pedaled their wares in assembly-line fashion to strung-out housewives. Women waited in line at the front door to be weighed, have their blood pressure taken, hand over their money to the doctor as he asked them how they felt, and then walk out the back door with a bag full of weight-loss amphetamines. That's all that was needed at the time to satisfy the state's medical code.

Timothy Leary's lysergic acid diethylamide, LSD, was just coming onto the scene, a drug of choice among California's flower children, its use encouraged by the Beatles' "Lucy in the Sky with Diamonds" and other hip tunes. However, "real" agents worked heroin. That's what I wanted to do. But that presented some problems.

For one, most of Philly's heroin dealers were either African- or Italian-American, and so were most of the successful undercover agents. They were more readily accepted by the drug dealers from their own tribe. Being of German-Irish-English stock put me at a distinct disadvantage. Since it was unlikely that I would be asked to work undercover in another agent's heroin case, I would have to make one on my own. That presented another problem. I didn't have any informants with which to make a case.

Crooks didn't like to meet strangers, so it usually took someone trusted, someone on the inside, another crook, to make an introduction of someone new on the drug scene. Only the best, most experienced undercover agents could get away with introducing themselves cold turkey. I never worked undercover before, not even in one of the exercises in basic agent training. So finding an informant had to be my top priority.

The best were defendant-informants, admitted felons over whose heads a stretch in the pokey was being held. With the most to lose, they were the easiest to control. But it was a Catch-22. To have a defendant-informant, I first had to make a case.

Then there were informants seeking revenge on someone who had done them wrong, and others who wanted to eliminate their competition. Those scoundrels were hard to trust. Some weirdo

☆ ☆

informants had perverse motives, like looking for an adrenaline high, or just wanting to hang around with cops.

The most common informants were the mercenaries, those who were in it for the money. But they could be treacherous too, willing to provide their services to the highest bidder. Whatever the informant's motivation was, it didn't matter to me. I would have been happy just to have one.

While I was pondering my dilemma, into the office staggered my first potential informant, my first chance to make a heroin case, my first opportunity to work undercover. Hallelujah!

He was ushered into the windowless interview room, but by the time the agent who had offered to help me and I had gotten there, he was slumped in the chair dozing, I slammed the door shut behind us to startle him awake. He mumbled something about knowing a street dealer nicknamed Peewee.

"How'd you meet this guy?" I asked.

"Sold me some dope," he slurred, "A couple days ago."

"Can you introduce me to him?"

"Sure. But it'll cost you."

"We pay for results," I said, "Not promises."

His motivation was obvious. His eyes were rheumy. He had the sniffles. The one side of his nose was bleeding, the skin having been scraped by wiping snot off with his jacket sleeve. He was obviously a mercenary, a heroin addict who needed money for a fix. The red flags began to unfurl. I knew I shouldn't trust a junkie. That's probably why the other agents wanted nothing to do with him. But, anxious to make my first case, I overlooked it.

I wrote him up as a Cooperating Individual, filled out a Personal History form, and took photos and fingerprints. I would send his prints to the FBI to make sure he wasn't a cop killer or a fugitive in another case. And if he double-crossed us, we'd have some personal information to give us a head start in tracking him down.

I checked our index card file. With no computers in those days, our records were typed on 3 by 5 cards, alphabetized by last names, aliases and nicknames, and held in the drawers of a wooden filing cabinet that looked like something you'd see in an old-time pharmacy.

I found a Donald Waters, aka Peewee, a small-time drug dealer who'd been recently arrested by the Philadelphia Police Department. He fit the physical description the snitch had given us. If this Peewee was the same guy, apparently out on bail on a heroin beef, a second offense could tack on more than a just few years at sentencing and maybe be the motivation I would need to get him to cooperate.

If I could turn him into a defendant-informant, I would have him introduce me to his source of heroin, and then keep moving up the ladder. Peewee was definitely on the bottom rung, but he could help me start making the climb.

I didn't think I would need an elaborate cover story. I just didn't want to come across as a junkie, like the guy who would be introducing me. If so, he would expect me to sample the heroin before buying it. I would have to convince him I was a businessman out to make a few bucks. But that line only goes so far.

I eventually came up with the undercover name Charles Howard Link, close enough to my real name that if it was called out in a crowd, I would react to it. I figured that I would wear my rust-colored polyester leisure suit, the fashion rage of the day, with a flowered shirt and penny loafers. Mr. Miami Vice, years ahead of his time.

The next night, I drove the informant to a diner in Camden, New Jersey, in a Cadillac Coupe de Ville seized from another crook that had been put into service just for undercover operations. Half a dozen agents had preceded us to set up surveillance in the neighborhood. We stood in the diner's parking lot. I felt the stainless-steel Smith & Wesson Model 60 five-shot .38 caliber revolver tucked in my waistband, a non-cop looking gun I had purchased with my own money for working undercover. I had wrapped rubber bands about the grip so it wouldn't slip down my pant leg, something else not to have to worry about. The only thing that bothered me now was that I would say something stupid and screw up the deal.

Peewee showed up on time. He was a small guy, as his nickname implied, with a medium dark complexion, medium length black afro, pencil-thin mustache and goatee. He looked street tough, like he could hold his own in just about any fight. He wore a loose-fitting shirt so I couldn't tell if he was carrying, but assumed he was.

His eyes darted around as we talked. I told him I wanted to buy some smack, and if it was as good as the informant said it was, that I'd be back for more.

"I can get you a bundle (twenty-five one-gram bags), but I need the money up front," he said. The going wholesale rate at the time was $7 a bag. I'd sell them for $10 each.

I remembered the golden rule that had been drilled into my head in basic agent training — don't front the money. I told him I'd show him the money once he showed me the dope. I figured the guy with the money should be calling the shots anyway, although to be safe I hadn't brought any money with me in case it was a rip off. He finally agreed, and we set up a meeting for the following night, same time, same place. When we parted, the surveillance team tried to put him to bed, find out where he was living, but he slipped away in the dark.

☆ ☆

I drove the informant back to the office and got him to dictate and sign a statement as to what had transpired that night. It would support my investigative report if the case ever went to trial. Then I gave him five bucks out of my pocket for cab fare home. It wasn't worth the trouble of writing up a Payment for Evidence or Information form for such a small amount of money.

My conversation with Peewee had me a little worried. It wasn't unusual for a drug dealer to want the buyer to front money, if only to make sure the buyer had money. Or maybe he needed the money to buy the dope from his source. Worse yet, maybe he intended to rip me off all along.

The next night I went by myself. Now that Peewee knew me, I figured I would distance the informant from the deal and lessen the chance of him having to testify. The last thing I wanted was for that junkie to be called to the witness stand. He would probably fall asleep.

I stood in the parking lot beside my car waiting and waiting. No Peewee. After about a half hour, one of the surveillance agents drove past and drew a finger across his throat — a not too subtle message for me to get the hell out of there. As much as I hated to give up on Peewee, it wasn't smart for a white guy to be standing on a street corner in that part of Camden with $175 in Official Advanced Funds in his pocket. I drove back to the office, disappointed.

The next morning the lead story in the newspaper jumped off the front page at me — "Donald L. Waters, aka Peewee, while out on bond awaiting trial in a narcotics case was arrested and charged with the slaying of a Philadelphia Bulletin newspaperman during an attempted hold-up outside a bar in North Philadelphia." And there he was. Peewee's mugshot above the fold.

Defendant Donald "Peewee" Waters

No wonder he didn't show up for the drug deal. He had been in jail on a murder rap. He had no intention of selling me anything. He had been planning to rip me off from the get-go. Fortunately, he had gotten locked up hours before we were to meet. Unfortunately for the newspaper deliveryman, he had met him first. That could very well have been me lying in the morgue.

You would have thought I would be reluctant to work undercover after that. But I knew it was risky business and a necessary part of the job. Now, even more so, I had something to prove to myself.

However, my next undercover stint had nothing to do with drug dealers. It was all about drug users. It would put me face-to-face with the anti-Vietnam War protesters I had tried to avoid in college. It was an historic weekend in the Nation's Capital when a little-known piece of the legacy of Richard "Tricky Dick" Nixon had occurred.

CHAPTER 5

BENT PENNY

A nti-war sentiment ran rampant on college campuses in the early 1970s. President Nixon had inherited an increasingly unpopular war. Having read the political tea leaves, he instituted a policy of "Vietnamization" designed to gradually turn the fighting over to the South Vietnamese and entered into peace negotiations with the North Vietnamese. But he couldn't end America's participation in the war fast enough to satisfy the anti-war protesters.

By the spring of 1971 tensions in Washington had reached the breaking point. The prior winter, Weather Underground terrorists detonated an improvised explosive device in a bathroom at the Capitol Building in retaliation for expanded military action into Laos. And just weeks before, a military tribunal found Army Lt. William Calley guilty of premeditated murder for the killing of innocent civilians in the village of My Lai. During the third week in April, Senator William Fulbright, Chairman of the Senate Foreign Relations Committee, began what was to become the last of his hearings on the Vietnam War. One of the proposals before him called for an immediate and unconditional withdrawal from Vietnam.

On the third day of the hearings, Vietnam veteran and future Massachusetts Senator John Kerry, claiming to represent 1,000

☆ ☆

like-minded veterans, accused the U.S. military of committing war atrocities. The following day Kerry and members of his organization, Vietnam Veterans Against the War, threw their Vietnam service medals onto the steps of the Capitol, an act Kerry himself later denied, but one that came back to haunt him thirty years later during his presidential bid.

A number of anti-war groups had coordinated weeks of demonstrations to coincide with Fulbright's hearings that were to culminate with a massive May Day rally in Washington, D.C. that organizers promised would shut down the government. The Nixon Administration wasn't about to let that happen. They also hoped by short-stopping the rally it would relieve the unrelenting pressure to abruptly end the war. They had developed a secret plan to document drug use by protesters in violation of their permit to assemble and called upon the Bureau of Narcotics and Dangerous Drugs to implement it.

It was a spring-feverish Friday afternoon when Group Supervisor Dick Johnson rounded up the few of us he could find. We sat solemnly in a smoke-filled conference room to receive the news. No one wanted to be there, not even Johnson.

"We've been ordered to confirm drug use by Vietnam War protesters in Washington tomorrow. You'll get your instructions once you get there," Johnson began. "Dress to fit in with the 'hippie' crowd, and don't take your guns, badges or credentials with you. Anything that can identify you as a law enforcement officer, leave it at home."

I was excited to hear that. It's not that I held any particular grudge against the protesters although I hadn't been pleased by reports of returning GIs being harassed, even spit on at airports. But by then, the Vietnam conflict was pretty much in my rearview mirror. For all I cared, the demonstrators could protest until

☆ ☆

their final exams were over. No, for me it would just be a chance to get out of town and do something different.

I could tell from the glum expressions around the room, though, that not many of my colleagues shared my enthusiasm. But it was that last statement by Dick Johnson that prompted a response. Special Agent Joe Braddock, a former Philly cop and Marine, growled, "If my badge and gun don't go, I don't go!"

Dick told him to settle down, not to worry, that we would receive special identification when we reported to the State Department the following afternoon. "And to get through security," he said, "Tell the guards you're there for the 'Bishop's Meeting.'" I perked up at that. It sounded like a code word, like a little "cloak and dagger" had been thrown into the mix . . . that is, until the next day when a Mr. Bishop from the White House opened the meeting.

About two hundred BNDD agents had trickled into the State Department's auditorium from offices throughout the mid-Atlantic region. Bishop, dressed in a dark blue suit, white shirt and red "power" tie, stepped to the microphone and called for our attention. "We have an estimated 200,000 demonstrators on the Mall," he said, "We expect a lot of drug use tonight, so brought you drug experts here to document it. No arrests. Just mingle with the crowd and observe."

He paused, prompting murmurs throughout the auditorium, and then raised his hand to quiet us down. "The Metropolitan Police are going to move in and disperse the demonstrators early Sunday morning. Encourage them to leave," he continued, "then go back to your headquarters and write down your observations."

A tall, high-ranking Metropolitan Police officer in full-dress uniform then approached the microphone. "When you see people using drugs, don't try to arrest them. Find a uniformed

☆ ☆

police officer and point them out. And show them this," he said, holding up his hand. "This bent penny will tell the police officers you're a federal agent and not a protester." I lined up to get mine.

Operation Bent Penny, May 1971. Reprinted with permission from *Vietnam* magazine, Operation Bent Penny, October 2011

I walked out onto Constitution Avenue toward the Lincoln Memorial and dove into the crowd of protesters, swallowed up like a stone tossed into the Reflecting Pool. The place was crawling with them. Although I wore jeans and a flowered shirt, and my hair was long, at least by my standards, I knew I didn't fit in. It looked like a beatnik convention.

I meandered toward the Washington Monument taking in the sights and smells. Trash had been strewn everywhere. The odor of marijuana permeated the air. How disrespectful of America's front yard, I thought, where some of our greatest national heroes are memorialized. Then someone tapped me on the shoulder.

I ducked, turned and grabbed the offending hand. It belonged to a scraggly-looking, wide-eyed teenager wearing a cardboard placard with a peace symbol hand-painted on it. "Hey man, want a drag?" he said with a sheepish grin, nodding to the joint of marijuana cupped in his free hand.

"No thanks," I said as I let him go and walked on. I couldn't believe anyone would be that blatant about using an illegal substance.

I had watched the demonstrations on TV after the military incursions into Cambodia, when National Guard troops at Kent State shot student protesters. I expected to see the same vitriol, vandalism, and violence as I had seen there. But this was no angry mob. It wasn't so much a political demonstration as a party. A "happening." Woodstock in Washington!

I navigated around the bedrolls and pup tents cluttering the landscape. College-aged kids sat in small groups, their protest signs propped against trees. While I heard an occasional shout of protest, for the most part they strummed guitars and sang folk music while circulating jugs of wine and joints of marijuana among them.

It wasn't only grape and pot. Warnings came over the public address system about bad LSD being sold on the Mall, and that the first aid stations were prepared to treat all types of drug overdoses. As the afternoon wore on, the announcements became more frantic. One begged parents to claim a small boy who had been found wandering alone, another pleaded for someone to come to First Aid Station #3 to identify a man who didn't know who he was.

This was all new to me. I had been trained to investigate hardened criminals. Many in the drug hierarchy didn't even use drugs and didn't trust people who did. Here I found myself in the midst of a horde of drug users, and the higher they got, the more open about it they became.

☆ ☆

It hadn't taken me more than a few minutes on the Mall to observe enough incidents of illegal drug use to fill a police blotter. Drugs were everywhere. The White House certainly didn't have to bring several hundred federal narcotics agents to Washington to determine that drugs were being used. A couple of Justice Department clerks could have accomplished the same thing. But if the White House wanted undercover agents with the expertise to infiltrate the demonstrators, they picked the right organization.

The BNDD wasn't made up of just stereotypical-looking cops. Its predecessor agency, the Federal Bureau of Narcotics, had been among the first federal agencies to hire agents from minority groups. No matter if it involved Italian organized crime mobsters, Black Harlem gangsters, Asian Triads, or Miami cocaine cowboys, we had agents who could infiltrate them. Young, pot-smoking hippies were no exception.

Making that very point, I watched as a conga line of protesters snaked its way through the crowd chanting, "One, two, three, four; we don't want your fucking war." Leading the line was Special Agent Jack Weiler.

Earlier in the week, the demonstrations had been centered at the Capitol and Supreme Court buildings. By late Saturday afternoon the majority of protesters had migrated to the open-air Sylvan Theater near the Washington Monument in anticipation of that evening's scheduled concert. As day slipped into night, bands took to the stage blasting rock and folk music over loudspeakers strategically located throughout the Mall.

The protesters sang and danced into the wee hours. Some of the "love children" practiced what they preached, in pup tents, under blankets or in sleeping bags under the stars, gyrating in not-so-discreet fornication, at times in sync with the music. The

Washington Post reported the next day that the demonstration lacked the fervency of previous anti-war protests and had turned into a "gigantic pajama party" — little mention was made of drug use.

While I saw a few confrontations between the police and protesters, there seemed to be more hassles between the police and BNDD agents. Special Agent Mike Horn learned that the bent pennies were of no use when he was stopped by two uniformed officers while walking back to the Mall around midnight. He pulled out his bent penny and they just stared. "What are you, a wise guy? Defacing American currency?" one of them asked before letting him go. And at one point Joe Braddock had been rounded up by the police and was about to be bussed to JFK Stadium for processing when he showed them his bent penny. After seeing the puzzled look on their faces, he flashed the BNDD badge he wasn't supposed to have with him, and they let him go.

Once the bands had packed up, quiet broke out on the Mall. Trash cans that had been set ablaze to take the chill out of the cool night air had been left to smolder. The repugnant smoke mixing with the reeking fumes from overflowing port-a-potties created an unbearable stench. I commandeered an "up wind" park bench and dozed off, to be startled awake at first light by an eerily familiar sound.

For a moment I thought I was back in Vietnam. A Huey helicopter flew overhead, the distinctive roar of its rotor blades reverberating throughout the Federal District. Then I watched busloads of police in riot gear line up behind the Sylvan Theater. A dozen mounted policemen with helmets and shields reined in prancing horses, looking like gladiators preparing for battle. More cops assembled at other locations along the Mall, and announcements started blaring over a loudspeaker mounted on

☆ ☆

a roving police car: "Your permit has been canceled. You must vacate the Mall by noon."

In the shadow of the Washington Monument protesters jumped from under blankets and ponchos and relieved themselves on the lawn, some completely naked, too groggy or too startled to hunt down a portable john. They didn't seem to need much coaxing to disperse. They threw on clothes, stepped into sandals, stuffed meager belongings into knapsacks, and were gone, leaving behind a thoroughly trashed National Mall.

I made my way to the BNDD gymnasium on Eye Street across the alley from headquarters on McPherson Square. Too early to find a coffee shop open, I sat with other yawning narcotics agents on the wooden basketball court scribbling observations of drug use on BNDD-6s, investigative report forms. They were never needed. The special event permits had already been revoked and the crowd dispersed long before we had finished documenting our observations. I suppose they may have been useful in the event of a legal challenge, but that never happened.

Nixon had called upon a reluctant BNDD leadership to launch Operation Bent Penny. "It wasn't something the BNDD leadership had thought to do," recalled Bob Nickoloff, Philadelphia's former Deputy Regional Director when asked about it years later. "It wasn't necessarily inappropriate — certainly within the law. And there was nothing to preclude us from doing it. But it was a waste of a weekend." Many of us agreed.

Philadelphia Special Agent Pete Davis put it this way: "We had more important things to do."

I'm sure there are those who will see this as yet another one of Nixon's abuses of power, an infringement on the protesters' right to free speech, and a black eye for drug law enforcement. I didn't see it that way.

☆ ☆

While most of the demonstrators appeared just to want to camp out, get high, maybe get laid while protesting the war, the possibility of them shutting down Washington was a serious threat. Their use of illegal drugs was in violation of the permit the organizers had signed. Therefore, they had forfeited their right to assemble. I thought the government's strategy, although unorthodox, was just fine.

Regardless, the weekend had been an awakening for this young agent. I hadn't joined the BNDD on a crusade to save the world from drugs. But I began to realize the extent of the problem. Drug use among returning Vietnam veterans had been widely publicized, perhaps because it further denigrated a war the media opposed. Now I had seen firsthand flagrant illegal drug use among anti-war protesters. It seemed to be the one thing these two groups had in common.

☆ ☆

CHAPTER 6

PHILLY POTPOURRI

Back in Philadelphia, my luck was beginning to change. With the exception of just one hiccup, unfortunately in another heroin case, I was starting to get my undercover act together. None of the cases were earth shattering; none would make the Hall of Fame. But I learned from each one, and my confidence continued to grow.

I don't recall how I came upon the snitch, but he introduced me to a guy who he said had been buying pills at the back door of a local pharmaceutical company. If I could make a case on him and he flipped, became a defendant informant, he could introduce me undercover to his source. That would be a big deal. But after I made two undercover amphetamine buys and we took him down, he clammed up. Facing prosecution, he still wouldn't give up his source of supply. So, the case went no further than his imprisonment.

During the post-arrest interview, I realized he was the younger brother of a building contractor for whom I had worked one summer during college, who had cheated me out of $100, a lot of money in those days. I never mentioned the connection to anyone, for fear it would appear as if I had targeted him out of revenge.

☆ ☆

Shortly after that episode, another informant introduced me by telephone to a marijuana dealer in Stamford, Connecticut. After a few recorded conversations, he said he could sell me 500 pounds of weed but wanted me to come to Stamford to finalize the deal. No doubt, he wanted to size me up. And budgets being what they were in those days, I didn't expect to get the money to go there. But I did.

I flew to Stamford and took a taxi to the crook's house, covered by agents from the nearby office. I must have passed the test because he agreed to have the marijuana delivered to me in Memphis, Tennessee. Why Memphis, I had no idea. I figured there was no way I would ever get the money to travel there. But for whatever reason, they financed that trip too.

A week later, after a preliminary undercover meeting in a local bar, three 'good old boys' showed me 500 pounds of Mexican loco weed in the back of their delivery van parked just off Beale Street. I could hear strains of BB King's "I Ain't Done Nothing Wrong" playing in the background as the arresting Memphis cops snapped the cuffs on them. Based on my account of the negotiations, the guy in Stamford was indicted too. The four of them pleaded guilty and each was sentenced to ten years in prison. In today's world, 500 pounds of grass might not have gotten them ten minutes in jail. The threshold quantities of drugs accepted for prosecution in many judicial jurisdictions have increased over the years, as has our tolerance for drug abuse.

Okay. Okay. I know it was kiddie dope. But it was a successful undercover buy, and that counts. So now I had successfully bought dope in two cases.

One day I rode with a posse that Special Agent Bill Glanz had rounded up to hunt down the intended recipient of a load of Southeast Asian heroin detected by the Military Police in the

☆ ☆

Army Post Office at Ft. Monmouth, New Jersey. It had been mailed from Bangkok, Thailand to a non-existent person at a phony address in Ft. Monmouth. We presumed someone on the inside was to pick it up. But after an extended surveillance, no one went near it.

Either word had gotten out that the heroin had been discovered, or our hastily arranged surveillance had been spotted. So, Bill seized the box and found seventeen pounds of pure white heroin inside, an amazing amount, worth millions of dollars on the street. At the time, I had no idea who had sent it, but in another two years the originator of this shipment would become the focus of one of my biggest investigations.

Good fortune followed me into that next summer. Mike Horn recruited me to work cases at the Jersey shore. This time I would be paid to frolic in "America's Favorite Playground," and it would give me a second opportunity to work undercover in a heroin case. That time, however, it didn't work out so well either.

The Philadelphia Regional Office covered Pennsylvania, Delaware, and the southern half of New Jersey. Despite a thriving drug market just a few blocks inland from the famed Atlantic City Boardwalk, a problem that some years later would justify the opening of a DEA resident office there, Philadelphia's agents seldom strayed into New Jersey very far from Camden.

Then Mike Horn worked out a deal with the Chief of Special Investigations of the Atlantic City Police Department. We would make a series of drug buys culminating with a roundup in the fall to let the citizens of South Jersey know that their law enforcement authorities had been hard at work — but long enough after Labor Day weekend so as not to scare away any tourist dollars. The police agreed to provide the informants and most of the undercover officers; the typically generous U.S. government,

Uncle "Sugar," would supply the money to make the buys and pay rewards to the police informants.

My job had been mostly surveillance, providing security while the cops made the undercover buys, and documenting them with surveillance reports to help corroborate the purchases for trial. But when one of the police informants said he could introduce any one of us to a guy who had a bundle of heroin to sell, Mike gave me the nod.

At nightfall I drove the informant to a largely abandoned high-rise tenement building. The other agents had set up surveillance in the area, for whatever good that would do in that rundown, dimly lit neighborhood. The informant and I walked up three flights of stairs into an empty apartment where a small, middle-aged, dark-skinned male sat on the floor. He pulled a single glassine bag filled with white powder from his jacket pocket and asked if I wanted to "taste" it. I handed him the hackneyed cliché, "I don't use it. I only sell the stuff."

I heard rumors that it wasn't unusual for undercover cops to sample the merchandise before buying it, either putting a pinch on their tongue or snorting it up their noses to be sure of its authenticity. But doing so was forbidden by every police department in America. It could scuttle a case if it came out in court and end an officer's career. And it wasn't too good for one's health either. I suppose I would have done it had someone put a gun to my head, but not just to make a case. I was never *that* desperate.

We settled on $175 for a bundle of twenty-five bags. He pulled out a pack of glassine bags wrapped with a rubber band from his other jacket pocket, counted out twenty-five and handed them to me. I gave him the money. I had a bad feeling not having tested it.

☆ ☆

I left the apartment with the informant and rendezvoused with the agents down the street. One of them sprinkled a small amount of white powder from one of the bags into a vial of Marquis Reagent. If it was heroin the field test would turn the powder purple. Instead, it fizzed. It wasn't heroin at all.

There probably was heroin in the one glassine bag the guy offered me to sample. He had filled the other bags with baking powder. By the time we got back into the apartment the rip-off artist was long gone. From my description, the cops later identified him as a local trash collector and heroin junkie — not exactly a member of the Black Mafia. He had cooked up the scam and I got burned by it. I wasn't having any luck at buying heroin. But I wasn't about to give up. I just chalked it up as another learning experience.

That summer's work was a success, though. Across the entire operation, nineteen suspects were ultimately indicted; fifteen of them rounded up on the second Friday in November and paraded through Atlantic City's iconic Convention Hall for processing. Trust me when I say there were no Miss America beauties among them. We nabbed the sixteenth defendant the next morning when he happened to walk into Gilberson's Diner while we were eating breakfast.

It had been more than two years since Operation Eagle went down, the Chicago case we learned about during basic agent training that portended the scourge of cocaine about to sweep across America. At the time, though, cocaine still hadn't reached Philadelphia. Then I was introduced by an informant to a young Latino male named Sergio Bustelo in a downtown Philadelphia bar who offered to sell me a kilogram of cocaine for $3,000.

I thought I hit pay-dirt when Bustelo let it slip that his source of supply was a guy in Queens, New York City nicknamed *Flaco*.

It might be an opportunity to move up the supply chain to Mr. Big, maybe the start of another Operation Eagle . . . until the New York Office reported back that the nickname was so common there were probably a thousand *Flacos* aka Skinnys of record living in Queens.

I thought the $3,000 price tag was ridiculous. My salary wasn't much more than $6,000 a year. But it was actually a bargain. And since it would be the first undercover purchase of cocaine ever made in Philadelphia, at least by the feds, the BNDD hierarchy gave me the go ahead.

I took Special Agent Jimmy Glauner undercover with me as my "money man" so I wouldn't be carrying all that dough if it was a rip off. The deal went down in the parking lot of a downtown bar. After I saw the coke, I signaled Jimmy and he brought over the money. It turned out to be quality stuff. A week later I called Bustelo to order up another kilo with the aim of taking him down but got no answer.

A day or two later Jimmy and I stopped by Bustelo's Baltimore Avenue apartment. The landlord said he had abandoned it. He had probably skipped town. He must have smelled a rat. We never found out what happened. Bustelo was picked up years later, pleaded guilty to the sale, and ended up serving a few years in the slammer. He never did give up *Flaco*.

At about the same time my luck at work was improving, I got lucky at love. Joy and I had been steadily dating for more than a year. With the Stingray's top down on a gorgeous Sunday afternoon, I pulled over onto the shoulder of the Northeast Extension of the Pennsylvania Turnpike and asked her to marry me to which she agreed. Joy set the date for April 8, 1972, exactly two years from the day we had first met. And then two days shy

☆ ☆

of our first anniversary we were blessed with our first child, a girl we named Amy Lyn, dearly loved.

But still, I didn't think the weight of having acquired a family had sunk in. Now I had others to care for. But I was driven by my work, which demanded a lot of my time. Drug traffickers didn't work nine-to-five, so neither could we. And I rationalized it by thinking I was doing the Lord's work.

It was a high-wire act, working long, odd hours — nights, weekends, and holidays — and now caring for a family. Many agents had difficulty keeping their balance and fell off, divorced. I would like to assert that I had done a good job of it. But looking back, it wasn't me at all. It was Joy's love, patience, understanding, and incredible tolerance that held our marriage and family together while I roamed about town, and soon the globe. Joy has always been my safety net.

I hadn't forgotten my primary reason for having joined federal narcotics — to work overseas. It was the BNDD's policy that a candidate had to have a minimum of three-years of experience in domestic enforcement before being eligible to go abroad. That made sense. They wanted to be sure an agent knew how to make a case before advising foreign counterparts how to make one. Subsequently, on my 1,095th day on the job, I applied for several overseas vacancies.

My Vietnam experience, having worked successfully overseas before, must have tipped the scale among other applicants. Within weeks I was one of three agents selected for Bangkok. I couldn't wait to get back to Asia. Philadelphia's Special Agent-in-Charge Art Lewis interviewed Joy to be certain she knew what I was getting her into. Then I was enrolled in a six-month Thai language training course at the State Department's Foreign Service Institute in Roslyn, Virginia, that was to begin in mid-April.

At the time, I had been working undercover on a guy we thought had some Italian organized crime connections. We met several times at a bar on Head House Square near 2nd and South Streets in Philadelphia where I had made a few small purchases of amphetamines hoping through surveillances of him to identify his source of supply. The office had New Jersey Bell Telephone Security install a second landline in our Pennsauken, New Jersey, apartment so I could receive calls from this schmuck after hours. The telephone was listed in the name of a fictitious company and backed up with a USPS mailbox address to make it untraceable. I asked Joy to answer the undercover phone whenever I wasn't home to make it appear realistic.

After being notified of my reassignment we had to take the case down, hoping that with the charges we already had against him he would cooperate. When we arrested him, we found an address book in his pocket with my undercover name and telephone number. Below it he had scribbled my real street address. He must have gotten it from somebody on the Mafia's payroll at NJ Bell Tel. I was ordered to vacate the apartment immediately. It was a rude awakening. I realized then that I had placed my family in danger and vowed never to let that happen again.

I didn't like being run out of our home but, if we had to relocate, the timing couldn't have been better. I moved Joy and Amy to Joy's parents' home in Drexel Hill until we could get clearance from the pediatrician for Amy to travel. Then I took off for Thai language school.

The timing of my transfer to Thailand was also fortunate in another way. It caused me to escape a transfer to New York City in which a number of Philadelphia's agents had gotten caught. Had I stuck around much longer, instead of Bangkok I could have easily ended up in the Big Apple.

☆ ☆

New York City was the center of the universe for drugs in those days. So you would think any narc would want to be stationed there. But with its high cost of living, and the nightmare commute from bedroom communities in Northern New Jersey that could be afforded on an agent's salary, for other than those born and raised in the area, most agents dreaded the thought.

Two momentous events had occurred while I was in language school. For one, the brief life of the BNDD ended. Nixon held the shotgun while U.S. Customs agents who had been working drug interdiction at the border were wed to the BNDD, and he named the new agency the Drug Enforcement Administration (DEA). He hoped this super agency would forever end the turf battles between narcotics and Customs' agents. It didn't.

The DEA kept the BNDD's responsibility for both domestic and international drug investigations, while Customs retained responsibility for drug interdiction at the border. Since the reorganization plan hadn't defined "border interdiction," a new set of Customs investigators continued to make incursions into the DEA's turf on both sides of it. They sent their informants overseas to smuggle drugs back to the border where they could seize them, and then they delivered the seized drugs to intended recipients in the heartland to be arrested. The turf battles continued. Only the name had changed.

The other momentous event was personal. After a few months on the job, I was promoted from the entry-level grade of GS-7 to GS-9 as a result of my score on the Federal Service Entrance Exam. That allowed me to escape a temporary promotion moratorium and be promoted to GS-11 in another year. By the time I landed in language school, I was ahead of my contemporaries grade-wise, and eligible for promotion to the journeyman grade of GS-12.

However, being in language school on my way overseas, out of sight, and presumably out of mind of my new Group Supervisor, John Wilder, my former boxing instructor in basic agent training, I figured he would save the grade for an agent who still worked for him and could do him some good. I don't think my boxing prowess had anything to do with it, but he promoted me anyway. He was just a good boss. And it wasn't only the extra money, although a salary boost never hurt anything. The journeyman grade would allow me greater independence of action once I got to Bangkok.

After months of grueling Thai language training, in early January of 1974, Joy, nine-month-old Amy Lyn, and I bade farewell to our families at Philadelphia International Airport. For me it would be the second time leaving home to go abroad, something that was to become a habit over my career. For Joy, who lived in her parent's home until we had married, other than for a high school class trip to France, it would be her first time living overseas.

Everyone's eyes had tears in them but Amy and me. Of course, Amy was unaware of where we were going, just happy for the attention she was getting; I was fixated on the next stage of my career, oblivious to the pain I was causing our parents. Joy, always the dutiful wife, never complained. Many years later, when we became grandparents ourselves, we looked back and wondered how in the world we could have snatched our parents' first grandchild away from them and moved her halfway around the world to a place they probably had never heard of before.

But we were young, and adventuresome, and saw the world as our oyster — curried, and sprinkled with a little *nam pla* (Thai fish sauce) and *phrik ki nu* (spicy hot peppers).

☆ ☆

CHAPTER 7

GOING POSTAL

The first case I worked on in Bangkok turned much of what I had learned up until then on its head. But before turning me loose onto the streets of Bangkok, my new boss, Fred T. Dick, summoned me and the other two newly assigned special agents to his office.

Fred had been brought in from Saigon and handed the top job in Southeast Asia. He brought with him his beautiful Vietnamese paramour (and future wife) and a collection of Asian artifacts that he displayed in his residence. Several of us referred to him, an epitome of an old "China hand," as "The Emperor" – but never to his face.

Deputy Director John Doyle escorted us to his office. Fred asked Bill Oakes, Brian Raftery and me to call off our names and last posts of duty, like an Army drill sergeant welcoming a batch of new recruits. He then signaled us to follow him down the hall. Ambassador William Kintner, dressed in a light brown elbow-patched tweed jacket, looking very much like the Ivy League professor he had been, shook hands and said, "When you get up in the morning, I want you to look in the mirror and ask yourself, 'Is there anything I'm going to do today that could possibly embarrass the ambassador?' If the answer is yes, go back to bed.

☆ ☆

Do I make myself clear?" Kintner then retreated to safety behind his oversized desk.

I never met an ambassador before. I didn't know what to think. Back in Fred's office he closed the door behind us and said in a hushed voice, "You heard the ambassador. Now listen to me. Go out there and make cases. Do I make **my**self clear?" Then he dismissed us with a wave of his hand and a stern, "Now get to work."

It hadn't taken me long to figure out that the DEA wasn't the most popular agency within the diplomatic community. However, over the coming months, Fred Dick taught me everything I needed to know about surviving in a hostile environment.

Many Thai government officials were involved in protecting, if not participating in the narcotics trade of that day. And whenever the DEA would surface evidence of complicity by politicians and military leaders with whom the State Department and the intelligence community had to work, it complicated their lives. But Fred wouldn't back off. And strong congressional support for the DEA's mission, gave them little room to maneuver.

Being an outcast agency, the "cowboys," as we were often called, had been stuffed into a few rooms in the rear of the Chancery's ground floor. However, the office of our "lightning rod" chief belied our status. Fred had inherited a tiny two-room suite on the second floor of the Chancery, just footsteps from the ambassador's office. Knowing that within the State Department's bureaucracy, proximity to the ambassador's office symbolized power, Fred wasn't about to give it up, even when the chancery began to sink.

Bangkok lies below sea-level, and the embassy floated on mud. When a crack appeared across the second-floor hallway and ran through the middle of Fred's office, he was asked to vacate for

☆ ☆

safety's sake while contractors pounded pylons down to bedrock upon which the building would eventually be cradled. But Fred refused to budge. He defended his turf from coveting diplomats like the Chinese warding off assaults by Genghis Kahn, fearing that if he ever vacated his office he wouldn't be allowed to return,

He took no guff from his host nation counterparts either. A heavy drinker, rumor had it that one night while hosting a party for some Thai police big shots he had one too many vodka martinis, got into an argument with one of them, and cold-cocked him. While the general might have deserved it — official corruption was undermining a lot of our cases in those days — there was no way Fred could sweep it under the oriental carpet. Word quickly got back to the ambassador who jumped on the opportunity to get rid of him. He asked Washington to have Fred removed, and the DEA obliged.

I had admired Fred's fierce determination to stand up to other U.S. government agencies and host nation counterparts to get the mission accomplished, despite the personal risk. His stern demeanor commanded respect. That's not to say I ever tried to adopt his management style. However, his order for me to "get to work" hadn't gone unheeded.

Senior Special Agent Bud Shoaf had a case ongoing at the Hyatt Regency Hotel on Silom Road, and after my meeting with Fred Dick, I jumped right into it. So new to Bangkok – I wasn't even sure how to get to the hotel – Bud asked me to take charge of the makeshift "command center" down the hall from the suspects' room. I was pleased at the thought of being locked up in a room full of Thai cops to practice my Thai. I needed it.

Upon arrival in Bangkok, we had checked into the Presidential Suite of the Presidential Hotel. It was in that hotel's hallway where Amy took her first steps, probably trying to make her way down to the coffee shop for some Thai fried rice. First thing Monday morning, not wanting to pay the exorbitant price charged for a hotel limo, I flagged down a taxi on Ploenchit Road. In my best Thai, I asked the driver very simply, "To go to the American Embassy, how much money?"

Apparently not expecting to hear Thai words coming from the mouth of a *farang*, a foreigner, he yelled, "No speak English," rolled up his window, and sped off. Seven months of studying the Thai language and that's the best I could do?

As it turned out though, there weren't many opportunities to practice the Thai language in the command center. The cops of the Metropolitan Narcotics Unit spent most of their time sleeping or eating. I couldn't blame them. They didn't make a whole lot of money, and I was fairly certain none of them had a plush mattress or air conditioning at home. Most Thai people slept on straw mats laid on teakwood floors, lucky to have an electric fan to ease the sweltering heat. And since the cops were supporting our case, we footed the food bill. They ate like they had gotten a tip on a famine.

So as not to run up a room service bill to a point that would send the boss into orbit, we gave them money to bring food back to the room — plastic bags full of Thai delicacies purchased from street vendors. With the aroma of fish sauce and garlic permeating the room, I was certain the hotel would have to call in ServPro to deodorize the room after we had checked out.

I had the tourist guide, hotel directory, and room service menu just about memorized, and was about to start on the Bangkok telephone directory when we got the word. "They're in the lobby headed for the coffee shop" came over the two-way radio from one of the agents pulling duty in the lobby. The crooks had finally left their room.

"Roger that," I said. "Let me know when they start back up." Then we went into action.

Two Thai cops dressed as hotel staff carried a huge ceramic lamp down the hall, entered the suspects' room with a passkey, and swapped it out for an identical-looking lamp. The replacement lamp had been hard-wired with a transmitter by our technician while the receiver sat on the desk in the command center with a tape recorder connected to it. I could hear the cops whispering over the bug, so I knew it was good to go. Now we would be able to put Bud's plan into action.

Days earlier, he had been tipped off by an informant that the two crooks were in Bangkok to buy a kilogram of heroin. They had been identified through hotel records as William Ward and Sylvia Baily. Our files were crammed with information on Baily who ran a prostitution and drug trafficking ring servicing American GIs in Germany. We had less information on Ward, a small time Seattle heroin dealer. Both were little fish in the international drug trade but swam in a pond with some trophy winners. If we could reel them in, Shoaf thought we might be able to use them as bait to lure some bigger fish onto the hook.

Now with their room bugged, he arranged for his snitch to deliver the heroin they had ordered. Where the informant got it from was anybody's guess. That's where it got a little screwy for me.

In a traditional drug case, the informant's source of supply is the target. We would have the informant introduce an undercover agent to his source of supply to order up, then knock off the source when he delivered the junk, try to flip him and have him introduce us to his source, and so on, moving up the supply chain to Mr. Big.

But this was Bangkok, the mother lode of heroin, and in those days just about any cab driver in town could take you somewhere to buy a kilo of smack. Our target was not the informant's source of heroin, but the wholesalers and distributors downstream for whom Ward and Bailey were purchasing it. The only thing we had yet to figure out was how they planned to get it to them.

The most common method of smuggling heroin out of Thailand was in the false sides of suitcases checked onto commercial airline flights. The suitcases could be purchased in just about any tourist shop. Departing passengers weren't routinely screened at airports in those days. So, there was little risk in getting dope out of Thailand. The risk came in getting it past customs when entering another country. That's why more often than not, heroin kingpins used mules to carry the suitcases, expendable people, not key players who could finger others in the ring if they got caught. Whether these two crooks had mules or not, we just didn't know.

Bud's informant would probably pay about $4,500 for the kilogram of 100 percent pure heroin and sell it to Ward and Baily for $5,000. Once it got to the States the kilo would be cut with diluents at each stage of marketing, and by the time it made its way through the wholesalers and retailers into the veins of addicts, its purity would typically run about two percent. The profits along the way were enormous.

I had just turned my attention back to the telephone directory when a rhythmic squeaking started coming over the receiver. It increased rapidly, and then the cops started giggling. It didn't take a voyeur to figure out what was going on. I got to the volume knob just as the moans and gasps reached crescendo. It's called "minimization," recording only those parts of a conversation pertinent to the case. The cops glared. I didn't have the words in Thai to explain to them why I turned it off.

☆ ☆

It was about 7 p.m. when the informant showed up in the make-shift command center with a bag of heroin. When Bud removed a speck of white powder with the wet tip of a toothpick and dipped it into a tube of Marquis Reagent, the liquid burst into a deep purple. No doubt about it, it was dyn-o-mite heroin. I turned up the receiver to be sure we captured every word. And then Bud let the informant out of the room. He walked down the hall; I could hear the knock. Then they let him into the room.

There wasn't a whole lot of conversation to record: A few grunts, some shuffling of paper, probably them opening the package to test the white powder, the snitch counting the money, the door opening and closing again. Then it turned quiet.

Defendants Sylvia Bailey and William Ward,
republished from the *Nation*, February 16, 1974.

Within minutes of the informant leaving, however, I was startled by loud bangs coming over the transmitter. It sounded like someone tap dancing on the desk. What in the world was that, I wondered? I turned the volume down for fear it would echo into the hallway, and then called Bud on the two-way radio.

"You need to come and listen to this," I said. When he got to the room, he couldn't figure it out either. The racket went on for almost an hour.

The next morning the crew in the lobby spotted Sylvia coming out of the elevator wearing a pair of large designer sunglasses and carrying a pale green tote bag over her shoulder. She started walking up Silom Road, stopped at the first mailbox, and dropped in a letter. Bingo. They were mailing it to the States.

The Metropolitan Narcotics Unit followed her and left a cop behind at each mailbox in which she posted a letter. Another policeman commandeered a postman and marched him up Silom Road, a block or two behind Sylvia, opening each mailbox and seizing the letters.

After she got back to the hotel, the cops hit their room. I followed them in but before long could hardly move. Even the Deputy Commissioner of the Metropolitan Police Department, General Saneh Sittipant, had squeezed into the room. We found a small postal scale, plastic baggies, and a manual typewriter sitting on the desk next to the bugged lamp. Aha, the source of the tap dancing. We would compare the print of the typewriter to the print on the envelopes as further proof of their crimes. We seized all of it as evidence.

Meanwhile, Bud went back to the embassy and prepared the 35 seized letters to be sent by Diplomatic Pouch to Washington, an ounce of pure heroin in each. The envelopes had been typed to persons at addresses in Seattle and Washington, D.C. with various fictitious return addresses. We asked the cops to keep a lid on any press release until the DEA was able to deliver the envelopes to the intended recipients after substituting most of the real heroin with sham. Almost two dozen crooks were subsequently arrested in the States.

☆ ☆

Ward and Baily were each convicted and sentenced to ten years in one of Thailand's gruesome prisons. With time off for good behavior, and the possibility of sentence reductions each year on King Bhumibol Adulyadej's birthday, the actual time they served would likely be far less.

Baily was content to go to her cell. But Ward said he knew his rights and demanded an appeal. Several months later a Thai Judicial Tribunal agreed with Ward that he had been unjustly sentenced and re-sentenced him to twenty years. Unlike in the U.S. judicial system, appeals in Thailand can go either way. Sometimes it's best just to accept your fate and move on.

Bud and I had been partners for nearly a year before he rotated back to the States. He had started the Metropolitan Narcotics Unit after realizing the Bangkok Police Department didn't have its own drug squad, and I inherited the responsibility to advise and assist them. Bud had also supervised a surveillance team of local nationals who were on call to assist in any agent's case, independent of the police, and that allowed us to develop our own investigations while protecting sources and methods.

It had been headed by a guy named Bandit. But when we suspected he had been living up to his name, we disbanded the team. Then we contacted the one former team member we trusted, and secretly formed a new team around him. I inherited the responsibility to supervise the new surveillance team as well.

And as a journeyman agent, I would be expected to carry my own caseload.

Just before Bud left, although he didn't realize it at the time, he also presented me with a parting gift, a golden opportunity, an informant who would lead me into what we call in our profession a "career case," an investigation upon which the reputation of an agent can forever rest. And then in the midst of that investigation, another case was dumped in my lap. It too turned into a "career case," a storied investigation of a gang that's talked about and written about to this day.

☆ ☆

CHAPTER 8

MINT LIST

We were expecting a knock at the door. When it came, my partner Matty and I gave the hotel room one last visual check. Everything seemed in place — my suitcase sat on the floor with the Amsterdam baggage tag clearly in view; my bogus Pan Am identification card lay on the dresser. I straightened my tie and took a deep breath. It was show time!

A middle-aged man with a receding hairline entered the room. He looked more like a pharmacist than a heroin dealer. With his untucked Hawaiian-style shirt I couldn't tell if he was armed or not. I didn't think so. I wasn't expecting trouble. After all, he had paid me to be there. We shook hands. He nodded in recognition to Matty.

I spread the schematic diagram of a Boeing 747 jumbo jetliner on the bed and got down to business. "Matty will hide your stuff behind these walls," I said, pointing to the bathrooms at the rear of the plane. Then we'll get it out when the plane lands and deliver it back to you wherever you want it." It was nonsense, of course. The dope was never going to leave Bangkok.

I had decided to have the informant skip the meeting to lessen the chance of his having to testify at trial. We knew this guy spoke some English. He seemed to understand well enough, nodding his head as I went along, although he didn't ask any questions. When I finished my spiel, he smiled and said he would be back in one hour then left.

Matty opened the door to the adjoining room and was assured by the crew next door that the conversation, although pretty much one-sided, had been recorded. I retrieved the two-way radio stashed in the closet, turned it on and set in on the desk. Whether or not the crook would return was anybody's guess. If he suspected something was amiss, he would be in the wind. We would just have to wait and see. That was always the hard part. The waiting. I sat down on the bed, fluffed a pillow behind my head, and let my mind wander off to when the investigation had begun.

Six weeks before, Bud Shoaf had gotten a call from his contact in the U.S. Army's Criminal Investigation Division (CID). Our combat troops had already been pulled out of Vietnam, and the supporting infrastructure in Thailand drastically reduced. Now it was the CID's turn to be yanked. Warrant officer Bill Cherry told Bud he had an informant he wanted to turn over to the DEA before he left town. Bud took me along. Since he too was about to rotate back to the States, I would inherit the informant.

We found Bill seated at a desk surrounded by a half dozen boxes full of files and knickknacks. The walls of his office were bare except for a sign that read, "Yea though I walk through the valley of the shadow of death I will fear no evil, for I am the evilest son of a bitch in the valley." I figured he wanted to leave it up until the day he left the valley.

Seated to his left was a ruddy Thai guy he introduced as Yongyut Kusum, one of the CID's local investigators and son of a retired Thai Army General. Bill put in a plug for him as a top-notch investigator who knew his way around, and we did end up hiring him soon after.

Seated to Bill's right was a pudgy, light-skinned Chinese-Thai male in his mid-thirties. Let's call him Sawat. In almost perfect English, Sawat said he was the owner of a commodity survey company. He explained his business as being hired by the potential buyer of a commodity, such as molasses in a ship's hold, to determine its quality and quantity so a fair price could be offered before being purchased and offloaded. Sawat said he learned the trade from Sukree Sukreepirom for whom he had worked before starting his own company. He said Sukree's business, Analabs, on Eckamai Road, was now just a front for his real business, that of heroin trafficking.

I thought maybe Sawat was trying to eliminate a business competitor. And I figured if Sukree was a street dealer selling heroin to GIs, the type of criminal the CID normally targeted, his customers were already on their way home. So he'd be out of business soon enough. But when Sawat said that Sukree wanted to send fifty pounds of heroin to the United States and was looking for someone to smuggle it there for him, he got my attention.

When we got back to the office, I asked Intelligence Chief Adrian Swain if we had anything on a Sukree Sukreepirom. I almost choked on my green tea when he said Sukree was on the MINT list — the Major International Narcotics Trafficker list — one of the crème-de-la-crème of the world's drug trade. I grabbed Sukree's file and started reading.

Sukree Sukreepirom aka Chao Pei Sui aka Lim Cheng was born in 1920 of Chinese parentage in Lampang, Thailand. He had been of record with the old Federal Bureau of Narcotics as far back as when the Bangkok office first opened in the early sixties and was suspected of having gotten into the drug trade ten years before that.

A chemist by trade, one report said Sukree was thought to be the first Asian to have ever manufactured white heroin — China white it's called, a water soluble, injectable heroin similar to the French Connection heroin marketed by the Mafia, but so pure it could put the old Corsican chemists to shame. He had reportedly been taught the process by Turkish chemists and must have vastly improved upon it.

There were reports that Sukree was wanted for heroin trafficking in Malaysia and Singapore, and that at one time or another had been under investigation in France, Laos and South Vietnam. But he had never spent a day in jail. He insulated himself from law enforcement by dealing with only a few trusted colleagues, like Malaysian Hoi Se Wan, another MINT-listed heroin trafficker who three years earlier had put out $10,000 contracts on the lives of two DEA agents responsible for the seizure of a total of ninety-four pounds of his heroin in San Francisco and Los Angeles. By anyone's definition, Sukree was a Mr. Big, the kind of guy every narc dreams of putting behind bars.

The next morning, I drove to Sawat's office located in an old Thai-style teakwood house in a compound along a canal off Sathorn Road. When I opened the front door, a tiny bell jingled that prompted a bald chap to pop up from behind the counter and say, "G'day, mate." He ushered me into what had been the dining room of the house where I found Sawat sitting behind a desk, his back to a bay window overlooking a garden.

I told him I needed to know more about Sukree, and more about his own background. Once I felt comfortable that he was telling me the truth, I wrote him up as a cooperating individual, and photographed and fingerprinted him with the kit I brought along. I would then send his prints to the FBI in Washington in the unlikely event there were warrants for him there.

As for a local records check, that wouldn't be wise. The Royal Thai Police didn't have a centralized data base. The only way to learn if Sawat was of record or reputation in Thailand would be to ask a Thai cop. But asking the wrong one could sign his death warrant. In fact, the Thai cops we worked with normally didn't want to know the identity of our informants. They knew if any of them disappeared, they would be the first ones we'd suspect.

I kicked around a few ideas with my group supervisor, Special Agent Paul Brown, as to how we might be able to take Sukree down. "What if Sawat tells him he has a friend in the airline business who can hide dope in commercial airliners?" I said.

"That might work," said Paul. "And I know just the guy who can help you pull it off." He introduced me by telephone to the Pan Am station manager at Bangkok's Don Muang Airport. I made arrangements to meet him that evening at his apartment.

Then I asked Paul if Matty Maher could work with me on the case. Matty had reported to Bangkok just a few months earlier from the Big Apple with the reputation of being a case maker. A glib New Yorker and a new face in town, he had another distinct advantage. While I had been finishing up Thai language training in Washington, he was beginning a year of Mandarin Chinese. With Sukree being Sino-Thai, Matty's Chinese language might just come in handy.

Matty didn't need any coaxing. We had already hit it off, having both signed up for the Marine Security Guard's touch football league. Although the Marine's definition of "touch" was more like "punch," and each of them was ten or fifteen years younger, we managed to hold our own. My wife, Joy, and Matty's wife, Eileen, who he affectionately called "The Giraffe," came out on Saturday mornings to watch our matches and soon became good friends — Eileen almost a second mom to our daughter Amy.

We talked it over. Matty, with his signature crewcut, could easily pass for an aircraft mechanic, someone with the know-how to hide drugs in a jetliner. I would pose as a Pan Am cargo supervisor who could track planes and see to it that we would have access on the other end to retrieve the drugs.

That night I met with the Pan Am station manager. "We won't put any drugs on your planes," I promised. "What I need are some identification cards to prove that my partner and I are Pan Am employees."

"I think I can do that. But I'll have to run it up my chain-of-command," he said. "Those ID's could get you onto any Pan Am flight in the world for free, and I would be on the hook. I could get you some Pan Am business cards easy enough if they would help."

"And some schematic drawings of a Boeing 747?" I added.

I called Sawat that night and told him about the scheme. He said he would run it by Sukree and get back to me.

"Tell him I want $5,000 for every kilogram shipped, and $5,000 up front to get me here from Tokyo to make the deal."

A couple of days later an excited Sawat telephoned me. "He gave me $3,500 toward your expenses. Not the $5,000 because he thinks you need to invest some money too. He's anxious to meet you. He asked me your name."

"What did you tell him?" I asked.

"The only name I could think of. The only other American I ever worked with: A. Edmund Blackburn."

"You've got to be kidding," I said. I hadn't thought to give Sawat my undercover name. My bad.

The next day we collected Sukree's $3,500 and placed it into evidence. I called the station manager and asked him to put the name A. Edmund Blackburn on my ID card and business cards, and Matty Marrin on Matty's, an undercover name he had used in New York City.

A day or two later Sawat again caught me off guard. He called to say Sukree wanted to meet with me that evening. That was crazy. Sawat had already told him I was based in Tokyo, so it wasn't like I could just materialize in Bangkok on a couple hours' notice. And we didn't have our Pan Am ID cards yet. However, Matty was supposed to be a mechanic at Bangkok's airport, so it would be hard to explain why he couldn't meet with Sukree.

The meeting was set for the Burapha Hotel on New Road, on the edge of Chinatown, only a block from Sukree's apartment building on Mahaesak Road. We rehearsed Sawat on the undercover story, and then I followed them to New Road and watched them enter the hotel.

I strolled past the front window. Several old men were seated in the lobby, on furniture that looked like it came from the set of a Charley Chan movie. No way could I go inside. I would stand out like a Buddhist Monk at a Baptist Missionary Convention. But it wasn't long before Matty and Sawat came out and got into their car. I followed them to an empty lot on Rachadamri Road across from the Sporting Club.

"I think he just wanted to make sure we existed. But the plan has changed," Matty said. "He wants us to take the heroin to Amsterdam. He must have had a partner down the hall because he would ask Sawat a few questions, leave the room, and then come back with more questions."

There were some indications that the guy down the hall might have been Sukree's buddy, Malaysian trafficker Hoi Se

Wan. But he hadn't shown his face, and we didn't know what role he might be playing, if any. It would be too risky to ask the police to check the hotel's records for Hoi. We would be lucky to grab Sukree. Putting Hoi in a position to be arrested as well would be too much to hope for.

I was disappointed the dope wouldn't be going to the States. Of course, we never intended for it to get that far. Sukree would have had to tell us who he wanted the dope delivered to. Just knowing who was to receive it would have been an intelligence coup. But Amsterdam came as no surprise. It was the hub for Asian heroin trafficking in Europe. And I couldn't lose sight of the fact that we would be taking down a MINT list heroin trafficker and grabbing fifty pounds of heroin which would be one of the largest seizures ever made in an undercover operation. We could turn over whatever we learned about his Amsterdam connection to Dutch authorities.

The problem was, neither Matty nor I had ever been to Amsterdam, and we needed to convince Sukree that we at least had some familiarity with the place when we discussed where to deliver the heroin. I ran it up the chain of command, and headquarters said no. It sounded to them like a boondoggle. But our regional management kept pressing, and finally they relented. Soon Matty and I were off to Amsterdam.

We decided the lockers at the train station would be the ideal location to deliver the heroin and found a few hotels that would do nicely as well. We checked out the Heineken brewery, but after sampling a few free beers as part of our research decided against it. And after a little window shopping in the red-light district where prostitutes sat in storefront windows advertising their wares, we decided against that too. We picked up street maps and tourist pamphlets to add to our collection of props

☆ ☆

and developed a pretty good conversational acquaintance with Amsterdam.

When we got back to Bangkok, I checked into a room at the Indra Regent, the closest hotel to Don Muang Airport, where many airline crews overnighted. Odds were Sukree wouldn't have a connection there to tip him off to a police presence. Another agent reserved the adjoining room where they had set up the make-shift command center, along with a few Thai cops to make the arrest and seizure. I called Sawat and asked him to tell Sukree where to meet me. There wasn't any concern for a rip off. After all, I was on Sukree's payroll.

Then a call came over the two-way radio that roused me from my daydream.

☆ ☆

CHAPTER 9

SERGEANT SMACK

Sukree Sukreepirom wasn't the only investigation on my plate. In the middle of it, Paul Brown handed me another case. I wasn't happy about it, thinking I already had enough to do. Besides, one of the main characters in the case was Herman Jackson who was doing thirty years in Leavenworth. He had been prosecuted in Denver for two kilograms of heroin that had been seized there, and eventually died in custody. The other character was Leslie "Ike" Atkinson who was sitting in a North Carolina lockup awaiting trial on state charges for conspiracy to distribute a kilogram of heroin that had been seized months before in Raleigh. With the two principals already in the can, the case was so cold even Bangkok's tropical heat couldn't thaw it out.

The agent handling the case had been transferred back to the States. Since every investigation needed to have an agent assigned to it, if only to do the required monthly status report, Paul was looking for someone to dump this white elephant on. What I hadn't realized at the time, though, was that in Thailand white elephants are revered. At birth, they become the property of the King. I should have been thanking Paul instead of complaining because, as it turned out, the case he threw into my lap was to become yet another "career case," a story that keeps being told, a legendary tale that doesn't want to end.

☆ ☆

I started wading through a file drawer full of folders going back to the mid-sixties. Leslie Atkinson, who everyone called Ike, also known as the Fat Man, had grown up poor in Goldsboro, North Carolina. At seventeen, he forged his mother's name to enlist in the Army and served in WWII and the Korean War. But while stationed in Germany, Atkinson switched his occupational specialty from quartermaster to that of fleecing fellow GIs out of their hard-earned money. After retiring in 1964, Atkinson remained in Germany with his so-called "band of brothers," a cadre of active duty and retired military NCO card sharks, to continue his avocation.

He met Sergeant Herman Jackson while the two were stationed on their twilight tours of duty at Ft. Bragg. Jackson retired a year before Atkinson and, with the war raging in Vietnam, moved to Bangkok to check out the action. He fell into a lucrative scam.

Rather than paying GIs in Vietnam with U.S. currency that could fall into the hands of the enemy to purchase weaponry, Military Payment Certificates were issued instead. The MPCs could only be used at military facilities and cashed in for U.S. dollars upon leaving the country. However, some Saigon merchants accepted them anyway. Jackson and other scammers commuted to Saigon to buy the MPCs from shop owners at deeply discounted rates and, being American citizens, were able to cash them in at face value upon leaving the country.

With the proceeds, Jackson opened Jack's American Star Bar that soon gained a reputation for the best soul music, the tastiest soul food, and the sexiest (Thai) soul sisters in Bangkok. It became the "in place" for Black GIs stationed in Thailand, and for those on Rest and Recuperation from Vietnam.

Between the MPC scam, the bar, and the prospect of thousands of GIs stationed in Southeast Asia anxious to gamble away their money, Jackson enticed Atkinson to join him. Another of the "band of brothers," retired Army NCO Jimmy Smedley, moved from Germany to manage Jack's bar. And since every local business was required to have a Thai business partner, Jackson took in Thai-Chinese Luchai Ruviwat as his local business partner and bartender. Luchai learned most of his English at the bar and spoke it like a homeboy.

Jackson and Atkinson soon tired of shuttling between Saigon and Bangkok on the MPC scam and were making good money between the bar and their crooked gambling tables. Then Jackson decided to go into another even more lucrative business.

With the help of his Thai paramour, Nittaya, Jackson began buying pure "China White" heroin from her uncle, Papa San. Atkinson got on board and tried his luck at smuggling some back to the States.

On his first run, Atkinson toted a duffel bag full of heroin onto a military transport aircraft headed from Thailand to the United States, a space-available courtesy extended to retired military personnel. When the plane stopped to refuel in Okinawa, due to a mechanical problem, Atkinson and the other passengers were transferred to another plane that had originated in Saigon and carried two coffins with the remains of U.S. servicemen killed-in-action. An informant had told law enforcement authorities in the States that there was heroin concealed inside the coffins. However, when the plane landed in Honolulu the coffins were searched and no heroin was found.

Nevertheless, the plane was diverted to Dover Air Force Base so that each of the passengers could be interviewed by the investigators with the original information. He was interviewed and let go. Inexplicably, Atkinson's duffel bag wasn't searched, making his first smuggling run a success. But his chance association with those coffins would come back to haunt him years later.

Jackson paid Papa San $5,000 for each kilogram of pure heroin. Once it got to the States, Atkinson diluted it and sold the resulting four kilograms of 25% pure heroin for $25,000 each, a pretty good return on investment — $100,000 for each pure kilo, less the purchase price and the cost of transportation, if any.

Atkinson sold the heroin to only a handful of dealers up and down the east coast, and that helped insulate him from law enforcement. His product was of such high quality; his customers were just as anxious to protect the identity of their source of supply as was Atkinson. To keep an even lower profile, Atkinson and his family lived in an unpretentious home on Neuss Circle in Goldsboro, North Carolina, although he reportedly spared no expense on decorating the inside of the house, drove an old, beat-up station wagon, and wore coveralls around town.

When Jackson was locked up in 1972, the dynamics of the business dramatically changed. With Jackson out of the picture, Ike was forced to do it all himself. Taking advantage of his retired military privileges, knowledge of military operations, and contacts within the military community in Bangkok, he began moving heroin by all manner to the States. And when Nittaya's uncle, Papa San, died, Atkinson turned to Luchai Ruviwat, Jack's former bartender at the by then defunct Jack's American Star Bar to procure his heroin.

Soon a hailstorm of heroin, a kilo at a time, cleverly concealed in the false bottoms of black leather "AWOL" overnight bags, began raining down on Goldsboro. The bags had been mailed in boxes through the Army Post Office system with the help of cooperating employees or hand-carried by soldiers returning to the States, some unsuspecting, some cheated at the card table and told their debts would be forgiven, and still others solely for money.

It was a daunting task for Atkinson. He had to commute between Goldsboro and Bangkok, approve, if not recruit the couriers, oversee the packing and shipping of the heroin, retrieve the incoming dope in the States, dilute it, distribute it, collect the proceeds, and then mail some of the money back to Bangkok to purchase more heroin. He had help from Smedley and a few others in the "band of brothers" who had migrated to Bangkok from Germany. But Atkinson did most of the heavy lifting himself.

It must have been jet lag. Atkinson was in Bangkok watching one of his "band of brothers" struggle to stuff a plastic bag of heroin into the false bottom of an AWOL bag. He impatiently grabbed the plastic bag and pushed it into place with the palm of his hand. They carefully sewed the bottom back in, filled the bag with old clothes, and mailed it in a box through the Bangkok APO to the aunt of an associate who was to pick it up when the box arrived.

Her nephew must have been running late. And when the package arrived, for some inexplicable reason, the elderly lady thought it contained a bomb. She called the police. Instead of finding explosives, they found the heroin . . . and Atkinson's palm print on the plastic bag. He was arrested, eventually convicted, and sentenced to nineteen years in a North Carolina penitentiary.

But Atkinson, if nothing else, was persistent. Motivated by greed, and no doubt wanting to maintain his status as a big shot in prison, he began running his operation from inside prison walls. By then most of our troops had been pulled out of Vietnam, and with military support operations in Thailand winding down, it didn't take a genius to figure out that his transportation system would soon evaporate. So, Atkinson decided to make two last heroin shipments, huge ones, large enough to set him up financially for the rest of his life.

When Paul Brown had assigned me the case, the name Atkinson wasn't totally foreign to me. He was the suspect behind the seventeen pounds of heroin Bill Glanz had seized from the mailroom at Ft. Monmouth, New Jersey, while I was stationed in Philadelphia. No one came to pick up that load, so the case never went anywhere. And then there was William Ward and Sylvia Bailey, the first case I worked on in Bangkok. Bailey had tenuous links to Atkinson from his years in Germany. But there was no direct evidence tying Atkinson to either one of those cases.

With no better ideas, I set the surveillance team of Thai locals out on the street to watch Jimmy Smedley, the only Atkinson associate I knew to be living fulltime in Bangkok. I wanted them to identify anyone Smedley was associating with, hoping it would develop some leads. The team was outfitted with binoculars and cameras and used motorcycles for them to navigate through the jammed Bangkok traffic. I even bought myself a motorcycle with my own money so I could watch the watchers and be certain they were doing their job.

But we were on the outside looking in, and not seeing much of anything. Breaking into the so-called "band of brothers" was harder than having money left in your pocket after getting up from one of Atkinson's crooked card games. What I needed was someone on the inside, someone who could tell me what was going on.

CHAPTER 10

DOUBLE TAKE

I had been waiting with Matty for Sukree Sukreepirom to return to the hotel when the call came over the two-way radio. It was Lt. Viraj Jutimitta of the Police Narcotics Suppression Center.

Reared by a German father and Thai mother, with a bachelor's degree from the University of San Jose and a master's degree in criminology from the University of California at Berkeley, Viraj was called by many of his peers the *tamruat farang*, the foreigner cop. He was an excellent investigator, spoke English as well as any of us — maybe better than some of us — and, most importantly, he was honest. That made him a threat to many of the higher ups in the Royal Thai Police Department. Fortunately for Viraj, he worked for General Pao Sarasin who was just as honest, and of high enough rank and social status to protect him.

Pao's family was one of the most influential and respected in Thailand. His father, Pote Sarasin, had served briefly as Prime Minister after World War II. Much of the family's fortune came through ownership of the Coca Cola franchise in Thailand. They contributed to charities, including building a wing at Bangkok's Police Hospital. They were referred to as the "Kennedys of Thailand." Pao was virtually untouchable.

Therefore, when it came to sensitive, high-level investigations, given the level of official corruption in Thailand in those days, Viraj was our "go-to guy." Despite being liaison to the Metropolitan Narcotics Unit, I asked Viraj to work with me on this case.

"*Khun* Chuck," said Viraj, the "*khun*" being a polite honorific used to address all males.

"Go ahead, lieutenant."

"He's with another guy. They're standing by a car with the trunk open. I can see boxes. I think we should grab them now."

Sukree had hopped into a taxi outside the Indra Regent Hotel. Viraj's men followed him to his apartment building where they saw him hook up with a guy who had been waiting outside and walk to the car. I wasn't so sure about them taking Sukree down before he delivered the heroin to Matty and me. If so, we would likely never find out to whom he wanted the heroin delivered in Amsterdam.

On the other hand, if they didn't grab him now, his buddy, whoever that was, would be in the wind. Under Thai law there was no such thing as conspiracy. Either the defendant was caught red-handed or had to be let go. Trusting his judgment, I told Viraj to go ahead. It turned out to be the right decision.

They nabbed Sukree and seized twenty-five kilograms of heroin in the boot of the car. And not a moment too soon, they nabbed his partner who was about to enter the Burapha Hotel. It turned out to be none other than Hoi Se Wan, the Malaysian fugitive who had put contracts out on the lives of two DEA agents. It looked like, in fact, it was Hoi's heroin that had been seized. So, we bagged two MINT-listed heroin traffickers for the price of one. But there were no high fives for Matty and me. It was very anticlimactic.

We had put Sukree, and by chance Hoi, into position to be arrested but weren't there to see them taken down — not that we could have participated, having no arrest or seizure authority outside of the United States. Subsequently, I decided the least I could do was stop by Viraj's office to take a look at our quarry.

Reporters jammed the room. Pao Sarasin's Deputy, Colonel Chavalit Yodmanee, beamed as he told them of the joy within the international drug law enforcement community upon learning the news that Sukree and Hoi had been arrested. Sukree sat next to a table piled high with thirty-five plastic bags of grayish-tan granular smoking heroin, the kind favored by Asian addicts. Hoi stood nearby.

(left) Defendant Sukree Sukreepirom sitting by 25 kilograms of heroin seized from Sukree and (right) defendant Hoi Se Wan

Sukree looked over and gave me a slight shrug as if to say, "You got me." He didn't look particularly worried. He was a businessman and probably figured getting caught was a risk of his trade. Hoi, though, looked glum. With furrowed brow, he stared down at the floor. He knew he was in big trouble.

The cops jumped to attention as Pao escorted Acting Director General of Police Pote Bekanan into the room and toward the table. With a smirk on his face, Pote brushed past Sukree with the back of his hand, and then inspected the heroin. It was probably only my imagination, but I could have sworn Pote had passed a

☆ ☆

message to Sukree that could have said, 'This is going to cost you plenty, pal.'

Pote had a bad reputation. He had been gifted with a golden parachute into retirement — eight months as Director General of Police before having to pull the plug. Rumor had it he intended to collect two million dollars in bribes to feather his retirement nest before leaving office. But considering the international notoriety of these two bad guys, I couldn't believe even the disreputable Pote would have the guts to take a bribe to let them go.

The next day another agent went with me to witness paying Sawat his reward. I could hardly stuff the half million Thai baht, the equivalent of twenty-five thousand U.S. dollars, into my briefcase. It was the largest amount of cash I had ever seen, the largest reward I had ever heard of. I handed it over to Sawat. Most cases came down to having a good informant. Sawat had earned every *setang*. I told him to call me if he was ever threatened, that I had made arrangements with the Counsel General for a U.S. visa if he ever had to flee. We shook hands. That's the last I ever saw of him.

Several weeks later Matty and I were called to the Ambassador's office. I was surprised to find Joy and Eileen already there along with the DEA's senior staff. As good fortune would have it, during the week the case was going down there had been a Southeast Asian drug conference underway in Bangkok, and Matty and I were asked to brief the participants. Among them were two White House staffers who had been so impressed with our case that when they got back to Washington, they drafted identical letters for the big boss to sign. Chargé D'Affaires Ed Masters read the letters of commendation from the President of the United States.

THE WHITE HOUSE
WASHINGTON

April 23, 1975

Dear Mr. Lutz:

I was pleased to learn of your outstanding dedication to the cause of combating international drug traffic, and I wanted to extend my congratulations for your most recent accomplishments.

I understand that through your efforts, twenty-five kilograms of heroin were seized by Thai police, and that the case further resulted in the arrest of two major international heroin traffickers.

Your exceptional performance has not only earned you the admiration of your colleagues in the Drug Enforcement Administration, but also the thanks of your fellow citizens. I am sure I speak for all of them in expressing appreciation for your devoted service to our nation.

Sincerely,

Gerald R. Ford

Mr. Charles H. Lutz
Special Agent
American Embassy
Bangkok, Thailand

I was flying high. Then three months after Sukree and Hoi had been arrested, I crash landed. I got the call at home. "He's out," said Viraj.

"Who's out?"

"Sukree. The prosecutor let him go. We didn't know anything about it until five hours after he was gone."

☆ ☆

Pao Sarasin complained vociferously. Media uproar ensued. The prosecutor claimed it had been Viraj's fault for not formally filing charges against Sukree within the statutorily allotted time period, that he had no choice but to release him.

Viraj claimed he had filed the necessary paperwork, but even had he not, that it was common practice for the prosecutor's office to inform the police of any paperwork shortfall well in advance of such a deadline, particularly when it involved a notorious defendant such as Sukree. We all knew what had happened. Palms had been greased.

In America, we think of official corruption as an aberration. In Thailand, what we consider corruption actually began as an accepted practice that dated back to the days when ancient kings of Thailand dispatched governors to the provinces. They received no salary from the king. The governed were expected to provide for them. It was the wealthy merchants who were able to do so, and thereby received the bulk of the services. Even with the advent of a civil service in Thailand, the governed were still expected to supplement the meager salaries of civil servants. What had changed was that the drug traffickers were now among the wealthy merchant class, and they could well afford to pay for the services they received.

Bangkok Post Investigative Reporter Anussorn Thavisin said it best. He wrote that Sukree's release reminded him of *Pla-Ra*, a traditional Thai dish in which assorted fishes are mixed with rice and salt, jammed into earthen jars, and fermented for as long as a year. In other words, it stank.

But all the complaints were for naught. Sukree had disappeared. No wealthy Thai had ever gone to prison in Thailand before. Sukree wasn't about to be the exception.

☆ ☆

Hoi Se Wan wasn't so lucky. Although a man of means who owned a bus company ferrying passengers between Haad Yai, Thailand and Penang, Malaysia, he was a foreigner with no apparent high-level connections in Thailand. And his partner in crime had apparently not wasted a Thai baht on him. No honor among thieves and dope peddlers. So Hoi was successfully prosecuted and, for all I know, died of old age in a prison cell.

Months later I got information that Sukree had fled to Aranyaprathet, a town near the Cambodian border. Investigative Assistant Yongyut Kusum and I drove there with photos of Sukree in hand. We interviewed the local police and hotel and bar owners, but nothing came of it. Had he been there, no one admitted it. The best that could be said was that we put Sukree out of business since he was never seen or heard from again.

I was taught an important lesson, though. I vowed never again to let any influential Thai in one of my cases be arrested in Thailand if there was any possible way to avoid it.

Also, that was to be my last undercover shot of any consequence. I had no regrets. That Presidential Commendation was definitely something on which I could hang my undercover reputation. And I found I enjoyed managing cases, the plotting and planning of investigations, much more.

Besides, I was about to meet an extraordinary special agent from San Francisco who made me realize there were others far better suited to work undercover than I. This guy could not only talk hungry dogs off meat wagons but could keep their tails wagging while he was doing it.

CHAPTER 11

HOMEBOY

The Herman Jackson / Leslie Atkinson case had been going nowhere. However, soon after we arrested Sukree Sukreepirom and Hoi Se Wan I received a call from Special Agent Lionel Stewart of the DEA's San Francisco Division. And that changed everything.

Lionel told me two GIs had been caught in Japan trying to smuggle a couple of kilos of heroin to the States. He said one of them cooperated and identified their source of supply as a former part-time singer at the now defunct Jack's American Star Bar. With that, my ears perked up. Lionel asked me if I thought I could find the guy. "No problem, man. If he's still in Bangkok, I'll find him." This could be the break I needed.

I tracked the guy down, an employee of the 3-M Company in Bangkok. On the news that I had found him, Lionel rushed to Bangkok with Assistant United States Attorney Dennis "Mike" Nerney in tow, the prosecutor in the Japan case.

I had borrowed the Consul General's office and sat Mike down behind the CG's imposing teakwood desk, with American and State Department flags unfurled behind him. I had called the kid to the American Consulate on a ruse, something about his work visa. When he showed up, Mike pulled off a bluff that would have made any championship poker player envious.

"I've got an arrest warrant in this hand and a 'get out of jail free card' in this hand," Mike said, holding up two scraps of paper. "Which one do you want? Either cooperate with these two gentlemen," pointing to Lionel and me, "or face prosecution in the United States."

Mike had told me the warrant was for aiding and abetting a conspiracy, a charge I hadn't even known existed and, without this guy's confession, a charge that probably wouldn't stick. Fortunately, the trembling young man saw the light and did the right thing.

He told us that the heroin for his two GI buddies had been sold to them by the former bartender at Jack's American Star Bar, Luchai Ruviwat. He agreed to introduce Lionel undercover to Luchai.

Mike promised us that if Luchai sold Lionel any heroin he would have him indicted under a provision of the Controlled Substances Act that makes it a crime to deliver illegal drugs anywhere in the world with the intention of it ending up in the States. But with no treaty that would allow Luchai to be extradited for a drug offense, it was only wishful thinking. I told Mike to go ahead, but that we would probably have to be satisfied with Luchai being prosecuted in Thailand.

We decided that Lionel would make two buys from Luchai; the first we would let ride, and the second we would take him down with, hoping he would cooperate and give up Atkinson, Smedley, and perhaps others. I suggested to Lionel that he tell Luchai that he has friends who work for Pan Am who would smuggle heroin into the States for him, capitalizing on the ruse that Matty Maher and I had used successfully in the Sukree Sukreepirom case. That would give Lionel reason to tell Luchai that he wanted to buy only a small amount of heroin the first

☆ ☆

time to test his smuggling system, and that if it worked, he would order up a second, larger load.

During a stroll through Lumpini Park, the Central Park of Bangkok, the informant introduced Lionel to Luchai as "Johnny," a San Francisco-based heroin dealer. He told Luchai he had known "Johnny" since his days in the Army.

During ensuing conversations with "Johnny," Luchai lamented that he hadn't been making much money in the dope business. He said the guy for whom he had been buying heroin gave him U.S. currency to make the buys. But instead of paying him for his services, he would allow him to keep the difference between the standard rate of exchange of twenty Baht to the dollar and whatever better rate of exchange Luchai could find on the black market. Then he would allow Luchai to use his own money to purchase heroin that he would ship back to the States for him and pay Luchai $25,000 for each kilo once sold, less the hefty shipping and handling fees. Atkinson had obviously kept from Luchai that he was getting $100,000 for each of Luchai's kilograms after diluting it.

"Johnny" negotiated with Luchai to buy a kilo of heroin for $4,700 and said he would give Luchai $50,000 for every kilogram of heroin Luchai wanted to invest with him to sell. Luchai saw "Johnny" as his chance to make some real money. The only snag was that Luchai wanted $2,000 of the $4,700 up front as earnest money for the first buy. Despite the admonition that had been drilled into our heads to never front the money, due to Luchai's status in the drug trade, I got permission for Lionel to do it.

Once again, I turned to Lt. Viraj Jutimitta of the Police Narcotics Suppression Center to work with me on the case. We meticulously documented "Johnny's" first purchase of heroin from Luchai that went down in Siam Square, a shopping area

☆ ☆

frequented by foreigners. Luchai showed up carrying what turned out to be an empty brown paper bag, figuring if it was a rip off, or a bust, that nothing would be found. After nothing happened, Luchai retrieved the heroin from the trunk of a car he had parked nearby.

It was after that first buy that Sukree Sukreepirom made good his escape. And after that, there was no way I was going to let Luchai be arrested in Thailand where he too could use his connections to get out of jail. So, I got permission to let the second, one kilogram buy of heroin ride as well. Next, we would have to figure out a way to lure Luchai out of Thailand to some country that would allow him to be extradited to the States.

It was soon after the second buy, though, that we learned "Johnny" had worked his magic. Luchai had become so convinced that "Johnny" was the real deal, that he told Lionel he was going to bring a kilo of heroin to San Francisco using his own smuggling system. "Johnny" told him if he did, he would not only pay him the $50,000 for it but take him to Las Vegas and introduce him to some showgirls. Little did Luchai know we were going to make his first trip to the States even more memorable than that would have been.

I flew to San Francisco to put the first two buys of heroin into evidence and help prepare for Luchai's arrival. "Johnny" picked Luchai up at San Francisco International Airport and drove him to Chinatown's Holiday Inn where we had reserved a room for him — outfitted with a court-ordered bug. Over dinner, Luchai told "Johnny" that his courier would be arriving in the morning.

The next day "Johnny" and Luchai watched Chalermpol Pitaktrakoon clear pre-alerted customs inspectors with a kilogram of heroin hidden in the false side of his suitcase. Then "Johnny" drove the two of them to a nearby motel to meet "Mister Big,"

☆ ☆

"Johnny's" boss, DEA Group Supervisor Pete Fong, followed by me and half the San Francisco office. Luchai was stunned when we cuffed him.

Defendant Luchai Ruviwat

I sat at the prosecutor's table during the trial to help Mike Nerney keep track of the witnesses and evidence. Star witness Lionel Stewart laid out the two buys he had made from Luchai in Bangkok, and the heroin seized from Chalermpol's suitcase.

At sentencing, Luchai's attorney pleaded for leniency, claiming Luchai's wife was dying of leukemia. He read Portia's plea from Shakespeare's *The Merchant of Venice*, "The quality of mercy is not strain'd . . . ." U.S. District Court Judge Oliver Carter apparently wasn't in a very merciful mood. He sentenced Luchai to 30 years in a federal penitentiary, and Chalermpol, who had confessed, to six.

Luchai was a big catch, a keeper for sure, Atkinson's source of heroin. But we had an even fatter fish to fry, the Fat Man himself. His doing time on a state charge was fine, but we were determined to pin a federal charge on him as well. Luchai refused to cooperate. So, in order to put Atkinson out of business for good, we would have to cast a bigger net.

During the negotiations between "Johnny" and Luchai in Bangkok, our surveillance team had continued to sit on Jimmy Smedley, Atkinson's right-hand-man. Almost every night they watched him eat dinner at Mitch and Nam's Soul Food Restaurant at Soi 16 and Sukhumvit Road, and then mosey over to the Thermae Massage Parlor, a rub and a scrub joint on Sukhumvit Road with a grimy bar in the basement, where he would party with whoever of the "band of brothers" happened to be in town.

Whenever Lionel was in Bangkok, we had a routine – an occasional round of golf, dinners at my apartment for which Joy often baked one of her world-class cheese-stuffed meatloaves, Lionel's favorite, and evenings at the Thermae. Of course, I would have to cover him there. I was becoming a regular at the bar.

It took the smooth-talking, affable "Johnny" no time at all to introduce himself to Smedley, and over time to ingratiate himself with many of the "band of brothers." One of those he had met was Freddie Thornton, a recently retired Air Force NCO. I never heard of him before. At one point Thornton invited "Johnny" to stop by his Bangkok house. They were shooting the breeze when in walked Luchai. Although Luchai had already sold two kilograms of heroin to "Johnny" and was about to smuggle a third to him in San Francisco, they pretended not to know each other. Neither wanted Thornton to know they were in cahoots.

By Thornton knowing Luchai, however, it was clear he was somehow involved in Atkinson's heroin business. We just didn't know how involved. Thornton had never said anything in front of "Johnny" to incriminate himself. So, we had nothing on him.

But I figured his cooperation might be of value. After we took down Luchai in San Francisco, I made a call to Bangkok to ask if the Royal Thai Police would be willing to expel him.

Cops from the 7th Sub-Division raided Freddie's house on a "writ of suspicion" — no court order was needed by the Royal Thai Police to search a residence in those days. They found a pistol that Thornton's paramour claimed was hers and a joint of marijuana that Thornton claimed wasn't his. But it was enough to expel him as an undesirable . . . conveniently onto a Pan Am flight with two DEA agents onboard, and the Hong Kong Police standing by at Kai Tak International to be sure he made his connecting flight to San Francisco.

Lionel and I met his flight and escorted him to the federal building. He told us he thought Atkinson was in the process of sending a huge load of heroin to the States, as much as a hundred pounds, and that if we let him go he might be able to learn the details.

Lionel and I were loath to do that, but there was no way we could hold him. He wasn't in our custody. We had nothing on him, so we took him upstairs to speak with federal prosecutor Mike Nerney who pulled off another one of his bluffs.

Mike told Thornton that he would let him go if he agreed to call Lionel each day to report his progress in finding Atkinson's load and submit to a debriefing by the Central Tactical Unit 9 in Wilmington, North Carolina. CENTAC-9 had been created by DEA headquarters to help coordinate the multi-jurisdictional investigation of Atkinson's enterprise, of which our case in Bangkok was one part. Thornton agreed to the conditions, and we had to let him go.

But if I had known then what I know now, I wouldn't have let Thornton out of my sight!

CHAPTER 12

AMERICAN GANGSTERS

While Freddie Thornton was telling Lionel Stewart that he was tracking down Leslie Atkinson's heroin in the States, back in Bangkok a huge load of Atkinson's heroin was about to be uncovered. And the circumstances surrounding that seizure would eventually reveal Thornton's treachery.

Army Staff Sergeant Jasper Myrick's tour of duty in Bangkok was winding down, and he would soon be on his way to Ft. Benning, Georgia. Days before, a teakwood bedroom set had been dropped off at his Bangkok residence. The weight of their household goods being less than what they were authorized to ship, Jasper told his wife that he had offered to take the furniture back to the States for a buddy.

An Army Inspector accompanied the movers to Myrick's home, a protocol instituted largely at the behest of the DEA to be sure no drugs were packed inside the crates. The inspector noticed that one of the finely carved teakwood nightstands had a rather crudely screwed-on bottom. He drilled a hole in it and out trickled white powder. He uncovered one of the largest hauls of pure heroin ever seized in Southeast Asia, 100 pounds in all.

☆ ☆

Thai 7th Sub-division Police Lieutenant Kulachate Na Ayuthaya, accompanied by Special Agent Brian Raftery, scoured dozens of furniture shops along Sukhumvit Road and eventually located the manufacturer of Myrick's furniture. The shopkeeper identified a photo of Smedley as the person who had ordered it. Special Agent Gary Fouse later learned from Myrick that it had been none other than Luchai Ruviwat who had delivered the furniture to Myrick's home before Luchai had left for San Francisco. Luchai had been a very busy man!

Lt. Kulachate arrested Smedley, and the accompanying DEA agents found a set of Myrick's military transfer orders in his briefcase. They also found a second set of orders in Smedley's briefcase for a Sergeant William Brown who had been transferred weeks earlier to the Eisenhower Medical Center at Ft. Gordon near Augusta, Georgia.

Still in San Francisco cleaning up the remnants of the Luchai Ruviwat case, I got a call from Matty Maher in Bangkok who told me about Brown's orders. Was the Myrick load the one Thornton had been talking about? Or could Brown be sitting on a second shipment? Lionel Stewart hadn't been getting anything of value from Thornton. All he kept telling Lionel was, "I'm working on it."

I alerted Don Ashton, the CENTAC-9 field supervisor at the Wilmington, NC office, and then hopped on a flight to Augusta. By the time I got there, Don's men had set up surveillance outside Brown's Ft. Gordon residence, while other agents were working on a search warrant. When we drove by Brown's house my heart sank. Sitting out on the back patio in the rain was a set of teakwood dining room furniture. We were too late.

We raided Brown's residence and seized the furniture, finding traces of heroin in the false bottoms. We arrested Brown. Thanks primarily to the investigative work of CENTAC-9's Special Agent

Paul Greensfelder, it was soon discovered that one of Atkinson's associates, using a fictitious name, had stayed at a motel near Ft. Gordon just days after Brown had settled in. Paul was convinced he had been the one who picked up the heroin from Brown.

Freddie Thornton had good reason to tell Lionel that he thought Atkinson was sending a large shipment of heroin to the States. And he wasn't lying each time he told Lionel that he was working on it. In fact, he had been in charge of it.

We arrested Thornton. He said after talking with the CENTAC-9 agents in Wilmington he had an epiphany. If he cooperated and told Lionel about Brown's household goods shipment, his life would not have been worth a Thai baht. And even if the DEA decided not to prosecute him, state and local authorities could. But if he followed Atkinson's instructions and delivered the heroin to Atkinson's daughter, Sharon, he would have enough money to party until the feds figured it out, and maybe they never would.

Lionel testified at Atkinson's federal trial in Raleigh to the facts surrounding the Luchai Ruviwat case, and Luchai's connections to both Thornton and Atkinson. I submitted into evidence the Thai newspapers that had been used to stuff the bags of heroin into the false bottoms of Brown's furniture. Presiding Judge Franklin Dupree asked to see one of the newspapers. He studied the Thai script for a moment, then handed it back to me and quipped, "Looks like the voter registration forms we used down here in the South a few years back."

Thornton was a key witness although his cooperation had come at a high cost. He pleaded guilty, and the judge suspended his five-year sentence. The federal prosecutors got him enrolled in the Witness Protection Program and later told reporters that if it had not been for Thornton's first-hand account, Atkinson probably wouldn't have been convicted. That might have been true, however I wasn't pleased. Thornton had back doored us and got off scot-free. CENTAC-9 never found the dope. And because of that, Brown's shipment, worth a cool $5 million on the wholesale market, had hit the streets causing more heartache, misery and pain.

Defendants Leslie Atkinson, Jimmy Smedley and Jasper Myrick,
reprinted from *Asiaweek* magazine,
"The High Times of Sgt. Smack," May 20, 1977

The verdict came in quickly. After calling Atkinson's drug ring "this cancerous growth that has come about our social order," Judge Dupree sentenced Atkinson to twenty-five years to be served in addition to his remaining North Carolina time. Atkinson's pregnant daughter Sharon and her husband Michael Arrington got fifteen years each although he ordered that Sharon be allowed to deliver her baby before reporting to prison. Brown and a half dozen of Atkinson's "band of brothers" were sentenced to ten years each. DEA Administrator Peter Bensinger told the media that these convictions would have "a major crippling impact on importation of heroin into the United States."

In Bangkok, Smedley's life sentence for the dope seized from Jasper Myrick was overturned on appeal, reportedly after paying a $50,000 bribe. He was deported from Thailand but prosecuted in Seattle and put behind bars for good. Myrick spent most of his 33-year sentence in a Thai prison.

Lutz, DEA Administrator Peter Bensinger, and Special Agent Lionel Stewart at the 27th annual Attorney General's Awards ceremony, Department of Justice, December, 1976.

A year later, Lionel and I flew to Washington to receive the Attorney General's Distinguished Service Award, the highest award a DEA special agent can receive, the same award Domenic Petrossi and Harry Fullett had received for Operation Eagle. We were singled out to represent the dozens of agents who had worked to close down Sergeant Smack's heroin empire. I was particularly pleased because my buddies in Philadelphia would learn that I had finally made a few heroin cases!

☆ ☆

I thought we had hammered the final nail in Atkinson's coffin, that he finally learned his lesson. But a dozen years later, in 1987, the incarcerated, ever-persistent Atkinson arranged through a nephew to have two kilograms of heroin delivered in Bangkok to a German diplomat to smuggle back to the States under diplomatic cover. The problem for Atkinson was that the diplomat, who had been introduced to him by a fellow inmate, turned out to be DEA Special Agent Wolfgang Preisler. For his trouble, Atkinson got another nine years tacked on to his already substantial term.

Atkinson was released in 2007 after having spent over thirty-one years in prison, almost half of his life. By then he was an old man, no longer thought to be a danger to society. He lived his last years in Raleigh near daughter Sharon. But before he died in 2014, he launched an academic war on one of his former customers, Frank Lucas.

Lucas was a major Newark/New York City heroin dealer. Years before, he told author Mark Jacobson that he had been the first Black trafficker to bypass the Italian Mafia, taking heroin from the farm to the arm, buying it directly from opium warlords in the Golden Triangle of Burma, Laos and Thailand, and smuggling it back to the streets of Harlem, at least once in the coffins of U.S. servicemen killed in Vietnam. That fairytale became the basis for the 2010 Hollywood blockbuster movie *American Gangster*, starring Denzel Washington as Frank Lucas.

Atkinson was outraged. He claimed Lucas had hijacked his reputation — that he, Ike Atkinson, was the true American gangster. He argued that he had been the source of heroin for Lucas and wanted his title back. While most self-respecting criminals claim their innocence, these two were arguing over which one was the bigger crook. It shouldn't come as any surprise, though. Lucas had made a fortune off his mythical tale, and Atkinson wanted a piece of the action. With these guys it was always about the money.

The truth was that Lucas traveled to Bangkok only once that we know of, to visit his source of heroin, Leslie Atkinson. There's no evidence he ever went to the Golden Triangle. For that matter, there's no evidence Jackson or Atkinson ever went there either. We know Jackson purchased his heroin in Bangkok from Papa San, and after Papa San died that Atkinson got it through Luchai Ruviwat. Where Luchai got the heroin, we never found out. But from the amount of money that we knew Atkinson was paying, it had to have been from someone in Bangkok.

As for heroin being smuggled inside coffins, there was no evidence it ever happened. The rumor started when an informant claimed heroin had been hidden in the coffins of two servicemen killed in Vietnam. However, when the coffins were searched in Honolulu, no heroin had been found. Atkinson was implicated in the affair after being unexpectedly transferred at Okinawa onto the plane carrying the coffins. Atkinson adamantly denied ever having done such a dastardly deed, saying he had much easier ways to smuggle his heroin.

Years later, in 1988, former Bangkok Regional Director Dan Addario added fuel to the myth with an article he wrote for the *San Francisco Chronicle* entitled "Supernarc: The Usual Suspects." He claimed to have witnessed in a Bangkok hospital heroin being pulled from the cadaver of a soldier killed in Vietnam, although Addario had served in Thailand long after our combat troops had been withdrawn from Vietnam.

True crime author Ron Chepesiuk finally put the matter to rest. In his 2010 book, *Sergeant Smack*, Chepesiuk's in-depth investigative reporting provided a logical argument as to why it

☆ ☆

hadn't happened. Jackson and Atkinson purchased their heroin in Thailand. They had U.S. military personnel and facilities at their disposal to smuggle heroin directly from Thailand to the United States with no reason to risk shipping it via a war zone. Even had they gotten their heroin into Vietnam, they had little chance of gaining access to the closely guarded Saigon mortuaries. And even had they somehow gotten heroin into coffins there, it would have been a logistical nightmare to retrieve it on the other end. There's simply no evidence it ever happened. The media, perhaps seeing it as yet another way to discredit the Vietnam War, perpetuated the myth with no due diligence.

Ron sent me an autographed copy of *Sergeant Smack* as a 'thank you' for my having helped him write it — autographed not by him, but by Leslie Atkinson. He said Atkinson wanted to talk with me, tell me he held no hard feelings for my investigative work. Ron told me Atkinson had spoken similarly with other criminal investigators who had dogged him over the years. I told Ron I wasn't interested, that I thought Atkinson was despicable.

Jackson and Atkinson had unleashed a tidal wave of heroin that helped plunge our country into a heroin epidemic. They had each sworn to defend and protect the United States of America but instead weakened it by subverting its military facilities, equipment and personnel for their personal gain. "Country Boy" Frank Lucas had terrorized communities in New York City and Newark with Atkinson's heroin, preying on the weak, living high off the misery of his victims.

These criminals had betrayed America by imprisoning thousands of its citizens in the chains of heroin addiction. They share a legacy of broken neighborhoods, broken homes, and broken lives. And not one of them ever displayed a shred of remorse.

With my two-year tour of duty in Bangkok coming to a close, I had a decision to make. I could extend for a third year and go home or take a home leave and return for another two years. Deputy Regional Director John Doyle helped to make up my mind. He told me of plans to create a second group of agents in Bangkok, and that if I re-upped for another two years, he would recommend me for the new supervisory position. But it wasn't meant to be.

We went on home leave to Philadelphia, just in time for the nation's 200th anniversary celebration. Joy and I went to hear President Ford speak at Independence Hall. And no, despite his kind letter, he hadn't recognized me in the crowd. Then one night John Doyle called me at Joy's parent's home with news. The Career Board had chosen someone else for the supervisory job. He said that since I had taken home leave with his assurance that I would get the promotion, he would try to get headquarters to let me come back for just a third year. I told him no, that Joy and I were looking forward to another two years in Bangkok.

While a disappointment, I thought maybe the promotion would have come too soon anyway. I'd been promoted to journeyman grade well ahead of my classmates, thanks to John Wilder. And after being in Bangkok barely a year, headquarters allotted Bangkok another Senior Special Agent position (GS-13). Being the most senior journeyman agent in the office, I got the promotion. So here I was with less than six years on the job, not only a senior agent but almost a supervisor which typically took at least ten years even to be considered. And realizing that a promotion into the supervisory ranks would put me behind a desk in the office for the rest of my career, I figured waiting a little longer might not be such a bad thing. I was having too much fun on the street.

☆ ☆

Joy, Amy and I flew home over the Pacific and made the return trip via Europe, taking us full circle around the Earth. Joy was almost seven months pregnant when we started the trek back to Bangkok, flying from Philadelphia to Madrid, and then riding the train to Barcelona, Bern, Vienna, and Rome, spending a few days for sightseeing at each location. Then from Rome we flew to stopovers in Istanbul, Teheran and New Delhi. During the hours' long drive from New Delhi to the Taj Mahal and back, on a washboard road clogged with pedestrians, donkey carts and dancing bears, we were certain the baby was going to be born in the back seat of the car along the side of the road.

However, Cindy Anne waited two months after we returned to Bangkok to peek out at the world. As Joy was being wheeled on a gurney into the Bangkok Nursing Home Hospital, her ex-patriot Austrian doctor met us in the parking lot and asked if I wanted to give her a hand. Surprised, but given Joy's okay, I scrubbed, put on a surgical gown, and followed the doctor into the operating room where I administered the oxygen to Joy during the delivery. To be honest, it was more than I needed to see!

Three and a half years earlier, when Amy Lyn had been born at Delaware County Hospital in Upper Darby, Pennsylvania, I was relegated to where I belonged — pacing the floor in the waiting room with the other expectant fathers.

It wasn't long after that when I got another call from San Francisco. This time the swashbuckling Lionel Stewart had another crook he wanted us to make walk the plank. Like Captain Hook's Mr. Smee, I was all in with that.

CHAPTER 13

THE ROYAL TREATMENT

The professor of Undercover Science was on the line. Lionel Stewart had been scheming to make an encore appearance in Bangkok and called to ask if I would aid and abet. He told me another San Francisco agent had flipped a defendant in a heroin case who said he could introduce Lionel by telephone to his source of supply in Bangkok. Lionel asked if I had ever heard of Preecha Leeyaruk.

By chance, before I even arrived in Bangkok, I had read about Preecha in Andrew Tully's 1973 book, *The Secret War on Dope*. He had been indicted in a Bureau of Narcotics and Dangerous Drugs case in Chicago for being the source of heroin to Frank August and eight members of August's criminal gang. But without an extradition treaty between the United States and Thailand for drug offenses, Preecha had been able to thumb his nose at the U.S. justice system.

Then a defendant in the Chicago case introduced a BNDD undercover agent to Preecha in Bangkok, and he was caught red-handed delivering 700 grams of pure heroin. But Preecha must have paid off some Thai officials because he walked, thumbing his nose once again, that time at the Thai justice system.

☆ ☆

Preecha made his living as a travel guide. He took GIs on R & R from Vietnam to see the Reclining Buddha, the Snake Farm, and the ruins of Ayutthaya; and then supplemented his income by selling them dope. According to Tully's book, Preecha had been on the Army Criminal Investigation Division's "top ten" list. Many GIs had come home addicted to heroin thanks to Preecha.

U.S. Customs investigators were quoted as saying Preecha was "perhaps the largest heroin trafficker in Bangkok with operations directly affecting U.S. servicemen and the United States. Preecha admittedly makes large payoffs to corrupt Thai police officials to continue in business." He certainly wasn't in the same league as Sukree Sukreepiron, Hoi Se Wan, or Ike Atkinson, but he had twice avoided facing the music. It was time to change his tune.

I told Lionel we wouldn't let Preecha walk again, that we would find a way to get him out of Thailand if I had to personally smuggle him out in a false-sided suitcase. So Lionel and I cooked up a three-act play we hoped might do the trick.

Act I: We'd get Preecha to deliver a load of heroin to Lionel in Bangkok. Assistant United States Attorney Mike Nerney, the federal prosecutor in the Luchai Ruviwat case, had already promised to indict Preecha in San Francisco if he sold dope to Lionel in Bangkok.

Act II: We'd get Preecha to travel to Hong Kong where he could be arrested.

Act III: We'd have Preecha extradited to San Francisco to stand trial. Through the DEA Hong Kong Office, I received assurances from the Royal Hong Kong Police if we could get him to Hong Kong, they'd send him on his way to the States.

After Lionel's call, I re-read the Preecha section of Tully's book. It mentioned the house off Soi 36, Sukhumvit Road that Frank August had rented while working for a helicopter repair

☆ ☆

company at Don Muang Airport. I realized then it was the same house my family had rented three years later, during our first year in Bangkok, because it described a secret room behind the living room bookcase where August had reportedly stashed his drugs. That was the same room in which we had stowed Amy's toys.

Once again, I called on my "go-to guy," Police Narcotics Suppression Center's Viraj Jutimitta, the same Royal Thai Police lieutenant who had worked with me on the Sukree Sukreepirom and Luchai Ruviwat cases. I told him what we had in mind. Viraj knew Preecha by reputation. I didn't need to remind him of Sukree's escape from custody that had left a bitter taste in both our mouths. He agreed to help orchestrate the play.

The stage was set for Lionel's encore performance. But none of us had foreseen how this three-act play was going to end before the curtain call.

I asked Lionel to set up the initial meeting with Preecha at the Nana Hotel — one of the Rest & Recuperation hotels for soldiers during the Vietnam War that by then had become a mecca for European backpackers. With so many foreigners floating around the hotel, surveillance of their undercover meeting would be a cinch.

I was surveying the scene from a high-backed rattan princess chair in the lobby when I noticed heads turn toward the front entrance. The curtain rose. Lionel aka "Johnny" made his grand entrance onto the stage, strolling with the grace and confidence of a leading man on the red carpet on his way to the Academy Awards. He winked at the star-struck girls as he passed them by.

"Johnny's" thin black leather jacket made him look a little out of place in the perpetual heat of Bangkok, like he had just gotten off a plane, which is exactly what we wanted Preecha to believe. He stopped for a moment at the glass door leading to

☆ ☆

the hotel bar to preen his slightly graying medium afro in the reflection. Then he walked into the pub and sat down on a stool.

We weren't expecting any trouble. It was the initial meeting. Just talk. No money was to change hands. But it was never smart to trust informants, particularly one sitting eight thousand miles away. So, I had my trusty five-shot stainless steel Smith & Wesson .38 tucked in the waistband of my safari suit, leaving nothing to chance.

I watched as the bartender set a brown-colored drink down in front of "Johnny." It had to be Courvoisier and Coke. I had told Lionel before that he was crazy to waste money mixing an expensive cognac with soda pop. But it fit the image of the successful San Francisco dope dealer he wanted to portray.

It wasn't five minutes before Preecha crept in. I recognized him from an old surveillance photo. He glanced furtively about, his pointy nose sniffing the air for any scent of danger, looking very much like the rat he was. He walked into the bar and sat down next to the only middle-aged male of African descent in the place. After no more than ten minutes, he scurried out of the hotel like a cockroach after the lights had been turned on. No need to follow him.

After finishing his drink, "Johnny" left as well. I waited a few more minutes in case Preecha had set up some kind of counter-surveillance around the hotel, and then caught up with Lionel on busy Sukhumvit Road. "I think he bought it," Lionel said, "I told him I had a Pan Am guy who can get the stuff from here to Hong Kong and friends in the tourist business in Hong Kong who can get it from there to San Francisco. He wants me to come to his place tonight for dinner."

"You've got to be kidding," I said. I'd never heard of a drug dealer inviting one of his customers home for dinner before.

"He says his wife makes real good Thai food."

"I'm sure she does," I said, but wasn't crazy about the idea. And covering Preecha's house, located in an alley, could be tough. But Lionel wouldn't be carrying any money. It would just be another chance to talk. So why not?

"Okay, but don't stay there all night. We've got an early tee time in the morning."

Preecha lived within walking distance of Lionel's hotel. I followed him in my car and watched Lionel stop at a street kiosk on busy Sukhumvit Road and then walk away with a small package. He told me later he bought some toys for Preecha's kids. He said by the time he left Preecha's house that night, they were calling him "Uncle Johnny."

Preecha agreed to deliver an initial kilo of heroin. "Johnny" told him if he didn't have any problems in getting it to the States, he'd be back for more. The hitch was that Preecha, just like Luchai Ruviwat, wanted money up front, in this case all five thousand bucks, the going price for a kilo of pure "China white" heroin. Lionel said Preecha wouldn't budge.

Having already set the precedent in the Luchai Ruviwat case, and not having gotten burnt, the bosses trusted my judgment and approved the whole enchilada. But letting five grand walk and possibly never seeing it again made me nervous. Careers had ended for far less.

Lionel set up another meeting for the Nana Hotel. I watched from the lobby as he handed over the money in a white envelope. Two days, and two restless nights later, Preecha delivered a kilo of heroin to "Johnny" in a brown paper bag in the Nana Hotel parking lot. Viraj's men joined us on surveillance, technically seizing the heroin after the deal went down and turning it over to

☆ ☆

me as evidence in accordance with the Mutual Legal Assistance Treaty between our two governments.

We had wired "Johnny" for sound with a Nagra recorder taped to his leg and video-taped the delivery from across the street outside Raja's tailor shop, evidence for a San Francisco jury to eventually consider. Since Lionel was heading back to San Francisco later in the week, I arranged for him to carry the evidence with him on his flight, turning it over to the agents in Hong Kong during his overnight layover and documenting the chain of custody each step of the way. With it, Mike Nerney would get Preecha indicted.

After a two-week intermission, Act II was about to begin. With Lionel back in town, we baited the hook with a scheme I cooked up that we thought might lure Preecha to Hong Kong, and maybe even get him to take a load of dope along with him.

They met again at the Nana Hotel bar. "Johnny" told Preecha that everything had gone okay with the first kilo, and then he changed the subject to his friend in the Hong Kong tourist industry who wanted to expand his business into Thailand. He said his friend was looking for a Thai partner in order to get the business license he would need to set it up. He told him he would talk to the guy about partnering with Preecha and thought the two might be able to do some business together.

Preecha said he was interested in meeting him, and then turned the conversation back to whether "Johnny" wanted to buy more dope or not. That's when "Johnny" laid the bad news on him. "My airline connection's been transferred. I got no way to get the stuff to Hong Kong," Then he told Preecha he would pay him an extra ten thousand dollars per kilo if Preecha could have it delivered to him in Hong Kong. He left Preecha to mull it over.

☆ ☆

Two days later Preecha called "Johnny" and told him he found a foolproof way to get the "goods" to Hong Kong but needed twenty thousand for each kilo delivered — five for the heroin and fifteen for transportation costs. "Johnny" got him down to seventeen total. They agreed on a one kilo trial run. "Johnny" insisted Preecha personally hand over the dope to him in Hong Kong, that he didn't want to meet any strangers, to which Preecha agreed, guaranteeing we'd be able to have Preecha nabbed. We were in business.

Under Thai law the police couldn't knowingly allow heroin to leave Thailand. But in this case, we had no idea how Preecha would be getting the dope to Hong Kong. All we knew for sure was that he planned to go there to talk to "Johnny's" friends about partnering in a travel business. Having the Thai cops escort him from Thailand wasn't necessary, but I invited Viraj to come along.

"Johnny" and Preecha sat side by side in the Pan Am jumbo jet's business class section; Viraj and I sat in economy as Act II came to a close. During the flight Preecha told "Johnny" the dope would arrive the following day. Whether it did or not didn't matter much, since we already had a prosecutable case waiting for Preecha in San Francisco.

After landing at Kai Tak International, the agents from the Hong Kong Office introduced Viraj and me to Chief Inspector Braithwaite of the Royal Hong Police Narcotics Bureau. We pointed out "Johnny" and Preecha standing in the immigration line. They took over from there. Our work was done. Viraj and I taxied to the Lee Gardens Hotel in Kowloon.

The next afternoon three Thai males arrived at the hotel. After checking in at the front desk they sat down in the coffee shop waiting for their rooms to be readied, each with a suitcase

☆ ☆

sitting by his feet. Preecha came into the lobby and signaled to one of them to follow him out onto the street. When the two returned to the lobby, another of the Thai males joined them from the coffee shop, a dark green hard-sided suitcase in hand. The three of them took an elevator to "Johnny's" floor.

The Hong Kong Police had bugged "Johnny's" room. They heard ripping at what turned out to be the lining of a suitcase, the heroin having been hidden behind its false sides. Once "Johnny" saw the white powder, he gave the signal and the door to the adjoining room flew open. Simultaneously, cops in the lobby detained the remaining Thai male sitting in the coffee shop.

After taking a look at their passports, Braithwaite got his boss on the phone, who got his boss on the phone, and the calls probably continued all the way up to the Prime Minister. As it turned out, Chumpol Maneenetr, Manit Prommanond, and Nisit Vejsiriyanan, the men who had been hired by Preecha to smuggle the heroin to Hong Kong, were Thai diplomats — actually former Members of the Thai Parliament traveling on diplomatic passports. That changed everything.

Due to the high-profile of the defendants, and the inevitable publicity, the Hong Kong Government reneged on its agreement to extradite Preecha to the United States. Instead, they decided to prosecute all of them in the Colony, wanting the trial to serve as a warning not to attempt to smuggle drugs into Hong Kong.

"Sorry old chap," Braithwaite told me, "We just can't let these blokes go." I called Mike Nerney in San Francisco to give him the bad news.

☆ ☆

Defendants Preecha Leeyaruk and his diplomatic couriers on their way to an initial appearance in a Hong Kong Court. L-R: Chumpol Maneenetr, Nisit Vejsiriyanan, Preecha, Manit Prommanond, reprinted from Bangkok Daily Time, October 12,1976.

Three months later Preecha, Chumpol and Manit sat side-by-side on the front bench in the ornately decorated Hong Kong High Court, their heads bowed, looking already defeated although the trial had yet to begin. Nisit, the one who had waited in the coffee shop, had been released on bail months before. There was no direct evidence tying him to the heroin, and he hadn't been fool enough to return to Hong Kong to declare his innocence.

Mike Nerney flew to Hong Kong with the kilo of heroin that Lionel had purchased in Bangkok on the off chance it might be of evidentiary value in demonstrating Preecha's predisposition to sell heroin. I had told Mike that he would be met by the Hong Kong police when he disembarked from the plane to relieve him of the heroin before he had to pass through Customs. But prankster Lionel talked Braithwaite into letting Mike sweat it out

☆ ☆

for a while in the arrivals area before showing up. "Some joke," a worried Mike Nerney later remarked.

Star witness Lionel Stewart stood in the well as Crown Prosecutor Peter Duncan led him through the details of his negotiations with Preecha in Bangkok, their travel to Hong Kong, and delivery of the heroin to his hotel room. Judge E.G. Baber, dressed in a British-style robe and horsehair wig, looking like an extra from the movie *Elizabeth*, expertly refereed the numerous objections launched by Defense Counsel E.C. Mumford who showed his frustration more than once, only to be warned by Judge Baber to behave.

During cross examination Lionel was exceedingly polite, much to the annoyance of Mumford. His casual demeanor and often glib responses clearly got under Mumford's skin. Lionel walked a high wire, teasing the Defense Council by occasionally giving him a glimmer of hope that he might stumble into a rhetorical trap, each time catching his balance in the nick of time. That kept Prosecutor Duncan amused, Defense Council Mumford mumbling, and Judge Baber struggling to maintain a straight face. Mumford even tried to muddy the waters by accusing Lionel of being a CIA agent, which Lionel deftly brushed aside.

After Lionel's testimony, Chief Inspector Braithwaite led a procession of Hong Kong policemen to tell of their "very proper" surveillance at the hotel, and their "very proper" arrests of the defendants in Lionel's room. A police chemist "very properly" testified as to the extraordinary purity of the seized heroin. Then the prosecution rested. It was Mumford's turn.

The Defense Council painstakingly led each of his clients through several days of tedious testimony, an agonizingly long process due to the pauses after each sentence to allow translation from Thai into the Queen's English and back again into Thai. I heard every question and answer at least twice. Each sentence wove an incredibly conflicting tale that I figured only the most naïve of the jurors could believe. Unlike in the United States, only a majority of them would be needed to convict.

Each defendant said they were good family men who had never been in trouble before. Each said they had no idea how the dope had gotten into the suitcase. One of them pointed the finger at Nisit, their "no show" cohort who had bailed out and was sitting safely in Thailand. Another said it was a case of mistaken identity, that they came to Hong Kong on holiday. We were "hoodwinked," cried Preecha once given his turn, which became the headline in the following day's *Bangkok Post*.

The seven-member jury found the three guilty. Judge Baber sentenced them to ten years in prison each, opining that trafficking in drugs is a "very grave crime" that brings "so much misery, horror and death into people's lives." Inspector Braithwaite told me the case had instilled great pride in Hong Kong's drug authorities. It had certainly sent embarrassing shock waves throughout Thailand.

I was disappointed that Preecha hadn't had to face the music in the States for what he had done to our GIs. But at the same time, I was pleased that our "fronting the money" had paid off once again, that we had succeeded in luring Preecha out of Thailand and, most importantly, that he had finally faced justice somewhere.

The Narcotics Bureau presented Lionel and I with small mementos of their appreciation, keychains with replica handcuffs and nightsticks engraved with our names and the initials of the Royal Hong Kong Police Department. I carry mine to this day.

☆ ☆

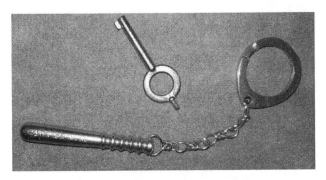

Keychain presented by Royal Hong Kong Police Department
in the Preecha Leeyaruk case.

Each evening after trial adjourned, Lionel, Mike and I would head to the Down Under, an Australian-owned bar and grill located on the site where the Ritz Carlton Hotel stands today, for cocktails and dinner. After the last curtain call on our three-act play, we went there to celebrate.

"Make mine a Courvoisier and Coke," I told the barmaid.

☆ ☆

CHAPTER 14

THE MOB COMES CALLING

He seldom left the room. He'd been entertaining some honeys all week, and his room service bill was beginning to approach the national debt. We knew he'd been to Bangkok at least once before to get the lay of the land, both literally and figuratively. This time was no practice run.

My job was to make sure he was successful, that the heroin he had been sent to procure got safely to New York and into the hands of the thugs who had sent him. But as the investigation unfolded, I made a chance call that helped save the case.

Anthony Porcello was to take delivery of a load of heroin and hand it over to a Mafia courier who would smuggle it to New York City. It didn't take a genius, just a guy willing to take the risk. Porcello knew if he didn't screw it up, his dream of becoming a "made man" in the Gambino crime family might very well come true. On the other hand, if the deal went south, he could find himself on the wrong end of an assassin's .22 caliber pistol.

His golden opportunity had come as the result of an agreement between the Gambino and Lucchese families, two of New York City's top organized crime syndicates. Both gangs had been buying heroin from their Mafia connections in Italy, but the international law enforcement community had been turning up the heat.

☆ ☆

In 1972 Turkish farmers had been forced to switch to the poppy-straw method of extracting opium from poppy plants to produce pharmaceutical morphine, which significantly reduced the amount of opium available to clandestine heroin laboratory operators. Then French authorities began cracking down on heroin labs in Corsica, while the Italians busied themselves rounding up many of the old Mafia dons. So, by 1977, the so-called French Connection was anemic, at best, and the American mob was looking for an alternate source of supply.

By then, the Shan State of Burma had surpassed Turkey as the world's leading cultivator of illicit opium. And the opium warlords in the Golden Triangle of Burma, Thailand, and Laos were churning out tons of "China white" injectable heroin at a record clip. Chinese Triad hoodlums lined up in Bangkok to buy it, determined to capture a bigger share of the world's heroin market. The American Mafia bosses figured they could muscle their way to the front of the line. But there wasn't enough room for two mob families in Bangkok without stepping on each other's Gucci loafers.

The Gambinos and Luccheses were about to go to the mattresses when Sicilian banker Michele "The Shark" Sindona stepped in to broker a deal. The Gambino family would purchase the heroin in Bangkok, Sindona would transport it to the States, the Lucchese mob would distribute it, and they would split the profits. Now all Sindona had to do was find a reliable courier to keep up his end of the bargain.

A trusted acquaintance of Sindona told him he knew of a TWA cargo manager, Antonio Conti, who could move heroin to New York City aboard commercial aircraft. Sindona spoke with Conti by phone several times and, once convinced he was for real, asked him to pick up a load of heroin from Porcello in Bangkok.

Conti was to drop it off at the Surfside 3 Motel in Howard Beach, Queens, New York.

What Sindona didn't know was that his trusted acquaintance was also a trusted acquaintance of the DEA, a cooperating individual, and that in real life the courier, "Antonio Conti," was supervisory DEA Special Agent Enrico Verdolin.

Washington was keeping a close eye on the case. If the Milan, Italy-based Verdolin could get the heroin back to New York City, and it resulted in some of the mafia hierarchy being arrested, it could put a serious dent in two of America's most entrenched organized crime families. The DEA in New York City had already identified several high-level Mafioso involved in the scheme. And once the heroin arrived, it might draw a few more out of the woodwork. Everything was set to go . . . except for one little devil of a detail that needed to be worked out in Thailand.

Not wanting the nation's reputation to be sullied by the nasty heroin trade, the Thai legislature had outlawed drugs from leaving the country — not that the crooks paid the law any mind. Only the nation's cops had to comply. On the surface, the law's intent appeared honorable, but its underlying purpose was anything but.

The law stymied one of drug law enforcement's most effective tools in defeating international drug trafficking: controlled deliveries. A widely accepted investigative technique, controlled deliveries had wiped out entire drug trafficking organizations. Once the drugs were in the possession of law enforcement, they would be transported to the intended recipients anywhere in the world and arrests would go down at both ends of the pipeline — those who had sent it, and those who had received it.

By banning controlled deliveries, Thai lawmakers weren't so much protecting the reputation of their nation as protecting their pocketbooks. Many politicians were complicit in the heroin trade — financing it, protecting it, profiting by it — and didn't want to have their business partners, or their business partners' customers, arrested. It wouldn't be good for business.

Fortunately, Pao Sarasin, Director-General of the Royal Thai Police Narcotics Suppression Center, greased the skids. "It wouldn't be a 'controlled delivery,'" he reasoned. "Once Porcello turns the heroin over to the DEA undercover agent, if the Thai Police maintain 'constructive possession' until it's placed into evidence in the DEA's New York City Laboratory, it will fall within the provisions of the Mutual Legal Assistance Treaty between our two countries." It was a bit of a stretch, but no one would dare question Pao Sarasin.

Once the dashing young Enrico Verdolin had checked into his room at Bangkok's Siam Intercontinental Hotel, I asked him to come to the American Embassy to bring us up to speed on the investigation. We taped a Nagra recorder to his thigh, and the microphone under his Italian silk shirt to record his conversation with Porcello, and then put him out on the street to hail a taxi to Porcello's hotel.

Porcello greeted "Antonio Conti" as he walked into the Hyatt Rama Hotel lobby, having been given a photo of him before leaving New York City. They sat down at a table in the bar and compared the halves of a dollar bill they'd each been given. Porcello told him the package would be ready for pick-up the following day.

The next afternoon we wired Enrico again, and this time he went to Porcello's room where Porcello handed him three hermetically sealed clear plastic bags of white powder that "Antonio" put in his briefcase. Porcello's job was done. "Antonio's" was just beginning. Enrico dropped the bags of heroin off with me, and then we dropped him off near his hotel. He would be leaving the following morning for JFK via Rome.

Heroin delivered in Bangkok to Enrico Verdolin by defendant Anthony Porcello. Standing L-R: Special Agent Gary Fouse, Verdolin, Lutz, Special Agent Helmut Witt, Royal Thai Police Lt. Khulachate Na Ayuthaya, Special Agent Dan Hoerner. Seated: DEA Investigative Assistant Yongyut Kusum.

When Enrico got back to his room the phone was ringing. It was Porcello. "I'm coming over," he said, and hung up. What was this all about? Had Enrico been found out? He called me and I scrambled the tech agent, Special Agent Helmut Witt, to the Siam Intercontinental to bug his room, and the few agents I could find to set up surveillance at the hotel. There wasn't enough time to get the cops involved.

Helmut had barely slipped out of the room when Porcello showed up, a brown paper bag in his hand. "I forgot to give you this," he told "Antonio," handing over a fourth bag of white powder. Porcello had held it back, probably for his personal use, most likely thinking he could blame "Antonio" for the loss. But he must have gotten cold feet when he realized what would happen if his boss didn't believe him.

☆ ☆

Porcello asked to see where "Antonio" had stashed the heroin he had already gotten. Quickly thinking, Enrico said he had already sealed it in the false sides of his suitcase. "Wow," said Porcello as he examined the suitcase, "No one will ever find it." Of course, there was no heroin in the suitcase, the three bags having been safely tucked away in my lock-bar cabinet back at the American Embassy.

As they talked, Enrico noticed the hastily installed room bug had fallen from under the coffee table. Without panicking, he stepped on it. Had Porcello noticed, it would have blown the deal and set Porcello on the run. That would have been a disaster. But having put his foot down, Enrico saved the day! And the next morning he flew off to Italy.

I had asked the Royal Thai Police 7th Sub-Division to work with me on the case. Police Lt. Kulachate Na Ayuthaya, the cop who had found the shop that made the furniture for Jimmy Smedley in the Atkinson case, was assigned as the one to maintain "constructive possession" of the evidence until submitted to the DEA Laboratory in New York City. We hopped on a Pan Am flight the following day, the heroin in a cardboard box sitting by our feet.

Enrico checked into a mid-town New York City Hilton Hotel under his undercover name, "Antonio Conti," with a phony Italian passport to back it up. Agents picked up his suitcase and dropped it back off after hard wiring it with a transmitter. They had also stuffed it with four bags of sham heroin and a small representative sample of the real stuff, not more than an ounce from the heroin Kulachate and I had turned over to the Laboratory. That way, only a small sample of the heroin would be lost in the unlikely event the suitcase disappeared — unlikely because New York Assistant Special Agent-in-Charge Tom Byrne had pulled out all the stops.

His plan was to have whoever picked up the suitcase at the Surfside 3 Motel followed to its destination, hopefully into the arms of some big shots in the Luchese organization. That's when the busts would go down. Tom had more agents sitting at Howard Beach than we had stationed in all of Southeast Asia. A police boat sat in the canal behind the motel, a police helicopter stood by to assist the vehicular surveillance. Everyone had their assignments . . . except me and Kulachate. We'd brought the evidence and wanted to be part of the action, but to Tom Byrne we were just excess baggage.

"Get in the car with the tech agent," Tom directed.

I wasn't happy about that, but he was right. We had no business being on the front lines. I didn't know my way around New York City, didn't even have a gun. And I was responsible for Kulachate who had no law enforcement authority whatsoever, and no diplomatic immunity if something went wrong.

With our fate dutifully accepted, Kulachate and I settled into the tech agent's G-ride. We rode to a side street within a block of the Surfside 3 Motel and parked out of sight but close enough to receive the signal from the transmitter hidden within the suitcase. We waited about fifteen minutes and then on cue an announcement came over the two-way radio. "The taxi's pulling up," said an agent who had an eyeball on the front of the motel. The taxi was owned by the DEA and driven by a New York agent.

"OK. He's getting out of the back seat with the suitcase," another agent announced as Enrico carried the suitcase into the motel. And that's exactly what we heard coming over the receiver: the door of the taxi creaking open then slamming shut, footsteps into the lobby, Enrico asking the clerk for the key to a room that he said should be reserved for a Mr. Conti, more footsteps, a door being unlocked then closed. And then total silence.

☆ ☆

"The taxi's pulling out," one of the surveillance agents broadcast. Now it was just a matter of waiting.

It seemed a lot longer, but probably ten minutes later when another agent announced that a black Pontiac was pulling into the motel's rear parking lot. The Luccheses no doubt had someone in the motel on their payroll who had notified the gang that Mr. Conti's suitcase had arrived.

"White male. Five-ten. Dark hair. Wife-beater T. He's out of the vehicle. Walking into the motel," an agent reported over the radio.

A few moments later we heard over the receiver the motel room door creak open, slam shut, and then footsteps.

"He's coming out. Putting the suitcase in the trunk," an agent announced over the air. "The vehicle's moving."

Then silence. Nothing. Not another sound.

For a moment I thought our two-way radio had gone on the fritz. After what seemed an eternity, Tom Byrne came over the air. "Anybody got him?" Again, silence. Then it hit the fan.

A cacophony of overlapping status reports began, transmissions being cut off by other transmissions. Surveillance vehicles scrambled in every direction in hopes of spotting the black Pontiac.

Stunned that the suspect could have so easily escaped what I thought was an impenetrable cordon, I told the tech agent there was no reason for us to just sit there. "We might as well join the search."

We drove down the main drag, Cross Bay Boulevard, and pulled up at a stop light. A dark green Pontiac sat in the left turn lane just ahead of us with its turn signal on. The driver looked straight ahead — Italian-looking, dark hair, wife-beater T. He fit the description of the guy we were looking for, but then so did just about every other guy I had seen in Howard Beach that day. Besides, his car was dark green, not black as had been reported over the radio. I don't know why, but when he made the turn on the green arrow, I noted his license plate. The light then changed for us and we drove straight ahead.

Agents were being dispatched to the addresses of every known suspect in the case in the event the Pontiac was headed to one of those locations. But it was nowhere to be found. We circled around the area hoping to pick up a signal from the transmitter in the suitcase. It was a longshot, but we had nothing to lose. As we doubled back toward the motel, I figured what the hell, and picked up the radio handset to call the New York base operator.

"Base. This is Bangkok One. Over."

"Go ahead Bangkok One."

"I need a license plate check," and gave him the number I had memorized from the dark green Pontiac.

Within minutes it came back that the plate belonged to Lucchese family associate Vittorio "Little Vic" Amuso with a street address in Howard Beach, within blocks of the Surfside 3 Motel. Amuso must have been driving around looking for a tail. The good news was he didn't spot one. The bad news was there wasn't one. We had been looking for the wrong color car.

We drove to Amuso's rowhome and parked outside. No sign of the Pontiac. No noise over the transmitter either. The tech agent then radioed New York base and asked them to look up the telephone number for Amuso's residence and dial the number. Over the radio we could hear the rings from the Base Station's phone, and simultaneously over the receiver we heard the exact muffled rings. That was good enough to get a search warrant, and within several hours agents had raided the house and found the suitcase in a hall closet.

☆ ☆

The New York office arrested Amuso and his partner-in-crime, Anthony "Gaspipe" Casso. They also arrested high-level Gambino-associate Vincent Napoli of Brooklyn, the one who had hired Porcello. The only loose end now was Porcello who was still partying in his hotel room in Bangkok, blissfully unaware of the events going on in New York City.

We pulled off the highway at a phone booth. I called the New York base and asked to be patched through to the American Embassy in Bangkok. "Gary, they've taken the case down here," I yelled, trying to be heard over the static on the phone and the roar of the traffic passing by. Special Agent Gary Fouse was my partner in Bangkok and the one keeping an eye on Porcello. "We don't have a warrant for him yet," I said. "See if the cops will throw him out of the country."

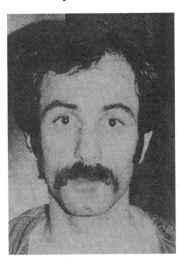

Defendant Anthony Porcello

By the time Kulachate and I left New York City for home, Porcello was on his way to the States. The cops had raided his room and found a small amount of marijuana. He was fined 200 Thai baht (U.S. $10) and turned over to the Thai Immigration

Division to be deported as an undesirable — conveniently onto a Pan Am flight to JFK, accompanied by a couple of agents to keep an eye on him.

Porcello and Napoli eventually pleaded guilty to avoid trial and were sentenced to ten years each in prison. However, Amuso and Casso beat the rap. While I wasn't called for the trial, and thus don't know the ins and outs of the prosecutor's case, I'm certain the lack of a continuous surveillance between the time Amuso picked up the suitcase and when it was retrieved from his hall closet had been a factor. Enrico Verdolin had been brought in from Milan to testify and recalled Amuso during a recess pointing his index finger at him and pretending to pull the trigger.

Amuso became a "made man" that same year, no doubt aided by his rise in stature after beating our case. Less than ten years later, by 1986, he rose to the top of the heap in the Lucchese crime family. He appointed his pal, Anthony Casso, as his underboss, and the two led what is considered by many organized crime experts to have been the most prolific killing spree in Mafia history. Both were indicted in 1991 for murder, convicted, and are serving life sentences. During the trial, the prosecutor referred to Amuso as "The Deadly Don."

Although our case hadn't put Amuso and Casso behind bars where they belonged, it had blunted an early attempt by the mob to find an alternate supply of heroin in Southeast Asia.

CHAPTER 15

A REGIONAL APPROACH

T hen I went from the wok, the stir-frying pan into the fire, from the Land of Smiles and Buddhist enlightenment into the land of the Pharaohs, a region of the world where civil unrest and sectarian violence dates back to the Crusades. This time my ambition got me into the Middle East, and into much more than I had bargained for.

We weren't back from Bangkok for six months when the overseas bug bit me again. I returned to a job at the National Training Institute as class coordinator for a special agent basic training class, and instructor for several of its courses. I also worked with a former CIA station chief to teach those about to go overseas how to coexist with the intelligence community. We barely settled into a house we had had built for us in Oakton, Virginia when I noticed a vacancy announcement for the narcotics attaché position in Cairo, Egypt.

It would be a promotion into the supervisory ranks, although in name only. Cairo was a one-man post of duty, the only one in the DEA at the time, which meant I would have only myself to supervise, a task that I thought I could handle. Since this was considered a hardship post, I didn't think many would apply. And since DEA Administrator Peter Bensinger would make the final call, if he remembered my name from the Attorney General's Award ceremony two years earlier, I would have a better than even chance of getting the job.

That night I explained the situation to Joy and asked her what she thought. "If we're going to go back overseas," she said, "we might as well do it while the girls are still young."

"You'd better sleep on it," I suggested. "If I apply, I might just get it." Hearing no objection in the morning, I tossed my name into the *taqiyah* (Arab skull cap).

I didn't know it at the time, but several years earlier General Sami Farag, Director of the Egyptian Anti-Narcotics General Administration (ANGA), had lobbied for a DEA office in Cairo. In his view, every civilized country in the world had DEA agents assigned to its U.S. Mission, and even in some not so civilized countries, and Farag wasn't about to let Egypt be denied.

While I don't pretend to know all that went into their thinking, Bensinger and the Chairman of the House Select Committee on Narcotics, New York Congressman Lester Wolff, took advantage of warming relations between Egypt and Israel in the wake of the Camp David Accord to satisfy General Farag's request. But for some inexplicable reason, the idea of a DEA officer in Cairo wasn't popular with the American Ambassador to Egypt, Hermann Eilts. In fact, he was dead set against it.

So Bensinger and Wolff traveled to Cairo to diplomatically shove a DEA office down the Ambassador's throat. Determined to have the last word, Eilts demanded the narcotics attaché be restricted to Egypt. "If there's not enough work for him here, he shouldn't be here," Eilts opined.

A special agent in Beirut who had been the liaison to ANGA made him the perfect choice to open the office. And now that his

☆ ☆

two-year tour of duty was coming to an end, the position was being re-advertised.

As luck would have it, my boss, Chief of Domestic Training Paul Malherek, was about to embark on a two-week trip to INTERPOL at St. Cloud, France, to evaluate delivery of a newly developed Intelligence Analytical Training Course by a DEA International Training team. But when his wife realized the date conflicted with events surrounding the high school graduation of one of their children, Paul had to back out. He asked if I could go in his stead. Springtime in Paris? How could I refuse?

I was lunching on a filet of horse meat with a side of ratatouille and sipping a glass of INTERPOL-labeled Bordeaux wine when I got word that Regional Director John Warner wanted to see me. He had responsibility for DEA offices in Europe, the Middle East, and South Asia, and I assumed had been asked for his opinion on the list of candidates for Cairo. The interview must have gone okay because not long after I returned from Paris, I was told I got the job.

There was no requirement for language training. Being a former British colony, English was commonly spoken among the Egyptian elite. And it would have taken me longer to learn Arabic than the two years I would likely be stationed there. Instead, I studied up on Egyptian history and current events.

I learned that Egypt was strictly a drug consuming country, the drug of choice being Lebanese hashish, a concentrated form of marijuana smoked in a hookah, a water pipe, so the burning embers wouldn't be accidentally inhaled. Being the world's connoisseurs of hashish, Egyptians demanded the very best quality — the middle grades going to Europe, the dregs to Canada. For some unfathomable reason, hashish had never caught on big in the United States.

☆ ☆

Egypt also had a stimulant abuse problem. The British had introduced amphetamines during construction of the Aswan Dam to increase the productivity of local laborers, WOGS as they became known, due to the letters on the back of their uniforms which stood for "Working on Government Service."

A relatively modest amount of opium poppy was cultivated clandestinely in the southern province of Asyut. That which survived ANGA's annual opium eradication campaign was consumed in-country.

So Egypt's drug problems had no impact on the United States, the normal criterion for stationing DEA agents abroad. And that made me wonder why we had an office in Cairo in the first place, although I wasn't about to argue since it would be the promotion I had missed out on in Bangkok.

I happened to read in the *Washington Post* that Alfred Atherton had been appointed the new ambassador to Egypt, replacing the retiring Hermann Eilts. While Henry Kissinger's shuttle-diplomacy was credited with the Camp David Accord, unsung hero Atherton had done much of the grunt work, and that was his reward. It gave me an idea.

Peter Bensinger was among the movers and shakers in Washington. Scion of a prominent Illinois family, he had held some important law enforcement positions in his home state before coming to Washington. With his pedigree and professional accomplishments, it struck me that the debonair Bensinger might like to meet Atherton who had become a Washington celebrity in his own right. And for me to meet the new Ambassador in the company of the DEA Administrator would make for a great introduction. I went up through the chain of command to Bensinger's office to ask if I could set up a meeting for us with Atherton.

☆ ☆

For fifteen minutes or so we sat in his office at Main State while Bensinger briefed Atherton on the international drug situation with a focus on the Middle East. Then, as if he hadn't heard a word Bensinger had said, Atherton stood up and said, "Peter, I have another appointment. Please have Mr. Lutz wait here until I call for him. I want a chance to look around in Cairo a bit before I decide whether to bring him out or not."

Bensinger seemed unfazed. I struggled to keep a smile on my face while shaking hands with Atherton. With my spirits descending faster than the elevator carrying us to the ground floor, I turned to Bensinger and asked, "What do you want me to do, Sir? My household goods are in storage, my house is rented, and we're booked to leave for Cairo in another week."

Bensinger then gave me my first lesson in Washington power politics. "Go," he said. This head of an administration had to pay no mind to a mere ambassador. So off we went.

Ambassador Atherton showed up in Cairo a few days after us. That Thursday, the end of the Muslim workweek, he stopped by the Marine (Security Guard) House during their weekly "happy hour" to introduce himself to the official American community gathered there. Atherton kept smiling as he worked his way around the bar shaking hands . . . until he got to me. In a low voice he said, "I want to see you in my office first thing in the morning." Uh oh, I gulped.

Atherton's secretary never looked up when I walked in. With her eyes glued to the paperwork on her desk, she waved a thumb over her shoulder pointing to the open door. She knew what was coming. I knew what was coming. Trouble.

Atherton sat in shirt sleeves behind an ornately carved wooden desk poring over a stack of cables. He never offered me a seat. After a few moments he removed his reading glasses and looked up. "I thought I told you not to come forward until I called for you."

Now telling a lie to an ambassador is dangerous business. They are the personal representatives of the President of the United States. I could have easily used Bensinger's "Go" as my excuse but wasn't about to front him off. So I said the only thing I could think to say after agonizing over it the night before: "When I received our diplomatic passports and visas, I assumed you had approved it."

"Harrumph," he muttered, and then said, "I'm going to call Washington and ask them to look into the matter."

"For whatever time I'm here, Sir, can I go ahead and do my job?"

"All right," he mumbled, waving me out of his office as he turned back to his reading. Having gotten the green light, at least for the time being, I got to work.

I had already met ANGA's Director-General, Sami Farag, and his Deputy, Mahmoud Zaki. ANGA is the oldest single-mission narcotics agency on the planet, established in 1929 by the Brits, one year before the U.S. Federal Bureau of Narcotics, and they were very proud of that distinction.

Farag and Zaki were polar opposites; Farag a wealthy Coptic Christian, Zaki a devout Muslim of modest means. Like many wealthy Egyptians, Farag thought of Egypt as part of Europe; Zaki, like most Egyptians, prided his Middle Eastern heritage. Farag and his family lived in a large apartment in Maadi, a British-built bedroom community south of Cairo, and owned a family farm in the Nile River delta near Ismailia that raised some of the finest pigeons in Egypt; Zaki lived in a modest rowhome in Heliopolis. Farag was a commanding, authoritative figure; Zaki a humble, pious man who knelt on his prayer rug for the *Salat*,

☆ ☆

the Muslim prayer, five times each day. Farag was at the top of his game; Zaki was still climbing — one day to replace Farag as ANGA director, and then to be appointed Governor of Asyut Province. Over time I was able to build good relationships with both of these fine men. Joy, the girls, and I were even invited to their homes for dinner on occasion, most unusual in Egyptian culture.

My predecessor had done what he could while stationed there, among other things setting up a system to track ships transiting the Suez Canal that might contain seaborne drug shipments. He was involved in several seizures of hashish being smuggled into Egypt from Lebanon. He also found plenty of time to hone his tennis game. There just wasn't that much to do.

After the first two months, I was getting as anxious to find something meaningful to do as a thirsty camel hunting for an oasis. I didn't want to spend two years of my life trying to solve Egypt's drug problems or learning to play tennis for that matter. Then I received notice of a regional conference in Paris and decided to make a case for some regional responsibility.

The sectarian war in Lebanon between Muslims and Christians had forced the closure of the Beirut office years earlier, and Ankara inherited Lebanon along with the rest of the Middle East. During my turn in the barrel with John Warner, his Deputy Clarence Cook, and my immediate supervisor Vic Maria, I told them I thought Narcotics Attaché Terry Dunne had his hands full with Turkey, one of the world's largest opium-producing countries, let alone having all the Middle East to cover. I argued for a piece of the *fatayer* (Middle Eastern meat pie).

"Your ambassador won't let you out of Egypt," Warner warned, the first time I heard of the concession that Bensinger and Wolff had made to Eilts.

☆ ☆

"But there's a new sheriff in town," I said, "Atherton may not even know about the deal," not fully believing it, Atherton having questioned my being posted to Egypt. "Let me give it a try," I pleaded, daring to venture into uncharted waters.

Before I left Paris, I realized I might have bitten off more pomegranate seeds than one man alone could chew. For they had handed me not only responsibility for Lebanon, the epicenter of hashish and heroin production in the Middle East, but Cyprus, Jordan, and Saudi Arabia — except for Israel out of concern that it might appear as if the DEA was being used as a political pawn to help bring Egypt and Israel get even closer together — and all of East Africa.

Vic Maria suggested I start with Cyprus. Sitting just forty miles across the Mediterranean Sea from Beirut, it would be a convenient spot from which to launch informants into Lebanon. So as soon as I got back to Cairo, I sat down and drafted a cable to the American ambassador in Nicosia requesting permission to travel there to establish liaison with the Cypriot National Police. Atherton got an informational copy of every outgoing cable, so if he had a problem with it I was certain I would be called in for another "see-me-first-thing-in-the-morning" meeting. I breathed a sigh of relief when that call never came.

I was soon off to Cyprus on the first of many trips there, including a vacation to that bucolic isle the following year with Joy and the kids. I worked closely with the chief of their narcotics unit, a top-notch cop who one day would become their chief of police. And over the next two years the groundwork was laid for opening a DEA office in Nicosia.

But the center of my universe quickly became Lebanon.

CHAPTER 16

THE LONE RANGER

Beirut was a war zone. For more than four years Lebanese Muslims and Christians had been fighting a new Crusade on its streets. Shortly after hostilities began, a DEA special agent had been kidnapped, mistaken for a CIA case officer. Fortunately, his true identity was sorted out in time, and he was released unharmed. But the DEA closed its Beirut office, deeming it far too risky to have agents stationed in Lebanon.

To exacerbate matters, shortly before my first visit to Lebanon, Iranian rioters had breached the walls of the American Embassy in Teheran capturing fifty-two of our diplomats. The Ayatollah called for Muslims around the world to rise up and slay the American devils. It wasn't a good time for an American to be living or working anywhere in the Middle East. However, as risky as it was, Lebanon commanded my almost undivided attention.

It was the hub of the world's hashish trade, and a center for Middle East heroin production. I was to see cannabis plantations in the Bekaa Valley irrigated and fertilized like Christmas tree farms, with bushes towering eight feet tall. And hidden in the same valley clandestine laboratories churned out heroin hydrochloride made from Turkish and Iranian opium destined for international markets.

I had landed aboard a Middle East Airlines flight from Cairo. Due to hijackings, Lebanon's MEA was the only air carrier that dared service Beirut in those days. Two of the embassy's local expediters, who I recognized from previous visits, greeted me. One grabbed my overnighter and took it around the Customs inspectors, while the other escorted me through Immigration via the VIP lane. But when they walked me out to the parking lot, instead of the bullet-proofed Cadillac limousine I had become accustomed to riding in, they led me to a beat-up old Pontiac muscle car with a guy slouched next to it wearing a Chicago Bulls t-shirt.

This looks like a kidnapping to me, I thought. But between the driver and the two expediters, it was three to one. I didn't have a weapon. No sense resisting. So I squeezed into the backseat and we took off through the airport parking lot toward the exit.

During that era, seventeen separate military groups operated in Lebanon and each group controlled a section of Beirut. We needed a scorecard to keep track of them all. Traveling between sectors was like crossing international borders except you didn't need a visa — only a good reason for being there. And Beirut had been divided in half. A two-block-wide strip of bombed out buildings ran like a spine down the city's center, a no man's land separating East from West Beirut, Christians from Muslims. The American Embassy was located in West Beirut, protected by Saudi Arabian military guards.

Cars were lined up waiting to get through the checkpoint out of the airport. We pulled around them and the expediter riding shotgun picked up a poster from under his seat and held it up to the windshield for the guards to see. One of them, an AK-47 slung over his shoulder, glanced over and nonchalantly waved us by. Once we passed through the narrow opening in the barbed-wire-topped cyclone fence, the expediter started to roll up the

☆ ☆

poster to put it back under his seat. Out of curiosity I asked to see it. He passed it back to me saying the Iranians controlled that particular checkpoint. My jaw dropped when I saw the Ayatollah's mug plastered on the poster. Had we been stopped, the number of American hostages being held by the Iranians would have surely increased by one.

Normally when we drove under an overpass or through certain neighborhoods in the Embassy limo, I'd be asked to lie down on the back seat so as not to draw the attention of snipers. That wasn't necessary in the backseat of a GTO, which I guessed was the whole point of their picking me up in it.

They dropped me off at the Mayflower Hotel in Hamra, West Beirut, where I normally stayed, within walking distance of the American Embassy. I checked in at the front desk. The embassy had made the reservation, so I made the point of telling the clerk I was with the DEA. I didn't normally identify myself as a narc. With that came certain risks, like anyone seen talking to me would be labeled a rat. Some might think my briefcase was stuffed with money to pay the rats, and that would make me a target for thugs. But the last thing I needed was for someone to mistake me for a CIA case officer. I really couldn't win.

Once in my room I pulled aside the shredded curtain and peered down onto the main drag. Not a good idea. I picked up the phone to ask the front desk to move me to a room overlooking a side street to lessen my exposure to car bombs. The telephone receiver disintegrated in my hand. Hotel workers had replaced the glass window in the room after the last bombing but hadn't noticed that shrapnel had shredded the phone while leaving it sitting on the nightstand seemingly undisturbed.

Most of my time in Beirut I was the Lone Ranger, which was technically a violation of DEA rules. It provided no one to witness my activities or attest to my reports. More important for me personally, there was no one to cover my rear end. But I had an ally in Tim Steen, a Royal Canadian Mounted Police officer, one of two Mounties stationed at the Canadian Embassy in Beirut. In those days, the RCMP handled both national security and criminal liaison. However, their "terms of reference" didn't allow them to handle criminal informants. So on those occasions when Tim ran across someone with information about drugs thought to be destined for the United States, he would give me a call.

On one of my dozen or more trips to Beirut, he let me know that a guy had called with a proposal for dealing with drug traffickers. "You want to talk with him?" he asked.

"Sure. When can we meet?"

"He's on the 'Christian side' (East Beirut) and says he can't get over here on his own. We can go over there tonight and pick him up."

Tim drove his personal vehicle across the Green Line, that block-wide spine of no man's land, the eerie stretch of blown out buildings and rubble marking the line between the two warring factions. We had no trouble leaving West Beirut or entering into East Beirut.

The want-to-be informer, Joseph, who turned out to be a Lebanese Christian militia member, was waiting outside a restaurant. He jumped in the back seat. As we approached the Green Line, Tim told him to lie down on the floor and cover himself with the blanket. We drove through the Christian checkpoint without incident, crossed the green zone, and then stopped at the Muslim checkpoint. One of the guards took our diplomatic passports into his shed while another circled the car inspecting it. After a few minutes, the one with our passports returned, handed them to Tim, and waved us through. I heard

✩ ✩

Joseph let out an audible sigh of relief from under the blanket. I think we all did!

Tim dropped us off at a local restaurant and kept watch outside. Over coffee, Joseph made a rather unique proposal: "Drug traffickers are ruining both our countries," he said, "Give me the names of the drug traffickers on your list and for $10,000 apiece I'll have them killed."

"How will I know they're dead?" I asked.

"I'll bring back an ear from each one."

"You'd better bring back two" I joked, "How else would I know you're not cheating me?"

He didn't think that was funny. He wasn't joking.

"It doesn't work that way," I said, "We arrest drug traffickers and seize their drugs. We don't kill them."

Joseph told me he would make his own way back to East Beirut. I never heard from him again.

✩ ✩ ✩ ✩ ✩ ✩

On one trip to Beirut, Tim and his wife, Marie, invited me to their apartment for dinner. We were sitting at the dining room table when suddenly machine gun fire opened up outside. Tracer bullets flew past the window, and several explosions from what sounded like grenade launchers rattled the windows. We hit the floor. Tim crawled out onto their concrete-walled balcony and motioned for me to follow.

Peering over the edge of the balcony, I saw the remnants of a building, its brick-and-mortar walls long gone, replaced by sandbagged bunkers on several floors. Catty corner, at the opposite end of the block, sat another building in pretty much the same shape. Tim thought the bombed-out buildings were occupied by opposing pro-Syrian and pro-Palestinian militiamen, shooting

☆ ☆

at each other to dutifully demonstrate loyalty to their individual causes.

Tim low-crawled back into the dining room to rescue the bottle of wine we had been drinking. Then we sat out on the balcony floor chatting and enjoying the fireworks while finishing off the bottle of local Chateau Ksara red blend.

☆ ☆ ☆ ☆ ☆ ☆

At some point during each visit, I would pay a courtesy call on the local cops. I didn't trust them. The chief of the narcotics unit wore a solid gold *Patek Philippe* watch which could hardly be afforded on a cop's salary. But it was a call I had to make, if for no other reason than to justify my being in Beirut.

During one of my calls, a hand-cuffed defendant was dragged into his office. The chief told me the guy had been picked up at the airport with a small amount of heroin and a U.S. visa in his passport. He said he figured I would want to talk with him. He asked the guy a few questions in Arabic, and when he got no response, POW, the chief cold-cocked him right in front of me.

He probably thought I'd feel indebted for his helping me. But I wasn't interested in small-fry crooks like that defendant. The ones I was interested in were too powerful for the police to mess with or, more likely, had the police on their payroll, like the benefactor who had given him that watch. Besides, having seen the assault meant more paperwork. I was obliged to report any prisoner abuse to the State Department for their annual Country Reports on Human Rights Practices.

Ambassador John Gunther Dean set aside an office for me in the Chancery, one that a year and a half after my last visit to Beirut collapsed in a suicide bombing killing sixty-three people. I had requested that headquarters send me the informant files from the defunct Beirut office. On each trip I tried to call one or more of the former informants. However, most of the lines had been disconnected; probably the informants had been disconnected as well, having fled the sectarian violence or been killed in the crossfire by rival drug gangs, militias or fanatical religious groups. I finally got through to one of them.

Mustafa agreed to meet me in my hotel room that evening. I could have asked him to come to the American Embassy but was certain the comings and goings of visitors was being closely monitored by any number of political, if not criminal organizations. So I gave him my hotel room number, something I wouldn't ordinarily do. I never met the guy, wouldn't know him other than by the photo in Mustafa's informant file, and didn't know if he would come alone. But I had no choice. If he stopped at the desk to ask for my room number, they'd know for sure he was a snitch.

Before leaving the Embassy, I borrowed a .38 caliber revolver from the regional security officer. The first time he had loaned me one he warned me not to pull it on anyone. "If someone bumps into you on the street," he said, "just say, 'excuse me' and keep walking. I'll guarantee you he'll have more firepower than you've got."

The informer was due at seven; fifteen minutes before then I walked down the hall, stood in the recess of a fire escape door, and waited. It was a few minutes after seven when the elevator door opened. I glanced down the hall and saw a short, mousy-looking guy about fifty, dressed in a dark brown suit a size too large for him, walk to my door and knock. He resembled the picture in the informant file. He was alone.

I sauntered down the hall, my pistol palmed in my pocket, and stopped behind him. "Mustafa?" When he nodded, I patted him down, found a semi-automatic pistol in his waistband, stuck it in mine, unlocked the door, ushered him in and dead-bolted the door behind us.

Mustafa said he worked at the port authority, and that the freighter *Lucky Star*, loaded with seven tons of hashish, was about to depart for the coast of Italy. "I'll know when she leaves," he said.

The smugglers used junk freighters to transport their dope. The old rusting hulks were expendable. They had no navigational aids, so the crews had to pilot by dead reckoning. The first sighting they needed to take after leaving Beirut harbor was a point of land off Larnaca in southeastern Cyprus. From there they would set sail for one of the Greek Isles, and then on to rendezvous with fast boats off the coast of Italy to have their cargo moved ashore.

I gave Mustafa my contact information in Cairo and told him to call me as soon as he learned when the ship would depart. Then I opened the door to let him out and handed him back his gun once he was in the hallway. After a few minutes, I headed out for the nearby British expatriate-managed Pickwick Pub, frequented by the manager's expat buddies. I needed a drink. No one there knew I was a narc — much safer for me to hang out there than in the Mayflower Hotel bar.

As for Mustafa's information, the last thing I planned to do was tell the Lebanese narcs anything about it. For one, they would want to know where I got my information, and I wasn't about to give up Mustafa's identity. And if I told them about the shipment, it was possible they would seize it before it left Beirut and sell the hash out the back door or extort money from its owners to let it go on its way. For all I knew, the cops could be investors in the shipment. Nope. I had a better plan.

The French had given the Cypriot narcs a twenty-four-foot open-air patrol boat with a .50 caliber machine gun on its prow that they kept tied up at Larnaca. Whenever they got word of a drug smuggling vessel coming within range (it had to be within the 12-mile limit for them to act legally, although they weren't big sticklers on the exact mileage), they would motor out, get the crew's attention by firing a few rounds over the vessel's bow, and then guide the ship to Larnaca's harbor. The smugglers would be arrested, the dope seized, and the vessel sold for scrap. The only thing the Cypriots needed to know was when a shipment was leaving Beirut.

Minutes after we took off from Beirut International the pilot announced he was turning back to Beirut. He didn't say whether there was a mechanical problem or that we had been hit by a missile. We circled over the Mediterranean dumping fuel. When the plane touched down on the runway, my fellow passengers clapped in appreciation for the pilot and crew, the custom upon any safe landing in the Middle East. Turns out the landing gears wouldn't retract after the plane had taken off and the pilot wasn't sure if they were locked down. But they held. Every time I left Beirut, I let out a sigh of relief. This time I had hardly taken a breath when the emergency had been declared, and here I was, back in Beirut.

We taxied to a remote part of the airport where waiting buses took us to the main terminal. I spent several hours sitting in the lounge sipping Turkish-style coffee while they readied another plane and fresh crew. Finally, we boarded, and this time made it to Cairo without incident.

Sure enough, Mustafa called me that night. He said the *Lucky Star* was setting sail at first light. I made the call to the narcotics unit commander in Nicosia. He grabbed his men, drove down to Larnaca, and the next morning did the deed.

Mustafa was due a payday. But I never heard from him again.

☆ ☆

CHAPTER 17

AFRICAN SAFARI

The *adnans*, calls to worship, sung five times a day by a *muezzin* from a minaret at the mosque down the street from our home in New Maadi, had become pleasant reminders of the exciting life we were living in Egypt. However, after the Iranian students had stormed the American Embassy in Teheran and taken American diplomats hostage, they had become constant reminders of the dangers that seemed to lurk everywhere. Ambassador Alfred Atherton had reassured the American community that "as long as Anwar Sadat is president, we have nothing to fear." Those words were no doubt remembered when several months after we had returned home, Sadat was assassinated.

The Muslim Brotherhood had killed him, outraged by Sadat's pact with Israel and his secular ways. Encouraged by the uprising in Iran that had swept an Islamic theocracy into power, and hoping for the same result in Egypt, members of the Muslim Brotherhood, masquerading as Egyptian soldiers, marched past the grandstand where Sadat was reviewing a military parade and opened fire. Sadat and eleven Egyptian and foreign dignitaries and their wives were left dead, including four U.S. military liaison officers. Another twenty-three persons had been wounded in the assault.

☆ ☆

☆ ☆ ☆ ☆ ☆ ☆

Even while Sadat was alive, and despite Atherton's assurances, tensions in Cairo ran hot. One night, angry shouts had startled us awake. Joy ran to check on the girls while I fumbled in the nightstand for my trusty stainless-steel Smith and Wesson. When I peeked out of our bedroom window, I watched four men dressed in white *gallabiyahs* (floor-length tunics) carry our kicking and screaming watchman, Mohammad, down the street, around the corner, and out of view. I figured they'd be back for us next.

I grabbed the two-way radio that had been issued to "official" families for use in an emergency so we would not have to rely on the notoriously unreliable telephone system. I keyed the mike and called the Marine security guard at the embassy. "Marine One, this is DEA One. Over."

After a few agonizingly tense moments, wondering if the radio was working, there came a reply. "Marine One. Over."

"Four men just kidnapped our watchman," I said, "Send help. Over."

"We'll get someone there as soon as we can. Out."

I pushed the couch against the living room door, went downstairs and propped a chair under the knob of the door leading to the walled-in garden, and checked all the locks on the windows. But it was all for naught. The garden wall could be easily breached, the fragile doors kicked in, and the huge picture windows smashed. But I didn't say anything to Joy, not wanting to alarm her any more than she already was. I then kept vigil at our bedroom window, gun in hand, waiting the return of the kidnappers.

It took quite a while before there was a knock at the door. I let the regional security officer's two local investigators into the

☆ ☆

house. "Sorry we took so long, but we wanted to check out the neighborhood first," one of them said. Then he explained what had happened. After they left, I sat Joy down on the couch.

"You're not going to believe this," I said, "Mohammad welshed on a gambling debt and his buddies tuned him up to get their money back."

The next morning, I found Mohammad at his guard post looking no worse for the wear — bruises, if any, masked by his ruddy, sunbaked skin. The frail watchman spoke little English, and me even less Arabic, so we couldn't discuss the incident. But I could tell by his sheepish expression he was embarrassed. He must have paid off his debt because he was never bothered again — at least not to my knowledge.

☆ ☆ ☆ ☆ ☆

One evening, as our first Christmas neared, there was a knock at the door. Through the peephole I saw three swarthy Egyptian men standing in the hallway. "Who is it?" I asked.

"Farag," one responded. Now I knew it wasn't General Farag. He was much shorter, stouter, and older than any of the three men standing outside the door. In Pidgin English one of the visitors said, "For you. General Farag."

"Put it under the door," I said, thinking it was a message. Dead silence.

Figuring they could easily break down the flimsy double-door, after a few awkward moments I opened it. There, sitting on the floor by their feet was a wooden crate full of chirping pigeons. Sami Farag had sent these delicacies from his Ismailia farm as a Christmas present. I carried them to the fire escape landing off from the kitchen. Joy put a bowl of water and some chunks of bread in the crate. We weren't sure what else to do for them.

The next morning Amy and Cindy giggled and poked their fingers through the crate's slats trying to pet them. When our Anglophile chef, butler and all-around housekeeper, Mohammad, (not the watchman Mohammad with the gambling problem) arrived for work that morning, I quietly asked him to cook a few of the pigeons for dinner that evening. We had never eaten pigeons before, and I wanted to be able to honestly tell General Farag what I thought of them.

Dressed in the spotless, starched white butler's jacket he always donned to serve our evening meals, Mohammad pealed a tiny brass dinner bell and announced with his very British accent, "Dinner is served."

Once we were seated, he ceremoniously uncovered a silver plate of steaming, stewed squab over rice. It tasted very good, not much different than dark chicken meat. We hadn't told the girls we were eating some of their pets. After dinner I told Mohammad to split the remaining birds between himself and Mohammad the watchman.

When I got home from work the next evening, I found Mohammad the watchman sitting on the floor outside his tiny room with two of the scrawny, de-feathered birds skewered and roasting over a small, Hibachi-style charcoal grill. He rose and bowed, his ear-to-ear, toothless grin telling me he thought he was about to meet the virgins in paradise.

☆ ☆ ☆ ☆ ☆

The U.S. Navy was an embarrassment. In the 1970s, there was so much drug use among sailors aboard ships that it was referred to by Egyptian locals as the "junkie navy." To combat the rampant drug abuse, the Naval Investigation Service, now called the Naval Criminal Investigative Service, developed an operation called Stable Boy to discourage the sale of drugs to sailors.

Informants would be recruited aboard ship then helicoptered ashore in advance of a port call. Once the ship arrived, the informants would go out on the street under local police surveillance to purchase drugs. When the drugs were delivered, the dealers would be taken down. Not only did Stable Boy reduce the number of drug sellers, it also spread the word to other dealers that selling drugs to U.S. sailors could be hazardous to their health.

The aircraft carriers *Eisenhower* and *Kennedy,* and the guided missile cruiser *Albany,* made port calls at Alexandria during my two years in Egypt. Each time, NIS Special Agent Ken Oglesbee from the Naval Air Station Sigonella, in Sicily, would be sent to Cairo in advance to set up the operation. I would hook Ken up with the ANGA narcs and we'd caravan to Alexandria, typically at night, which in itself was an adventure.

Egyptian motorists didn't often use headlamps on the highway for reasons of economy and courtesy. They thought that not using them would preserve the life of the headlamp as well as the car's battery. They also considered it impolite to follow someone with headlamps on and chance the light glaring from the rearview mirror into the eyes of the driver ahead. So other than the lead vehicle of the caravan, it was lights out for the three-hour journey. Driving my Peugeot 504 at sixty or seventy miles per hour in the dark, following the red pinpricks of the riding lights ahead, was mesmerizing for me and quite a white knuckler for my passengers.

During one of the port calls, with Stable Boy well underway, Ken had been called to the ship's sick bay to interview a sailor who had been badly beaten up while ashore. When Ken returned

☆ ☆

to our makeshift command center in a local hotel room, he told us the sailor said he had been pummeled by an Egyptian guy. Ken said that when he asked him what had started the fight, he mumbled through swollen jaws, "I don't know. All I said to him was, 'I want to buy some hashish.'"

☆ ☆ ☆ ☆ ☆ ☆

Opium in Egypt is as old as the Pyramids. General Farag was trying to crack down on its cultivation and proposed a law to allow for the confiscation of the land upon which opium was found, in addition to fines and imprisonment for the cultivators.

In early 1980, I accompanied ANGA Deputy Mahmoud Zaki by train to Asyut to observe their annual eradication campaign. Opium poppies were cunningly concealed among ripening crops of cotton and wheat and irrigated by water from the Nile River. There had been confrontations in the past between the police and heavily armed clannish villagers who generally resisted any government authority. But while I was there, there were no confrontations.

ANGA seized about two hundred acres of opium poppies during that year's campaign, twice that of previous years, which I dutifully reported to Washington. However, it was still a modest amount by world standards, and all of it likely consumed in Egypt.

☆ ☆ ☆ ☆ ☆ ☆

One day I picked up the phone in the office and got an offer from Washington I couldn't refuse. It would be my first opportunity to explore the Dark Continent.

Special Agent John Coleman was on the line, headquarters staff coordinator for the Middle East. "The Sudanese National Police Chief wants us to evaluate their drug trafficking situation in hopes of getting some assistance," he said "Can you go there? I'll pay the freight."

That was *raq sharqi* (belly dance music) to my ears. "No problem," I said, hoping it would be the first of many more African safaris.

A week later, just after midnight, my flight landed in Khartoum. An Embassy expediter whisked me through Immigration and Customs, and then stuffed me in the back seat of a waiting embassy car for the ride to the magnificent Grand Holiday Villa Hotel located at the convergence of the Blue and White Nile Rivers.

Over its 100-year history, the venerable hotel had hosted luminaries as renowned as Queen Victoria and Winston Churchill. I walked up the marble staircase into its ornate, open-air lobby, envisioning the former British Governor of the Sudan, General Charles Gordon, climbing those very stairs to attend the hotel's grand opening. Slain years later in a Sudanese rebellion against colonial rule, nevertheless a statue of Gordon stood on the hotel's grounds.

The night clerk sorted through a deck of 3 X 5 cards in a small wooden box, pulled one out with a flourish, and with a slightly British accent said, "Yes, Mr. Lutz, we have your reservation. But we have no room."

I tore out of the lobby and intercepted the driver before he could speed from the parking lot. He took me to a cinder block hotel within several blocks of the American Embassy, probably owned by a relative. It was almost 2 a.m. by the time I checked in.

The small, dark, musty, windowless room had a bare concrete floor and an air conditioner jutting from one of the windowless walls that roared like a lawn mower. But at least there was indoor plumbing. I flopped down on top of the straw mattress to get a few hours of sleep, afraid to pull down the sheet for fear of what I might find. A knock came at the door seemingly minutes later. It was my 7 a.m. wake-up call.

After a cold shower and shave (there was no hot water), I donned a fresh safari suit, got directions at the front desk, and plodded my way to the American Embassy, careful not to stumble over crumbling curbs or step into one of the many potholes. Along the way women in colorful skirts squatted on the sidewalks selling cooked rice and Turkish-style coffee. They had few customers but looked happy enough to be chatting with fellow hawkers as their children played nearby, some in rags, others naked.

I finally reached the American Embassy that occupied the top three floors of a private office building, one of the tallest structures in town. A hand-written sign taped to the elevator door read, "Out of Order."

Already soaking wet from the heat, I climbed the five or six flights of stairs to where a Marine Guard eyed me warily from behind bullet-proofed glass. I slid my Diplomatic Passport through the teller's tray. He checked it against a visitor's log, slid it back to me with a temporary badge, and then pressed a button that released the heavy steel turnstile. Once inside, he directed me to the top floor.

"Come in, come in," said Ambassador William Kontos as he beckoned me to sit down. He asked his secretary to summon the Political Officer who had been assigned as my escort. Once he arrived, he outlined the meetings that had been arranged for me.

At my first appointment, we were ushered into a small waiting room outside the police chief's office. His men brought out bottles of Coca Cola and glasses of ice. We drank the warm

☆ ☆

soda from the bottles — not daring to touch the ice. No telling if it had been made from boiled water.

They brought out albums with photos and newspaper clippings of drug seizures for us to peruse — mostly of khat, a weed often associated with marijuana. It's actually a mild stimulant, not a hallucinogen, closer to the coca bush leaves found in the Andes Mountains of South America. And it's chewed like coca leaves in order to release its active ingredient. Like marijuana, though, it grows wild. The World Health Organization just that year had classified khat as a drug of abuse. But it was not abused in America, so of little interest to me.

After an hour or so, my escort suggested we leave. "He's not going to show. Let's go get some lunch," he said. I reluctantly agreed, since it had been the chief who had requested my visit.

We drove to the Grand Holiday Villa Hotel where I was to have stayed. The *Maître d'*, dressed in a white tunic, wide brown leather belt, and gold embroidered pointed leather slippers, ushered us to a table in a luxurious dining room overlooking the majestic Nile. We dined on a buffet of local dishes fit for a Turkish Pasha, including a delicious lamb stew with okra and stewed onions, rich in the spices introduced to Sudanese cuisine by Ottoman and Arab traders over the centuries.

Our next stop was at the airport. A tall, ebony-skinned military colonel proudly described the security features at the airport but knew nothing of illegal drugs. His duty was to prevent weapons from reaching the Christian Sudanese in the southern part of the country that could help fuel another civil war. There had been seventeen years of war in which Christian and animist leaders in the south had fought for independence from the Egyptian and British-aligned Muslims in the north, followed by a seven-year tenuous peace after the south had been granted semi-autonomy.

We returned to the Embassy where I was introduced to several counselors and attachés. By then I was desperate to learn about the country's drug problem, not having met a single Sudanese official who could tell me anything about it. Ironically, the success of my mission would have to depend on information I could have gotten through a few telephone calls between Cairo and Khartoum.

The consensus was that khat and prescription drugs sold over the counter, a common practice in Africa, Asia and the Middle East, constituted their local drug problems. A drug consuming nation, the Sudan had no impact on its neighbors, let alone the United States. At the end of the day I walked upstairs to out-brief Ambassador Kontos.

"The Sudanese drug problem doesn't warrant any in-country DEA support," I said, "but I'm going to recommend that several of their police officers receive investigative training at our international academy in Washington." The ambassador seemed pleased with that. Then I sheepishly told him that I hadn't met the chief of police, hoping he wouldn't think my trip a total loss.

"Don't worry about it," he said, with a wave of his hand brushing it aside. "They don't show up for meetings with me either."

I took a shower back at the hotel, changed into a white safari suit, checked out, and was driven to the American Club where its restaurant, bar and swimming pool served as a haven for the American community. From there the Defense Attaché, whose brother Dale Laverty by chance was a DEA special agent stationed in Miami, was to take me to his home for dinner.

On the way to the American Club a haboob passed over the city, an intense sandstorm that darkened the sky like a solar eclipse. Headlamps and streetlights came on. When I got out of

☆ ☆

the car at the Club, I noticed that my white safari suit had been stained red by the haboob sand. Nevertheless, a pleasant evening was had, and I was dropped off at the airport near midnight for my return flight to Cairo.

As the plane circled Cairo in preparation for landing, I watched the spectacular Pyramids of Giza silhouetted by the rising sun, the Sphinx dutifully standing guard.

We flew over the "city of the dead," which was coming to life. Otherwise, homeless Egyptians lived in the cemetery's tombs built by wealthy Egyptians to provide shelter for their beloved in the afterlife. The tombs now housed the most destitute of Cairo, squatters who for the most part eked out their meager existence by scavenging Cairo's garbage dumps. I could see several women washing themselves outdoors, modestly wrapped in sheets, dousing the suds off with buckets of water.

As the plane lined up over Heliopolis for its final approach, morning traffic was just beginning to flow. The streets would soon be crowded bumper-to-bumper with cars, diesel-belching buses, and donkey carts vying for space on the narrow streets. The faithful would be called to morning prayers by *muezzins* over loudspeakers from mosques throughout the city. Vendors would be selling *ful* to passersby, the traditional Egyptian breakfast porridge of boiled fava beans mashed with onions, tomatoes and various spices, cooked in huge brass-handled copper tubs.

As we touched down on the airport's runway, the typical applause broke out. I thought to myself, *Boy, it's great to be home.*

☆ ☆

CHAPTER 18

HEADQUARTERS HODGEPODGE

I got another call from Washington. This time it wasn't about a trip to Africa.

Staff Coordinator John Coleman explained that the DEA's request to establish an office in Cyprus hadn't been approved by the State Department as yet, that the bosses wanted me to hold tight in Egypt until it was, and then direct transfer to Nicosia to open it up. Although two years in idyllic Cyprus was tempting, the grapevine had it that the office wasn't going to be approved for at least another year. Spending a third year in Cairo was just too much to ask of my family.

"If you don't extend in Egypt, we'll have no choice but to bring you back to headquarters," he said, figuring the threat would get me to stay. Most agents would walk over hot coals in their bare feet to avoid a tour of duty there; but I told him to throw me into that briar patch. It played right into my hand. Not only would the headquarters staff time check off a prerequisite for further career advancement, but our home in Northern Virginia also awaited.

I must have done something right while in Cairo because when I reported for duty in Washington, former Paris Regional Director John Warner, who by then was director of international operations, pulled me in to be his special assistant. However,

☆ ☆

I had barely gotten my feet planted in that job when the very existence of the DEA came under threat.

In 1977, Attorney General Griffin Bell commissioned a study by the FBI as to the feasibility of folding the DEA into the FBI. However, Administrator Bensinger and his team had barred the door. So the FBI bided its time until Bensinger was gone. Then in 1981, backed by Associate Attorney General Rudy Giuliani, they dusted off the plan and launched a three-pronged attack designed to overcome any resistance.

They had the Department of Justice grant the FBI concurrent jurisdiction to enforce the Controlled Substances Act domestically. The DEA Training Academy, which Jimmy Carter had transferred to his home state of Georgia while President, was appended to the FBI Academy on the U.S. Marine Corps Base at Quantico, Virginia. And finally, they wheeled a Trojan horse across the DEA's moat stuffed with senior FBI executives to capture the key leadership positions. Bud Mullen was appointed the administrator, Jack Lawn his deputy, and they seized the top internal security and finance positions as well.

This new cabal created a committee that was to turn the DEA into an FBI clone. Most significantly, headquarters' geographical desks were transformed into drug functional desks, which actually made good sense to me. The domestic East and West Desks that had been responsible to oversee investigations of all drugs in their areas of responsibility were replaced by heroin, cocaine, methamphetamine and marijuana desks with responsibility for those specific drugs nationwide. The desk officers would develop expertise in a given drug, enabling them to link investigations more easily in multiple jurisdictions and implement drug-specific enforcement strategies. And the new regime cloned the foreign program after its own which, in my view, made no sense.

☆ ☆

Based on the FBI's Legal Attaché model, DEA's foreign regional management system was abolished, and the regional staffs dragged into headquarters, much to the delight of the State Department. Each of the DEA's overseas offices was to report to a foreign geographical desk at headquarters. While structurally well-suited to the FBI's liaison programs abroad, it left critical decision-making of the DEA's overseas enforcement and intelligence operations in the hands of staff officers who often had little insight into the environment in which the operations were being conducted, and were typically many time zones away, in some instances half a world.

They even changed our titles in line with that of the FBI. Special Agents-in-Charge, SAICs, became SACs. Domestic Regional Offices became Divisions, and overseas Narcotics Attachés became Country Attachés, which I never understood and have refused to acknowledge to this day.

What no one had anticipated was the uproar the *coup d'état* would cause among state and local police organizations that knew the "9 to 5" FBI agents were distrustful of them and unwilling to get their hands dirty with them on the street, but quick to take credit for their work. Also, the FBI had underestimated the DEA's resourcefulness. Their incremental approach allowed time for the cunning DEA to conjure up a defense.

Special Agents Dave Westrate, who had been on Bensinger's 1977 team, and Bob Penland came to the rescue of a DEA in distress. Armed with sharpened pencils, they undertook a study that argued the value of retaining a single mission narcotics agency and proved the relative productivity of the DEA's enforcement efforts over the FBI's. Their report turned heads, most importantly the heads of Bud Mullen and Jack Lawn. Perhaps a little Stockholm syndrome had set in as well, although

☆ ☆

I like to think the effectiveness of DEA's worldwide operations enlightened them. But for whatever reason, Bud Mullen and Jack Lawn became strong advocates for retaining the DEA as an independent agency, stronger than some of the DEA's own who had shamelessly envisioned expanded post-retirement job opportunities by being retired as FBI agents.

Thanks to Mullen and Lawn, the following year Attorney General Janet Reno called off the dogs, announcing the DEA would remain a "specialized, single mission agency." It was like magic. In 1981 the FBI had held us in their clenched fist. Then when they opened their hand a year later, presto, we were gone.

During the early stages of the coup, I was transferred to the newly created Cocaine Desk. When they began looking for volunteers for two-month long stints in South Florida to help counter the waves of illegal drugs washing onto its sunny shores, I raised my hand. I missed the street, its fast pace, never knowing when or how a day would end. And where better to learn my job as a cocaine staff coordinator than as a supervisor in what had become America's front line in the battle against cocaine.

☆ ☆ ☆ ☆ ☆ ☆

Florida had been sinking under the weight of the cocaine and marijuana being corralled onto its shores. General aviation aircraft were landing drugs from Colombia and Jamaica on highways, byways and abandoned airstrips. Boats delivered even more via rivers, harbors, inlets and coves. Some drugs even floated ashore, belched up from the bowels of sunken ships or ejected from smuggler aircraft on aborted smuggling runs.

City fathers argued that it was unfair for them to have to shoulder the burden of fighting the importation of drugs destined for consumption in all of the lower forty-eight. They rightfully complained that it was a national problem that demanded a national solution.

Ronald Reagan appointed VP George H. W. Bush his (unofficial) drug czar. Among other measures, Bush created the Florida Joint Task Force that sent dozens of DEA and customs agents from around the country to process the seized drugs, freeing up the permanently assigned DEA, Customs, and Coast Guard personnel to go out and find more. I was sent to Ft. Lauderdale to help coordinate the effort in Broward County.

One night a Coast Guard surveillance aircraft spotted three guys floating in a life raft close to the Florida Keys. As the pilot flew overhead, the three began paddling for dear life — not to make it to shore, but to distance themselves from the six bales of marijuana and the tail section of their airplane that was following their raft. And the more furiously they paddled, the stronger the draft they created, and the tighter the formation became. They were lucky to have survived the crash but couldn't escape from the proof of their crime. My job was to see that the defendants and evidence were properly processed for trial.

I had been reviewing that report, and those of other overnight seizures, when my secretary buzzed. "Customs is transferring a call," she said. I picked up the phone.

"If you wanna' catch 'em, get over here right now," the caller demanded.

"Who's this?" I asked.

"Never mind. Just get over here now." He gave me an address and hung up.

Crank calls are commonplace in the drug business, particularly during a full moon when the crazies come out. Although an anonymous tip occasionally pays off, it happens so infrequently that no agent in his right mind wants to take one.

But I figured taking nuisance calls was just another part of my Task Force duties.

"Omar, I've got something I need you to check out," I said, handing the address to DEA Special Agent Omar Aleman who had been detailed from El Paso, Texas. He grabbed a Task Force Customs agent and headed out the door. I turned back to the reports at hand.

Not a half hour later Omar called over the two-way radio sitting on my desk, "Boss, you need to get out here." It didn't take a minute for me to make it out the door.

I screeched to a halt in front of the address on NE 20th Avenue. A sleek, pale green Lincoln Continental sat in the driveway next to a couple of beat-up, old pickup trucks. A man sat in the back of a Ft. Lauderdale PD squad car parked at the curb. I found Omar in the backyard eyeing a 46-foot sport fisherman, *Miss Deb*, tied up at the dock, a dozen gas cans sitting on the deck to extend its range.

"When we drove by, we didn't see anything suspicious," Omar said, "So we parked down the street and walked back to the house. Someone inside must have spotted us because one guy jumped out of a window and two others bolted out the door. We caught one of them and turned him over to the locals. They're looking for the other two."

The one they caught was a former Monroe County (Florida Keys) deputy sheriff who knew better than to say a word. Within the hour the guy who had been renting the house turned himself in. We identified the third suspect from the Georgia license plate on one of the two trucks in the driveway. The locals nabbed him a few hours later.

Omar went to get a search warrant for the house, and I asked the locals for a drug detector dog to check out the Lincoln. When

Omar returned with the warrant, we found thirty-five pounds of pure cocaine in plastic bags sitting on top of the washing machine.

Suitcases bulging with cocaine, stuffed into the trunk of a Lincoln Continental, Ft. Lauderdale, Florida.

When the dog handler arrived, he led his German Shepard around the Town Car. She sniffed and whined and scratched at the trunk. I thought the poor dog was going to have a nervous breakdown. Based on the dog's alert, I sent another agent to the courthouse to get a warrant for the car. Sometime before two in the morning, with Assistant U.S. Attorney Lurana Snow standing by my side, we popped the trunk lid and found three suitcases bulging with another 215 pounds of cocaine; all told, the second largest cocaine seizure in Broward County history.

One of the defendants flipped and said the cocaine on the washer had been their share for receiving the shipment from an air drop at sea and bringing it ashore. The cocaine in the Lincoln rental was to be picked up by a Colombian national they knew only as Alex.

Cocaine seized in record Broward County cocaine seizure.
Ft. Lauderdale Police Department drug detection dog
and unidentified dog handler pictured.

We processed the defendants and dope overnight, and in the morning prepared for the preliminary hearing. Of course, the Customs supervisor who had transferred the call to us was now kicking himself for having given away a record cocaine seizure.

Through the car rental agency, Omar was able to identify Alex, and a week later found him. All four pleaded guilty. It was just as well for Alex, much safer for him to be ensconced in a federal prison than have to explain to his ruthless Colombian bosses the loss of a million-dollar drug shipment. Doubtless, there would have been some unpleasant consequences.

☆ ☆ ☆ ☆ ☆ ☆

For the last of those three years in headquarters, I was assigned to the Office of Inspections under Marion Ramey, one of the original FBI interlopers. Our job was to make sure offices operated within the rules and regulations spelled out in the Agents Manual. It was a job that took me to places in the

U.S. and around the world for weeks at a time that I might not otherwise have gotten to see.

Domestically, I was assigned to inspection teams in Chicago, Phoenix, Atlanta, San Diego and New York. While in New York City, I got several reminders of why I never wanted to be assigned there. We ate breakfasts at a luncheonette across from the office. Each morning I noticed that a bicycle chained to a light pole outside the shop was missing yet another piece. By the time we left, all that remained of the bike was its frame. And, during one lunch hour several of us rushed to the aid of a messenger who had been struck by a car, only to watch someone ride off on his damaged bike. It's a town that can wear anyone down.

Internationally, Special Agent Jack Macready and I survived an earthquake while inspecting the Tokyo office and toured the DMZ between North and South Korea with Joe Braddock who, by then, was the Narcotics Attaché in Seoul. But my most memorable overseas journey was with Special Agent Al Johnson to Guadalajara.

We spent time there with Enrique "Kiki" Camarena who less than a year later, in February 1985, was kidnapped, tortured and murdered. We had eaten several meals together, one at a restaurant in which a table full of thugs, guns in hand, came in to eat. We backed out of the restaurant after eating our meal. I played a round of golf with Kiki on the weekend, and his wife took me shopping on Sunday morning to buy presents for my family.

In the aftermath of the murder, Bud Mullen and Jack Lawn conspired with Customs Commissioner Willie von Raab to virtually shut down the U.S.-Mexico border by insisting that every single vehicle crossing it be thoroughly searched. Truckloads of spoiling avocados lined up for as far as the eye

☆ ☆

could see. Although lobbying of the White House and Congress by American farmers and businessmen dependent on Mexican labor and goods eventually forced them to relent, their action had sent a strong message to the Mexican Government that we weren't about to simply stand by. Soon after, Mullen retired but Lawn continued to relentlessly badger the Mexican government to investigate the crime, and publicly criticize the official corruption that had contributed to Kiki's death. The pursuit of the murderers of Kiki Camerena continues to this day.

An annual national Red Ribbon Day is dedicated to Kiki's memory and has come to symbolize the perils and sacrifices in our line of work. The DEA will never forget Kiki. His passing was a sad moment in our history, but the relentless effort to bring his killers to justice has become a source of great pride for the DEA as well.

With my assignment to Inspections winding down, I needed some domestic supervisory experience to check off the final prerequisite for advancement into mid-level management. By then, my old San Francisco pal Lionel Stewart was Secretary to the Career Board. Unbeknownst to me, he submitted my name for the coveted position of Resident Agent-in-Charge of the Reno, Nevada office.

When the announcement came out, I told Joy what I thought would be good news. But she was anything but joyful. Visions of gambling and prostitution danced in her head, thinking it no place to raise our two daughters. It took a sustained effort to convince her that Reno was more like the Garden of Eden than the City of Gomorrah. Thankfully it turned out to be so.

CHAPTER 19

SPEED KILLS

"Call the Sheriff!" I asked my secretary. "Tell him we need to meet."

Sheriff Vince Swinney oversaw the Washoe County Narcotics Task Force, led by Sparks Police Department Lieutenant Dave Saville, which included officers from every law enforcement agency in the County. With only five DEA agents in the Reno office, it was hard to conduct even a decent moving surveillance without local assistance. So gaining their continued support was critical if I hoped to do my job. Meeting the sheriff was first on my "to do" list.

When I entered his office, I thought I had walked onto the set for a Western movie. From under a wide-brimmed Stetson hung by a peg on the wall dangled a holster with a long-barreled six-shot "peacemaker" revolver. Pictures of Indians decorated the office, no doubt Paiute, Shoshone and Washoe, all native to the area. Swinney sat with his legs propped up on his desk, his pointy-toed cowboy boots forming a "v" through which he was able to take aim at his prey. I half expected to hear someone yell, "Action!"

"Howdy," he said, as if reading from a script.

"Good morning, sheriff," I said with a smile. "I'm the new DEA chief, and I'm very happy to be here in 'Nevaahda.'"

"The first thing you need to learn, son, is how to pronounce the name of our state. It's 'Nevatta'!"

It felt like being scolded by my third-grade schoolteacher.

"Do you have your tickets for Saturday's rodeo yet?" he went on.

"What rodeo is that, sheriff?" I asked.

"This Saturday. I got some tickets right here," he said, pulling a stack from his desk drawer. "The Sheriff's Posse sponsors a rodeo each year to raise money for my office."

I had never been to a rodeo before and didn't want to go to one now. Joy and I had plans to drive up to Lake Tahoe on Saturday to check out a property we hoped to rent at Incline Village while we house hunted in Reno.

"I'll take two adults and two children," I said, not wanting to dig myself into an even deeper hole.

The meeting with Swinney was still nagging me when we drove to the fairgrounds. But it didn't take long for my spirits to pick up. Not a cloud hung in the bright blue sky, no humidity loomed in the high-desert air, and a cool breeze blew off the Sierra Nevada Mountains. We parked and found seats in the open-air arena just in time for the "Grand Entry."

A dozen riders galloped around the arena carrying American and Nevada flags; red, with white and blue banners streaming behind them. Cowboys walked in, waving their hats. A prayer was said for the safety of the contestants, and the "Star Spangled Banner" sung. The show was about to begin.

A calf released from a pen tore across the arena enjoying its new-found freedom, while a cowboy on horseback zeroed in on it. He lassoed the calf around its neck, jumped from his horse, and wrapped three of the calf's legs together while his well-trained horse backed up to keep the rope taut. Six cowboys competed in all. The winner rode triumphantly into the arena tipping his hat to the appreciative crowd.

Barrel racing, another timed event, came next. Teenage girls raced on horses around barrels trying to come as close as possible to save time, but not so close as to tip one over and incur a penalty. The winner, a young lady dressed in a white blouse and hat with gold piping, was awarded the prize. She pranced her horse to the edge of the stadium where her proud parents reached down to congratulate her to the roar of the audience.

Next was the steer wrestling contest, the most dangerous of all. Competitors jumped headfirst onto huge bulls and wrestled them to the ground, trying at all costs to avoid those menacing horns. After each contest, rodeo clowns came to their rescue, taunting the steers until the cowboy could get away. Each contestant sauntered back to the corral beating the dust off his jeans with his hat, keeping a wary eye over his shoulder all the while.

Before intermission they called for the children who had registered for mutton busting to report to the sign-up desk. I had almost forgotten. When we had walked into the arena I noticed a hand-written sign reading, "Mutton Busting Contest — Children Eight Years Old or Younger." Neither Joy nor I had a clue what it was about, but I wanted our girls to experience everything they could of the Wild West. Amy was eleven, so I signed up Cindy despite a mild protest from Joy.

"They're not going to do something that would get kids hurt, would they?" I replied.

So with a brave smile that belied my shared concern, I took Cindy by the hand and walked her down through the portal. They told the dozen kids that whoever rode a sheep the farthest would win. All but two of them were boys; all but Cindy dressed

☆ ☆

in cowpoke gear. With a white blouse, pedal pushers and tennis sneakers, she looked like a city girl – that she was– at a dude ranch.

We paraded with our children into the arena. I helped Cindy lie down on the back of her mount, wrap her arms around the sheep's neck, and grab hold of its scruff. Then a whistle signaled the start of the race. A few fell off immediately. Several were stepped on and sobbing, being comforted by a parent. Others stayed aboard for a few yards before tumbling off.

Cindy's lamb must have been a "mutton for punishment." It staggered under Cindy's weight almost to the far wall before the poor thing collapsed. The crowd went wild.

I stood with Cindy for the award presentation, waving to Joy and Amy in the stands. And guess who came over to hand out the prize. Yup! None other than Sheriff Vince Swinney. From then on, we were *dos amigos*.

☆ ☆ ☆ ☆ ☆ ☆

Marijuana had been the big drug problem in Northern Nevada. General aviation aircraft, puddle jumpers, flew the weed in from Mexico, often at night to lessen the chance of detection. They landed on makeshift runways on the high-desert floor illuminated by kerosene lanterns. The fellow I replaced in Reno had himself been put to flight after it was learned he had taken flying lessons at the DEA's expense to patrol the vast desert for clandestine airstrips. With the strengthening of Southwest border security, those risky flights had faded into history.

By the time I arrived in Reno, instead of flying over the border, smugglers relied on the more traditional methods of smuggling drugs into the States — concealed in trucks, trains, buses, and automobiles, backpacked over the wall, and waded across the Rio Grande. And they had begun to carve tunnels under the border as well. One group specialized in recruiting senior citizens vacationing in Mexico to carry loads of marijuana hidden in their RVs, Ma and Pa Kettle being far less likely to be searched at the border. I'm sure that weed paid for more than just a few knee replacements.

There was plenty of cocaine in Northern Nevada too. The casinos in Reno, Sparks, Carson City and South Lake Tahoe attracted drug dealers anxious to sell to high rollers and low rollers alike. And it wasn't restricted to tourists.

In one of our cases an informant told us of a Reno skin cancer doctor who was buying cocaine in Southern California and selling it locally to support his habit. We were trying to identify his source of supply when I halted the investigation because our informant told us the doctor was so strung out on cocaine he would have to snort some before surgery to steady his nerves. We never did identify his source of supply, and he got only a slap on the wrist from the judge. But his license to practice medicine was suspended, which to me was the best possible outcome of the case.

The Nevada side of Lake Tahoe is one of the most beautiful places on earth. We lived at Incline Village for several months while our home in Reno was being built. But Lake Tahoe had its share of drugs too. An agent was assigned to the South Lake Tahoe Task Force, and before I left Reno, I dedicated another agent to work the north end of the lake where a number of wealthy drug traffickers lived as well.

We arrested one of them, a cocaine kingpin named Javier Francisco Ocando-Paz aka Jose Ferrer who rented a large home in Incline Village for himself and his young wife Elvira. Ocando-Paz was wanted in a Colorado case involving the broken off negotiations for sale of cocaine to an undercover DEA agent in which a small amount of cocaine had been seized in his hotel room. He was also a fugitive from his native Venezuela, wanted there for the seizure of 135 kilos of cocaine, and for suspicion that he had financed another shipment of 600 kilograms.

We seized $75,000 cash and three expensive automobiles at the home and found documents for a safe deposit box at a local bank in which we later found diamonds, emeralds and rubies worth an estimated $3 million dollars. Civil forfeitures have become very unpopular in the media in recent years, but seizing the ill-gotten gains of drug traffickers definitely took the fun out of it for them.

Northern Nevada had some heroin as well. But during my almost two-year tenure in Reno, methamphetamine was king. Speed, the poor man's cocaine, was the favorite of outlaw motorcycle gangs in the San Francisco Bay area. We found many bathtub labs in private homes and trailers in Reno, Carson City, even Lake Tahoe, after getting calls from annoyed neighbors — meth's distinctive, unforgettable odor while being "cooked" being all but impossible to conceal. But most of its production occurred in rented hunting cabins high up in the Sierra Nevada Mountains, far from snooping noses.

Special Agent Lew Thomas was wired into the local meth scene. He would get a call whenever any law enforcer in Northern Nevada got the faintest sniff of a possible meth lab. That put us into every lab seizure in Northern Nevada, on average about one a month. And since the DEA's performance measuring stick in those days put laboratory operators at the top of the list, cuffing a meth producer every month kept the office statistically afloat. The real crime, though, was that once we found a lab it would be declared a toxic waste dump, and the taxpayers would have to cough up the money to clean up the "spill."

☆ ☆

Cooking speed is dangerous business and raiding meth labs can be perilous too due to the hazardous chemicals used in the process. Many labs were discovered after they had exploded, having given the cooks a "speedy" departure to the next "high" life.

And in those days, we didn't know the physical harm that could be done by breathing in the toxic fumes, the stench of which stuck to our clothing. Joy made me keep my "lab clothes" in the garage. Today, meth labs are raided by agents and technicians dressed like astronauts.

Raiding meth labs was also dangerous because of the nature of the beasts that operated them. Bikers armed themselves like Navy Seals — not only to protect themselves from grizzly bears, but also from grizzly gangbangers looking to rip them off. High on speed, they felt invincible. For this reason, we always brought along an overwhelming number from Lieutenant Saville's Task Force to ensure the safety of all involved.

We had found a home in Northern Nevada. Our house was perched on a hill with a panoramic view of Reno and the entire Washoe Valley. The girls learned to ski as part of their school's curriculum. Amy learned to play softball, and Cindy t-ball. Amy won the Washoe County spelling bee contest and had gone on to the finals in Las Vegas. If it hadn't been for our family's roots on the East Coast, we would have happily retired there.

However, in less than two years I was selected to be an Assistant Special Agent-in-Charge of the Miami Field Division. Getting to Miami had been my goal since the Florida Joint Task Force. But when the promotion came, it was bitter-sweet.

I left Joy behind while the girls finished the school year and was tooling down I-20 in my Corvette roadster, somewhere in the Texas panhandle, when a flash came over the radio —

"Federal agents shot and killed in Miami." I thought they had to be DEA. However, later broadcasts clarified that it had been two FBI agents who died in a gun battle with bank robbers.

Nevertheless, in that era of the cocaine cowboys, I knew I was heading from the Wild West into an even wilder Southeast.

CHAPTER 20

COCAINE COWBOYS

I got the job I had hoped for, planned for, and prepared for — an Assistant Special Agent-in-Charge position in Miami — and South Florida was every bit as exciting as I had remembered it. It was the gateway for Latin Americans on their way to Disney World, and a mecca for the Cuban refugees who had risked life and limb fleeing Castro's totalitarian regime. And they had spiced it up with their salsa music, rumba dance, fat cigars and *Mores y Conquistadores* (black beans and rice).

Meanwhile, Colombian traffickers who had been selling cocaine to Cuban hoodlums finally realized who had been making all the money and decided to take over domestic distribution themselves. In 1979, Colombian Queenpin Griselda Blanco staked out her claim with the gangland-style massacre of some of her competitors at Crown Liquors in Dadeland Mall. Metro-Dade undercover officers Sonny Crockett and Rico Tubbs wouldn't begin to hunt down narco criminals on TV until 1984. The real Miami Vice had begun playing itself out that very day, five years earlier, at Dadeland Mall. It was the beginning of the cocaine cowboy era, a fight over market share of drug-addled Americans. What a pity!

Colombian traffickers were ruthless. Their take-no-prisoners strategy for anyone who dared oppose or cheat them left a deadly wake. Many of our investigations began with the discovery of a dead body, and then we would work alongside homicide detectives to identify the victim's role in the drug trade which often told them the possible motive for the killing.

The drug lords dealt with informers most brutally, silencing them along with their spouses, children, parents, grandparents, even the family pets, to send a message to dare not even think about ratting on them. One gruesome practice became known as the "Colombian necktie." After extracting details of the betrayal, the throat of the brutally tortured informer would be cut and his tongue pulled out through the slit.

The day I checked into a Miami hotel, Group Supervisor Herb Williams called to say his team just seized 275 kilograms of cocaine, which he described as fairly routine, although larger than our record Broward County seizure four years earlier. The cocaine had been offloaded in duffel bags from a forty-foot, converted shrimp boat moored to a dock behind a house in a Biscayne Bay neighborhood. When Herb's group of agents and Metro-Dade detectives attempted to enter the house, three men bolted out the back door and jumped into the canal. One doggie paddled to the opposite bank and was caught. The other two must have been better swimmers because they were never seen again. Herb said the *Miami Herald* was already looking for the story, and that I would probably be interviewed the next day, after the funeral.

It would have been appropriate under any circumstance for me to have spent my first day on the job in Miami seeking divine guidance. Instead, I was at church to attend the funeral service honoring the life of one of the FBI agents slain the week before. The choir sang "Amazing Grace" until the pews filled to capacity. While I was relieved it hadn't been a DEA agent slain, we were all saddened at the loss of yet another law enforcement officer killed in the line of duty.

I had been selected by the Career Board to take over what remained of the Florida Joint Task Force. However Regional Director Pete Gruden thought ASAC Jerry Hochman, who had previously worked closely with U.S. Customs at JFK International before being transferred to Miami, was better suited for that job. So he swapped us, and I ended up with an all-star cast of enforcement Group Supervisors: John Andrejko, Mike Kuhlman, Lew Rice and Mike Vigil. They all eventually rose into management positions, three of them into the Senior Executive Service. They made me look good while I learned my job.

It wasn't just cocaine seizures that made the headlines; cash money was there for the taking. The cocaine industry generated so much of it that traffickers sometimes had a harder time getting the cash out of the country than getting the drugs in. In one typical case, agents knocked on the door of a suspected cocaine trafficker's house and asked permission to look inside. The occupant signed a "consent to search" form, and almost a million dollars in cash was found stuffed into laundry detergent boxes stacked in a closet. The woman said the money wasn't hers and didn't know who it belonged to. They gave her a receipt and told her to have the owner come to our office to claim it. Of course, no one ever did, and it was eventually forfeited to the government.

And there were more than cocaine cases to be made. One investigation which had started long before I got to Miami targeted British marijuana and hashish entrepreneur Dennis Howard Marks. Marks had flaunted his former ties to British intelligence services, threatening to reveal state secrets if ever prosecuted. Special Agent Craig Lovato began his relentless pursuit of Marks while stationed in Madrid, a case that eventually spanned fourteen countries.

Craig had allied himself with Scotland Yard, much to the chagrin of British Customs which claimed sovereignty over that nation's international drug investigations. I flew with Craig to London to negotiate a truce between the agencies, an agreement that contributed to Marks eventual prosecution. A 1984 book by David Leigh described Mark's escapades: *High Time: The "Shocking" Life and Times of Howard Marks*. After reading it, I sent Craig a note saying, "Terrible book! I'm counting on you to re-write the ending" — which he did. Actually, it was authors Paul Eddy and Sarah Walden who wrote the final chapter in *Hunting Marco Polo: The Pursuit of the Drug Smuggler Who Couldn't Be Caught by The Agent Who Wouldn't Quit*. The title says it all.

There were a few laughs. Colombian traffickers often consolidated loads to economize on smuggling runs, each putting their mark on their packages to distinguish them once they arrived in Miami. One of the enforcement groups made a case in which several of the kilogram bricks of cocaine had the word "broccoli" written on them. Some wise-guy trafficker must have known that George H. W. Bush hated broccoli and thought maybe his narcs wouldn't go near it.

And there were some tears as well. In that violent era, I was fortunate to have had only one shooting among my groups that year. Cocaine was such a big business that independent contractors began cooking it up in Miami. John Andrejko's group had set up an undercover storefront to sell precursor chemicals to them. During the investigation, they followed deliveries of chemicals to a house where they thought a lab was operating. Agents knocked at the front door.

☆ ☆

Dominican national Sammy Garcia answered the door carrying a small child in his arms and invited the agents inside. Then he darted down the hallway, pulled out a pistol, and started shooting. In an exchange of gunfire, two bullets slammed into the chest of one of the agents knocking him to the floor, his body armor saving his life. A third bullet struck him in the right eye. One of the other agents shot Garcia five times, killing him. They found a cocaine lab in a bedroom. Fortunately, the child was unharmed. The deceased had been wanted in Brooklyn for the murder of the child's mother.

With sight left only in only one eye, the wounded agent wasn't physically qualified to remain on the job. However, Administrator Jack Lawn said he would be a special agent as long as Lawn was the boss. The agent steadily rose through the ranks and one day took charge of the Miami Field Division. And Lawn's esteem continued to rise.

☆ ☆ ☆ ☆ ☆ ☆

Not long after my arrival in Miami, SAC Pete Gruden had been tapped for an assistant administrator position in Washington and replaced by Diogenes "Dodge" Galanos. With the increasing cocaine pandemic and the advent of crack cocaine, headquarters began increasing the size of the Miami Field Division, rivaling New York in the number of agents assigned. When Dodge retired back to San Diego, and Deputy SAC Sam Billbrough opted for the SAC job in Philadelphia, the inimitable Tom Cash was sent to head up the newly invigorated Miami Field Division. "If you can't run with the big dogs," Tom used to say, "stay on the porch." And there were plenty of big dogs running on the streets of Miami.

☆ ☆

Miami Field Division, 1987. L-R: DEA Administrator Jack Lawn, ASAC Tom Kennedy, Assoc. SAC Johnny Phelps, SAC Tom Cash, FBI Director William Sessions, Assoc. SAC Lionel Stewart, Lutz.

Tom had a wealth of knowledge about drug trafficking in the region. Never shy about sharing it, media outlets took every opportunity to interview him whenever a cocaine cartel boss snorted, or an international marijuana trafficker sneezed. I don't know if there's ever been a book written or a TV documentary produced about the drug trade in those days, in which Tom Cash isn't quoted. If I learned anything from Tom, it was to use the press to our advantage, get out front to tell our side of the story, and stay on message. Tom brought with him two Associate SACs. One was Johnny Phelps, the other, none other than Lionel Stewart, my old partner from the Leslie Atkinson and Preecha Leeyaruk cases in Bangkok.

As part of the reorganization, a new Assistant SAC position was created to handle the Caribbean operations that Sam Billbrough had been managing. Every ASAC in the office put in for it. However, being the only one with foreign experience and, just as importantly, military experience, with the Department of Defense just having been brought full tilt into the drug interdiction fray, I hit the jackpot.

I was given essentially the same responsibilities that Bangkok's Fred Dick had after being unceremoniously removed from Thailand. In those days I volunteered to attend annual meetings of the Florida chapter of our retired agent's association to keep the old timers abreast of drug trafficking patterns and trends, and the comings and goings within the DEA. Fred was a regular attendee. So I got to know him on a first name basis, which was pretty heady stuff. Over time, and a few drinks, Fred cleared up some of the rumors that had shrouded his time in Southeast Asia. Sorry to say, I'm still sworn to secrecy.

As the newly appointed ASAC for Caribbean operations, I could roam the DEA offices in Nassau, Kingston, and Santo Domingo at will, while Joy and the girls remained safely ensconced in the Broward County community of Coral Springs. It was the best of both worlds for both me and my family.

One of the first challenges of my new position was to develop a coordinating mechanism between the U.S. military and the DEA to de-conflict their interdiction operations with our controlled deliveries from Colombia. We routinely recruited informants to pilot drug loads for the Colombians so the recipients could be arrested in the United States upon delivery of the drugs, and those who had sent them indicted for future prosecution. Without adequate coordination, these controlled deliveries could easily be mistaken for actual smuggling runs and be taken down, not only risking our investigations but also the lives of our informants. I needed to make sure that didn't happen.

We worked it out. One general officer told me not to worry, though, that they would have the drug smuggling corridor from Colombia through the Caribbean shut down within a year. I wished him luck.

They blockaded Colombia with Navy ships for starters, but that didn't last very long. The Colombian government ranted and raved, calling it an act of war. The State Department saw it as diplomatically incorrect. So, the military backed off, settled down, and joined with U.S. Customs and Coast Guard in acquiring suspected smuggler aircraft with their airborne and shipboard radars, sorting out the good guys from the bad, and following them to their destinations to be intercepted by law enforcement authorities. And they followed smuggling vessels as well, even semi-submersibles. They're still at it today, thirty-five years later.

Each of the foreign offices I had inherited developed programs to meet the drug trafficking situation in that country. The stock-in-trade of Narcotics Attaché Ernesto Perez at the Santo Domingo office, for instance, was the Joint Intelligence Coordination Center, a program set up by former Narcotics Attaché John McFarland to monitor the comings and goings of drug traffickers by air and sea into the Dominican Republic. The local police collected data from immigration records of arriving air and sea passengers and electronically bounced the names off the DEA's El Paso Intelligence Center (EPIC). To maintain the integrity of the information, hits would be returned to the locals through the DEA's Santo Domingo Office, preventing any corrupt policeman from going on a fishing expedition in EPIC's database to see what we might have on his buddies. Fugitives would be arrested, and known traffickers surveilled.

☆ ☆

Jamaica grew some of the best weed on the planet, and what wasn't toked by tourists and indigenous Jamaicans was destined for the United States. Narcotics Attachés Jim Williams, and then Steve Widener set eradication as a top priority, as was the identification of major weed traffickers, like the notorious Norris Barnes, wanted on marijuana smuggling charges in New York and Miami.

Special Agent Pete Sarron had been introduced undercover to Barnes. It was a smiling Norris Barnes, anxious to get started on a promised day of deep-sea fishing, who hopped onto one of the DEA's seized boats at Montego Bay. The boat had been wired for sound before being placed into service. Barnes admired the rod and reel Pete gifted him once on board, purchased with Official Advanced Funds. But he stopped smiling when they reached international waters and the cuffs were snapped on. He was hoisted onto a Coast Guard cutter that I had asked to stand by and sailed to Miami through an arraignment and into a holding cell. Barnes cried foul, claiming he was kidnapped, but the judge was hearing none of it. He was eventually convicted and did his time in the pokey.

But it was the Nassau office that took up most of my time. The Bahamas had been a smuggler's paradise dating back to the rum running days of Prohibition. As federal efforts made it riskier to fly drugs directly into South Florida, air smugglers began landing on sparsely inhabited isles among the 700 in the Bahamian chain, and then moving the drugs to Miami by fast boat under cover of darkness.

Pablo Escobar's confidants, Carlos Lehder and George Jung, had pioneered the technique. In 1978, Lehder purchased Norman's Cay as a waystation, and Escobar International Airport became busier than Washington's Reagan National on a

Friday afternoon. They should have built a control tower because hulks of smuggler aircraft can still be seen submerged in the shallow waters off Norman's Cay, having crash-landed just short of the runway. The Bahamian government was forced to shut Norman's Cay down three years later after a vacationing Walter Cronkite happened by in his yacht and reported to authorities the heavily armed fortress he had observed there. But drug loads kept landing elsewhere in the Bahamas.

Heavyweight boxer Mike Tyson liked to say, "Everyone has a plan until they get punched in the mouth." Beginning in 1982 the DEA's Operation Bahamas, Turks and Caicos (OPBAT) began landing punches. Teams of Royal Bahamian Police officers, accompanied by DEA permanent staff supplemented with a half dozen special agents recruited from domestic offices on months-long deployments, would board U.S. Army Blackhawk and Coast Guard H-3 helicopters and be vectored by U.S. Customs and Coast Guard tracker aircraft from their bases in Nassau and Georgetown to suspected smuggler aircraft landings. The crews would be arrested, the drugs seized, and the planes confiscated.

OPBAT had been a tough call for the Bahamian government. Although it was the Bahamian cops who made the arrests and seizures, allowing armed American agents to accompany them, with the operations being commanded from within the bowels of the pink-washed walls of the American Embassy in Nassau, was seen by many locals as an infringement on their national sovereignty. However, with the government on defense from withering allegations of official corruption, even that their Prime Minister had turned a blind eye to the cavalcade of drugs moving through his country, they relented. They figured if OPBAT failed to solve the problem, they'd have the Americans to blame. It did anything but fail.

Narcotics Attaché Bill Simpson was transferred from Nassau shortly after I took over, and John Pulley replaced him as the Narcotics Attaché. John continued to receive the support of the Iron Lady of the Bahamas, American Ambassador Carol Hallett, and then gained the support of her successor, Chic Hecht, a former Senator from Nevada. They refereed the occasional dustups, and that made the job a lot easier.

The middle-aged, burly Pat Shea, a former University of North Carolina football lineman, ran OPBAT. *People Magazine* published a feature article on Shea, calling him "Batman of the Bahamas." John Pulley told the reporter that Pat's OPBAT was making the Colombians do things they didn't want to do. "We're putting a crimp in their style," he said.

Pat's wife spoke to them from a slightly different perspective. "Pat thinks he's still in the Marines. He puts on camouflage and jumps out of helicopters. He thinks he's young again."

The missions weren't without risk. In 1984, an OPBAT helicopter crashed at sea killing Special Agent Larry Carwell and four of his Bahamian police colleagues. Their bodies were never recovered.

As OPBAT matured, in order to bolster the acquisition of targets, customs launched aerostat balloons to supplement the tracker ships and aircraft — the first one on Grand Bahama Island, then at Georgetown, with a third planned for Great Inagua. The balloons, tethered by cable, flew thousands of feet in the air with radars that could sort out legitimate flights from suspected smuggling runs over thousands of square miles of ocean. But nothing is perfect. They had to be lowered in bad weather and for routine maintenance. An aerostat balloon launched in the Florida Keys had been infamously doused with iridescent paint so the traffickers could see, day or night, whether the balloon

☆ ☆

was up or down and adjust the timing of their smuggling runs accordingly.

To avoid the seemingly ever present OPBAT helicopters, the smugglers adjusted. Aided by the advent of the GPS, and with cell phones in lieu of high frequency radios, they began to air-drop loads to waiting boats which would ferry the drugs ashore, avoiding the necessity of landings. That made it more difficult for the OPBAT teams to interdict the loads. Subsequently, the Coast Guard got permission to shoot to disable the boats, another punch that foiled their best laid plans. And to add insult to their injuries, I got permission to buy SCUBA gear and pay for diving lessons so the Nassau agents could retrieve abandoned cocaine and marijuana from sunken smuggler boats and aircraft before the locals could get to it.

OPBAT had been tacking up "Do Not Trespass" signs in the Bahamas. And by 1987, the Colombian cartels had been waffled so many times they were getting punch drunk. During the three years I oversaw it, OPBAT seized more than 165 tons of cocaine and almost 1,000 tons of marijuana.

As much as the cartels loved the geographical proximity of the tranquil Bahamas to South Florida, and the docile Bahamians, OPBAT forced them to look elsewhere. That's when they hit upon Haiti — and that's when Port-au-Prince became my next new frontier.

CHAPTER 21

VOODOO MAGIC

Heads turned when the distinguished-looking couple strolled into the living room. He was nattily dressed in white, from his three-piece suit, starched shirt, and silk tie, down to his patent leather shoes, in stark contrast to his ebony dark skin. She was rotund, light-skinned, likely of French descent, Haiti being a former French colony, and wearing a flowing white gossamer gown which made her appear as if she was floating alongside him. The salt-and-pepper couple paused in front of one of the many TV sets scattered about American Ambassador Brunson McKinley's residence, all tuned to the election results. Michael Dukakis was running slightly ahead of George H. W. Bush, as the early returns along the East Coast were being tabulated.

Ambassador McKinley had invited Haiti's elite to watch America's democracy in action — only a dream in this poorest of nations. And since I was on one of my routine trips to Haiti, he invited me to attend as well. So, I walked over to the gentleman and extended my hand. "I'm with the Drug Enforcement Administration in Miami," I said. "Who are you?"

"Voodoo," he mumbled. I wasn't sure I had heard him correctly; but after he repeated it, I realized what he had said and learned later he was Haiti's Voodoo High Priest. Between his

☆ ☆

Pidgin English and the few words that I knew in Creole, it didn't take but a moment for us to run out of things to say. I pointed toward the buffet table and bade him farewell. He smiled and wished me good luck.

With OPBAT seizing cocaine and marijuana at record pace in the Bahamas, our intelligence had indicated Colombian traffickers were seeking alternative routes. When it was learned they were sending loads of cocaine aboard ships from Venezuela through the Eastern Caribbean for onward movement to the States, we set up an office in Bridgetown, Barbados, led by Narcotics Attaché Al Williams, to thwart it. And when we noticed that seizures of cocaine off Haitian junk freighters in the Miami River were beginning to spike, Port-au-Prince became my next port of call.

Our intelligence indicated several hundred Colombians had already migrated there, and clandestine airfields were popping up on the landscape like chicken pox blisters. One such airstrip was on a ranch in the Port-au-Prince suburb of Fermathe owned by the infamous Colonel Jean Claude Paul, Commander of the elite Dessalines Battalion, the Palace Guard.

His unit had been named for Jean-Jacque Dessalines, the first leader of an independent and free Haiti. It was the best trained and equipped unit in Haiti's military, and many would say the most brutal. It was rumored that when "President for Life" Jean-Claude "Baby Doc" Duvalier had been forced into exile the year before, Colonel Paul recruited many of his Tonton Macoutes into the Dessalines, the secret band of thugs that had kept the Duvalier family's repressive regime in power for almost thirty years. Paul was considered the most powerful man in Haiti and had become the Colombian cartels' go-to guy.

☆ ☆

Jean Claude Paul, his brother Antonio Paul, and his former beauty-queen wife Mireille Delinois, had already been indicted by a Miami grand jury for shipping 100 kilograms of cocaine destined for Florida. The load had left Paul's airstrip, been successfully airdropped to a waiting fast boat in the Bahamas for a run into South Florida, and then disappeared. Colonel Paul had five men killed while in pursuit of the missing drugs and was holding a sixth man personally accountable for the $800,000 he had invested in the load. Knowing he was on Paul's hit list, the sixth man wisely switched sides and spilled the beans. But the indictment did us no good since our extradition treaty with Haiti covered all manner of crime but drugs.

When headquarters agreed to open a permanent office in Haiti, as with Bridgetown, the responsibility to set it up and manage it fell to me. I made several trips to Port-au-Prince to negotiate office space in the Embassy, and the Career Board tapped Special Agents Walter Brown and Juan Rodriguez to man the office. Walter was a Vietnam veteran and that gave him some international experience and a passing acquaintance with Port-au-Prince, it having been built by the French using the same plan they had followed to build Saigon. Juan was one of the San Juan, Puerto Rico agents who had made regular visits to Haiti to liaison with local law enforcement authorities. As a result, we wouldn't be starting from scratch. And Juan spoke Spanish fluently — the language of our Colombian quarry.

The two began searching among local agencies trying to find counterparts they could trust. The pickings were slim. Early on, they struck the police from the list, their reputation of corruption and unprofessionalism having long preceded them.

Although it was highly unusual for the DEA to work with foreign militaries, Haiti was a highly unusual situation. The

☆ ☆

military had its own corruption problems, but they controlled the airport that would be the key to our initial intelligence collection strategy. And with military security forces having quasi-law enforcement powers, by default the head of security at Haiti's International Airport, the "spit and polish" Army Major Antoine "Tony" Atouriste, became our principal counterpart. While he may not have been the ideal suitor, he had no warts we could find.

For the "grand opening" of the Port-Au-Prince Office, I wanted to do it up right. I asked my Coast Guard colleagues in Miami to land one of their H-3 helicopters at the airport, park a trailered command center along its perimeter, and station a Coast Guard Cutter off the southern coast of Haiti to have its radar acquire suspected drug smuggling targets arriving from Colombia. It was to have been a two-week Haitian OPBAT, a show of force. But it didn't turn out that way.

The fanfare must have scared off the air smugglers. So in the down time, in order to create some goodwill, the Coast Guard transformed the airport into Magic Kingdom East. Military and police officers queued up for helicopter rides. Few had ever gotten a bird's eye view of their country; most had never flown before.

Our initial objective was to paint a broad-brush picture of what was going on in Haiti. So we cloned a Joint Intelligence Coordination Center at the airport modeled after the prototype in Santo Domingo. Due to the unreliability of communications systems in Haiti, we connected it to the DEA's El Paso Intelligence Center via short-wave radio modem. What became immediately apparent once we started checking flight manifests against the EPIC database was that herds of Colombians arrived daily, many of them associated with one Colombian cartel or another. And while painting the picture, we began to sketch some enforcement successes onto the canvas as well.

Walter, Juan and Tony engineered the first undercover operation ever conducted in Haiti. Posing as corrupted soldiers providing security for a drug transporter, Tony's uniformed men pretended to guard the smuggler's plane after it landed on a beach in Jacmel. They watched as the Colombian crew offloaded a ton of cocaine onto their Army deuce-and-a-half truck, and then turned their rifles on the startled crew and whisked them away with the dope to Port-au-Prince.

Cocaine seized from a hidden compartment in the hold of a Colombian freighter at Port-au-Prince, Haiti.

Several months later we got word that a Colombian freighter in route to Jacksonville with a load of cocaine hidden onboard was refueling at Port-au-Prince. Tony commandeered dockworkers to offload its cargo. A line of bare-footed men toted tons of cement over their shoulders, one bag at a time, down wooden planks to the dock under a scorching tropical sun. Walter and Juan were sweating too, concerned that if no dope was found, they'd lose credibility with Tony. But after the final bag of cement had been manhandled from the ship, a ton of cocaine was found in a secret compartment welded beneath the ship's hold.

One day Ambassador McKinley telephoned me in Miami with an extraordinary request. "I need you to come and pick up the police department's seized drug inventory," he said, "The Chief's afraid it's going to be stolen and that he'll be to blame."

The chief had shown me his "evidence vault" on one of my courtesy calls — his office bathroom that he kept locked with a skeleton key. I assumed much of what they had seized would be missing, having been sold out the back door. But I figured at least we would keep whatever drugs remained from getting onto the street.

I sent several agents on a Coast Guard C-130 to Port-au-Prince to retrieve the dope. Meanwhile, other agents scoured reports of drug seizures by the Port-au-Prince police department to see what amount of drugs there should have been. When the DEA Laboratory technicians in Miami weighed and tested each bundle of cocaine and marijuana, low and behold, virtually every gram of dope was accounted for, save for a few kilos of sham cocaine that could have been substituted for real cocaine by scheming dopers before that load had been seized. Maybe we had read the Chief of Police all wrong.

Despite its grinding poverty and the rape of much of its forests, Haiti was still a beautiful country. Royal Caribbean owned a pristine beach at Labadee on the north end of the island nation, hidden away and barely accessible even by the locals, save for a nearby tribe they paid to work there. In that era of the AIDS epidemic, Royal Caribbean chose to describe to its cruise passengers the Labadee stopover as "a day on a tropical isle," never uttering the word "Haiti."

☆ ☆

We heard rumors that some unidentified crew members aboard Royal Caribbean passenger ships were ferrying cocaine from Labadee to Miami. I suggested to Walter that we go there to check it out. Even the DEA's sturdy four-wheel drive Land Cruiser could barely navigate the rocky trail over mountainous jungle terrain to get us there from Cap-Haitian. Once at Labadee, we offered rewards to several of the locals to get word to Walter of any suspicious activity. But nothing ever came of it.

Like Thailand, Haiti was becoming known for its coups d'état. We decided to plan one of our own. Harkening back to my days in Bangkok luring the likes of Luchai Ruviwat to San Francisco and Preecha Leeyaruk to Hong Kong, we began thinking about ways to entice the indicted Colonel Jean Claude Paul from his sanctuary in Haiti to a place from where he could be extradited to Miami. But Paul's former wife beat us to the *punch*, or I should say to the *soup*.

Walter had picked me up at the airport on one of my visits. We were headed up to my favorite hotel in Petionville, the Montana, where Tony was to meet us, when we were forced to the side of the narrow mountain road to allow a line of Army trucks to pass us by on their way down to Port-au-Prince. A half a dozen sullen-looking soldiers sat in the back of one of the trucks with a flag-draped coffin at their feet. By chance, it had been Colonel Paul's funeral cortege.

While sipping a Prestige beer in the hotel's Bougainvillea outdoor dining room, peering down on the squalor of Port-au-Prince far below, I lamented the fact that the colonel hadn't met his demise in the federal courthouse in Miami as we had been scheming.

"I always thought he would be killed by some Colombians he had cheated," Walter opined.

☆ ☆

"Actually, it was his former wife who did him in," Tony said, "She poisoned him with a bowl of homemade pumpkin soup."

The Haiti JICC had some tangible successes as well. On one of my "management by flying around" trips to the Caribbean, I hopped a ride from Santo Domingo to Port-au-Prince with the hierarchy of the Dominican Republic's armed forces who were on their way to help celebrate Haiti National Day. When we landed, Walter told me the JICC had identified a passenger who had arrived the previous day aboard a general aviation aircraft from Bogota as a fugitive in a Ft. Lauderdale case. Tony had the Colombian national under surveillance at a local hotel and offered to arrest him if I wanted to take him with me to Miami. I borrowed handcuffs from Walter, and that next morning Tony marched the fugitive in shackles across the tarmac and up the stairs onto my Eastern Airlines flight. I cuffed him to the seat next to me, under the steadily watchful eyes of my fellow passengers. It's what we called an informal extradition.

It wasn't long after that when a highly placed informant told the DEA in Colombia that the word on the streets of Medellin and Cali was, "Don't go to Haiti, DEA's everywhere." And we watched seizures in Miami of cocaine arriving from Haiti plummet. The kingpins had turned their sights to their own new frontier.

The Colombians loved the Bahamas. The peaceful islanders were only interested in making a few dollars. But OPBAT had made their prized route an obstacle course. And when they hedged their bets on Haiti, in two short years our little, two-man office rousted them from that once viable alternative. We had prevailed in the Caribbean but started a war in Mexico. Mexican criminal gangs had long been involved in marijuana cultivation and black-tar heroin production and in smuggling contraband

☆ ☆

across the Southwest border. Now the Colombian cartels reluctantly turned to them to aid in their cocaine trafficking.

The Mexican gangs demanded a larger role in smuggling operations, and a bigger share of the enchilada. And the Mexican gangs fought each other with their own brand of ruthlessness over the privilege of helping the Colombians. Our success in the Caribbean had forced an alliance in Mexico that created a far more formidable adversary for Mexico and the DEA than we could have ever imagined, a war that continues to this day.

I sometimes wondered if that Voodoo high priest who wished me luck at Ambassador McKinley's residence in 1987 had anything to do with our success in Haiti. If so, it sure would have been nice to have had some of his Voodoo magic in Mexico.

☆ ☆ ☆ ☆ ☆ ☆

Following the ouster of Baby Doc Duvalier and successive regimes of strongman military rule, in 1990, Catholic priest Jean-Bertrand Aristide had been democratically elected President of Haiti. But he barely made it through seven months in office before being escorted out of the country by General Raoul Cedras who then began purging the military of those deemed loyal to Aristide and to Aristide's American lackeys. That put Major Tony Atouriste in the general's crosshairs.

Tony sought political asylum in the U.S. for him and his family. However, Congress was up-in-arms against the Haitian military after the overthrow of Aristide, and the State Department wasn't about to issue visas to any of them.

"Any chance you could help him?" asked Walter Brown on a call from Port-au-Prince. "I think we owe him."

By then, I was stationed back in Washington and able to intervene through some contacts I had made at Main State. The Atouriste family made it safely to Miami.

CHAPTER 22

TO THE ENDS OF THE EARTH

We got some heartbreaking news from New York. Special Agent Everett Hatcher had been murdered.

He had been negotiating undercover for the purchase of cocaine from Italian organized crime associate Costabile "Gus" Farace, a prison-tattooed, muscle-bound punk, but one with important underworld connections. Farace's father was a Gambino associate, and he had cousins in both the Bonanno and Colombo crime families. Farace had spent the prior seven years of his life in prison, sentenced in 1982 for beating a homosexual man to death after forcing him to commit sodomy. While doing time, Farace had befriended fellow inmate Gerry Chilli, a captain in the Bonanno gang. Recently released from prison and under Chilli's tutelage, Farace was trying to get his drug business back up and running. DEA and FBI investigators hoped that Hatcher's drug buys from Farace would eventually lead them to Chilli.

But Farace's "Wimpy Boys" street gang alerted Farace that the guy who had introduced Hatcher to him might be a snitch. Pumped up on coke, Farace foolishly broke one of the few rules customarily observed by the Mafia — never kill a cop; it brings too much heat. And did it ever! For months after the cold-blooded assassination, wise guys couldn't look in their rear-view mirrors without seeing a fed. And the intense, unrelenting scrutiny was costing them money.

The DEA's boss in New York, Bob Stutman, put Mafia "boss of bosses" John Gotti on notice: "If you want us to back off, turn the guy over." Instead, the arrogant Gotti told underlings, "You wanna' be wise guys? You gotta' take the heat. It's all part of doin' business." And Chilli's loyalty to his protégé-in-hiding remained steadfast.

We got word in Miami that Chilli had a second home in suburban Coral Springs. Agents kept the house under surveillance twenty-four-seven hoping Farace would show. Then we learned that Chilli also owned a vacation getaway in the Cayman Islands. Adding to the possibility that Farace might have fled there, the New York Office learned that his sister would soon be traveling to Grand Cayman with her fiancé. Subsequently, I led a team of DEA and FBI agents to the Caymans. If Farace was there, we would find him.

Farace's sister had booked a room at a motel on Seven Mile Beach. The Royal Cayman Islands Police Service set us up in a nearby oceanfront timeshare and got permission for us to bug the sister's room. But all we learned from the wire was that her fiancé was studying for his plumber's license.

Then we found Chilli's vacation cottage in a quiet George Town neighborhood. The local cops waited down the street in case of trouble. Under cover of darkness a tech agent picked the lock on the front door, and the two of us slipped in. I tiptoed through the house checking closets and under beds to be certain we were alone while the tech agent installed a bug in the base of a living room lamp. Done within minutes, he locked the door behind us. If anyone showed up, we would overhear them. I figured planting the wire and keeping an eye on Farace's sister was about all we could do. Then I thought about Little Cayman.

☆ ☆

It's a remote, ten-square-mile spit of land fifty miles northeast of Grand Cayman with a year-round population of less than a hundred people. There were a few exclusive vacation estates on the island owned by reclusive millionaires. Could one of the mansions be owned by a Mafia don? Could Farace be hiding out there?

To cover that base, the next day I hired a pilot to fly me to Little Cayman. He landed the two-seater in a cloud of dust on a dirt strip in view of the exclusive Southern Cross Club, a world-renowned fishing and SCUBA diving destination. I walked over to the resort's clubhouse, found the manager, and showed him a photo of Farace. He said he'd never seen him before.

"We'll go to the ends of the earth to find this guy," I told the manager. Then I looked around at the barren, wind-swept landscape and thought to myself, *you know, I think I'm already there.*

As it turned out, Farace had never left New York City. The DEA had gotten a judge to revoke the parole of Farace's cousin who then flipped and admitted to being the wheelman on the night of the murder.

"Gus shacked up with Chilli's daughter right after the killing," he said. "Then he began bouncing between the few friends he thought he could trust. That's when I lost track of him. You feds were always one step behind."

After nine months of harassment, the mob's patience finally ran out. Chilli was facing a new FBI racketeering charge that could get him another fifteen years to life, and his daughter had been hauled in on charges of harboring a fugitive and faced a dredged-up marijuana beef from years before. Gus Farace's "godfather," Gerry Chilli, decided it was time to give him up. With the apparent blessing of John Gotti, he got Farace's father to unknowingly set the scheme in motion.

☆ ☆

Joseph Scalfini, a relative of one of Gotti's closest aides, offered to drive the unsuspecting Farace to a meeting with his close friend Louis Tuzzio. When Scalfini stopped the car in front of Tuzzio's house in Brooklyn, a van carrying Tuzzio and two other hoodlums pulled up alongside the passenger-side door pinning Farace inside. Sixteen rounds riddled the car before the hit men raced off. Farace rolled out of the passenger side door, shot in the face, chest, neck, spine, right arm, upper abdomen, pelvis and buttocks. It was the mob's way of turning him over to the DEA without any chance of him ratting them out — dead on delivery.

DEA's Stutman had gotten it right when he told reporters the next day, "Farace died where he lived . . . in the gutter."

☆ ☆ ☆ ☆ ☆

It wasn't too many months after that when Tom Cash called me to his office with some troubling news. "You'd better sit down," he said. "You're being transferred to headquarters."

He told me in so many words that I was being yanked from the best job in the DEA to take over perhaps the most unpopular operation in the history of drug law enforcement. I hadn't requested it. It wasn't a promotion. Worst of all, it would force me to uproot our teenage daughters from their friends, particularly difficult for Amy who in 1990 was a rising high school senior. But I was given no option. They said my paycheck would be in Washington if I cared to pick it up.

At my farewell party my secretary read a poem she had written that I thought captured well my four-year tour of duty in Miami:

☆ ☆

ODE TO SIR CHARLES

After four short years
of joining your peers
at Ralph's for lunch,
time's come to leave this bunch!

Your days of travel to Caribbean places
will soon be replaced with different faces.
No more long hours with the phone in your ear,
as in the jungles, there's none to hear.

ASAC-3 won't be calling to say,
"Is the Ambassador in today?"
'cause you'll soon be ensconced at OC [Cocaine Desk],
as headquarters saw fit to decree.

Your Sir Charles title will go by the wayside,
as C/A Pulley finds a new ASAC to chide.
It's back to basics as you don jungle attire,
and hit South America with your unique kind of fire.

Your writing skills are some of the best,
and giving speeches an excellent attest
of showing just where your strengths lie,
for which you'll be remembered as time goes by.

Norma! Be sure to put my middle initial "H" in,
as C Lutz without it has a funny din!
Attention to detail is your first name,
certainly, someday it will add to your fame.

Snowcap's gain is indeed our loss,
for we do hate giving up our boss.

We wish you well and Godspeed,
may He take care of your every need.

Much good luck!

Norma

I'd been given pretty much free rein to manage Caribbean operations. To thank Tom Cash, and my immediate supervisor Johnny Phelps, I presented each with a copy of James Michener's *Caribbean*. In it were tales from many of the islands I had come to know. Inside the cover of each book I wrote, "Thanks for letting me off the porch!"

Then I was off to the jungles of South America.

CHAPTER 23

SNOWCAP

Bolivian para-military strike force police (*UMOPAR*) caught the *cocaleros* totally off guard. Accompanied by DEA special agent advisors, they had located and destroyed eight coca base laboratories in the Chappare region. The coca leaf market collapsed as Colombian buyers fled, and that denied the cartels much of the coca base they needed to make their cocaine hydrochloride. Operation Blast Furnace had been the first concerted effort to go after coca base production, and the DEA's top leadership wanted to sustain the disruption.

The cocaine that had been transiting the Caribbean and landing on South Florida's shores came from Colombia but hadn't originated there. The process began along the eastern slopes of the Andes Mountains where coca bushes thrived in the volcanic soil. Bolivian and Peruvian peasants stomped the ripened coca leaves in plastic tarp-lined pits, *pozos*, filled with a solution of kerosene, water and sodium carbonate to leach out the coca alkaloid. The putty-like precipitate, coca paste, would then be dissolved in buckets of sulfuric acid, potassium permanganate and water, and dried to make coca base. The potentially more dangerous final step to cocaine hydrochloride employed ether or acetone, and hydrochloric acid to crystallize it, and was done mostly in clandestine laboratories in Colombia, although a few enterprising Bolivian and Peruvian traffickers had tried their hands at it.

Over cocktails at a Panama City, Panama hotel bar, after a long day of reviewing Operation Blast Furnace's results at the DOD's Southern Command, several DEA senior executives hatched a much broader plan. They wanted not only to attack the coca base labs in Bolivia and Peru, but also reduce the amount of precursor chemicals supplying the labs and disrupt transportation of the finished product to Colombia. They thought their idea had the potential to cripple the entire cocaine industry. They named it Operation Snowcap.

The Department of State loved it. Snowcap would be the perfect complement to their Andean Strategy of coca bush eradication and crop substitution to wean peasants off coca cultivation. They lobbied officials of a dozen South and Central American governments to allow DEA special agents to accompany their law enforcement authorities in carrying out the plan. Having noted the large footprint that had to be laid down in Bolivia to support the six U.S. Army Blackhawk helicopters used to ferry raiding parties in Operation Blast Furnace (one hundred and sixty soldiers), they even offered to furnish the needed helicopter support – Vietnam-vintage Huey slicks.

The Department of Defense envied Snowcap. They would much rather have been the "point of the spear," as Southern Command's General George Joulwan liked to put it, conducting the operations instead of supporting them, but were precluded from doing so by policy and law. So, the Special Operations Command offered to train the DEA advisors in jungle survival techniques, basic Spanish language, and provide logistical support such as transportation to and from the cooperating

☆ ☆

countries. They even detailed Special Operations staff officers to DEA headquarters to help coordinate their support.

But while the interagency community adored Operation Snowcap, many within the DEA hated it. Some SACs complained that it drained needed manpower from domestic investigations. Others expressed concern that it strayed too far from the DEA's traditional investigative and intelligence collection roles overseas. However, DEA Administrator Jack Lawn liked the idea, and he had the final say. After a few years, though, even some of Snowcap's staunchest supporters had become concerned.

Perhaps it had been the preference of the Vietnam War hero who had originally been put in charge of it. Or maybe it was the influence the attached military staff at the DEA headquarters had on the operation. But for whatever reason, DEA's senior leadership thought Snowcap had moved too far into the DOD orbit, that its wheels had come off the law enforcement track. A red flag went up when 82 mm mortars were requisitioned for the defense of Peru's Santa Lucia base camp. That's when they decided to make a change, and that's when I got dragged back to Washington to take it over. Ironically, the military service and international experience that had gotten me my dream job in Miami caused me to lose it.

During Snowcap's early years, I had been pretty much minding my own business in the Caribbean. I heard rumors that it was more of a paramilitary than law enforcement operation and was being directed from headquarters rather than by narcotics attachés in the field. But now that I was taking it over, I thought it best to withhold judgment until I had a chance to take a firsthand look.

I traveled to the Ranger Training Brigade at Ft. Benning, Georgia, the unit delivering the modified jungle survival course to

Snowcap volunteers. The brigade commander briefed me on the course of instruction. It was physically demanding, as it should have been. And the Army Rangers taught the fundamentals of staying healthy and safe in a jungle environment. But when the colonel got to the segment on raid planning, I called a time out. "Teach them how to get to the targets safely," I said, "but leave the raid planning to us. Our job is not to have our counterparts move, shoot, and communicate to destroy the enemy, but to arrest drug traffickers and seize evidence for trial."

After being satisfied that future recruits would no longer be exposed to military raid planning, next on my list was to see what was happening down range. So, I headed south for the first of what was to become my quarterly "management by flying around" tours.

The trip started in La Paz, Bolivia, which, at 12,000 feet elevation, is the highest capital city in the world. The airport is actually a thousand feet higher than the city, requiring an unusually long runway for takeoffs in the thin air.

My headache began as soon as the plane's door opened. A nurse greeted us with an oxygen tank for anyone who needed a shot. They probably did a brisk business in coca tea in the airport lobby; although I never tried it, not wanting to risk a positive drug test back home.

I paid a courtesy call on Ambassador Bob Gelbard, not your typical State Department bureaucrat. Bob could be as direct at times with his diplomatic counterparts as he was with me. At least I always knew where the Snowcap program stood with him. And despite his occasional bluster, I counted him as a fan.

After that formality was over, I went down to the jungle; from one elevation extreme to the other. On that first trip, the DEA pilots flew me by the wreckage of an Eastern Airlines Boeing

☆ ☆

727 partially buried in a glacier on the side of Mount Illimani. At 19,600 feet, it was too high up for helicopters to land, and too steep for rescuers to make the climb. Consequently, the plane and twenty-nine frozen bodies remained there, one the wife of a former American Ambassador to Paraguay.

We landed at steamy Chimore, in Chappare Province, where one of the two teams stationed in Bolivia bivouacked at an UMOPAR base camp. This was the primary illicit coca bush growing region, and the team there focused on the production side of the equation. They destroyed the *pozo* pits that fed the coca paste labs whenever they were found, much to the chagrin of the locals who depended on them to supplement their meager, hand-to-mouth existence. But their primary targets were the trafficker's coca paste and coca base labs.

This team had been supplemented with U.S. Border Patrol Tactical agents, BORTAC, who worked with the *UMOPAR* on roadway interdiction of precursor chemicals. Each Snowcap team also had a professional medic and communicator assigned.

On that first trip, I no sooner got settled into the barracks when the bell rang. An informant had provided the coordinates for a clandestine coca base laboratory located deep in the rainforest. We boarded helicopters and landed in a clearing where pre-positioned motorboats awaited us. Labs were normally located near rivers to provide a source of water for the conversion process. We motored down the river under triple canopy jungle to within striking distance of the lab.

To be honest, this really wasn't a raid. In fact, I never went on an actual raid. I wasn't trained for it. And the last thing a Snowcap Team Leader wanted was to get the boss hurt — it wouldn't look good on an annual performance evaluation. No, the raid had occurred the day before, and the lab operators had long since faded into the jungle. The *UMOPAR* had sat on the lab overnight awaiting my arrival so I could see what one looked like *au natural*. After my inspection, they salvaged everything of value and torched the rest.

Clandestine coca base laboratory, Chapare, Bolivia.

Although I never went on a lab raid, I did have a few exciting adventures during subsequent trips to Bolivia. Once a DEA pilot, who shall remain nameless, let me take control of a DEA Casa STL (short takeoff and landing) cargo aircraft in flight, although he had the good sense not to let me attempt to land it. Another time I made the scenic drive from Chimore to Cochabamba in one of our trusty Land Cruisers. For almost four hours, we drove through dense jungle on a narrow, rutted dirt road fractured by landslides; forded meandering streams flowing across the highway; maneuvered around broken-down trucks; and prayed our way over quite a few rickety wooden bridges.

On that first trip, though, after a dinner of C rations and an overnight on a canvas cot at Chimore, I was off to Trinidad by DEA Casa. The team at Trinidad focused on the transportation of the coca base to Colombia. They captured and disabled the smuggler's general aviation aircraft, cratered clandestine airstrips, and conducted riverine interdiction operations aided by the expertise of U.S. Coast Guardsmen detailed to the team. They resided at the Gonadero Hotel in downtown Trinidad (it doesn't take a great imagination to figure out what they nicknamed it). That Saturday night, Trinidad looked to me like any rural town in America — young men rode their motorbikes round and round the town square trying to catch the eye of the young maidens strolling along the boulevard in their finery. After two nights at the Gonadero and the inspection of a recently captured smuggler aircraft, I was off to Lima.

My visits to Peru didn't start out quite so dramatically as in Bolivia. For one, Lima's at sea level. And there was no command performance demanded by the Ambassador. However, the threat of Abimael Guzman's *Sendero Luminoso*, Shining Path, and the *Tupac Amaru* communist guerrillas roaming the hillsides contributed a different sort of drama. These terrorists owed much of their existence to extorting what they could from the coca industry and didn't appreciate Snowcap trying to put their benefactors out of business. Officers of the Peruvian National Police (PNP) often wore ski masks during operations to hide their identities, and thereby protect themselves and their families from retaliation.

There was just one Snowcap team in Peru, based at Santa Lucia, a Peruvian Air Force Base in the Upper Huallaga Valley, in the heart of Peru's coca bush growing region. The team worked with the PNP on the full range of coca paste and coca base lab location and destruction, and on the interdiction of coca base transportation to Colombia. As Snowcap operations forced traffickers to move their activities out of the range of the Santa

Lucia-based helicopters, a secondary base camp was established in the Town of Pucallpa, near a Peruvian Navy Base, from where riverine operations could also be staged. And we rented a safe house in Lima for in-and-out processing of the agents and some occasional rest and recuperation.

Snowcap team at Santa Lucia, Peru, February, 1991. Standing L-R: Special Agent Tracy Haig, Special Agent Tony Silva, Director of Int'l Ops Paul Higdon, Peru Narcotics Attache Mike Kane, Special Agent Vito Guarino, Lutz, Special Agent Frank Balazs. Kneeling L-R: Special Agent Steve Gunzenhauser, Special Agent Juan Rodriguez, Snowcap Team Leader George Feeney.

Legitimate coca bush cultivation had been restricted to certain areas of Bolivia. However, in Peru it was all legal. So instead of eradication, the State Department relied solely on crop substitution, encouraging farmers to plant corn and tomatoes instead of coca. But, coca bushes, being hearty plants, needed little tending. And once its leaves had been chemically converted into coca base, unlike vegetables, there was no need to tote it by pack animal over rugged mountain trails to market before it spoiled. The traffickers came to pick it up.

☆ ☆

And because it was legal to cultivate coca bushes, the leaves couldn't be touched until they'd reached a *pozo* pit. If the strut of a State Department helicopter so much as broke the branch of a coca bush while setting down in a field, the farmer was entitled to compensation. After the harvest, the farmers would spread the leaves out on tarps to dry in the sun. Occasionally a frustrated State Department helicopter pilot would accidentally fly a little too close to the drying leaves scattering them to the winds.

After a few days in the Upper Huallaga Valley, my takeaway from that first trip, and many subsequent trips to Bolivia and Peru, alleviated any concern I may have had that Snowcap volunteers had been conducting arrests and seizures. Although well-armed for their own protection, I was assured they always remained one step behind their host nation counterparts. Maybe they had pulled the llama wool over my eyes, but I found no evidence they were overstepping their bounds.

While the Snowcap teams were outwitting wily drug traffickers and seizing their dope, calming outraged townspeople, foiling fanatical terrorists, traversing harsh terrain, and avoiding dangerous critters, my travails were all in Washington. I always thought they had the better deal. There were battles to be waged within the DEA.

Early on, I put aside my concern that recruitment of new Snowcap volunteers would put me at odds with domestic Special Agents-in-Charge for I had learned that soon after Snowcap had started, a supportive Congress allocated 277 additional special agent positions to compensate the DEA for Snowcap's drain on domestic manpower. These added positions provided more special agents than would be recruited during the entire life of the program, with no more than thirty-five agents deployed to the field at any one time during my tenure. With that ammunition,

☆ ☆

I knew I could fend off assaults from disgruntled SACs. The problem for many SACs was that the new positions hadn't necessarily been allocated to the Field Divisions that supported the program with manpower, and those SACs had a right to complain — but not about Snowcap.

The bigger problem for me was the pervasive perception that Snowcap was a rogue, paramilitary operation far outside of the DEA's traditional role. I made it clear to my staff that as much as we relied upon military support, Snowcap was strictly a law enforcement operation. I once overheard a DOD staff officer refer to my office as the "demilitarized zone," so figured the message had gotten through. I focused the staff on the recruitment of new volunteers, preparation of teams for deployment, logistical support to deployed teams, and reporting Snowcap accomplishments, and left field operations to the narcotics attachés. But I knew if Snowcap was to survive, it would have to be better integrated into the mainstream of the DEA's mission. Then in 1992 the Kingpin Strategy appeared as a godsend.

The Kingpin Strategy targeted the vulnerabilities of the Colombian cartels — their need to transport drugs, finance operations, purchase chemicals, and communicate with subordinates. I argued that their dependence on coca base was yet another vulnerability that Operation Snowcap was already exploiting. And more than just destroying labs, Snowcap had developed a sophisticated network of informants that had identified the hierarchy of coca paste and base production in Bolivia and Peru linked directly to the Pablo Escobar's of Colombia. I don't think Kingpin guru Bobby Nieves ever completely bought into the idea. So, while we may have stood out in the Kingpin Strategy like a gorilla in a cage full of monkeys, interdictors among investigators, at least I had put Snowcap in the same menagerie.

And there were occasional battles in Washington within the interagency community. One skirmish involved the Departments of State and Defense and the CIA that made me think for a moment I had entered the Twilight Zone. Diplomats were calling for war, and warriors were calling for peace. As it turned out, the ultimate decision hadn't mattered one way or the other institutionally for the DEA. But had I come down differently on the issue, it would have mattered to me.

When in 1993 President Clinton shifted the focus of government efforts from the "transit zone" to the "source zone," the DOD's Southern Command stationed ground-based radars in northern Peru, Ecuador and Southern Colombia to track smuggler aircraft flying drugs along the "air-bridge" from Peru so they could be intercepted once they landed in Colombia. Then the Peruvian government unexpectedly authorized its Air Force to shoot down suspected smuggler aircraft, and the Colombians followed suit. Concerned that a death could make their employees legally liable, the DOD suspended its intelligence sharing with them.

Bob Gelbard, the former Ambassador to Bolivia, who by then was the Assistant Secretary of State for International Drug and Law Enforcement Matters, cobbled together a meeting to hash it out. At the conference, I went out on a limb. Without senior leadership instructions, I came down with the DOD on the side of peace. I too was concerned for liability. If our agents contributed intelligence that resulted in "shoot downs" and someone got killed, they would be left holding the bag. And in my mind, the penalty didn't fit the crime anyway. There was no death penalty on the books for smuggling drugs. Therefore, I ordered Snowcap not to share information with the Peruvian Air Force.

Gelbard tossed the matter to the Department of Justice to determine the liability matter. Months later, the DOJ ruled that "shoot down" did indeed create a substantial liability risk. As a result, the following year Congress passed legislation that provided relief from liability. The "air bridge denial program" resumed. However, by then, Operation Snowcap had ended.

Over the next five years, the DOD radars and CIA Citation tracker aircraft guided Peruvian Air Force fighter jets to suspected targets. Fourteen drug smuggler planes were shot down, five more forced to land, with three confirmed fatalities. Then on April 20, 2001, the program was shut down for good. The unthinkable occurred.

Baptist missionaries Jim and Veronica Bowers and their two children were flying back to their adopted home of Iquitos, Peru, in a single engine "float" plane. After leveling off at 4,000 feet, a Peruvian A-37 jet that had been vectored to the aircraft by a CIA tracker aircraft approached from the rear and fired 7.62 mm rounds from the jet's machine gun into the aircraft. Veronica and infant daughter Charity were killed instantly. Despite a bullet wound to his leg, the pilot set the plane down safely on the Ucayalli River. Jim and son Cory were miraculously uninjured. The State Department immediately suspended the operation. To my knowledge, it has never resumed.

It wasn't that we didn't have enough to do with Snowcap in Bolivia and Peru when another challenge was thrown in our path.

☆ ☆

CHAPTER 24

CADENCE

D EA Administrator Rob Bonner called an emergency meeting. The senior staff gathered around his twelfth-floor conference room table to hear what was being billed as a grim situation. Being the Chief of Drug Suppression, I had been invited to attend.

Latin America Desk Chief Felix Jimenez briefed the group. As a result of our success in working with Mexican authorities to stop "fast flyers," commercial jets converted into drug cargo planes, from flying from Colombia deep into Mexico, Colombian traffickers had switched tactics once again. He said the DOD's Southern Command had been watching general aviation aircraft land on dirt strips in the jungles of Guatemala, and that the Guatemalan authorities had no means to deal with the invasion. The cocaine was being loaded onto trucks destined for Mexico. Guatemala's border with Mexico was a sieve. Bonner looked around the room for answers.

After a few moments of silence, I spoke up from my seat against the wall. "I could send a Snowcap team there and, with a few helicopters and some dedicated aircraft tracking resources, they could use OPBAT airmobile interdiction tactics to intercept them."

That evening I got a call from Bonner's executive assistant. "He wants to call the State Department tonight to propose the operation you suggested. He needs a name for it." I grabbed my dictionary and within minutes called him back.

"Operation CADENCE," I said, "It's an acronym for 'Central American Drug Enforcement Centers.'"

"Perfect."

After Bonner got the okay from State, he dispatched me to Guatemala City to sell the American Ambassador on the hybrid program. Once that was accomplished, my staff got to work. With the help of the Guatemala City Office, within two months we had a safe house set up, host nation counterparts identified, and a CADENCE team on the ground — or should I say in the air. And did they ever kick butt.

Southern Command's seaborne and airborne radars and a U.S. Customs tracker aircraft based at Soto Cano, Honduras, began vectoring the CADENCE team to suspected smuggler aircraft landings on make-shift dirt runways in remote areas of Guatemala. They captured one cocaine-laden aircraft after another.

Guatemala offload of cocaine.
Photos courtesy of Special Agent Steve Gunzenhauser.

In a panic, the Colombian drug lords demanded the landings be made at night to lessen the chance of their precious cargo being seized, albeit a much riskier proposition for the pilots. State quickly adapted, acquiring night vision goggles for their pilots and installing special lighting for the helicopters. Soon the chase was back on.

More tons of cocaine were seized or scraped off airstrips as the number of crashed airplanes began to mount. When the smuggler aircraft began landing farther and farther from Guatemala City to out-distance the range of the CADENCE helicopters, we randomly staged operations in towns far from Guatemala City.

Based on the success we were having in Guatemala, we had concerns that the traffickers would start looking to other Central American countries to exploit. Also bordering Mexico, Belize was a natural. So, I traveled to Belize City to ask the American Ambassador there to lobby the Government of Belize to allow a CADENCE advisor to prepare them for possible CADENCE deployments. Eventually, we sent advisors to El Salvador and Nicaragua as well. Within two years, the Colombian kingpins had pretty much given up on Guatemala. And the groundwork had been laid in other Central American nations to counter future threats if need be. The crisis was over almost as quickly as it had begun.

☆ ☆ ☆ ☆ ☆ ☆

I often wondered why Snowcap hadn't ever been invited into Colombia. Going after cocaine hydrochloride labs in the jungles of Colombia wasn't much different than chasing down coca base laboratories in Bolivia or Peru, except perhaps for the level of violence associated with the drug cartels, the revolutionary FARC, the Marxist ELN, and a vigilante group called *Los Pepes*. However, the Shining Path and *Tupac Amaru* in Peru were no

☆ ☆

slouches when it came to violence. Perhaps the reason was that we had already invested so much in ending the drug industry in Colombia, that it seemed like overkill.

But I wanted to put a boot on the ground there, and in 1993 wrangled a two-man team onto the Guajira Peninsula where "Colombian Gold" marijuana flourished and from where many of the marijuana flights to the Caribbean originated. Later, a three-man Snowcap team led by Special Agent Bob Hartman was dispatched to work with Colombian authorities to crater clandestine airstrips in the Vichada Region of Colombia near the Venezuelan border. However, despite our broadening efforts, and panoply of successes, both Snowcap and CADENCE came under threat from the incoming Administration.

Jack Lawn had used his influence to get Operation Snowcap up and running. Rob Bonner had adopted Snowcap as if it was his own, boasted of CADENCE successes and allowed Snowcap to expand into Colombia. Thanks to Deputy Administrator Steve Greene, and Deputy Assistant Administrator Doug Wankel who had kept the wolves from my door for four years, I was even recognized for my work with an Administrator's Award for Exceptional Service. Then Attorney General Janet Reno and Administrator Tom Constantine came to town and brought with them a philosophy that threatened to end both programs.

They believed it was the responsibility of each nation to solve the drug problem within its own borders and that the United States should not be risking the lives of its agents to solve others' problems. I thought that naïve considering it was our demand for illegal drugs that created the problems for these nations. None of them had the resources to cope with the drug production and drug smuggling industry we had inspired. Their governmental institutions had been corrupted by drug money to the extent that our presence became necessary if anything was to get done. Even the honest cops appreciated our looking over their shoulders, if only to give them an excuse for having done the right thing should they be challenged by corrupt politicians. To me, Snowcap and CADENCE were matters of us helping them to help us.

I tried to make those points during several briefings for Constantine. I invited him to meetings with returning Snowcap and CADENCE teams to get firsthand accounts of the drug trafficking situations downrange and their successes in disrupting them. I even maneuvered to similarly brief Janet Reno during her visit to headquarters for the DEA's twentieth anniversary celebration.

Briefing of Attorney General Janet Reno during DEA's 20th Anniversary celebration, 1993. L-R: AG Reno, DEA Administrator Bonner, Lutz, and Snowcap Team Leader Scott Meadows.

For the festivities, a Snowcap team had transported an entire coca base laboratory (minus the coca base) back from Bolivia and stood it up in a room in DEA headquarters just off the main lobby. They rented palm trees from a local nursery, hung plastic

☆ ☆

birds from their branches, and even piped in jungle sounds to create a most realistic scene. However, the parrots squawked as I briefed Reno. They must have known the handwriting was already on the lab's thatched walls.

☆ ☆ ☆ ☆ ☆ ☆

I felt a loyalty to Snowcap and CADENCE and had to justify to myself why I should leave. By then, I'd been the longest serving drug suppression chief, as long as I had been in any one position during my entire career. If I was going to have any career left in me, it was time to move on.

It had also crossed my mind not to press my luck. As dangerous as these programs were, no one had perished during my watch. The only serious injury had been an agent shot in the foot when his team was ambushed by an angry mob in Bolivia; the only Snowcap fatality the loss of Special Agent Pilot Rickie Finley in a 1989 plane crash in Peru the year before I took over the program.

When the job of deputy director of International Operations opened up, I tossed my *sombrero* in the ring. Matty Maher, my junior partner from the Sukree Sukreepirom case in Thailand, became my new boss. He had shot up past me into the senior executive ranks to the position I coveted. When he retired soon after, I found myself the acting director, which gave me almost daily contact with Constantine.

Tom invited me to sit in on virtually every meeting he had with foreign officials and in one instance with the newly appointed American ambassador to Colombia. My esteem for Constantine quickly rose after he chastised the ambassador for asking him to go easy on the newly elected Colombian President. "Give me a chance to work with him," the ambassador pleaded.

"I work for the American people, and they're tired of us giving the Colombians more chances," Constantine said. And he continued to blast the Colombians for their ineptness and corruption.

I escorted Tom on his first trip overseas to an International Drug Enforcement Conference, in 1994, to Quito, Ecuador. Technically, aside from travels to Canada, it was his second trip abroad. He told me his first overseas travel had been to attend a law enforcement conference in Israel while Commissioner of the New York State Police. But when he landed at Tel Aviv he was told a state trooper had been shot and immediately hopped on the next flight back to JFK.

He even invited Joy and me to join him and his wife at a Christmas party hosted by the Canadian Embassy in Washington. We were getting along very well.

Then Constantine announced that New York SAC Bob Bryden was to be his Chief of Operations. Bob had been choir director of the anti-Snowcap chorus within the DEA, and I feared the curtain was about to drop on the Snowcap / CADENCE symphony. The only thing postponing the inevitable was the need for them to find some plausible justification to shut down two programs the Departments of State and Defense had come to love.

Bob selected Jim Milford as his Director of International Operations, and I assumed Jim would want to bring in his own deputy. While I was pondering my next move, arguably the worst tragedy in the DEA's history occurred.

It had been only a few months since I had been transferred from Snowcap when three Snowcap Special Agents hopped aboard an ill-fated flight from Santa Lucia to Pucallpa, Peru. In route, they decided to check out some information that an informant had given them about some drug activity occurring just off the flight path. The pilots diverted the plane and followed a stream flowing from a canyon. By the time they realized they were boxed in, it was too late. Casa cargo aircraft aren't designed to make vertical climbs. Apparently, the plane stalled, and fell nose first into the jungle. All radio contact was lost.

We sat in the Command Center for hours on end waiting for news, hoping it would be a rescue mission, and not a recovery. Constantine dispatched both Milford and Air Branch Chief Donnie Marshall to Santa Lucia to coordinate the search. Then the next day, recognizing my long association with the program, in an act of true kindness, Tom dispatched me to Peru as well.

By the time I got to Santa Lucia, the crash site had been located. In a truly international effort, a Chilean commercial airline pilot had picked up a signal from the downed plane's black box that pinpointed its location. Soon after, a Peruvian Air Force pilot spotted a glint of steel creviced among trees on a heavily forested mountain, and a Peruvian helicopter crew braved howling winds to courageously lower an officer to the ground who confirmed that all onboard had perished. But they couldn't land the helicopter on the rugged, treed cliff.

A team of agents with a Snowcap medic and communicator had set out on foot to the crash site but were forced to turn back by a raging stream, steep slopes and impassable boulders. And so, in another truly heroic effort, Group Supervisor Frank Balazs from the Lima Office, a former Snowcap volunteer, led a group of agents to the crash site, lowered by jungle penetrator, a device used extensively during the Vietnam War to hoist battlefield survivors from the jungle floor, from a wind-swept, hovering helicopter to the downed aircraft. Members of the by then extracted overland team were inserted next onto the crash site,

☆ ☆

followed by necessary equipment and supplies. They spent an overnight extricating the remains from the aircraft and chopping down trees so a helicopter could hover close enough to the ground the next day to remove them all.

After a memorial service in Lima, Jim Milford and I escorted the remains of Special Agents Frank Fernandez, Meredith Thompson, Jay Seale, Frank Wallace, Jr., and Juan Vars aboard a U.S. Air Force C-5A *Starlifter* to their grieving families at Andrews Air Force Base, and a hero's welcome officiated by Janet Reno and Tom Constantine.

I felt bonded to Meredith Thompson. She had worked in one of my groups in Miami and called one day to ask my advice as to whether she would be a good fit for Snowcap. I had encouraged the bright, athletic special agent to apply. That routine act of mentoring weighed on me now. There's a memorial golf tournament each year for Meredith that raises money for the survivors of all lost agents. I played in the initial tournament with Meredith's father, a fine gentleman whose graciousness during his grief will always be remembered.

I got to know Frank Fernandez while he worked for me as a Snowcap Team Leader. In a quirk of fate, Frank is memorialized in a Hollywood movie — the screen adaptation of Tom Clancy's book, *Clear and Present Danger*.

Long before the plane crash, the film crew had come to Washington to record scenes for the movie. I had been asked to brief them on how cocaine lab raids in South America were actually conducted, and by whom. In the book, Clancy had mistakenly attributed such work to the FBI. I set the record straight, and a DEA narcotics attaché is featured in the movie.

While I was briefing the film crew, there were Snowcap teams at Quantico Marine Base preparing for deployment, what we

☆ ☆

called a "mount out." I asked Frank to escort the movie-makers there to see the real stars in action. Frank started dating one of the film crew staff, and she got him a small part in the final scene. Frank can be seen as the Congressional staffer sitting on the top row in the Congressional chamber, second from the left, as Harrison Ford spills the beans on the movie's White House-sanctioned illegal military ops in Colombia.

I didn't know Jay Seale, although I'm sure we must have met; and knew of pilots Frank Wallace Jr. and Juan Vars only by their stellar reputations.

Constantine had the added compassion to take me with him to the funerals of Snowcap Special Agents Frank Fernandez, Meredith Thompson and Jay Seale, for which I'll always be grateful.

☆ ☆ ☆ ☆ ☆ ☆

The crash marked the end of the Snowcap and CADENCE programs, but the Snowcap concept survived. Years later, after former Snowcap Team Leader Mike Braun had risen to be Chief of Operations, he resurrected it in Afghanistan and called it FAST, Foreign Assistance and Support Teams.

However, there's one thing that annoys me to this day. Tom Constantine put a false narrative into the DEA's 25th anniversary book to justify his shutting down Operation Snowcap, a narrative that has been repeated in each anniversary book since. He claimed Snowcap was ended because agents were "participating in enforcement operations," and that the program was causing a "serious drain" on domestic field division manpower.

Of course they participated in enforcement operations. That was why they were there – to advise and assist. The only question was whether they had exceeded their authority. There was no evidence they had. They were either backing up their counterparts or acting in self-defense.

And the latter part of his statement is simply not true. Congress had given the DEA more than enough special agent positions to compensate for any disruption the program may have caused to domestic operations.

Ironically, OPBAT had been operating in the Bahamas for fifteen years by then and continues to this day, using similar enforcement tactics and relying on volunteers recruited from domestic offices, although in fewer numbers and without specialized training. I don't ever recall hearing similar complaints about OPBAT.

I've tried to have Constantine's language eliminated in successive anniversary books, but to no avail. I hope someday it will be. The men and women who served honorably in Operations Snowcap and CADENCE, and particularly those six who paid the ultimate price while doing so, deserve better.

Not long after the crash, my career took yet another unexpected turn.

CHAPTER 25

STRANDED

My days at headquarters were numbered, a transfer back to the field inevitable. However, having moved seven times with the DEA already, I wasn't all that anxious to pack up and go.

I had the prerequisites to qualify as the Special Agent-in-Charge of a small Field Division and, given the good relationship I had established with Administrator Tom Constantine, thought I might have a pretty good shot at one. With both girls at Virginia Tech, I definitely wanted to stay east of the Mississippi. The Washington, D.C. Field Division would have been ideal. Then Chief of Operations Bob Bryden threw me a curve ball. He offered me a job east of the Mississippi River all right — Far East of it. The SAC job in Bangkok!

I hadn't given returning to Thailand a second thought since we left there in 1978. Of course, it would be a promotion into the hallowed ranks of the Senior Executive Service, at a pay grade equivalent to that of a two-star general, nothing to sneeze at. But I knew it would be a non-starter with Joy. For that reason, I told Bob, no thanks. Then Constantine called me to his office.

"I want you to take my place at an upcoming United Nations Drug Conference in Wellington, New Zealand," he said, "and,

☆ ☆

while you're out there, go to Thailand and look around. Wait until you get back to give Bob your final answer on Bangkok." He was no fool. He knew it would get my international juices flowing.

☆ ☆ ☆ ☆ ☆ ☆

Once in Bangkok, I looked up some of my former Royal Thai Police colleagues who by then were running the show — like Viraj Jutimitta from the Sukree Sukreepirom / Hoi Se Wan, Luchai Ruviwat and Preecha Leeyaruk cases, who was by then a full colonel in the Police Narcotics Suppression Center. It would be a homecoming.

After a few days of reminiscing, and a few rounds of golf, I called Joy and told her I thought it could work. I made the case that we weren't seeing much of the girls between their studies, part-time work, and partying — not necessarily in that order. And with the satellite phone in the SAC's apartment that could patch us through to them as if we were calling from Washington, and that newfangled World Wide Web that everyone was talking about, we would be able to stay in touch. The girls would get to travel to Bangkok each Christmas at government expense, and I told Joy she could fly back to the States for holidays, birthdays, anytime she wanted for that matter. But the clincher was when Amy and Cindy heard the words "Christmases in Thailand." They encouraged us to go, and Joy finally, reluctantly agreed.

I asked the Training Division to arrange a Thai language refresher course for me. They said they couldn't, that according to their records I spoke Thai too fluently.

"But that was almost twenty years ago," I said. "Since then, I've only used it to order food at Thai restaurants." They said I would have to be tested by the State Department to prove I couldn't speak Thai at that level.

☆ ☆

"So, let me get this straight," I said. "I have to take a test and flunk it to get what I want? I think I can handle that."

It turned out that the refresher course was actually a waste of time. All my Thai counterparts spoke far better English than I could ever hope to speak Thai.

☆ ☆ ☆ ☆ ☆ ☆

Bangkok was nothing like I had remembered it. In the intervening years, it had exploded from a town of canals and teakwood homes into a western-style metropolis with high rise condos, office towers, shopping malls, and wall-to-wall cars, trucks, buses, motorbikes and motorized rickshaws.

They had banned elephants from the city because it slowed traffic — like the baby elephant we rented from the Erawan Hotel that had lumbered its way up Sukhumvit Road to our home on Soi 36 to give the kids rides at Amy's first birthday party — although it was hard to imagine Bangkok traffic moving any slower.

The changes in Thailand that had amazed me more, though, were the drug trafficking patterns. My predecessor had pulled the bamboo mat out from under the world's most prolific heroin producer, ending the thirty-year reign of Opium Warlord Chang Chi Fu, *nom de guerre* Khun Sa. It was estimated that he had been producing half of the Golden Triangle's heroin, and Operation Tiger Trap put him out of business.

It was Khun Sa's infrastructure in Thailand that had been targeted. A federal grand jury in the Eastern District of New York indicted the ones who had been residing in Thailand, exporting his heroin, collecting the proceeds, and buying the beans and bullets for his private militia, the Shan United Army. And since none of them were Thai citizens, they were all deportable to stand trial in the States. Without them, Khun Sa's heroin couldn't be sold, he didn't know who owed him money for what, and soon his hungry soldiers began to fade into the jungle. Eight months after I arrived in Thailand, after we sent the last of his Thailand-based crew packing for New York City, and his chief chemist had been arrested, Khun Sa surrendered to the Burmese government. He lived the remainder of his life under house arrest in Rangoon, his empire in ruins.

With Khun Sa out of the picture, the production of Golden Triangle heroin plummeted, no longer dominating the heroin market in the United States, not even the drug market in Thailand. Methamphetamine had replaced heroin as the substance of choice among Thai druggies. So instead of stumbling over heroin cases as we had in the 1970s, the cops were tripping over meth cases.

The agents, of course, wanted to make cases. And since heroin cases had become relatively scarce, they were fine with working on meth. But I felt strongly that the American taxpayers hadn't sent us to Thailand to solve the Thai's methamphetamine problem, but to ensure that Asian heroin didn't return to the streets of America. That's not to say we didn't have an interest in helping our counterparts. It had always been a matter of us scratching their backs if we expected them to scratch ours. But I insisted heroin remain our top priority. That wasn't very popular with some of the agents in the office.

Despite the rise of methamphetamine, it wasn't as if heroin had disappeared. There were still a few heroin laboratories in the Golden Triangle and patches of opium being cultivated to keep those labs operating. The State Department continued to support the Royal Thai Police Department's annual opium eradication campaign to reduce the supply of opium. I had been invited to tag along on one of the raids.

We flew commercially to Chiang Mai, and the next morning boarded a Thai Police helicopter that shuttled us to a mountain top in Northern Thailand, just a hand grenade's throw from the Burmese border. As our helicopter hovered for landing, the Thai Border Patrol policemen guarding the clearing turned away from the billowing clouds of dust the rotors had stirred up. Once it settled, a police colonel led us through a line of trees into a field of spectacularly beautiful, purple-flowering opium poppy. Each bulb had been scored, and opium sap oozed from the scars. Some of the gum would have been smoked by the Hill Tribesmen who had cultivated it — the bulk sold to traders who in turn would sell it to chemists to convert into morphine base and then heroin.

Scored opium poppies in the mountains of Northern Thailand, part of the Golden Triangle of Thailand, Laos and Burma.

The cultivators hadn't done anything to conceal their handiwork. They didn't have to. In such difficult terrain it was unlikely a foot patrol would have ever stumbled upon it. And the acre-sized plot was surrounded by towering trees, so the aerial

☆ ☆

patrol that spotted it two days earlier had been either very good or very lucky. Now the planters' luck had run out. We had come to chop it down.

Al Nugent, the State Department's Chief of the Narcotics Assistance Section, had arranged the field trip. He had also invited the newly appointed head of the Joint Interagency Task Force West, Coast Guard Admiral James McClelland, to join us. Based in Alameda, California, JIATF West had been created by the Department of Defense to support drug law enforcement activities in Asia and the Pacific. They detailed an intelligence analyst to my office. They were building drug intelligence centers for the DEA's police counterparts in Bangkok, Songkhla, and Chiang Mai. And they had been training Border Patrol policemen assigned to drug interdiction. It would be Jim's first visit to Thailand, and he brought with him his special assistant, DEA Special Agent Lloyd Clifton. We were joined by the DEA boss in Chiang Mai, Ed Kelley. It was a great opportunity for some male bonding!

We were handed machetes and began chopping down stalks. As they fell to the ground, the cops dragged them downwind, piled them high, and set them ablaze. It was a good thing we were upwind, or we might have been able to fly back to Chiang Mai on our own!

Based on the size of the plot and the density of the plantings, we probably kept a quarter ton of opium, potentially 50 pounds of heroin, off the streets. But after an hour of toil, we had had enough.

The sun was beating down as it approached its apex; it was getting hot, even in the relatively thin air at 4,000 feet elevation. And it was only for show anyway, a photo op to document the cooperation between the governments of Thailand and the

☆ ☆

United States in wiping out the narcotics scourge. We had more than enough pictures and if we left soon, we'd be back to the hotel in plenty of time for "happy hour."

As we walked from the field a cloud settled around us like a shroud, shrinking visibility to a couple of feet. We groped our way to the helicopter to wait it out. An hour passed. Then another. The sun was dropping. It was getting chilly. The helicopter couldn't take off until the fog lifted. If we waited much longer, we'd be stuck.

The prospect of having to spend the night there began to sink in. We weren't dressed for it. We had trousers on, thankfully not shorts. I had worn dungarees. But we all had on short-sleeved shirts — Al, a pink Ralph Lauren polo. And while Lloyd, Ed and I wore sneakers, The admiral sported penny loafers. We looked more like fraternity brothers at a beer bash than a team of government officials on an opium eradication raid. We hadn't expected to be hazed; we certainly hadn't planned on an overnight camping trip.

I checked around for food. The only thing onboard the helicopter was a few candy bars the pilots had brought along. Of course, the police carried field rations that I was certain they would share with us so we wouldn't starve. But we had just about drunk up all the water we had brought along, and what little was left filled the canteens of the Border Patrolmen. Who knew where that water had come from?

I noticed Lloyd sizing up the sleeping quarters. He was a big guy, a little taller than me, and a lot broader. I figured two of us could lie across the passenger seats, and one on the floor. And assuming the pilot and co-pilot found shelter with their comrades, the other two could sleep sitting up in the cockpit chairs. We would have to draw straws as to who slept where. I wasn't feeling very lucky.

Then there were the pesky natives to worry about – the Hill Tribesmen who had planted the opium poppy. No doubt they were pissed to see their months of work go up in smoke. For all I knew, we were already in their sights. No telling if they would try to exact a penalty on their now stranded enemies. Their primitive weapons, long rifles with bird shot and bows and arrows, were no match for the carbines of the Border Patrol policemen. But by sneaking up on us in the fog or under cover of eventual darkness, they could be on top of us before we knew it.

I actually felt sorry for the Hill Tribe people. They were as much victims of the drug trade as anyone. In addition to eradication, Al and his State Department cronies were big on crop substitution to wean them off opium cultivation. But for those who lived in such remote, mountainous areas, agricultural products were seldom the answer. Similar to the plight of the coca farmers in the South American Andes Mountains, once harvested, without roads to get their produce to market, it rotted. And what little could be carried out in backpacks wouldn't earn enough money to support their families. Like coca, poppies were hardy plants, easy to grow, and the shelf-life for opium gum was ten years once sealed in plastic. And like cocaine base, the opium farmers didn't need to worry about getting their goods to market. The opium traders came to buy it. Although the farmers never saw the huge profits generated from the international drug trade, they made a lot more money than they would have from selling corn and tomatoes.

We huddled. Al asked if we were more comfortable staying there overnight or trying to walk out. Although we were in radio contact with the Border Patrol substation at the base of the mountain, they couldn't drive up to get us. There were no roads. But they said they would meet us at the bottom of the mountain if we could make it down and then drive us to town. And since it would probably take a couple of hours to walk down, we didn't have much time to decide. Hiking down the mountain through dense jungle was risky enough, but in the dark it wasn't even an option. We voted. "Let's go," I said. And with that, we made a run for it.

Where the planters had blazed a narrow, trampled-down dirt path, we lined up in single file. Two-armed Border Patrol officers took the point; two more brought up the rear. The pilots stayed with the helicopter, guarded by the remaining Border Patrol policemen. We started our descent. It was late afternoon. Although the sun was still up, it was dark under the triple canopy foliage. Our clothes were damp from the day's exertion and the misty fog and chilled by the late afternoon thin air. I was glad to be moving. It was getting cold.

We had rocks and branches to negotiate, fallen tree trunks and limbs to climb over, and mountain streams to ford. We broke branches from trees and fashioned them into canes. Several times we lost the trail and reached cliffs too steep to negotiate, having to double back and start down again. It was very discouraging! We tried to be quiet but probably sounded like a herd of water buffalo as we slipped, stumbled, grunted and groaned down the steep mountain. Exotic birds called to each other; no doubt never having seen such a sight. I kept thinking that maybe it was the Hill Tribesmen signaling to each other. More likely, I had seen too many Tarzan movies!

As we pushed on, we bent back bushes and branches that, despite our best efforts, snapped back in the faces of those behind us. Every fifteen minutes or so, we stopped to rest . . . but not for long. There were the Hill Tribesmen to worry about, and the ever-dimming light. It was much safer to keep hustling along. The admiral was having a tough time of it, though. His feet were killing him. He thought he had developed a blister on one foot, Coast Guardsmen not being accustomed to forced marches, I supposed.

During one of the rest breaks, Jim pulled off his loafers and soaking wet socks. Instead of a blister, two six-inch leeches hung from the side of his left foot. We burnt them off, careful to make them release their vice-like jaws rather than yank them off and cause even deeper wounds. He wrung out his bloody sock, put it back on, and toughed it out as we continued down the mountain.

After an hour or so we reached a small village with a dozen grass huts perched on stilts. Pigs wallowed in small sties. Startled chickens strutted about squawking and pecking in the mud, too nervous to look our way. I noticed a few Hill Tribe women peeking out from behind the sheet-covered doorways of their huts, their kids hiding behind their skirts. There were no men to be seen. No doubt they had faded into the jungle, and I was certain they were watching us. There was no reason to stop. We kept moving on.

It took us another hour to reach the base of the mountain where we rendezvoused with the Border Patrol convoy parked on a muddy trail. Actually, the convoy consisted of an open-air jeep and a commandeered Nissan pickup truck. From his looks, the truck's surly driver hadn't volunteered for the job. But we were tired, cold, hungry, and happy to cram onto the tiny bed of his old pickup with a camper shell to protect us from the wind. The truck bounced and skidded on the rutted gravel road, finally gaining purchase on a paved highway, a welcome sign that our adventure was nearing an end.

☆ ☆

We got back to our hotel in downtown Chiang Mai at about 9 p.m., our faces and arms scratched, shirts with pulls and tears, burrs and brambles stuck to our trousers, and shoes damp from fording streams. We looked like the survivors of a tsunami, pleased to be back to civilization, safe, and almost sound. All I could think of was taking a hot shower and climbing under a warm blanket.

We walked to the front desk to pick up our keys. Jim was first in line. My eyes followed him as he walked toward the elevator, his left shoe leaving bloody imprints across the lobby's oriental carpet. I wish now that I had snapped a picture, but we had had enough photo ops for one day.

☆ ☆ ☆ ☆ ☆ ☆

In addition to Thailand, I had responsibility for the DEA's interests in Laos, Cambodia and Vietnam. Laos was a priority. Our intelligence indicated Operation Tiger Trap had chased several of Khun Sa's heroin chemists to the wilds of Northern Laos where they set up their labs. We had an office in Vientiane until 1975 but shuttered it when Saigon fell and the communist Pathet Lao took over. Recently our two-man office at Udorn Thani, in Northeastern Thailand, began to regularly liaise with the Laotian police. But that wasn't good enough. We needed to build a closer relationship.

Of the other Southeast Asian countries, Cambodia wasn't playing any role in international drug trafficking that we knew of, so it was of little interest to me. I hadn't given any thought to Vietnam. Then a decision by the State Department suddenly moved Vietnam to the top of my list.

☆ ☆

CHAPTER 26

RECONCILABLE DIFFERENCES

It hadn't taken the United States twenty minutes after World War II to begin rebuilding Germany and Japan, countries that between them had wreaked more havoc on the Earth than any other two in world history. After the Vietnam conflict, it took us nearly twenty years to admit that the Socialist Republic of Vietnam even existed. There had been reason for the delay.

We had left South Vietnam in the hands of a communist regime during the Cold War which was a bitter pill to swallow. There was embarrassment over not having won it, the first time in our proud military history, despite never having lost a major battle. And, we had great empathy for the thousands of Americans who had lost loved ones there.

I hadn't given Vietnam much thought over the years. When I took up my post in Southeast Asia in 1995, I didn't know a thing about the illicit drug situation in Vietnam. The Golden Triangle of Thailand, Laos and Burma, where much of the world's heroin had originated, and Bangkok, its gateway into international markets, were the compelling threats. However, when Washington finally found the political will to normalize relations with Vietnam, this veteran found himself right in the middle of it.

☆ ☆

During the Gerald Ford Administration, the People's Republic of Vietnam had agreed to cooperate in recovering our missing-in-action "to the fullest extent possible." In early 1995, Bill Clinton's State Department took the first step toward normalizing relations by establishing a Liaison Office in Hanoi. Then the State Department began searching for an issue to begin dialogue with the Vietnamese they hoped would lead to broader cooperation. They settled on illegal drugs, a plague in both our houses. If the North Vietnamese agreed, it would fall to me, Mr. Drugs in Southeast Asia, to begin the dialogue. Suddenly, Vietnam had jumped to the top of my list.

Bob Gelbard, State's head honcho for international narcotics and law enforcement matters, and Steve Greene, the deputy administrator of the DEA, were tapped to lead the initial negotiations. I knew Gelbard from when he had been Ambassador to Bolivia, and later from having debated with him over the "shoot down policy" in Peru. I knew Greene, the former narcotics attaché in South Vietnam since he had been evacuated to Bangkok in 1975 as Saigon was falling.

I became excited about returning to Vietnam, but also apprehensive. Certainly, they would know that I had been an Army Intelligence Officer during the war. I was concerned they might hold my prior service against me, making my job much more difficult, if not impossible.

Gelbard and Greene arrived in Bangkok in early June. After a whirlwind tour of Thailand's piece of the Golden Triangle, Vientiane's "Valley of Jars," and Cambodia's "Killing Fields," on Wednesday, June 14, 1995, we landed at Hanoi's Noi Bai International Airport. From there the police escorted our motorcade into the belly of the beast.

☆ ☆

I was surprised at the beauty of Hanoi. We passed dozens of lakes, tree-lined streets, and a few old French villas scattered about. Motor scooters buzzed about the streets like swarms of bees. The city along the Red River was low-lying, protected from surrounding waters by numerous dikes. During the war I wondered why we hadn't blown them up to flood the city and put the North Vietnamese out of business. Being the noble country we are, we hadn't taken such drastic action. After seeing Hanoi, I was glad we hadn't.

We checked into the historic Metropole Hotel with its wooden-floored rooms, shuttered windows, and ornate balconies, a throwback to French colonial times. The hotel sat on Sword Lake, named for the magical sword that the Turtle God who lives there had loaned to an ancient Vietnamese Emperor to vanquish an invading Chinese army.

Joy Lutz at Sword Lake in Hanoi, with Ngoc Son temple on Jade Island in the background.

Our Vietnamese hosts wined and dined us and took us on a city tour intended to leave no doubt in our minds that their country had survived the war quite well despite our superior

☆ ☆

might. They showed us Ho Chi Minh's tomb, the carcass of a B-52 shot down over Hanoi, and the statue of a shackled John McCain that had been erected on a bank of Truc Bach Lake into which his Navy jet had crashed after being shot down.

During some free time, Steve Greene, also a Vietnam veteran, a Marine, and I slipped away to pay our respects at the *Maison Centrale* Prison, the "Hanoi Hilton," known locally as Hoa Lo Prison, where many American POWs had been held captive. During one of my subsequent visits to Hanoi, I happened by the prison compound and witnessed the last pile of rocks from the prison being removed. The prison had been knocked down to make way for Hanoi Towers, a high-rise business office and shopping complex, save for its gatehouse that was to be turned into a museum. Maison Centrale Prison was built by French Colonialists who imprisoned Vietnamese dissidents there during France's almost 100-year rule.

Lutz and DEA Deputy Administrator Steve Greene standing in front of the gatehouse of Hoa Lo Prison, nicknamed the "Hanoi Hilton." (right) The last pile of rubble from the walls of the "Hanoi Hilton." The prison's gatehouse can be seen in the background.

☆ ☆

Our formal meeting the next day with the Foreign Minister didn't go according to the State Department's script. After some diplomatic foreplay, Bob Gelbard tossed our proposition onto the table: cooperation on drug control as a pathway toward formal recognition. But before the Minister could even open his mouth to reply, President Clinton knocked Gelbard's diplomatic legs out from under him. That very day, the White House had signaled to the Vietnamese its decision to normalize relations with Vietnam, no mention of drugs being made. Either Clinton didn't know of State's strategy or knew of it and made the announcement in spite of it. Less than a month later, on July 11, 1995, formal recognition was granted in a White House ceremony.

While the announcement undermined what leverage Bob had, and his mission wouldn't be the historic breakthrough toward a normalization of relations he could have added to his record of diplomatic achievements, he did succeed in opening the door to cooperation on drugs. The Vietnamese saw no reason not to work with us. Their police would get the training and equipment they needed to help curb their domestic drug abuse problem. And the DEA stood to gain intelligence on drug trafficking organizations linked to drug gangs in the United States, and potentially the cooperation of Vietnamese authorities in intercepting Thai trawlers smuggling heroin through their waters to Hong Kong.

Over the next three years I returned ten times to Hanoi to continue the dialog and pave the way for a DEA office there. On each visit I schmoozed with the nation's chief of police and local law enforcement authorities to strengthen our friendship. I tagged Special Agent Tom Harrigan to commute between Bangkok and Hanoi in order to build the working relationships we would need to have any enforcement successes. In 2000, a little more than a year after my tour of duty in Southeast Asia ended, a DEA office was opened in Hanoi to carry on the work and remains open to this day.

Special Agent Ly Ky Hoang accompanied me on each of my eleven visits. Ly had been chief of the Saigon Police Department's narcotics squad during the war and had worked closely with the DEA. When Saigon began to crumble, Steve Greene was instrumental in having Ly and his immediate family evacuated to America. The DEA hired Ly as an Intelligence Analyst and, once he was able to prove his qualifications, was entered into basic agent training to become a criminal investigator. At first, I was concerned that his being a former South Vietnamese government official would complicate matters. But his thorough knowledge of the history, culture and government personalities in Vietnam, along with his native language ability, proved to be true assets in accomplishing our goals.

President Clinton nominated Douglas "Pete" Peterson to be America's first Ambassador to the Socialist Republic of Vietnam. It took a year for him to make it through the Congressional wickets, but his arrival breathed new life into the normalization process. Peterson had been a POW for six years and, like fellow POW John McCain, was a driving force in Washington to normalize relations. His commitment to the effort was evident by his having given up his Florida seat in the House of Representatives to become eligible for the Ambassadorial appointment. I don't know if marrying a Vietnamese-Australian woman had been part of the strategy to ingratiate himself with the Vietnamese, but it didn't hurt his cause one bit.

My duties also took me to Ho Chi Minh City, which many of the locals still call Saigon, to meet with that city's chief of police. That gave me the opportunity for the first time in almost 30 years to visit some of my old haunts. The city had grown dramatically in the ensuing decades, its streets jammed with cars, buses and trucks jockeying for space — the mirror opposite of low-rise, slow-paced, motor scooter-infested Hanoi. The pragmatic socialist government knew better than to mess with the capitalistic industry of Ho Chi Minh City, the engine of the nation's booming economy.

But Ho Chi Minh City wasn't without its disappointments. The War Remnants Museum boasted captured American tanks and aircraft and spewed accusations of American war crimes that painted us in the worst possible light. There were young men roaming the streets, having been sired by American GIs and abandoned by their Vietnamese families. And the shell of the American Embassy had been left standing as a monument to North Vietnam's ousting of America — Peterson made its razing a precondition for opening an American Consulate on the site.

Many of the venues I remembered had changed or were gone altogether. A wooden hammer and sickle hung behind the front desk of the Rex Hotel, a reminder of the era that followed ours. The open-air, rooftop O Club — with its $2 steaks and nightly entertainment — had been a favorite of mine during the first six months of my one-year tour of duty. Now the Club's white metal tables and chairs lay on the roof in rusting heaps.

Ly and I couldn't find the Ponderosa, the French villa that headquartered the 525 Military Intelligence Group from where I had commuted to my first job — Operation Hurricane — preparing to defend Saigon from another Tet Offensive. And we couldn't find the compound at the foot of the Binh Loi Bridge where the 519th Military Intelligence Battalion had been housed.

We drove a rental car into the boonies, thirty-five miles east of Bien Hoa, to Xuan Loc. It had been home to the 18th ARVN Infantry Division, and where I spent my second six months in country. I told Ly that my former MACV Team 87 compound wouldn't be hard to find since it sat just across the road from the airstrip from where my "Firefly" helicopter search-and-destroy missions had been launched. I figured by now it would be the town's airport. But when we got to Xuan Loc, we were told there was no airport.

After driving around in circles, we stopped an elderly woman with red, betel nut-stained teeth carrying two buckets of coal balanced on a long pole cradled over her shoulder. She said she remembered the old airstrip and pointed across a field toward a stand of trees. We parked and walked through the tree line into a small village where Ly asked the first fellow we found if he could direct us to the airstrip. "You're standing on it," he told Ly, pointing to our feet. It was now the "main street" of their small village, Mother Nature having done a much more thorough job of crumbling its tarmac than any VC mortar team had ever done.

Main Street. Scene from the village in Xuan Loc built on the former MACV Team 87 airfield.

The fellow told us he had been a ground pounder in the 18th ARVN Infantry Division and invited us into his grass hut for tea. His old Army helmet hung on a stake at the front entrance, its only decoration. We sat on the dirt floor as he served us hot tea in tiny, chipped cups and then proudly took us on a tour of his mushroom farm.

☆ ☆

Unidentified mushroom farmer, former 18th ARVN infantryman, standing in front of his grass hut in the village at Xuan Loc.

Before we left, I bought the entire jar of hard candy at the tiny wooden kiosk that served as the village's general-store and café and handed it out to the kids who had gathered to gawk. I also left a handful of Dong with the store's owner in the name of my comrade-in-arms, enough money, Ly told me, to pay for him and his buddies to drink rice wine for a month.

Having found the old airstrip, I was able to orient us to the MACV compound. However, when we drove by, it was totally overgrown. A guard was posted at the front gate, an AK-47 slung over his shoulder. A sign on the gate read NO PHOTOGRAPHS. It might have been a supply depot by then, perhaps for weapons or ammunition. Although I would have loved to peek into my former lair, Ly thought it best not to stop.

Back in Ho Chi Minh City we drove to Ly's childhood home. His parents had emigrated to the states some years after Ly but were allowed to take with them only one suitcase apiece. Consequently, they had to leave virtually everything they owned behind. The woman who now occupied the house welcomed us in to look around. Ly's parent's furniture sat exactly as it had when he grew up there, including the tiny, lacquered table Ly ate on as a child. Tears welled up in his eyes, and Ly asked me to take some moving pictures for his parents. I realized then that even those who had escaped the communist takeover had paid a price.

With rare exceptions, the Vietnamese people seemed to hold little animosity toward Americans. Other than the propaganda in the War Remnants Museum, the only instance of bitterness over the war I had personally observed occurred in late 1996 when I spoke at the graduation ceremony of the DEA's first international training course in Hanoi. I had just started my remarks when a scuffle arose in the back of the auditorium. One of the students was escorted from the room. Afterward, the Director-General of Police apologized profusely, explaining that the officer's brother had been killed in the war and that the officer had become emotionally distraught. I can only imagine after having spent a week with American instructors, the fellow must have had second thoughts about his country's closer ties to the United States.

I had taken Joy with me on that trip, and that evening we attended a banquet hosted by the Minister of Interior to thank the training team for its work. In a government hall along Sword Lake, they laid out an array of local delicacies fit for an Emperor, followed by rounds of toasts to each other's organizations and to the improving relationship between our two nations. After raising our glasses, the hosts had us interlock arms with theirs and say in English, "Bottoms up," before tossing down each shot of cognac. The toasts went on for some time. I don't remember getting back to the hotel!

My three years of working to improve relations with the Vietnamese government forced me to put aside any ill-will I may have held for my former enemies. It gave me a different perspective of the war, one that crystallized while sipping a *Bière 33* at the R & R Hanoi Tavern, an ex-patriot American-owned bar in Hanoi. A Vietnamese guy sitting next to me struck up a conversation. He spoke English pretty well, and I'm certain just wanted to practice a bit. At one point I asked him what he thought of the war. "Which one?" he asked.

His response got me thinking. For most of the Vietnamese people living today, the war with the Americans is just another chapter in their history book, following chapters about their wars with China, France, and Japan. They paid a dear price during the protracted war with us. Some estimate total human losses at more than one million during that era. But the survivors, for the most part, had moved on.

America paid a high price as well. More than 58,000 brave Americans lost their lives upholding an international peace accord, while taking a stand against the advancement of communist aggression during the Cold War. It took much longer for us to move on. However, during the twenty-five years that followed, the relationship between our two nations has blossomed.

Today our primary concern in Asia is containing the ambitions of the Chinese. There has never been any love lost between Vietnam and China, despite China having backed them in the war against us. In this fickle world we might find it helpful one day to have the Vietnamese on our side. Maybe they could get the Turtle God in Sword Lake to loan us his magic saber!

CHAPTER 27

THE ELEPHANTS WERE FIGHTING IN LAOS

Laos was a hard lychee nut to crack. In fact, it took a "military" invasion.

General Barry McCaffrey had been rampaging through the Pacific leaving nothing but devastation in his wake, reminiscent of the famed left hook of his armored cavalry brigade during the first Iraq War. But instead of routing Saddam Hussein's Republican Guard, this time he had some DEA narcotics attachés on the run. Apparently he hadn't been getting the answers he'd been demanding. I was the next target in his sights.

McCaffrey was on a tour of Asia and the Pacific in his role as the nation's Drug Czar, a job bestowed upon him by an embarrassed Bill Clinton. Rumor had it that the uniformed McCaffrey had been seeking directions in the Eisenhower Old Executive Office Building next to the White House in the early days of the Clinton Administration when a young staffer haughtily rebuffed his inquiry. "Oh, we don't talk to soldiers," she huffed and walked off. I don't know if the staffer ever got her just due, but the President appointed McCaffrey to a Cabinet position to be certain he put the slight behind him, and out of the media's view.

McCaffrey found himself a world away from the one in which he had thrived. He had no troops under his command at the Office of National Drug Control Policy — only policy wonks. And the hierarchy within the interagency community didn't appreciate his commanding presence. While he might be the President's drug strategist, in their view, he wasn't in charge of anything. The field generals in the war on international drug control roamed the halls of the Departments of Justice, Treasury and State, not the ONDCP.

And unlike soldiers, drug agents didn't snap to attention when McCaffrey entered a room. When given an order, they had the audacity to ask, "Why?" But this most highly decorated combat veteran did have the ear of the President, and that had to be reckoned with.

In the aftermath of Operation Tiger Trap, our intelligence indicated some of Khun Sa's heroin laboratory operators had fled from Burma to remote areas of Northern Laos to set up their factories. There wasn't even a rudimentary law enforcement presence in that region. American Ambassador to Laos Wendy Chamberlin was well aware of the threat as a result of my liaison visits to Vientiane. I had pressed her time and again to allow us to re-open the DEA Office that had been forced to close after the fall of Saigon twenty years earlier. But my entreaties had fallen on deaf ears.

The strong-willed Ambassador preferred the ongoing weekly liaison visits by a DEA agent from our Resident Office in Udorn Thani, Thailand. She told me her State Department Narcotics Assistance Section (NAS) was engaged in opium eradication and crop substitution, thank you, and that she wasn't about to give up another one of the precious positions within her limited staffing ceiling for drug control.

I knew it would take more than liaison visits to build the kind of close working relationships with the Laotian Police we would need to tackle the emerging drug threat. It became a test of wills between Wendy and me, and not surprisingly, the Ambassador was winning. I figured if I played my hand right, I might be able to use McCaffrey's visit as my trump card.

However, trying to maneuver a titan like McCaffrey against the Ambassador could be risky. An old African proverb warns, "When elephants fight, it's the grass that suffers." I was hoping it wouldn't take a fight, just a little trunk twisting, and figured the risk would be well worth the potential reward.

The evening before McCaffrey was to arrive, his advance man, future Fox News Military Affairs Analyst Lieutenant Colonel Ralph Peters, on loan to McCaffrey from the Pentagon, paid me a visit. He had watched the briefings given by my peers during McCaffrey's Pacific odyssey thus far and assured me things weren't going well. "Let me give you some advice," Peters offered. "When the boss shows up tomorrow, just tell him what's going well, what's not going well, and what he can do to help. He likes it when people get right to the point." That sounded like pretty reasonable advice, and I stayed up half the night reorganizing my briefing.

The next morning McCaffrey sat ramrod straight at the head of my conference room table surrounded by his aides. A map of Southeast Asia hung on one wall, slides of the key points I wanted to make were to be projected on the screen behind me as I spoke. The tension in the room was palpable. You could have heard a lotus blossom petal drop before I started to speak.

"The availability of Southeast Asian heroin has plummeted," I averred. "Our cooperation with the Royal Thai Police has never been better." I confidently detailed the enormous impact my predecessor's Operation Tiger Trap had. And I detailed the progress we began making in building working relationships with our law enforcement counterparts in Vietnam which I knew, as a fellow Vietnam veteran, he would be interested to know. Then I switched gears.

"Laos is the challenge," I said. "Our intelligence indicates several of Kuhn Sa's heroin laboratory operators may have fled to Northern Laos to set up shop there. We need to re-establish a permanent DEA presence in Vientiane to begin building the relationships with counterparts we'll need to hunt them down." When I finished speaking there was dead silence.

I was relieved that my head was still firmly attached to my shoulders. On the other hand, I was concerned that perhaps I hadn't made my pitch for Laos persuasive enough. But we had to move on to meetings with the American Ambassador to Thailand, William Itoh, and then General Noppadol Somboonsap, Commissioner of the Thai Police Narcotics Suppression Center. I figured I would have another bite at the pineapple soon enough.

That night McCaffrey joined Joy and me at the wedding reception of another one of my principal counterparts, Prija Champaratna, Chairman of Thailand's Office of Narcotics Control Board. I had arranged the invitation in coordination with McCaffrey's office — truth be told, so Joy and I wouldn't have to miss the reception. Prija was delighted to have an American Cabinet Secretary attend his elegant dinner cruise on the Chao Praya River. In Thai culture, attendance at a wedding by high-ranking officials not only infers status but can be an omen of good fortune. And it gave Joy the chance to meet General McCaffrey, and even dance with him at the reception. The police launch that shadowed our yacht to provide security motored McCaffrey back to his hotel mid-cruise so he wouldn't have to stay up half the night.

The next day the Royal Thai Police flew McCaffrey and me up to Northern Thailand to tour the Burmese border. We received a primer from my old pal, PNSC Colonel Viraj Jutimitta, on the history of Southeast Asian heroin trafficking. Other than a courtesy call on American Consul General in the old walled, former capital city of Chiang Mai, it was strictly a Thai Police show. The following morning, we were off by commercial jet to Vientiane.

Buckled into the seat next to McCaffrey, I took the opportunity to brief him again. I parsed my words, careful not to badmouth Ambassador Chamberlin, still not knowing McCaffrey's leanings, and fearing my comments might get back to her. After all, whatever the result of McCaffrey's visit, I would still have to work with her. Once again, McCaffrey kept his thoughts to himself.

Ambassador Chamberlin met us at planeside and escorted McCaffrey to her black Cadillac limousine for the brief ride to her residence for lunch. I was seated at the dining room table next to McCaffrey who sat directly across from the Ambassador. She presided over the luncheon with conversation of the current government's policies toward drugs, spoken tactfully, in vanilla terms in this unclassified setting, as would be expected of any experienced diplomat. The retired general smiled and spoke politely in kind. Had he ignored me completely, or was he just biding his time? This was D-Day for me, and I didn't have a clue how it was going to end.

After we finished eating, with charts set on an easel beside him, NAS Chief Al Bryant briefed the narcotics program in Laos. He boasted of the State Department's opium poppy eradication campaign denying tons of opium to drug traffickers, and of his crop substitution program successfully weaning Hill Tribe farmers from opium cultivation to strawberries and corn. He conveniently skipped mentioning the tons of Golden Triangle opium still available to heroin laboratory operators in what was still the world's third largest opium producing country.

I couldn't take it any longer and started to speak up when under the table McCaffrey tapped my knee. I held my tongue. At the end of Bryant's briefing a beaming Wendy Chamberlin asked, "So, Barry, what do you think of my narcotics program?"

McCaffrey looked the Ambassador straight in the eyes and said, "Madam Ambassador, if you don't have a DEA agent on your staff, you *don't have* a narcotics program!" I thought she was going to pass out. I bit my lip trying not to smile.

That afternoon McCaffrey met with the Lao Minister of Foreign Affairs. In typical diplomatic fashion the two sat side by side, flanked by their delegations facing each other forming a "U." Ambassador Chamberlin sat closest to McCaffrey, with her staff seated in descending order by rank. Not being diplomatically accredited to Laos, I sat at the far end of the American row.

McCaffrey and the Minister exchanged pleasantries, and then McCaffrey pointed in my direction and asked, "Do you know Mr. Lutz?" Of course, the Minister had no idea who I was. He put on his glasses and strained to see to whom McCaffrey was referring. I politely waived. "Mr. Lutz could be your best friend," McCaffrey continued. The Ambassador glared as Barry went on to explain that as the DEA Chief in Bangkok, I had the wherewithal to help them solve their drug problem.

That night the Lao People's Democratic Republic hosted a dinner in McCaffrey's honor at the stately Dhavara Hotel. During conversation at the table, McCaffrey broached the idea of a permanent DEA presence to his drug control counterpart. And when they turned to the Ambassador for her opinion, she waived the white flag. He had worn her out. The Laotians offered no objection to the offer, and the deal was sealed over a toast of not-so-dry red wine. Maybe McCaffrey hadn't made a lot of friends in law enforcement circles, but that day he made an admirer out of me.

It took a few months to get an agent on the ground, needing the ink on the approvals to dry. I never again discussed McCaffrey's visit with Wendy Chamberlin, seeing no point in rubbing it in. The General's victory in Laos wouldn't even be a footnote to his distinguished career, but it was a big deal for me. I had gotten the elephants to fight . . . and the grass was no worse for the wear.

☆ ☆ ☆ ☆ ☆ ☆

A year after McCaffrey's visit, JIATF West's director, Jim McClelland, and Lloyd Clifton came back to town, two of the guys I had hiked down the mountain with from that opium field in Northern Thailand. This time they accompanied me to Ban Houaysai, in Northern Laos, for the dedication of a new substation of the Laotian Narcotics Bureau. Ambassador Chamberlin flew up from Vientiane with her Deputy Chief of Mission for the ceremony, and we made plans to speed down the Mekong River in long-tail boats to Luang Prabang the following day.

That evening after the ceremony, we went to a thatch-roofed bar overlooking the Mekong River for "happy hour." After a few Beerlaos, the sun began setting behind a mountain in neighboring Thailand. Wendy laid her head down on the table to watch from under the low hanging roof as it bade its farewell. Lloyd snapped a photo that unintentionally made her appear as if she had passed out surrounded by a half dozen empty beer bottles. If I had that photo when I was negotiating the re-opening of the Vientiane office, I probably wouldn't have needed McCaffrey's help!

☆ ☆

The next morning the ambassador wasn't feeling well, likely from something she had eaten at the reception after the dedication ceremony, and flew back to Vientiane. In the company of the Deputy Chief of Mission, we careened down the Mekong River in small, long-tail boats, crash helmets strapped on our heads, dodging huge boulders in the river while marveling at the pristine forests and beaches along the way. We stopped to have lunch at Pak Beng with the governor of that province who had trekked there thinking the ambassador was with us.

While walking to the open-air restaurant, their version of a Southern cash n' carry, we had to step aside to allow a line of chained working elephants pass by. A mahout sat on the neck of the lead elephant whacking the beast with a stick, looking like a racehorse jockey wielding a crop. The last elephant in line, a lame baby elephant, struggled to keep up. It was a memorable sight during an unforgettable journey through that Land of a Million Elephants.

Laos never developed into the significant heroin source country our intelligence had indicated it might become. I like to think that re-opening the DEA office in Vientiane and establishing the narcotics police substation at Ban Houaysai had something to do with it. Unfortunately, the office only lasted half a dozen more years before the Laotian government's cooperative attitude soured, and it closed once again.

☆ ☆ ☆ ☆ ☆ ☆

Cambodia was the "ugly sister" of the nations in Southeast Asia. Phnom Penh was a difficult city to visit, the capital of one of the poorest countries on Earth. Amputees from their many upheavals begged on every street corner, a legacy of Pol Pot's brutal Khmer Rouge regime. It has been estimated that Marxist

Pol Pot slaughtered one fifth of his nation's population between 1975 and 1979, including its intellectuals, in an attempt to create the agrarian utopia he had envisioned. The Socialist Republic of Vietnam's invasion of Cambodia in 1979 forced Pol Pot into the jungle. Apparently even they couldn't abide his brutality.

When I first arrived in Bangkok, the trip to Phnom Penh with Assistant Secretary Bob Gelbard and Deputy Administrator Steve Greene opened the door to cooperation. Over subsequent trips, a relationship developed that just before I was to return to the States proved fortuitous, perhaps lifesaving.

For one of my side trips there, I had been invited to tour the thousand-year-old Buddhist shrine of Angkor Wat, so I took Joy along with me. Don't ask me what I was thinking, but while in Phnom Penh I took her to see Tuol Sleng Genocide Museum, a former school converted into a torture chamber where heart-wrenching photographs of Pol Pot's victims lined the walls. And we were appalled by the tower of human skulls at the Killing Fields where human bones still protruded up from the ground upon which we walked.

We drove with a police escort to Siem Reap. When we arrived at our hotel, Cambodian Army trucks raced by carrying dead and wounded from a battle with remnants of Pol Pot's Khmer Rouge nearby. Nevertheless, we toured the magnificent temple ruins of Angkor Wat the following day, but I was greatly relieved when we safely returned to Phnom Penh that evening.

Near to the end of my tour of duty in Thailand, an informant in Bangkok provided information that a ship was to be loaded with marijuana in the Gulf of Siam before heading for the Washington State coast. The Thai Police Narcotics Suppression Center hired a boat, and its officers planned to capture the mothership once loaded. Instead, Cambodian military forces captured the Thai

☆ ☆

police, claiming they had strayed into Cambodian territorial waters.

Thailand and Cambodia had no diplomatic ties at the time. In fact, they were close to war over a border dispute. The relationships we had established in Cambodia saved the day. I asked my deputy, Bill Simpson, who I had known since we briefly worked together in the Bahamas, to call upon one of our Cambodian contacts to intervene on behalf of the Thai, in coordination with the American Ambassador in Phnom Penh. After a few tense days, the Thai cops were released unharmed and flew home. His deft handling of the crisis clearly demonstrated why I had confidence in Bill to succeed me.

☆ ☆ ☆ ☆ ☆ ☆

After my tour of duty had ended, my picture was hung on the wall alongside those of the other former bosses in Bangkok, including that of The Emperor, Fred T. Dick. I have to say, I'm pleased to be hanging around in such memorable company.

I was offered none of the jobs I had put on my wish list. Instead, I was brought back to headquarters for a fourth tour of duty, which must be a record. That wasn't a problem, though. We still had our home in Oakton, Virginia. And, having lived there off and on over the past twenty years considered ourselves Washingtonians.

I was assigned to a Deputy Assistant Administrator position, pretty high up in the pecking order. But I had even higher aspirations.

CHAPTER 28

EXECUTIVE SECRETARIAT

As the Deputy Assistant Administrator for Operations Management, I was responsible for the multi-million-dollar budget of the Operations Division, nothing I had been trained to do. Fortunately, my competent, professional staff kept the books in balance. I also ran the Command Center, and wordsmithed changes to policies and procedures in the Agents Manual, two jobs I thoroughly enjoyed doing. Even so, it was difficult to concentrate in my tenth-floor office with its million-dollar panoramic view of the Washington skyline. What kept me truly buoyed, though, was the thought that there might be one more promotion left in store.

While I had been in Bangkok, I heard stories of Tom Constantine running senior executives off the job. That wasn't the Constantine I had known, although he hadn't come to the DEA with the best of reputations. The standing joke at the time was that the New York State Police had thrown a farewell party for him . . . after he was gone!

I already knew he was no fan of the DEA's foreign program, particularly Operation Snowcap. However, we had gotten along well while I was the Acting Director of Foreign Operations. And he had promoted me into the Senior Executive Service. So, he must have thought I had some managerial potential.

☆ ☆

Constantine was also well aware of some of my successes in Bangkok, among them getting the Vientiane Office re-opened and making progress toward establishing relationships with the Vietnamese. He personally approved my request to establish the first Sensitive Investigative Unit outside of Latin America, composed of thoroughly vetted Thai cops with whom we could share highly sensitive information. He knew the first extradition of a Thai national to face drug charges in America was conducted under my watch – former Thai Parliamentarian Thanong Siripreechapong who had been indicted as the source of seventy-three tons of Thai stick marijuana seized by the U.S. Coast Guard off the coast of Washington State. And he might have known that I had proposed the International Law Enforcement Academy in Bangkok to match the ones in Europe and Central America, with construction of it well underway by the time I left Thailand. Further, while I was back in Washington for a National Heroin Conference, he asked me to travel to Rangoon when I got back home to brief a congressman traveling on a visit to Burma to be sure he got the right scoop on the drug trafficking situation in the Golden Triangle, a chore normally reserved for assistant administrators and above. That assured me he still had some confidence in me.

However, managing field operations and briefing congressmen were child's play compared to managing the Operations Division budget. There was never enough money to go around. It was a balancing act, moving funds from one pot to another to keep enforcement operations afloat. I could never satisfy everyone, and I was soon to learn that not pleasing the big boss had serious repercussions.

At one point, several of the Field Divisions were about to park their G-cars for lack of gas money. One of my staff members spotted some unused funds in a marijuana eradication account. Before moving it, I discussed the transfer with the Chief of Operations. But when I moved the money, it was as if I had stepped on the third rail.

I had taken a day off to accompany Joy to a Health Fair at the DC Convention Center when I got paged. Constantine wanted to see me. I drove Joy home, then drove to headquarters and was ushered into his office. Constantine told me he got a call from one of his state police buddies that I had ripped off his marijuana eradication money. You would have thought I had taken it at gunpoint. What seemed to me a trivial matter completely changed our relationship. After that, I couldn't do anything right.

But there were rumors he was about to retire, so I figured I would wait him out. Constantine's heir apparent, Deputy Administrator Donnie Marshall, with whom I had worked during the plane crash tragedy in Peru, stopped by my office one day to suggest I stick around, implying that once Constantine was gone a promotion to an Assistant Administrator position might be in the cards. The problem was that I didn't have a whole lot of time left to play. I was closing in on the mandatory retirement age and didn't want to risk spending my last two years on the job in Operations Management.

I was mulling over what to do when I noticed a bulletin that intrigued me. The Department of Justice was looking for a senior executive to head up an interagency organization to implement the President's General Counterdrug Intelligence Plan (GCIP). A new interagency organization was being set up within the Department of Justice from scratch. Its director would work pretty much independently, and that's what really attracted me. With no sure thing to lose, I let my interest be known and snagged the job. My friends thought I was crazy, but it turned out to have been a great move.

The GCIP had been devised to improve coordination, cooperation and information sharing among federal law enforcement agencies, between the DEA and the Intelligence Community, and between federal law enforcement agencies and state and local police. There were systemic reasons for them not to do so. The individuals who got the results usually got the promotions, and results could mean budget enhancements, even survival for an agency. So why give up an ace in the hole — their intelligence information.

The White House interagency study that had led to the GCIP found the intelligence community pretty much had its act together. They had a single, centralized intelligence-sharing structure with standardized practices and procedures, and an interoperable technology system between agencies. The law enforcement community did not.

Badge carriers had gotten into the intelligence game late. Once law enforcement realized the value of it, agencies had independently developed intelligence programs and systems to meet their individual needs. The differing systems couldn't talk to each other; their intelligence analysts, having been trained using different methodology and terminology, couldn't talk to each other. The three national drug law enforcement intelligence centers didn't have clearly defined roles and responsibilities, were duplicative in some areas, and competitive in others.

The 17,000 state, local and tribal police agencies, upon which domestic drug law enforcement greatly depended, were in an even greater quandary. Most of them operated autonomously, many with overlapping jurisdictions, and were supported by a multitude of authorities, procedures and systems. In addition to that, the several state and local intelligence centers worked independently of each other.

The GCIP specified seventy-three action items to make improvements to the nation's drug intelligence structure that would better support operators in the field and policymakers in Washington. Overseas, it designated Deputy Chiefs of Mission to coordinate counterdrug efforts.

It created a Counterdrug Intelligence Coordinating Group (CDICG) to oversee progress in implementing the plan, with a full-time staff to do the leg work, incredulously named the Counterdrug Intelligence Executive Secretariat (CDX), which made it sound like a subsidiary of the Soviet KGB. I was appointed director of the CDX.

My deputy director was a senior executive from the CIA, a former station chief, later replaced by senior intelligence analyst Dave Lodge; my chief of staff was a senior executive from DOJ's Justice Management Division, Miles Matthews. I had a staff of mostly mid-level managers and supervisors from the DEA, the FBI, U.S. Customs, the Coast Guard, the Defense Intelligence Agency, two officers representing state and local police, and part-time detailees from the National Security Agency and the Defense Information Systems Agency. We took over the entire floor of a cushy, downtown Washington office building, just a few blocks from the White House.

What I hadn't known when I volunteered for the CDX position was that the Department of Justice hated the GCIP. It wasn't that they thought improvements to the counterdrug intelligence system weren't needed. They hated it because the Office of Narcotics Drug Control Policy, headed by their arch enemy, my hero from Laos, Barry McCaffrey had thought of it, and wanted to run it. The Drug Czar had done his homework, getting the backing of every Cabinet Secretary in Washington for the plan, so there was no way the DOJ could shut it down. Instead, they demanded to have the operators, not ONDCP policy wonks, in charge of it.

ONDCP Director Barry McCaffrey visiting the CDX, Washington, DC, 2001. L-R: CDX Chief of Staff Miles Mathews, DEA Intelligence Chief Steve Casteel, McCaffrey, Lutz, CDX Deputy Director Dave Lodge.

The job didn't make me the most popular guy in town. There was distrust in the intelligence community for the ability of law enforcement organizations to protect their sources and methods, and distrust in the law enforcement community for the CIA which was alleged to have supported their military and political allies at any cost, turning a blind eye to, even protecting at times, their involvement in drug trafficking in Southeast Asia during the Vietnam War era and in Central America during the communist insurgencies in Nicaragua and El Salvador. Where there had been instances of cooperation between the CIA and the DEA in the field, the chasm had been bridged by carefully crafted, legal and policy guidelines or, more often, by personal relationships.

And there was the generation-old animosity between Customs and the DEA that needed to be overcome. But in my eighteen months at the CDX, we did make some progress.

We started off with a week-long retreat at the CIA's Camp Peary near Williamsburg, Virginia, to get our CDX act together and divvy up the workload. Then we visited thirty cities across the nation to identify "best practices" in information sharing.

We established a Training Advisory Committee to standardize hiring and career advancement paths for law enforcement intelligence analysts and a Curriculum Working Group to develop a standardized law enforcement analytical training course. To better define the roles and responsibilities of the national intelligence centers and, in coordination with the National Drug Intelligence Center, national guidelines were created to enhance exploitation of seized documents. We created a Systems Policy Review Group to develop common criteria and define architectural and data standards for law enforcement information sharing systems. In order to facilitate connectivity for information sharing with and among state and local authorities, a State and Local Law Enforcement Advisory Board was formed. And we prepared Semi-Annual Reports for the CDICG to inform the Cabinet of the progress being made, and an Annual Report to Congress.

I got new DEA Administrator Asa Hutchinson to speak at a meeting of state and local police organizations that we had convened at the Willard Hotel in Washington, DC. That wasn't the last time I was to meet Hutchinson. Shortly after his presentation, Joy and I received an invitation from him and his wife to attend a Christmas party at a luxurious estate on the Potomac River in Arlington, Virginia, once owned by reclusive

Hollywood movie mogul Howard Hughes. I assumed the entire DEA senior staff had been invited.

It was a glamorous affair. The who's who among Capitol Hill Republicans sang Christmas carols accompanied by Attorney General John Ashcroft at the piano. Fox News Special Report anchor Brit Hume read the Christmas Story. We dined on exquisite heavy hors d'oeuvres and a huge white cake in the shape of the Capitol building and were each gifted a hand-painted Christmas tree ball.

However, when we first arrived something seemed odd about my host's demeanor. Although he politely introduced me to the Attorney General, Asa looked at me as if I had crashed the party. As it turned out, I was the only DEA person in the room. That was strange. Later that evening it struck me why.

Although detailed away from the DEA, I had been invited to attend the annual DEA senior executive retreats that since Constantine's tenure had been piggybacked onto the International Association of Chiefs of Police conferences, that past fall in Toronto, Canada. While I was at an early morning meeting, Joy attended an IACP-sponsored prayer breakfast and happened to be seated next to Asa's wife. They hit it off, and she insisted Joy accompany her that day on a guided tour of Toronto which had been arranged for her by the Royal Canadian Mounted Police. As it turned out, it hadn't been me at all who had been invited to the Christmas party. Apparently unbeknownst to Asa, his wife had invited Joy. I was just tagging along.

While working at the CDX, there had been some perquisites. Barry McCaffrey once arranged for the senior staff to dine in the White House Navy Mess, directly below the Oval Office.

☆ ☆ ☆ ☆ ☆ ☆

And thanks to my CIA deputy, we luxuriated at a week-long conference held at the exclusive, all-inclusive Casa de Campo Resort on the far eastern tip of the Dominican Republic where we gathered DEA narcotics attachés and CIA station chiefs from Central and South America to acquaint them with the GCIP, review their authorities to work together, and in one instance insist on the development of essential interpersonal skills.

I was within a few days of leaving for a similar conference in Bangkok, this time taking Joy with me, when the tragic events of 9-11 unfolded. My deputy ran into my office and asked me to turn on the TV. We watched the World Trade Center's North Tower smoldering, thinking it had been the result of pilot error. But when the South Tower was struck before our very eyes, we knew it was no accident.

That wasn't the first time I had heard the name Osama Bin Laden. During my time with Operation Snowcap, I represented the DEA on occasion as a member of Richard Clarke's Counter terrorism Committee at the White House. The DEA had been invited to participate because of Latin American narco-terrorism. However, after the 1993 World Trade Center bombing, the Committee focused almost exclusively on the threat posed by radical Islamic terrorists. Although I stopped participating in 1994, I'm certain that focus continued. It was obvious the committee hadn't seen the 9-11 attack coming, at least not when, or in the manner in which it had come.

In the spring of 2002, just before I retired, I participated on behalf of the CDX in the IACP's *Summit on Criminal Intelligence Sharing* which addressed the critical need to share information on all manner of crime. I was glad to see it was starting to sink in. After reading *The 9-11 Commission Report,* I thought what a pity the CIA and FBI hadn't had a "General Counter terrorism

☆ ☆

Intelligence Plan" to follow prior to 9-11. It might have saved 3,000 lives.

September 11, 2001, forever altered an untold number of lives. It certainly changed mine.

☆ ☆

CHAPTER 29

THE AGENCY EVERYONE LOVED TO HATE

We had been warned that no one in the airline industry would welcome us. Airport directors across the country were upset about losing overall authority for airport security. Airline station managers were concerned that stricter passenger and baggage screening might delay flight departures — on-time performance being critical to the "hub and spoke" system of the larger airlines (and to their annual performance ratings). The FBI wasn't pleased to be losing its authority to investigate airport security incidents, and local police departments weren't happy about being booted off the gravy train of overtime pay for off-duty cops in many jurisdictions. Being as unpopular as it was, it sounded like the perfect job for me.

When radical Islamic terrorists attacked the World Trade Center and Pentagon on September 11, 2001, taking the lives of three thousand innocent people, it shattered confidence in our air transportation system. Before then, hijackers had forced pilots at gunpoint to Cuba where political statements were made, ransoms paid, and the airplanes released to fly home. Pilots were under strict orders to obey hijacker's demands to preserve the lives of the passengers entrusted to them. However,

☆ ☆

the 9-11 hijackers didn't follow precedence. They held flight attendants hostage with box cutters until allowed access into the cockpits where they murdered the crews and turned fully fueled commercial airliners into guided missiles.

Not knowing what might be coming next, the government dispatched soldiers to guard the nation's airports, with M-16 assault rifles in hand. That couldn't be left to stand, so Congress rushed to enact legislation that would tighten airport security under civilian government control. Within a record twenty-nine days, President George W. Bush signed into law the Aviation and Transportation Security Act creating the Transportation Security Administration (TSA).

The Act transferred passenger and baggage screening to the TSA that had long been the responsibility of the airports and airlines. It gave the TSA certain regulatory powers of the Federal Aviation Administration. It forced the FBI to cede authority to investigate airport security incidents, and local police forces to surrender overall airport security duties. But the urgency to enact the legislation hadn't stopped partisan bickering.

To satisfy their constituency, the Republicans wanted to continue outsourcing screening to private companies as the airlines had done but managed and supervised by a small cadre of federal government employees. To satisfy their base, the Democrats wanted all TSA employees to be federal workers since low paid government workers tended to vote their way. To unclog the bottleneck, Bush compromised. Screeners would be government employees at all but five airports of various sizes and risk levels, among them San Francisco and Kansas City. After two years, the performance of the two systems would be compared, at which time airports could opt out of federal screeners. Congressman John Mica of Orlando, Chair of the

☆ ☆

House Transportation Sub-committee, had the responsibility to oversee the fledgling TSA. He was also the Republican's point man for getting airports to opt out of a federal workforce.

That compromise didn't turn out to be such a good deal for the Republicans. Since all airports worked under the same TSA standards and rules, after two years no appreciable difference was found between the performance of federal and private screeners. And having the federal government assume total liability for security incidents was far too attractive for airports to give up. There would be only one exception — Ely, Nevada. With only a few daily flight departures, the airport manager wanted screeners to do maintenance chores in between flights, like mowing the grass, which wasn't in a federal security screener's job description.

I was within a year of mandatory retirement when the TSA was created. In the emotional context of that time, like most Americans, I would have sacrificed almost anything for a chance to get even with Al Qaeda, to right the wrong of 9-11. Working for nothing, however, was not one of them.

By law, if I took another federal job after retirement, my salary would be reduced by the amount of my retirement annuity. However, the new Act waived the annuity offset for Federal Security Directors for up to five years in order to give the TSA time to develop its own cadre of senior leaders. When I heard that, I was the first from the Drug Enforcement Administration to get in line.

Bush tapped John Magaw to be the TSA's Administrator. He had been chief of his father's White House security detail, went on to become Director of the Secret Service, and then Director of the Bureau of Alcohol, Tobacco and Firearms after the botched Branch Davidian compound siege in Waco, Texas.

☆ ☆

I met Magaw a few times. I briefed him years earlier when he made an official visit to Bangkok and ran into him again at several International Association of Chiefs of Police conferences. I wrote him a letter offering my services. But not satisfied with leaving it at that, I visited Carol Hallett, the former Ambassador to the Bahamas, who by then was president of the powerful Air Transport Association. She offered to put in a good word for me with Magaw, which couldn't have hurt a thing. Soon after, I was interviewed and then offered the job of Federal Security Director (FSD) at Orlando International Airport. I couldn't have been prouder.

Orlando was the fifth largest airport in the nation in terms of departing passengers, typically the only ones the TSA had to screen, and had the seventh largest screener workforce, over one thousand. It certainly wasn't going to be a "retirement" job.

While I was thrilled to be part of the effort to respond to the tragedy of 9-11, I wasn't enamored with the location of my assignment. We left Florida in 1990 with no intention of ever returning. However, in the tenor of those times, I couldn't bring myself to tell the TSA that I would only go where I wanted to go. If they needed me in Orlando, Joy and I agreed, that's where we'd go.

We sold our home in Oakton, Virginia, the house we moved into four times over the twenty-five years we had owned it, never expecting to return to Washington. And with Amy and Cindy both married by then, we prepared to move our empty nest to the Sunshine State.

I entered only the second FSD training class, a week-long course on airport operations, regulations and security. Drilled into our heads was the critical need to satisfy the many airport stakeholders — airport directors, airline station managers, even airport shopkeepers — all of whom, they said, would be gunning for us. Sitting alongside me in the class was a former New York Port Authority senior officer on his way to JFK. He had been standing in the lobby of one of the World Trade Center towers when it collapsed, killing his boss who was standing beside him. There was also a retired California Highway Patrol colonel headed for San Francisco and a retired FBI special agent going to Louisville. I didn't believe any one of us would be intimidated by airport stakeholders.

Then over cocktails one evening after class, my boss, TSA's Chief of Operations, added one additional dissatisfied stakeholder to my list. He told me Orlando would be one of the two toughest airports in the country for FSDs — Charlotte, because its airport director had publicly proclaimed his opposition to the TSA taking over security at his airport; and Orlando, because it was in Congressman John Mica's home district. He talked about Mica's role in discouraging airports to keep federal employee screeners. I realized the most convenient way for Mica to succeed would be to discredit the federal workforce at Orlando, and there would be plenty of them to take aim at. "Good luck with Mica," he said. I started to get a bad feeling.

It had been late afternoon on my last Friday in Washington when my boss called me to his office. I assumed he wanted to offer a few parting words of advice. But when I entered his office, he closed the door behind me. "How much of an inconvenience would it be for you to detour to Louisville on your way to Orlando?" he asked.

He went on to explain that he had just relieved the FSD at that Kentucky Airport. The fellow's fiancé, an FBI intelligence analyst, had been flying to Louisville on weekends to house-hunt and must have been running late. According to the local newspaper account, on that previous Sunday evening the FSD had escorted her around screening to get her onto her flight back to Washington. One of the airport's screeners dropped a dime.

"Louisville is going to be one of the first two airports in the nation to be 'federalized,'" he said. "I need someone there Monday morning to be in charge. Will you do it?"

"Of course I will." When I got back to my desk, I called Joy. "You're not going to believe this," then went on to explain.

Monday morning, I stood tall alongside the Louisville airport director as we announced to the media how smoothly passenger screening had transitioned to the TSA the night before. My boss called from Washington to say he was pleased. Then I got a call from Steve Crawford in Orlando, one of the FAA Inspectors transferred to the TSA who had been holding down the fort pending my arrival. "You're not going to believe this," he started out saying, which was becoming an all too familiar refrain.

Steve explained that the company contracted by the TSA to test Orlando's existing screeners against the new hiring standards had descended that past Friday night on Orlando unannounced. Finding insufficient space to set up their operation in the airport's Hyatt Hotel ballroom, they negotiated for the hotel's interior parking garage. It had been closed to the public since 9-11 due to the risk it posed of allowing a car bomb to be introduced into the heart of the airport terminal and was being used only by the most senior and trusted airport personnel.

Over the weekend the resourceful human resource company set up an air-conditioned tent in the parking garage, installed dozens of computer workstations, hired a couple of off-duty cops to provide security, and were ready for business first thing Monday morning. However, no one at the hotel had thought to mention anything about it to Airport Director Bill Jennings.

When Jennings pulled into the parking garage early Monday morning, he was astonished to find a tent taking up most of the parking spaces. As he approached the tent to find out what was going on, one of the policemen on duty blocked his path and shouted, "You can't enter here. Government property." Jennings went ballistic and demanded to speak with a supervisor. A heated argument ensued with the two contractors-in-charge.

I called Jennings, whom I had yet to meet, introduced myself, and asked how we could resolve the flap. We agreed that he would write a letter of complaint that I would forward to the TSA headquarters as soon as I got to Orlando. I called my boss and told him of the problem and the resolution. Only the next day, it got worse.

"The deal's off," Jennings called to say, "unless you get these two knucklehead contractors out of my airport." Then he read that morning's *Orlando Sentinel* headline — "TSA Almost Arrests Airport Manager." I called my boss again, and he agreed to have the two contract supervisors yanked.

But here I was, fiddling in Louisville while Orlando was burning, and it wasn't until nearly week's end when I was finally released from Louisville. I rendezvoused with Joy near Macon, Georgia, and we arrived in Orlando that Saturday.

First thing Monday morning, I met with Bill Jennings. With the two miscreant contractors gone, his dander had settled a bit. A tall, dignified Black man, Bill had worked his way up from the bottom of the Greater Orlando Aviation Authority (GOAA), and was now its longest serving chief executive. Quite a remarkable accomplishment. And Bill was politically well-connected. He once told me that while growing up, he and Cuban refugee Mel Martinez, Secretary of Housing and Urban Development, former Orlando Mayor, and future U.S. Senator, used to skinny dip together in a local stream. A nice enough guy, Bill and I agreed to meet for breakfast once a week to avoid future dustups.

Bill was overseen by the GOAA Board, consisting of the Orlando Mayor, the Chairman of the Orange County Board of Commissioners, and five members appointed by the Governor of Florida — from among the who's who of Orlando. The GOAA Board's purpose in life was to see that the conventioneers and "vacationeers" continued to visit the magical kingdom the golden rodent had created. Mickey had transformed Orlando from a highway junction wedged between cattle ranches and orange groves into one of the world's most popular tourist destinations. The airport was an engine of its prosperous economy. The GOAA Board was determined that visitors be pampered as they flew in and out of Orlando. So was I.

Although my first crisis at the airport had passed, my head was spinning with the changes taking place within the TSA. Of most immediate concern was screener hiring. The new law had set minimum standards for security screeners. Whether they be government or private company employees, they had to be American citizens, twenty-one years of age or older, speak English at the eight-grade level or above, have sufficient strength and dexterity to lift suitcases and wand passengers, not be colorblind in order to identify volatile substances that appear on x-ray screens in different colors, and have no serious criminal record.

The TSA had expected to hire the screeners who had been working for the airlines on 9-11 and provide them better supervision and training. But as the testing unfolded, it was discovered that nationwide, startlingly, only ten percent of the existing workforce could meet the newly established minimum hiring standards. New applicants qualified at a similar rate.

At Orlando alone that meant more than seven hundred new screeners would have to be hired to bring the total up to the authorized number. It was a recipe for disaster. Of the new hires, some had never been in an airport before, let alone conducted security screening in one. Little wonder there were long lines at security checkpoints during that first, on-the-job-training year.

Then, just after I settled into Orlando, George Bush fired John Magaw. According to press releases, Magaw had been too slow to hire screeners for the nation's 429 airports — by June 2002, only 1,200 of the 45,000 screeners that would be needed had been hired. Truth be told, Magaw had begun to set up the TSA as the law enforcement organization the Bush Administration and the majority in Congress had envisioned, but the airline industry preferred a kinder, gentler TSA. They lobbied Congress for a change at the top, and Washington caved in. Magaw must have been bitter, but his parting remarks were anything but. "I'm leaving quietly because your work is too important," he wrote to us all.

Even more disturbing to me, Congress had stripped the TSA of its law enforcement functions. Through their respective lobbying efforts, the FBI had won back its responsibility to investigate airport security incidents, and local police authorities regained their responsibility for overall airport security. My promised team of criminal investigators and uniformed police officers disappeared. Overnight, the Transportation "Security" Administration morphed into the Transportation "Screening" Administration. That wasn't the job I had signed up for.

Nevertheless, the urgency of the task at hand kept me going. The law required the TSA to "federalize" screening at the nation's airports within one year, thought by many in the airline industry to be an impossible goal. What enabled us to meet that goal at

☆ ☆

Orlando was the bright and dedicated staff I had inherited from the FAA. Among them was Trygve Reeves, a Tuskegee University graduate with a dozen years in the Army and several years of airport regulatory experience at Orlando, whom I appointed as my Assistant Federal Security Director (AFSD) for Regulatory Affairs; and Steve Crawford, the Interim Security Chief, whom I dubbed the AFSD for Screening, the "screening czar," by far the most demanding job in the office.

I hired Orlando's Resident-Agent-in-Charge Rick Scovel away from the DEA to be my AFSD for Law Enforcement. Although the TSA's law enforcement responsibilities had been stripped away, Rick was needed to coordinate responses to security incidents at the airport with federal, state and local authorities, and investigate complaints by and against our employees.

Despite the overwhelming number of novice screeners, the rollout of passenger screening went smoother than I had expected. Everyone on the staff chipped in, typically working ten-hour days. By the end of July, the 308 qualified screeners held over from the private screening company, plus the first *tranche* of new screeners hired and trained, supplemented with members of a TSA mobile training team, federalized half of Orlando's 129 checkpoints. By the end of August, with another several hundred new screeners hired and trained, we federalized screening at the other half of the checkpoints, well ahead of the November 19 deadline, the first of the major airports to have done so. It was a proud moment for the entire team.

However, the intensity of screening was still an issue. Passengers wanted to be safe but didn't want to miss their flights. The sensitivity of the equipment could be adjusted, for example, in detecting metal. While we didn't want to let any lethal weapon through the checkpoints, neither did we want to slow down the lines by having to dig paper clips out of briefcases.

Security industry experts weighed in. Some thought the TSA screening was too lax, that we should adopt the Israeli-style screening process of interviewing every single passenger. That worked well for El Al's several daily flights, but it wasn't practical for the one million airline passengers traveling in America each day.

Other critics thought the TSA screening was too strict, particularly when it came to the elderly and young children. Of course, I have seen illegal drugs smuggled in wheelchairs and diapers. Explosives were no different. We put that argument to rest in Orlando when one of the screeners detected a fully loaded handgun sewn into a teddy bear being carried through a checkpoint by an eight-year-old girl.

Cartoon by Jeff Parker, published in *Florida Today*, 2003, reprinted with permission from imagn.com.

So now that passenger screening was under control, it was a good time for me to taxi down the runway for some rest and recuperation. To celebrate my retirement from the DEA after thirty-two years of service, before I had even hired on with the TSA, Joy and I had signed up with friends from Vale Methodist Church in Northern Virginia to take a Russia river cruise from St. Petersburg to Moscow.

Shortly before we left, I found a $10,000 bonus in my paycheck from the TSA's new Administrator, Jim Loy, for the passenger screening success. I was astonished to learn that bonuses came in that large of an amount. I had never received more than $2,500 while working for the DEA. That money was going to buy me a whole lot of Russian vodka!

When we returned from the cruise, there was no time to rest on passenger screening laurels. Baggage screening loomed, and it was going to make passenger screening seem like a stroll down Disney world's Main Street.

CHAPTER 30

BAGGIN' IT

Passenger screening down, baggage screening to go. I was confident we'd get that done too, and on time. And we did! But frustrations and misunderstandings mounted along the way. Some were the natural by-product of standing up an enormous federal agency in an extremely short period of time; others were the result of what human beings can't seem to stop introducing into every large bureaucratic endeavor — politics. For the most part, I successfully navigated these types of obstacles throughout my career with the help of professional colleagues across all walks of government service. But whenever politics gets thrown into the game, wild cards come into play.

The TSA had developed a long-range plan to help airports integrate explosive detection devices into the conveyor systems that carry checked bags from ticket counters, through the bowels of an airport, to departing aircraft. It would take a minimum of two years to build such an in-line system at Orlando, and that wouldn't be soon enough to satisfy the year-end deadline.

As a result, fifty-six SUV-sized explosive detection machines, and one hundred fourteen explosive trace detector stands were about to be deployed at Orlando's ticket counters until the in-line system could be completed. The GOAA Board was apoplectic. They cringed at the impact this so-called "lobby solution" would have on the aesthetics of their beautiful airport, albeit temporarily. Airline station managers had a more practical concern: that the machines would take up much of their coveted passenger queuing space. Fingers began to point.

Airport Director Bill Jennings traveled to Washington to beg the TSA's senior leadership for a pass on the December 31st deadline that would allow Orlando to go directly to the in-line system once completed. But they wouldn't budge. The GOAA Board was no doubt embarrassed that, even with their political clout (read John Mica), they couldn't forestall those dreaded baggage screening behemoths from invading the airport's lobbies. To make matters worse, the machines were late to arrive and would have to be hastily installed. Weeks before the deadline, the *Orlando Sentinel* quoted Jennings as saying that come New Year's Day, "the airport will be gridlock . . . a sea of bags."

In what appeared to be payback to the TSA, the *Orlando Sentinel* published an editorial: "The Tenant from Hell." It accused the TSA of not paying rent for the space they occupied at the airport, owing the GOAA nearly $400,000 for police services rendered, not agreeing to pay $30,000 in screener parking fees owed, not defraying the cost of extra buses needed to shuttle screeners to and from the employee parking lot, and refusing to pay $300,000 in damages to airport computers after a TSA sub-contractor accidentally set off the airport's sprinkler system.

It didn't matter that it had been an entirely different federal agency, the General Services Administration, not the TSA, that was behind in the rent; that it had been the GOAA that had refused to take parking payments directly from screeners while headquarters negotiated a contract with a company to collect the money to pay for parking; that the TSA had never been asked to

☆ ☆

defray the cost of additional shuttle buses; that it was the GOAA that had forgotten to bill the TSA for police services; and that the water damage reimbursement had been stalled because the GOAA refused to accept the customary depreciated value of the computers, and instead insisted the TSA pay the full cost for new ones. The damage had been done. Jennings swore to me he hadn't been the one who leaked the story. Obviously, it had been someone in the GOAA.

TSA news conference at Orlando Airport

Despite those bumps in the tarmac, though, come New Year's Day, rather than a sea of bags, the airport was a Sea of Tranquility. Owed to thorough preparation, and some emergency measures I'd been authorized to employ in the event of piled up bags, the crush of passengers and baggage eased through the airport like the floats along Pasadena's Tournament of Roses Parade route.

At a subsequent media event, four airline station managers stood at my side, two from the largest air carriers at the airport, and told reporters what a great partnership they had with the TSA in Orlando. Afterward, the American Airlines station manager

☆ ☆

told me that, in his view, TSA Orlando had set the standard for screening with the best team of any major airport in the country. *Condé Nast Traveler* magazine rated Orlando as one of the most passenger-friendly airports in the nation. None of that had happened by accident.

For one, we had established a Security Consortium of senior stakeholders that met weekly to sort out problems and find solutions. At Bill Jennings' suggestion, we also started the Screening Process Improvement Team (SPIT). Representatives, two each from the airport, the airlines and the TSA, spit out some excellent ideas for streamlining screening processes.

And, we set up more employee committees than you could shake a screening wand at — a Screener Steering Committee to ensure that shift scheduling was done fairly, a Hardship Committee to adjust the work schedules of screeners who faced personal difficulties, a Morale Committee to advise management of the impact that changes in policies or procedures were having on employee morale, a Customer Services Advisory Committee to improve screening processes for passengers, and a Safety Action Team to encourage safe practices by all employees. We even established an Employee Club that, among other things, hosted a "Thanksgiving Feast" for employees who had to work that day. We gave out Employee of the Month, On the Spot, and Achievement awards. In addition, I frequently held Town Hall meetings in the airport to answer questions of employees, and entertained press conferences to answer questions from the media.

Based on a prototype started by the Denver Airport, during my second summer in Orlando, we created a checkpoint lane for families with young children, a KIDZ lane, decorated with posters and toys. Screeners used hand-puppets to entice youngsters through the metal detector, wrapped a fuzzy caterpillar around a hand wand to make it look less intimidating, sat kids in tiny chairs if they needed special attention, and rewarded them with "A Great Kid" sticker when finished for a job well done.

We started a newsletter, the "MCO Insider" (MCO being the Orlando airport's code, based on it once having been McCoy Air Force Base). The eleven issues published during my tenure provided needed information to employees, announced events and, perhaps most importantly, dispelled rumors.

In addition to fine-tuning passenger and baggage screening, we completed a study of the threat to the airport posed by shoulder-mounted, man-portable antiaircraft missiles, MANPADS. Based on their range, we determined where terrorists could find cover and concealment in proximity to the airport and shared that information with state and local police. We also identified perimeter vulnerabilities in anticipation of attempted terrorist infiltration onto airport grounds.

We built a good relationship with the local law enforcement community. Rick Scovel and I attended monthly law enforcement community breakfasts. I was appointed to a Security Advisory Board at the Orange County Sheriff's Office. Val Demings, Chief of the airport's police detachment, future Chief of the Orlando Police Department and then U.S. Representative, presented me with an Orlando Police Department shirt with my name and title embroidered on it (that I kept in my car in case I ever got pulled over by the cops). And I got to brief Florida Governor Jeb Bush on Orlando Airport's security measures.

But despite all the successes, the challenges continued to mount. For one, Congress had appropriated funds for the TSA to pay up to seventy-five percent of the cost of installing the in-line, checked-baggage explosive detection devices at airports that

☆ ☆

would end the hated "lobby solution" at Orlando and elsewhere. Airports across the nation decided that the taxpayers should pay more. Relying on their influence with Representative Mica, the GOAA Board led the charge to increase the government's share to ninety percent. They won the battle; but lost the war.

Orlando had been ninth on the list of ten airports when Congress allocated funds sufficient to pay seventy-five percent of installation costs. However, when at the GOAA Board's behest Congress raised the percentage to ninety percent, there was only enough money to fund eight. Consequently, Orlando slipped from the list. The GOAA Board was flabbergasted. Jennings told me they were convinced it was the TSA's payback for them having gotten John Magaw fired — which was the first time I heard they had anything to do with that.

The next glass slipper to drop was a misunderstanding that lowered my stock with John Mica. An influential Orlando hotelier had proposed that the TSA allow his guests to check in for their flights at the two hotels he owned on International Drive. After boarding passes and baggage tags had been issued by the air carriers at the hotels, the checked bags would be transported to the airport by a private, bonded company. The advantage for passengers would be more leisure time before heading to the airport with only the security checkpoint to negotiate once they arrived. For local businesses that meant passengers would have more time to shop along International Drive. For the airlines it represented good customer service. For me, we could screen the passengers' bags at our convenience before their flights' departures. It was a win, win, win situation that I championed with TSA headquarters. However, I received resistance from the TSA regulators in Washington who said it was against the rules.

☆ ☆

The idea languished for months until Mica convened a meeting at the Orlando Airport to demand resolution. My immediate supervisor flew down from Washington to represent the TSA. When no reasonable argument could be made against the idea, Mica slammed his fist on the table and gave the TSA just three months to get it done. She told him we would get it done in one. I had won! At least I thought I had. However, Jennings told me days later that Mica thought I had been the obstacle all along and that my boss had been sent to Orlando to overrule me. Jennings promised he would straighten it out with Mica. I called my supervisor and told her what was going on. She said not to worry. I was worried. Several months later the third strike was called on an inside pitch.

In January 2004, with little fanfare, a new deputy executive airport director showed up. The position had been vacant for the year and a half I had been in Orlando. Bill Jennings told me several times, "I don't need no stinkin' deputy." However, he made noises about retiring, and I assumed a deputy had been sent over as his heir apparent. Jennings sat him in the corner.

He and I got along just fine. I suppose because we were both pariahs at the airport. At one point he told me I needed to get out of the airport more often and offered to introduce me to some of the movers and shakers around town. I thought it might prove useful in improving the TSA's image and, quite frankly, my own. He introduced me to the Director of the Orlando Tourist and Convention Bureau who weeks later invited me to a luncheon of the Home Builders Association which was planning a convention at the Orlando Convention Center. I was seated next to the Director of the Chamber of Commerce who, a few weeks after that, invited me to be an "honored guest" at a Chamber luncheon.

By then, Congress had capped TSA's nationwide screener workforce at 45,000, and it was announced that, along with most airports, Orlando would be taking a modest hit. The official line was that the TSA was "rightsizing" the number of screeners at each airport. My staff had already begun converting a number of full-time positions to part-time in order to supplement checkpoints during the peak hours and was confident we'd be able to absorb the cut.

During the Chamber luncheon I was asked to comment on the prospects of our handling the upcoming summer rush with fewer screeners. Had I expressed anything but confidence in our ability to keep the airport flowing, it would have not only contradicted TSA's senior leadership, but given ammunition to the Henny Pennys who would have started frantically crying once again that the airport's roof was about to fall in. So, I simply told them I thought we would do just fine. My remarks ricocheted back to the airport and up to Washington and several weeks later I was summoned to an unusual Saturday morning, one-on-one meeting with Acting TSA Administrator David Stone.

After a few pleasantries, Stone got to the point. "Bill Jennings says he's not getting along with you. And it's my responsibility to make a change whenever a Federal Security Director and an airport manager aren't getting along."

"I don't agree," I said, "I think your responsibility is to back up your FSDs until it's proven they've done something wrong. If I've done anything wrong, you won't have to remove me. I'll quit." I asked that a management review be conducted. But I was on shaky ground, essentially a contractor whom he could have fired on the spot.

Stone was in a bind. A retired Navy one-star and the former FSD at Los Angeles International Airport, he was brought to

Washington to work in Congressional Affairs. No doubt having impressed Congressman Mica, he was tapped to replace Jim Loy when Loy moved up to become Deputy Secretary in the newly created Department of Homeland Security. Stone might not have known if Mica was involved in Bill Jennings's version of events; but Stone must have known that if Mica was, and Stone took no action to remove me, he'd stand little chance of getting the Administrator's job permanently.

And he had to know it was politics at play. Because instead of firing me, Stone offered me the FSD job at any other airport in the country where there was a vacancy. He told me the FSD position at Lihue Airport on Hawaii's Island of Kauai had just become available, and while it was at a much lower paygrade than Orlando, he would see to it that I kept my senior executive-level pay. Or he could use me to help set up the new Transportation Security Operations Center (TSOC) in Northern Virginia. Since that wouldn't be an FSD position, he said he would arrange for a special dual compensation waiver. He asked me to think it over and let him know which job I preferred.

On the flight home, I couldn't get visions of swaying palm trees, hula-dancing wahines, or Don Ho singing "Tiny Bubbles" off my mind. But having moved Joy so many times during my career, I knew it was only fair to let her decide. With Amy and her family living in Michigan, and Cindy and hers in Northern Virginia, I began to wonder what working in the TSOC was going to be like.

When I got back to Orlando, I confided in AFSD Rick Scovel what was going on. He offered to ask the powerful local sheriff to intervene with Mica on my behalf. And I could have called Homeland Security Deputy Secretary Jim Loy, who I knew from

☆ ☆

my Snowcap days when he was Coast Guard commandant, to ask him to speak with Stone. But I decided to do neither.

I accomplished in Orlando what I had been hired to do. Without any law enforcement authorities, it wasn't the job I had signed up for. I never wanted to be a passenger and baggage screening guru and facing two more years of that wasn't an appealing prospect. It was time to move on.

I did, however, confront Bill Jennings, if only to get the true story of what had happened. His hands trembled as he apologized for having gone behind my back, saying he had been under orders from the GOAA Board. Bill said my remarks at the Chamber of Commerce luncheon had gotten back to them and, despite Congressman Mica's public protestations of a bloated TSA, the Board had been working with Mica behind the scenes to get the number of screener positions at Orlando restored and thought my comments had undermined their efforts. Bill wouldn't say whether Mica had been directly involved in having me removed.

Shortly after informing my staff that I would be transferring to Washington, a senior GOAA executive called and asked to meet with me in one of the parking garages. "I can't be seen with you," he said.

In a scene reminiscent of *All the Presidents Men,* he told me not to beat myself up over it, that I had done nothing wrong. "It's politics," he said, as he glanced over his shoulder to be certain no one else was within earshot.

Stone sent a gracious, but disingenuous press release to the *Orlando Sentinel* that read, "Lutz is being transferred as part of an effort to bring more field experts into the headquarters operation."

Shortly thereafter, Congressman Mica was asked by the *Sentinel* how he thought things had been going at the airport.

☆ ☆

"So far, so good," he said. Then, without mentioning me by name, he cryptically added, "As an elected official in Congress, you sometimes have to throw your toys out of the tub to get attention."

I was disappointed. I had led a charmed career until then. But I wasn't going to let it take away from all we had accomplished. I recalled former Administrator John Magaw's parting words when they let him go, "I'm leaving quietly because your work is too important." I was determined to leave Orlando with that same dignity.

I spent my final year and a half with the TSA as Chief of Operational Support at the TSOC in Northern Virginia. My boss, Ernie Christensen, a former Navy Top Gun, asked me to link the TSOC with other law enforcement and intelligence community command centers in Washington, and with modes of transportation other than air, such as the trucking industry. I did the best I could. But I couldn't help thinking that my career had come full circle from my days in Saigon, sitting on the bench, wanting to get into the game.

Christensen told me that Stone wanted him to keep an eye on me to be sure I hadn't been embittered by my transfer from Orlando, implying there might be another position for me in the offing. But in April 2005, Stone announced he was leaving; the *Washington Post* said he had been asked to leave. By early June, he was gone.

A few months later I got a call from the acting chief of operations (my old boss had stepped down from chief of operations to take an FSD position — it seemed as if everyone in the TSA headquarters was "acting"). He told me my "up to five years" contract with the TSA would end. I should have thanked him. I wasn't enjoying the work. To be honest, I had stuck around for the money.

☆ ☆

In a memo, the TSA explained that reorganization of the TSOC had eliminated my position, thanked me for my expertise, and expressed gratitude for my service. I suspected Stone's replacement, the new acting administrator, had been looking around for some senior executive slots he could encumber to start building his own team. If so, that was fair. I was given a generous six weeks of severance pay and, in my last paycheck, a $1,000 bonus from Ernie Christensen, his way of saying farewell as he too walked out the door.

It had been a wild ride. The rush to erect the largest, new government agency since World War II had been chaotic. And, although it hadn't ended the way I would have preferred, it was an honor to have been part of one of the most remarkable bureaucratic achievements in our nation's history.

In January 2002, the TSA had started with just thirteen employees. Eleven months later nearly fifty thousand, mostly on-the-job trainees, including myself, had taken over passenger screening at the nation's airports, and baggage screening soon after. And from that foundation, the TSA matured into a professional organization. Not only have there not been any events similar to 9-11, seldom are complaints heard from passengers any longer.

☆ ☆ ☆ ☆ ☆ ☆

During my year at the TSOC, I had several lunches with former DEA agents who worked for the State Department's Antiterrorism Assistance Program (ATA), one being the son of my former secretary in Cairo. I thought all along that when my work at the TSOC was over, the ATA would be the perfect place to end my full-time working career — back overseas, where all my adventures had begun. The time to make that decision was at hand.

My buddies told me the ATA was looking for someone to fill a new in-country Program Manager position at the American Embassy Manila, dual-hatted as the State Department's Counterterrorism Advisor to the Government of the Philippines. I thought with my military, law enforcement, and airport security experience, along with my many years of working overseas, I would be a shoo-in. I interviewed, and they hired me on the spot.

It didn't take long to learn that the new ATA position had been unpopular with the former U.S. Ambassador to the Philippines who wanted to use that slot for some pet project. And I knew my personal philosophy of law enforcement authorities assuming a larger role in the fight against international terrorism in developing countries, like the Philippines, wasn't going to be popular with host nation armed forces, or even with my military colleagues at the American Embassy.

It sounded like the perfect job for me! In fact, I wouldn't have wanted it any other way.

CHAPTER 31

A Filipino Finale

I t was a mess. Muslim separatists, communist insurgents, and international terrorists had been roiling the island nation for years. Using terrorist tactics, they competed to get the government to cave to their various demands. Dozens of bombings had killed hundreds of innocent civilians. We needed a scorecard to keep track of who was doing what to whom and why. And if things didn't change soon for the better, it was only going to get worse.

Muslims had occupied the southernmost islands of the Philippines for more than a thousand years, centuries before the first Spaniard set boot there. During their 350-year colonial rule, Spain granted the Sultan of Sulu semi-autonomous reign over the followers of Islam in Mindanao and elsewhere on the Sulu archipelago.

When Spain ceded the Philippines to the United States after the Spanish-American War, America didn't know what to do with her. We weren't a colonial nation and didn't want to become one, having not much more than a century earlier unshackled ourselves from the British Empire. For that reason, we cloned a government after our own, and set the locals on a path toward independence. Interrupted by World War II, it was granted

☆ ☆

on a date in 1946 not set by chance, July 4th. Several Filipino colleagues told me they thought America had set them free too soon after the war, before the country had gotten its political act together.

Philippine independence also spawned a dream among local Muslims that one day they too would have a state of their own. By the 1970s that dream had become a nightmare, having metastasized into a full-blown separatist movement. Two primary groups emerged: the Moro National Liberation Front (and its splinter group, the Moro Islamic Liberation Front), and the Abu Sayyaf.

Added to the list of malcontents was the Communist Party of the Philippines and its military arm, the New People's Army that looked to overthrow the democratically elected central government and turn the country into a communist state. More recently, the radical Islamic terrorist group Jemaah Islamiyah had taken sanctuary in the southern Philippines and negotiated haven for other international terrorist groups like Al Qaeda.

The Armed Forces of the Philippines (AFP) had been taking the fight to them, attacking their base camps and training sites. In 2005, after the government of the Philippines lifted the twelve-year suspension of military cooperation with the United States they had imposed after ousting American-backed Ferdinand Marcos, the U.S. Army deployed fifteen-hundred troops to assist them. However, the enemy seldom confronted them, slinking off into the brush once the cavalry arrived. In fact, there hadn't been a single act of terror committed in the jungles of Mindanao.

Terrorists preferred to hit "soft targets" in metropolitan areas, places where civilians gathered, like shopping malls and modes of transportation. They wanted to instill fear in the general populace to force the government to capitulate to their demands.

☆ ☆

How better to accomplish that than with mass casualties of civilians. And the responsibility to protect innocent civilians in metropolitan areas was that of the police, not the military.

I was hired on a one-year contract by the State Department's Bureau of Diplomatic Security to fill a new, in-country Program Manager position in their Antiterrorism Assistance Program (ATA). My job would be to intensify training to Philippine law enforcement authorities and thereby improve their capacity to fight terrorism. But when I arrived in the Philippines, I found the police standing on the sidelines.

It wasn't for lack of training. The ATA had been training them for twenty years, along with other U.S. agencies and the Australians as well. There were two obstacles keeping the police out of the fight: the law, or rather the lack of one, and Philippine government policy.

Terrorism wasn't illegal in the Philippines. An anti-terrorism law that would penalize anyone conspiring to commit acts of terror and give the police the legal tools they needed to proactively investigate terrorist organizations, such as court-ordered communications intercepts, had been languishing in their Congress for a dozen years, tabled over the definition of terrorism which some feared could be used to indict all Muslims, even those innocently striving to build an independent Islamic State through democratic means.

Since terrorist leaders weren't the ones tossing the bombs, their fingerprints couldn't be found at crime scenes. Without the plotting and planning of terrorist acts being illegal, the police could only investigate the means by which the terror had been created — the bombings and kidnappings — and only after they had occurred. They were just sweeping up the debris.

The more vexing problem was that of Philippine government policy. The government, being run by former military officers, had put the AFP in charge. With the responsibility came the resources, and the hungry AFP dog jealously guarded its rice bowl, growling at anyone who ventured nearby. Law enforcement had been shunted aside.

Identifying training requirements and coordinating its delivery was the job description of an ATA Program Manager. Influencing foreign government policy was not. Fortunately for me, the State Department's Counterterrorism Bureau (CT), the organization that set policy for the ATA, had been itching to play a bigger role in the field. So, they dual-hatted me as the Counterterrorism Advisor to the Government, the only one in existence, hoping it would give me the clout I would need to invigorate their heretofore moribund Anti-terrorism Task Force (ATTF), Philippine law enforcement's sinking flagship in the war on terror. To make it happen, though, there would need to be a change in government policy. That became **my** itch to scratch.

During my first week in Manila, I was introduced over breakfast to Undersecretary Ricardo "Ric" Blancaflor who was to be my principal counterpart. An attorney, former Army officer in the Judge Advocate Corps, Blancaflor was the President's point man for counterterrorism. As such, he was head of the ATTF, a task force in name only though, because no agency participated in it.

The pending anti-terrorism legislation would create an Anti-terrorism Council, headed by the Executive Secretary, the equivalent of our Vice President, to which the ATTF would report. And the new law would require selected agencies to assign representatives to the ATTF, which would be critical to building an effective interagency team to go after terrorist organizations. Getting the anti-terrorism law passed was Ric's top priority.

☆ ☆

To try to influence that, Blancaflor arranged for me to speak with influential congressmen to explain how provisions similar to those in their draft law were being successfully employed in the United States. Later on, he got me seated with several of their Supreme Court Justices at a Manila Country Club reception to impress upon them the importance of the proposed law, should its passage face a court challenge. And I did some speaking at service clubs around town to gin up public support.

Meanwhile, training remained "Job One." There were seven ATA training courses scheduled for 2006 plus consultations for the Philippines National Police (PNP) on computer forensics and explosive detection dog training, and for the Bureau of Fire Protection to resupply their Special Rescue Unit with chemical, biological, radiological and nuclear weapons response preparedness equipment. There were also slots to be awarded for courses at the International Law Enforcement Academy in Bangkok which, by then, had expanded from counterdrug to teaching counterterrorism.

For each training course I had to solicit the names of nominees from selected agencies in sufficient time to obtain human rights clearances from Main State. For in-country courses, I also needed to secure training venues, contract food catering services, pick up and store course materials, and make hotel reservations and transportation arrangements for the instructor teams. I even had to purchase old jalopies and find secure, safe places to have them blown up in post-blast investigation segments of several training courses. For the consultations, I had to grease the skids with the appropriate host country officials and then accompany the consultants to each of their meetings in the event any follow-up would be needed. It was a handful. I was only a one-man band.

The curtain would rise in February on ATA's premier course, the nine-week Preventing, Interdicting and Investigating Acts of Terrorism (PIIAT) with a second PIIAT, a slimmed down six-week version, scheduled for June-July. They ran the full gamut of counterterrorism subjects, the perfect vehicles for laying a foundation for interagency cooperation and identifying candidates to participate in an invigorated ATTF once the new law was enacted.

I secured the National Defense College of the Philippines (NDCP) as the training venue for both courses. Over the years, most ATA classes delivered in-country had been delivered there. Located in Camp Aguinaldo, headquarters of the AFP, it was a terrific training site, and the NDCP President, Commodore Carlos "Chuck" Agustin a gracious host. He had long ago attended an ATA course and was proud to be hosting them now.

In the past, the American Embassy's Regional Security Officer (RSO) had allowed the PNP to allocate most of the classroom seats among their officers, save for a few he allotted to the Philippine government agencies that helped him keep American officials and U.S. government properties safe. But for these two PIIATs, I took control of each slot. The RSO wasn't pleased, and neither were the PNP's high muckety-mucks. But there had been no need for the PNP to worry. They got their fair share.

Seats went to the PNP's Task Force *Singlahi,* the unit that led their counterterrorism efforts, such as they were. Two went to their Bomb Data Center that investigated the crime scenes of terrorist bombings. The PNP Intelligence Group that kept track of terrorist organizations got a seat as did the Criminal Investigation and Detection Group that conducted their general criminal investigations. The Aviation Security and Maritime Groups were included in the mix as was their Transnational

☆ ☆

Crime Unit that did cyber forensic analyses. And the paramilitary Special Action Force (SAF) that doubled as their SWAT (Special Weapons Assault Team) wasn't neglected.

I divvied up the remaining seats to organizations I thought also needed to be included in the ATTF, among them the National Bureau of Investigation (NBI), the nation's premier investigative agency, modeled after the FBI, and the FBI Legal Attache's principal counterpart agency. In discussions with the NBI Director, I was surprised to learn they had no unit dedicated to terrorism. I promised him ATA would train and equip such a unit if he decided to create one. Within weeks, the NBI's General Intelligence and Investigation Division became the Antiterrorism Division.

I included the Bureau of Customs and Immigration that would be needed in the ATTF to follow terrorist migration and the movement of their supplies, and the Anti-Money Laundering Council to follow the terrorist's money. And probably for the first time in any ATA course, I offered a seat to the AFP's Intelligence Service, thinking their representative would serve as an important link between the ATTF and the AFP.

There was no doubt in my mind that the military had been overlooking potentially valuable evidence during their jungle raids and could benefit from crime scene management training — the identification, preservation, and custody of evidence. Our Guantanamo Bay Detention Camp had been built for that very reason because U.S. soldiers hadn't collected sufficient evidence to build prosecutable cases against many of the terrorists captured in Afghanistan and Iraq.

Ideally, the PNP's Special Action Force should have been integrated into AFP units in the field, not only to manage crime scenes after raids but to interrogate prisoner-suspects. However, that was too high a hurdle to attempt and, even had they agreed, the numbers of SAF that would need to be trained would far exceed the ATA's ability to provide it. Instead, I suggested to the DOD's Pacific Command that crime scene management training be included in the curriculum provided to the AFP, delivered by either the Navy Criminal Investigative Service or the Army's Criminal Investigation Division.

Law enforcement authorities in the Philippines suffered from some of the same ills as law enforcement organizations in the United States. On PIATT's opening day, I harkened back to my days at the Counterdrug Executive Secretariat, introducing the students to words from the General Counterdrug Intelligence Plan — that the only way to win the war, in this case the one on terror, was for agencies to coordinate, cooperate and share information. Those words became my calling card.

Taking a page from the DEA's history of developing task forces, I told them if there was any hope of winning the war on terror it would be by working together, that law enforcement was a team sport. I extolled the benefits of agencies bringing their collective knowledge, capabilities, and laws they enforced to bear on the enemy.

And I explained the DEA's premier Kingpin Strategy of having dismantled Colombian drug cartels by attacking their vulnerabilities — a strategy that could as easily be applied to terrorist organizations.

In perhaps another unprecedented step, I supplemented the PIATT instructor staff throughout the course with a cast of local characters. I asked Ric Blancaflor to detail the provisions of the pending anti-terrorism law and his vision for the ATTF. I had the Embassy's legal attaché explain the role of the FBI in counterterrorism, both at home and abroad. I gave the narcotics attaché an opportunity to explain the Philippine Drug Enforcement Agency's network of strategically located Maritime Enforcement Communication Centers that the DEA had helped them build to track drug smuggling vessels, upon which I thought the ATTF could piggyback. And when I noted that the lesson plans were based solely on U.S. law, much of which didn't apply under Philippine law, I invited Philippine State Prosecutor Geronimo Sy to put the course's legal instruction into a local context for the students.

New American Ambassador Kristie Kenney officiated at the graduation. Ric Blancaflor arranged for the Undersecretary of National Defense to host a banquet for the graduating class. He also arranged for Executive Secretary Eduardo Ermita, the nation's Vice President and future head of the Anti-Terrorism Council once the new law passed, to host a separate dinner for the instructors at a suburban Makati restaurant. These two events provided my first opportunities for one-on-ones with executive branch policymakers who sat at the highest level of their government.

For each dinner I had arranged to be seated next to the host to expound on what I thought was the proper role of law enforcement vis-à-vis the military in their nation's war against terror. I told each of the importance of the pending anti-terrorism legislation that would give the police the tools they needed to proactively disrupt and dismantle terrorist organizations.

I told them that terrorists are criminals, that in western countries it's the law enforcement organizations that combat them, not the military. I pointed out that it had been Spain's Guardia Civil that solved the 2004 train station bombing in Madrid, and Great Britain's Scotland Yard that just that past summer had put a stop to the London subway bombings. I reminded them each that in the United States, it's the FBI and state and local police that are responsible to combat terrorism; that we don't even allow our military to operate within our borders, except under the most extraordinary of circumstances. I said that in the Philippines, the military and the police needed to be working together.

Executive Secretary Eduardo Ermita, the second highest government official in the land, himself a former Undersecretary of National Defense and former Deputy Chief of Staff of the Army, was a hard man to sell. He said he didn't think the police were up to the task. I told him if the police received the same level of training and support as did the AFP and had the legal tools to do the job, they could be very capable. He had trouble arguing with that.

But I knew there was still a long way to go to convince him, if ever.

CHAPTER 32

OVER THE FINISH LINE

I had taken the job in the Philippines to end my career on a high note. I used just about everything I had learned during my long career to make it happen. And it turned out even better than I could have imagined.

It was an unaccompanied tour of duty. They didn't let me take Joy along which was the first time in our married life we were separated. I never understood why. I thought dodging daredevil drivers on Edsa Highway during my daily commute to work was more hazardous than any of my professional duties. But new grandmother Joy shed no tears, content to visit me there. And I was entitled to home leave after six months. But we got to see each other more often than that.

Six weeks after I landed in Manila, over the phone Joy told me that Penn State had been selected to play Florida State on New Year's Day in the Orange Bowl — Joe Paterno versus Bobby Bowden, the two winningest coaches in major college football. It would be one for the ages. "If you don't come home for the game," she said, "you'll never forgive yourself."

She was right. So, I put in for a few days of annual leave around New Year's, flew to Washington, and then hopped on a flight with Joy to Miami. We had dinner at Joe's Stone Crabs in South Beach and the next night watched the Nittany Lion's classic, triple-overtime victory over the tenacious Seminoles. That same evening, the game having ended long after midnight, I dropped Joy back off in Washington and was sitting at my desk when my boss called from Washington on Thursday morning. He didn't even realize I had been gone.

Then in April, Joy came to visit for our 34th wedding anniversary. The Philippines had done a remarkable job of preserving World War II history, and I decided we would explore some of it during her stay. I occupied a two-bedroom furnished apartment at Essensa Towers in the upscale Manila suburb of Fort Bonifacio. I had been told that Imelda Marcos, by then a member of Congress, owned a condominium at Essensa Towers. I met her once at a Makati restaurant but never saw her set a dainty foot inside Essensa Towers in any of her hundreds of pairs of shoes.

My apartment overlooked the American Cemetery. We walked the meticulously groomed grounds where circular rows of crosses and Stars of David mark the graves of the 17,206 heroes buried there, and where another 36,286 missing-in-action are memorialized. And we studied the colorful mosaic murals depicting the WWII naval battles in the Pacific Theater.

That first weekend, Joy and I took a fast boat to Corregidor at the mouth of Manila Bay, once an important strategic fortress that modern warfare had stripped of any military value. A Disney-style tram motored us around the island, by crumbling barracks, and past rusting artillery pieces standing like sentries waiting for another shot at history that will never come.

We paid our respects at the U.S. War Memorial dedicated to the Americans and Filipinos who had died on Corregidor. Then we visited the Japanese Memorial at the opposite end of the island, dedicated to the Japanese, Filipino and American war dead. I was impressed that the Japanese had honored their former enemies . . . impressed that is, until I was told by the NDCP's Chuck Agustin that the recognition had been demanded by the Government of the Philippines as a precondition for them to build it.

We toured Malinta Tunnel where General Douglas MacArthur holed up during the Japanese invasion. We photographed his statue on the beach from where he had escaped to Australia, his index finger raised, promising to return.

On Sunday we drove to Intramuros, the city inside the walls of Manila's Fort Santiago, where three years later MacArthur made good on his promise. Built by Spanish conquistadors during their reign, the Japanese made their last stand there, where thousands on both sides met their maker. The fort had been restored — there's even a golf course on what had been its moat, where I played golf on many a Sunday afternoon with the Philippine International Golf Society, the PIGS. The bullet holes in the flagpole preserved at the nearby American Embassy are some of the few remaining testaments to the ferocity of the fighting during the Battle of Manila.

The next weekend we made a little history of our own. Saturday morning, we drove to Taal Lake and sailed in a rickety wooden outrigger to the volcano at its center. We rode horseback up a precariously steep and narrow trail to the volcano's rim. Later we lunched on some Spanish-inspired ground pork-stuffed bitter melon and Filipino garlic fried rice at a hillside restaurant overlooking the peaceful lake. Then we drove by the magnificent chalet that Ferdinand Marcos had built for an overnight stay by Ronald Reagan — who refused the accommodation after witnessing the nation's poverty firsthand. By late afternoon we checked into our hotel, disappointed to be assigned a dingy, dank, and dark room. Thinking better of it for our anniversary, we drove back to Ft. Bonifacio for a wonderful seafood dinner at a local restaurant and then popped a cork on a bottle of wine in my apartment to celebrate our 34th.

The highlight of Joy's visit, though, was her last weekend when we stayed at the American Ambassador's residence in Baguio. Perched high on a mountaintop overlooking the city, it had been built as a summer respite for the rotund Governor of the Philippines and future President of the United States, William Howard Taft, who couldn't tolerate the tropical heat. Since independence, it has served as the Ambassador's alternative residence and weekend get-a-way for Embassy employees.

Filipinos say the ghost of Commanding General Tomojuki Yamashita, the Tiger of Malaya, still prowls the stately mansion. During the Japanese occupation of the Philippines, he used it as his headquarters. After the war, Yamashita was tried for war crimes in that very house, and later executed for his war crimes in a prison outside Manila. But the locals believed his ghost found its way back to Baguio and has been haunting the historic mansion ever since. I wasn't buying it. I don't believe in ghosts.

Staying in the mansion was like living in a museum. The furniture and artwork in the estate date back to Taft's day, save for a painting of Yamashita's trial hanging over the fireplace. We chose to sleep in Yamashita's bedroom. From the window he would often climb out onto the roof of the portico to address his troops assembled on the front lawn below. A patch in the closet floor concealed a fireman's pole that would have whisked him down into a network of cavernous escape tunnels below had the need arisen.

☆ ☆

We were lying in bed reading when suddenly my toiletry kit, that I was certain I had set securely on the shelf over the sink, tumbled to the bathroom floor, its contents clanging across the tile like warning bells. I'm sure Yamashita's ghost had nothing to do with it. It was no doubt the chilly mountain air, or maybe the romantic setting. But after I dimmed the lights, we snuggled just a little bit closer.

☆ ☆ ☆ ☆ ☆ ☆

In early May, Ambassador Kenney floored me. She had sent an extraordinary cable to Washington. In it she said I had gained access, improved law enforcement capabilities, and shaped Philippine government policies far beyond expectations.

Using the PIIAT as her example, she complimented my having invited host-nation experts to assist in teaching alongside the ATA instructors, and the Embassy's law enforcement agencies to speak to the class. She went on to say that the enthusiasm of the students at graduation was "palpable."

Ambassador Kenney said I had gained the confidence of Undersecretary Blancaflor to identify for him the "best and brightest" from among the students for future assignment to his ATTF. She said she was confident Blancaflor would provide me an office at the Malacanang Park facility, across the Pasig River from the Presidential Palace, once it was renovated.

Most astonishingly, she ended the cable by saying that in order to sustain my success I needed a staff. In all my dealings with Ambassadors over the years with the DEA, never once had one ever suggested an increase in staffing.

I knew immediately who I wanted to be my local assistant, the Director of the Emergency Management Institute at the NDCP, Ronald Dizon. A young, bright Filipino who spoke perfect English,

☆ ☆

Dizon was already familiar with our training scenarios having helped me set up the classroom for the PIIAT and monitored a few of its courses. And his expertise in emergency management was right in line with the ATA's mission. He enthusiastically jumped at the chance. Dizon's boss Chuck Agustin, on the other hand, wasn't happy.

Weeks later I was enjoying dinner at a Makati restaurant with Agustin while he regaled me with tales of the horrors of Japanese occupation of Manila during his childhood. He ended by saying that, despite their cruelty, he had been able to forgive them.

"Chuck," I said, "If you can forgive the Japanese for World War II, you can certainly forgive me for stealing Ronald Dizon away from the NDCP." He chuckled. He knew it was a great opportunity for Ronald.

It took until the end of July to get Ronald onboard and, with barely two months left on my tour of duty, I took him with me to Subic Bay, the former U.S. Navy base, to help prepare for an upcoming Post Blast Investigation course there. He quickly learned the ropes.

☆ ☆ ☆ ☆ ☆ ☆

I had never been pleased with the image that hosting ATA courses at the National Defense College projected – that of the military training the police. As ideal a physical location as it was, and as good a friend Chuck Agustin had become, I almost immediately began looking for alternative venues. It finally paid off.

My search led me to the Philippine Public Safety College at Fort Bonifacio, the academy for entry-level policemen. It was a natural – cops teaching cops. Its President was the flamboyant socialite, philanthropist, and author, Dr. Margarita "Tingting" Cojuangco, who I later learned was a former governor, an aunt of former President Benigno Aquino III, and a presidential assistant to the then President of the Philippines, Gloria Macapagal-Arroyo. Cojuangco was anxious to host ATA courses at the PPSC. However, the limited training space could only accommodate the smallest of ATA classes. In the end, we agreed they would host the Cyber Forensics Course later that summer and an Instructor Development Course in the fall, the last two courses of my tenure.

I took every opportunity to impress upon her the proper role of the police in countering terrorism. When I learned the PPSC didn't have a single anti-terrorism course, in fact not a mention of counterterrorism anywhere in its basic curriculum, I suggested they include confiscation of cell phones during arrests and crime scene searches. I knew that valuable intelligence from cell phones and computers was being lost. Every Filipino had a cell phone. They were way ahead of the United States in the number per capita. Having had no reliable landline system, they went directly to it when cell phone technology hit the marketplace. And since it was cheaper to text rather than to speak over the mobile phones, no doubt a wealth of text messages could be exploited for all manner of crimes.

Tingting Cojuanco was so enamored with this new relationship that she tried to cement the deal by setting aside an office for me at the PPSC. It was tempting since it was within walking distance of my apartment. But I didn't need it. Instead, I used some of the money that had been allocated to renovate the new ATA office and warehouse space at the Embassy's Seafront annex compound in anticipation of my hiring Ronald Dizon to have built a PPSC anti-terrorism library in that space.

Invitation to Philippine National Police Academy ceremony,
April 19, 2006.

Tingting also arranged a day in my honor at the Philippine National Police Academy in Cavite Province, the police department's "West Point." One warm fall afternoon, police cadets paraded across the drill field to the beat of a marching band and saluted as they passed the grandstand. The parade was followed by a luncheon with the cadets in the mess hall. It was quite an honor.

On my next to last morning in Manila, when I had arrived for work, the Regional Security Officer whisked me to the Presidential Palace, saying it was for a meeting requested by

Executive Secretary Ermita. I could only imagine that he wanted to wish me farewell. On the way over, I thought it would be my last opportunity to convince him of the role the police should be playing in the nation's counterterrorism efforts. But when we got to the palace, I was led into the Ceremonial Hall where almost all my colleagues, and dozens of former ATA students had assembled.

Undersecretary Ric Blancaflor spoke eloquently about the progress made in the past year. I brushed aside a tear when he ended by thanking me for defending and believing in the Filipino people. He then presented me a huge, decoratively etched mounted water buffalo horn with my name inscribed on its base, certainly the most unique recognition I had ever received. Chuck Agustin followed with a plaque from the NDCP. Even the Fire Department gave me an award, presented by Jose Embang, then chief of the Makati-based Special Rescue Unit and future chief of the Philippines Bureau of Fire Protection. Caught totally off guard, I stumbled through a few remarks ending with the words I was certain everyone was sick of hearing: "To win the war on terror, you must coordinate your investigations, cooperate with each other, and share information."

Then with Ambassador Kinney by my side, Executive Secretary Ermita draped the Philippine Department of National Defense's Medal of Achievement around my neck; the highest award that can be bestowed on a non-Filipino, I was told. I thought it ironic to be receiving an award from the AFP.

When the citation was read, praising the capacity-building of law enforcement authorities and the improved interoperability among agencies that had been achieved because of my work, and thanking me for supporting passage of their anti-terrorism legislation, I couldn't help but sadly reflect on the fact that while progress may have been made, neither of my goals had been realized. The police had yet to be installed into their rightful place in the war on drugs, and the anti-terrorism law still hadn't been enacted. The ceremony seemed a little premature. But it must have been an omen.

Armed Forces of the Philippines Outstanding Achievement Medal award ceremony at Malacanang Palace, Manila. L-R: Ambassador Kristie Kenny, Lutz, Philippine VP Eduardo Ermita.

For just a few weeks after I returned home, I received an email from Ric Blancaflor saying that Philippine President Gloria Macapagal-Arroyo had issued a proclamation putting the police in charge of protecting civilians in metropolitan areas. Perhaps Ermita had a change of heart. More likely, it had been the work of PPSC's Ting Ting Cojuangco behind the scenes.

Then several months after that, I received an invitation in the mail to attend the President's signing of the "Secure the State and Protect Our People from Terrorism Act" in the Ceremonial Hall at Malacanang Palace on March 6, 2007. The law had finally passed.

☆ ☆

Mission accomplished! Those were the two outcomes I had worked toward, had hoped for, and the high notes that accompanied my tinikling (Filipino folk dancing) into retirement.

☆ ☆ ☆ ☆ ☆ ☆

After that, I did some consulting work, including half a dozen trips back to Manila on behalf of a firm selling telecommunications interception equipment. I spent three weeks in Riyadh, Saudi Arabia with Mike Horn, from my BNDD days in Philadelphia, conducting an institutional development assessment of the Ministry of Interior's General Directorate for Narcotics Control. Even the Saudis had a drug problem; seizing a considerable amount of hashish — and whiskey as well. And, in Charlestown, West Virginia, I critiqued the pilot offering of a two-week training course being delivered to a class of intelligence analysts at the West Virginia State Police Academy. I did some private investigating. And for almost ten years I conducted background investigations for the Department of State. I swore off taking up unpopular causes!

But it had always bothered me that our first Commissioner of Narcotics was largely a forgotten man. Hardly anyone alive had ever heard his name. He had even been disowned by his descendants in the Drug Enforcement Administration. Worse yet, the few who did remember him were the marijuana legalization advocates who had made him their poster child for what they hated about America's drug laws.

Restoring the record and reputation of this unpopular man was long overdue. And it was right up my alley.

CHAPTER 33

THAT OLD BASTARD

Maybe my being a Libra had something to do with it – always seeking balance, harmony and fair play. After I retired, I realized too many of the men and women who served our country ably and well in drug law enforcement had been all but forgotten. The most prominent "missing in action," the one that bothered me the most, was the man I thought of as our nation's first drug czar.

No building bore his name; no memorial honored his memory. There wasn't even a picture of him in the Drug Enforcement Administration headquarters building, save for among the relics in the DEA Museum. He had been the father of drug law enforcement, but even among his descendants in the DEA, Harry Jacob Anslinger was a forgotten man. It didn't seem fair. I wanted to know why.

I read everything about Anslinger I could get my hands on, including the three books he had written, books by agents who had worked for him, and the definitive biography of him by Penn State History Professor John McWilliams. I watched movies from his era, such as *To the Ends of the Earth* starring Dick Powell, in which Anslinger makes a cameo appearance. And, of course, *Reefer Madness,* which many mistakenly believe

☆ ☆

Anslinger had produced. I spent several days at Penn State's Paterno Library poring over the more than thirteen cubic feet of papers Anslinger's family had donated. And I visited the DEA library, disappointed to find only a thin manila folder of newspaper clippings from his day.

From what I read, he had been a giant of a man. In 1930, after Herbert Hoover carved the Narcotic Division out of the Treasury Department's Bureau of Prohibition to create the Federal Bureau of Narcotics (FBN), America's first single-mission anti-narcotics agency, he appointed Anslinger its first commissioner. Charged with enforcing the Harrison Narcotics Act of 1914 and the regulatory provisions of the Narcotic Drugs Import and Export Act of 1922, for more than thirty years Anslinger guided America's drug policy during the economic, political and social turmoil of the Great Depression, World War II and much of the "Cold War," and during the beginning of the 1960's Cultural Revolution. He served five presidents, last appointed by John F. Kennedy who held him beyond mandatory retirement age until a suitable successor could be decided. He was a Representative to the United Nations from its inception until long after he retired. However, few people living today had ever spoken his name.

Why he had been forgotten, estranged from the DEA, wasn't all that hard to figure out. It had been reorganizations of the nation's drug efforts that had done him in – reorganizations that agencies like the FBI never had to endure.

Six years after Anslinger retired, in 1968 Lyndon Johnson uprooted the FBN from its bedrock in the Treasury Department, transferred it to the Department of Justice, and merged the Food and Drug Administration's Bureau of Drug Abuse Control into it to form the Bureau of Narcotics and Dangerous Drugs (BNDD). Few remnants of Anslinger's legacy survived.

Then in the early 1970s, Richard Nixon doubled the number of BNDD special agents to help fight a heroin epidemic, in what was referred to as Nixon's war on drugs. And the former FBN agents within the new BNDD who had ever worked for Anslinger became a very small number indeed. That was the beginning of the end for Harry Anslinger's legacy.

The end came in 1973 when Nixon held the shotgun while wedding the U.S. Customs agents who had been working drug interdiction at the border to the BNDD to create the DEA. So as not to make the Customs agents feel like second class citizens, the DEA's leadership chose not to identify the new organization with the history of either agency. That's when Anslinger slipped from view. I thought it a terrible injustice.

When I searched the Internet, though, I found that not everyone had forgotten him. The pro-marijuana legalization crowd certainly hadn't. They had made Anslinger their poster child for what they believed to be the unfairness of America's drug laws, in particular the Marijuana Tax Act of 1937. The truth was that Anslinger never wanted the sale of marijuana to be a federal crime.

In the 1930s, drug laws across the country were in disaccord. Anslinger campaigned for States to adopt a model Uniform State Narcotics Act to bring conformity to drug crimes and punishments. The Act contained a marijuana provision that, if adopted, would take the FBN off the hook. That would allow Anslinger to keep the two-hundred-seventy-one agents he had inherited from the Bureau of Prohibition focused on his priorities – heroin from Europe, cocaine from Chile, and opium from China.

By the mid-1930s, starting in New Orleans, defense attorneys began to use "marijuana intoxication" as a legal defense in violent crime cases. "My client didn't know what he was doing when he stabbed her, Your Honor. He was high on marijuana." So as part of his strategy to get the States to adopt the model law, Anslinger dramatized the trials wherein the marijuana intoxication defense had been used. He paraded the gory details of self-alleged marijuana-induced violence before Congress and the media in hope of getting the model law adopted. It backfired.

Alarmed citizens demanded more be done. And since most of the marijuana originated in Mexico, Border States demanded the feds take charge. So, Congress forced Anslinger to draft the Marijuana Tax Act. It required a tax be paid by legally authorized handlers of pot, similar to the way the possession of opiates had been treated under the Harrison Narcotic Act. Congress asked Anslinger what had taken him so long. The potheads never forgave him.

Now don't get me wrong. Anslinger was an unapologetic opponent of smoking marijuana. He just didn't want his agency to have to enforce its prohibition. In fact, seven years after he retired, Anslinger participated on a Playboy panel in which he called the smoking of marijuana a gateway drug, physically and mentally harmful and addictive. And guess what? After fifty more years of experience and study, much of modern science agrees; including the Food and Drug Administration, upon which we've relied since 1938 to tell us the efficacy and safety of the drugs we use. The FDA says smoking marijuana has no accepted medical use, a high potential for abuse, and can be harmful, both mentally and physically, particularly for our youth.

While there are an increasing number of pharmaceuticals being produced from the ingredients found in cannabis, none of them are smoked. Smoking marijuana is not medicine. Some say it reduces pain. So does Johnny Walker Black Label. But whiskey isn't medicine either. Harry Anslinger had said nothing for which he need apologize.

Instead of being ridiculed for his stance on marijuana, he should be celebrated for his many remarkable achievements.

Anslinger was a pioneer. Given his State Department background, and the fact that the opiates and cocaine were being smuggled from abroad, he recognized the need for international cooperation on drug control. Almost immediately upon becoming the FBN commissioner, he created the "Committee of One Hundred," a secret panel of officials from Canada, Great Britain, Germany, Switzerland and France to share information on drug trafficking activities, the forerunner of today's International Drug Enforcement Conferences.

That same year he sent his first agent "overseas," to El Paso, Texas, to implement an information exchange agreement with Mexico. And after sending agents to Europe on case-specific missions, in 1935 he permanently assigned the first narcotics agents abroad – to Rome to focus on Mafia deportees who were shipping heroin to the States, and to Paris to target French Corsican laboratory operators who were producing the heroin and their sources of opium in the Balkans. Interrupted by WW II, in 1950 Anslinger reopened the offices in Rome and Paris. By the time he retired, there were FBN offices in Marseille, Beirut, and Istanbul with plans underway to open ones in Mexico City and Bangkok as well.

Anslinger was a patriot. During World War II he stockpiled tons of opium in the Treasury Department's vaults, enough to produce the morphine needed to meet the medical needs of American and allied soldiers alike. During the war he assigned twenty-five percent of his agents to protect domestic military bases from drug dealers. After the war, Anslinger detailed agents to General MacArthur's staff in Tokyo and to occupational forces in Germany to assist in post-war international drug control.

He also contributed to the development of an intelligence capacity within the War Department. He assigned some of his best agents to help William "Wild Bill" Donovan stand up the Office of Strategic Services, the predecessor agency of the CIA. One of his men acquired land for OSS training facilities — one site in Virginia, near Williamsburg, which is now known as Camp Peary; and another in Frederick County, Maryland, which is now called Camp David.

Anslinger was a diplomat. He was America's first observer to the League of Nations' Permanent Central Opium Board and for twenty-four years, seven of them while in retirement, he was our representative to the United Nations' Commission on Narcotic Drugs, chairing it for one year. He's credited with passage of the U.N.'s Single Convention that became the model for drug laws around the world, including our own Controlled Substances Act of 1970, which remains the law of the land to this day. He was considered by many of his contemporaries as the world's leading expert on international drug control.

Anslinger was the bane of the Mafia. If for no other reason, he should be remembered for that. The Mafia dons hated him. They called him "That old bastard" and "Ass-linger." No wonder! His relentless pursuit of them put more than three hundred organized crime felons behind bars. Anslinger fueled the 1951 Kefauver Hearings that first brought the Mafia to the public's attention. He supported prosecutions following the 1957 raid on the syndicate's meeting at Apalachin, New York. And it was FBN defendant / informant Joe Valachi who exposed the inner

☆ ☆

workings of the Mafia before the 1963 McClellan Hearings which forced a reluctant J. Edgar Hoover to finally admit that the La Cosa Nostra even existed.

When Anslinger learned that exiled "boss of bosses" Charles "Lucky" Luciano had slipped into Cuba, he told Fidel Castro that if Luciano was allowed to remain, all medical supplies to his island nation would be cut off. The then not-so-lucky Luciano found himself on the next Italy-bound boat. Shortly before he died, while poking a finger at Anslinger's picture in a magazine, Luciano blustered to an FBN undercover agent, "If it wasn't for that guy, I'd be back on top in New York."

Anslinger had his critics, other than the pro-marijuana legalization crowd. He lent an agent to the CIA in the 1950s to assist them in "Cold War" mind-control experiments, called MK Ultra, to determine the feasibility of using lysergic acid diethylamide, LSD, for those purposes. Some of the guinea pigs were volunteers; others were unsuspecting. The critics assume Anslinger knew everything that was going on. However, it would take a leap of faith to believe the CIA, or even his own agent for that matter, had told him everything. And even had he known it all, LSD wasn't classified as a Schedule 1 Controlled Substance until 1971, almost ten years after Anslinger had retired.

I was about to launch a crusade to try to restore the record and reputation of Harry Anslinger when I noticed an allegation on the Internet that gave me pause. He was being called a racist. Having already read so many misrepresentations and false allegations about Anslinger on the Internet, I had my doubts. However, I didn't want to champion him if that allegation was true, if for no other reason than out of respect for the many Black agents I had worked with during my career. For this reason, I resolved to find the truth.

CHAPTER 34

OUT FROM THE SHADOWS

If I was going to restore the record and reputation of Harry J. Anslinger, I would have to satisfy myself that he wasn't a racist. No easy matter.

The original accusation had stemmed from a 1940s Federal Bureau of Narcotics (FBN) wanted poster that described a rogue informant as a "ginger-colored nigger." A copy of the poster was among Anslinger's papers at Penn State's Paterno Library. I read where complaints about the poster had reached the White House and that several congressmen wanted his scalp. Whatever his explanation — an oversight, his signature auto-penned or signed off on by a subordinate in his absence — it must have satisfied Franklin Roosevelt because he kept Anslinger on the job. That didn't clear him in my mind by a long shot, but it did ease my concerns just a little.

Other accusations surfaced on the Internet. He was alleged to have called Mexican Americans "degenerate Spanish-speakers." But I was able to put that to rest when I read that those words had actually been taken from a letter sent to Anslinger by the editor of an Alamos, Colorado newspaper, and mistakenly attributed to Anslinger.

Then there was an accusation that he targeted a group of Black drug dealers for having had sex with white female students at a mid-western university to whom they had been selling marijuana. Anslinger related the investigation in his 1964 book, *The Protectors.*

The way I read it, the local FBN office had initiated the case after another student told police about the situation and vowed to break it up. Then a newspaper reporter threatened to break the story, raising concerns among university administrators about the damage an exposé would cause the students. The local police eventually arrested the principal marijuana dealer and two of his underlings for the unrelated burglary of a pharmacy, and that broke up the gang. There was no indication Anslinger had influenced the case in any way. In his account, Anslinger expressed support for improving race relations, saying that cause would not have been well-served had the case been exposed by the press, or led to prosecutions.

As I delved further, I realized Anslinger had actually been a pioneer in hiring minorities. During a time in our history when we separated ourselves from one another not only by wealth but by ethnicity and color, Anslinger deftly used his Civil Service "Schedule A" hiring authority to employ dozens of minorities for their "special skills." He often boasted, "Because criminals come in all sizes, shapes, and colors, so do our agents."

In 1930, he hired Special Agent Gon Sam Gue, believed to be the first Chinese American employed by any law enforcement organization in America. He hired Italian Americans, Arab Americans, Hispanic Americans, and at least one American Indian. A Jewish pharmacist became a trusted special assistant. And in 1950, before any other federal law enforcement agency had seen fit to do so, Anslinger hired the first African-American special agents, five of them, thirty in all during his tenure as commissioner.

I was able to track down one of those first five Black agents, William B. Davis. Davis had written a feature article in the 1992 edition of "The Connection," a publication of the DEA's Association of Former Federal Narcotics Agents (AFFNA), in which he described the indignities heaped upon him and other Black agents during his initial assignment to New York City. I drove to his home in Potomac, Maryland to ask him about it.

Bill was quite definite about his former boss. "Yes. There were racists in the old FBN," he said, "but Harry Anslinger was not one of them." Bill said he had personally met Anslinger four or five times during his twelve years with the FBN, and that each time Anslinger had treated him with respect. He said their final meeting came about after Anslinger had learned that Davis was planning to resign from the FBN. He had called the journeyman agent to his Washington office to ask him why. Bill's response to his questioning reflected his respect for Anslinger. "Because I want to be a diplomat like you," he said he had told Anslinger.

Davis said he cast about for a new path, and selected Anslinger's old home, the State Department, in which to continue his career. He spoke five languages, including Russian. It was a wise decision; Davis would retire after a distinguished career.

Contributing to the mischaracterization of Anslinger as a racist, in *The Strength of the Wolf,* author Douglas Valentine distorted Davis's story, saying Davis had quit the FBN because he had been held back from promotion because he was Black. Yes, he had been held back all right, but it had nothing to do with his race. Civil Service rules prohibited employees hired under "Schedule A," like Davis, from being promoted beyond the journeyman grade unless they first passed the Federal Service Entrance Examination. The State Department, being exempted from Civil Service rules, had no such restriction.

☆ ☆

During our conversation, I asked Bill about the case about which Anslinger had dedicated almost an entire chapter in his book, *The Protectors*. In it, Anslinger tells the story of Davis working undercover against members of the notorious 107th Street Gang of Italian mobsters in New York City, and credits Davis with taking down some of its key members, making him out to be the hero that he is — hardly the act of a racist. Davis knew nothing of the book. When I returned home, I mailed him a copy of the chapter.

During our meeting, Bill told me he had been the senior partner and mentor to another one of the FBN's early Black agents, one hired out of the mailroom in New York City. "I taught Art Lewis everything he knows," Bill said with a grin. Well, I thought, if that was so, he must have done a pretty good job because Lewis had risen to become an Acting Deputy Administrator of the DEA, and the Philadelphia Division's conference room is named in his honor.

I called the retired Art Lewis, for whom I worked during my last year in Philadelphia, and told him what Davis had said about his having taught him everything he knows. Art laughed but didn't deny it. Then I told Art the reason I visited Bill. I explained that based on my research, and particularly on Bill's comments, I was beginning to believe Anslinger had not been a racist at all. "What do you think?" I asked the man who I knew to have never had a problem speaking his mind.

"I think you're on the right track," Art said.

I later had the opportunity to speak with another one of the early Black agents, Bill Jackson. Joy and I sat at a table with Jackson and his daughters at a 2013 AFFNA Conference dinner in Reno, Nevada. I asked him what he thought of Harry

☆ ☆

Anslinger. Upon hearing his name, the elderly, disabled Jackson smiled, shook his head, and said, "He was tough."

We'll never know what was in Harry Anslinger's heart, whether he hired minorities solely for pragmatic reasons, to get the job done, or had some higher purpose in mind. What we do know is that Anslinger gave opportunity to many who otherwise would not have had it, and there's no evidence he ever disparaged a single one of them.

I have to admit, though, that Anslinger hadn't done so well on the distaff side. Anslinger shared the sentiment of the day that law enforcement was a man's world, although he did allow wives of agents to accompany them to undercover meetings. The only female FBN agent during Anslinger's era whom I ran across in my research was Helen Bass, the Special Agent-in-Charge of the FBN's Denver office. Bass was a personal friend of Eleanor Roosevelt who had apparently foisted Bass on Anslinger. However, Anslinger thought so highly of Bass that he used her in his campaign to get States to adopt the Uniform State Narcotics Act.

☆ ☆ ☆ ☆ ☆ ☆

In November 2012, after the citizens of Colorado and Washington State voted to legalize marijuana for recreational purposes, I said to Joy, "You know, Harry Anslinger must be rolling over in his grave." A week later, after attending a Penn State football game at Happy Valley, we stopped in Hollidaysburg, Pennsylvania on our way home.

Anslinger had been born in nearby Altoona and spent his final years in Hollidaysburg, dying in 1975 at the age of eighty-three. We found his former home downtown and then his grave alongside his wife's in the picturesque Presbyterian Cemetery overlooking the town. I was surprised at the modest headstone for a man of such great accomplishment.

I remembered reading in Professor McWilliams' biography that Anslinger had specifically requested a funeral service with only family and close friends in attendance. No government officials or foreign dignitaries were present to eulogize him, not even a representative from the DEA – probably to honor his wishes (or, perhaps, his estrangement from the DEA had already begun). It was while I was standing in the cemetery that I decided it was high time Anslinger be brought out from the shadows. However, my first attempt failed.

For more than twenty years I had been part of a group of Penn State alums, the Crime, Law and Justice Alumni Advisory Board, mentoring criminal justice undergraduate students. Each year I would sit through an awards ceremony during which, among others, the Society of Former Special Agents of the FBI presented one of its scholarships to some deserving Penn State student. Despite all his warts, they had named the scholarships for J. Edgar Hoover. Not only did the grants help the students, but garnered positive recognition for the FBI.

The DEA's retired agent's association had no such program. I proposed they start a similar, but more modest program considering the relative size of our two organizations and name the scholarships for Anslinger. Unfortunately, but understandably, the AFFNA Board decided to keep its limited funds focused on the noble cause of supporting the families of slain agents.

At a subsequent Crime, Law and Justice Alumni Board meeting, I asked our faculty advisor, Criminology Professor John Kramer, if he happened to know John McWilliams, the author of Anslinger's biography. To my delight, he told me that, by chance, their wives were best of friends. Kramer set up an opportunity

☆ ☆

for me to meet McWilliams over a drink, and then arranged a dinner with our wives to compare notes. Although McWilliams and I didn't agree on every aspect of Anslinger's career, our discussions gave me an idea.

I contacted Sean Fearns, Director of the DEA Museum, and proposed a lecture on Anslinger in the Museum's Lecture Series. I asked Professor McWilliams to be the keynote speaker and planned to deliver some remarks of my own. Standing in the Shadows: The Legacy of Harry J. Anslinger was presented on October 15, 2014.

Seventeen of Anslinger's descendants attended, pleased and proud to have their revered ancestor finally remembered. One nephew turned over to the museum some Anslinger memorabilia he had stowed away, and after the lecture spoke extemporaneously to the audience about recollections of his favorite uncle. By the way, Bill Davis also attended the lecture to prominently display his support for Anslinger.

The lecture can still be seen online at https://museum. dea.gov/video-archive/standing-shadows-anslinger. The DEA Museum also proudly displays artifacts from Anslinger's years at the helm. Some of them can be seen online at museum.dea.gov/ exhibits/online-exhibits/anslinger. Better yet, pay a visit to the newly-renovated museum — 700 Army-Navy Drive, Arlington, Virginia.

On one of my trips to Penn State, I stopped by Hollidaysburg to find a plaque that McWilliams had mentioned in the biography. The year after he retired, Hollidaysburg threw a party, Harry J. Anslinger Day. There was a picnic, testimonials, the high school band played, and the mayor unveiled a plaque for the hometown hero he promised would hang in the Blair County Courthouse in perpetuity.

But when I arrived at the courthouse to see it for myself, the plaque was nowhere to be found. The security guards shrugged. I inquired at the County Commissioners' office. None of them knew of it or had ever heard of Anslinger for that matter. I searched the hallways and found the holes in the wall where the plaque had once hung. The building engineer told me it might have been taken down during renovations some years back and ordered a search, but to no avail.

I located an *Altoona Mirror* news article from that day describing not only the appearance of the plaque but the exact wording on it. I found another ally in retired Special Agent Tom Raffanello, then president of the AFFNA Board, who agreed to have AFFNA fund the cost of duplicating it. On the bronze pages of an open book are words borrowed from a letter written by JFK at the time of Anslinger's retirement inscribed.

Plaque presented to Harry Jacob Anslinger.

Months later, a dozen of Anslinger's family members, all three Blair County Commissioners, the DEA Museum's Director, and the Resident Agent-in-Charge of the DEA's Harrisburg office joined me to watch the Hollidaysburg Mayor ceremoniously install the replica plaque on the courthouse wall at the very spot where the original had hung, along with a photo of Anslinger standing with John F. Kennedy in the Oval Office. A Penn State

☆ ☆

mentoring buddy, Robert Donaldson, agreed to periodically check on it to be sure it's not tampered with. Coincidentally, Robert's law office is located across the street from the Blair County Courthouse in a storefront that once housed a coffee shop frequented by Anslinger in retirement.

I would have preferred the DEA headquarters building be named for him but knew that wasn't going to happen. There had been one too many intervening reorganizations to tie him directly to the DEA. So, I wasn't disappointed when the DEA agreed instead to name the International Conference Room after him. I thought it fitting. I flew up to Washington to join with the DEA's deputy administrator, and several of Anslinger's family members for the dedication ceremony. His name is now on the door, and a plaque on the wall with his picture and the words from a letter written by Kennedy upon Anslinger's retirement:

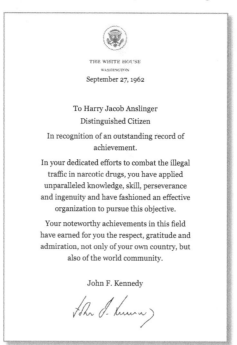

THE WHITE HOUSE
WASHINGTON
September 27, 1962

To Harry Jacob Anslinger
Distinguished Citizen

In recognition of an outstanding record of achievement.

In your dedicated efforts to combat the illegal traffic in narcotic drugs, you have applied unparalleled knowledge, skill, perseverance and ingenuity and have fashioned an effective organization to pursue this objective.

Your noteworthy achievements in this field have earned for you the respect, gratitude and admiration, not only of your own country, but also of the world community.

John F. Kennedy

In the DEA's first three anniversary books, its twenty-fifth, thirtieth and thirty-fifth, there hadn't been a single mention of Anslinger. For the fortieth anniversary book, I was asked to write his epitaph. It, and a comprehensive history of drug law enforcement going back to its earliest days, appears in the book.

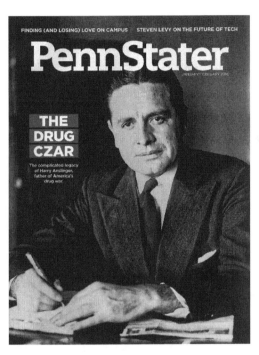

Penn Stater alumni magazine, "The Drug Czar,"
January/February 2018, reprinted with permission from the
Penn State Alumni Association.

Finally, I asked his Alma Mater to bring him out of the shadows as well. During my six years on Penn State's Alumni Council, I had the pleasure of getting to know the editor of the alumni magazine, *The Penn Stater*. Despite the controversy on college campuses concerning Anslinger's role in marijuana prohibition, it didn't take much to convince her that a story should be written about this 1959 Penn State Distinguished Alumnus. The cover story of the January/ February 2018 edition, titled "The Drug Czar: The Complicated Legacy of Harry Anslinger," tells the controversial story of his career, and the efforts to restore his name.

Harry J. Anslinger had been unfairly smeared with unsubstantiated allegations of racism to discredit him and thereby his cause. When the reputations of men and women are soiled, their accomplishments cheapened, and they are no longer around to defend themselves, it takes a concerted effort to repair the damage. Men like Anslinger helped shape our national character and make us into the nation we are. If we allow him, and others like him, to remain unfairly libeled and relegated to the shadows of history, we chance to forget what patriotism and good citizenship all are about.

A lot has changed in the almost sixty years since Anslinger retired. The Mafia's control of illegal drugs gave way to the drug lords of Southeast Asia, the Colombian cartel kingpins, Mexican drug gangs, and South Asian and Middle Eastern narco-terrorists. And over that span of history the BNDD and the DEA has had some remarkable successes, many that Harry Anslinger could never have imagined. But it was he and his FBN that paved our way. We can't afford to forget that.

But enough already of these unpopular causes!

☆ ☆

AFTERTHOUGHTS

I chose two giants of American history to bookend my memoir. I began with a quote from Theodore Roosevelt, whose image of rugged individualism and taming of the wilderness inspired me as a lad. And I ended it with the story of Harry Anslinger, the visionary of modern drug law enforcement who set the course for my career.

The pages in between reveal an insider's view of the three most controversial undertakings of my lifetime: the wars in Vietnam, on drugs, and against international terrorism, across five decades of federal government service. They became contentious despite their good intentions. It was their unintended consequences that became the problem.

VIETNAM

The Vietnam War began with good intentions. The Soviet Union had gobbled up Eastern Europe, including half of Germany. Nikita Khrushchev blazingly threatened nuclear annihilation, basing missiles at our very doorstep in Cuba. I recall sitting on the cloakroom floor of my elementary school classroom during air raid drills waiting for the all-clear bell to sound.

In Asia, China had fallen to Mao Zedong. And Harry Truman took a stand in South Korea to thwart communist aggression from the North, a conflict almost universally supported by the American public.

Facing a similar situation, Dwight Eisenhower sent military advisors to South Vietnam under an international accord to keep Soviet Union- and Chinese-backed Ho Chi Minh at bay until nationwide elections could be held to determine the country's future. However, after continual violations by North Vietnam,

☆ ☆

John Kennedy secretly increased the number of advisors to keep that domino from falling. As he put it, "Keeping South Vietnam free is our finger in the dike." And then a frustrated Lyndon Johnson sent conventional troops to try to cower the North Vietnamese to the peace table.

Although we never lost a major battle, we were unable to win a defensive war against an unconventional and elusive enemy. And being the honorable nation we are, we steadfastly refused to invade North Vietnam. That wasn't part of our mandate. Johnson's miscalculation, however, turned a peace keeping mission into a quagmire and, with a rising number of casualties, the American public against it. The enemy waited us out. We walked away, the first war in our history we hadn't won, a bitter pill to swallow.

But no matter the disappointment, we had demonstrated once again our willingness to fight to keep another ally free during a very hot Cold War, which perhaps forestalled communist aggression elsewhere in the world. Who knows what the map of Asia, perhaps of the world, would look like today had we not laid down a marker there?

I salute all my brothers who fought in Vietnam and sacrificed for the cause of freedom.

ILLICIT DRUGS

Although we have won many battles in the war on drugs, it may never end, already the longest conflict in our history. It is a noble cause, well worth fighting, not just for the health and wellbeing of Americans but for the dignity of mankind. Many entities are blamed for the predicament we are in.

Fingers point at drug producing countries. But they are victims of the scourge we have created, their institutions corrupted by the money our seemingly insatiable demand for mind-altering substances generates.

Many blame law enforcement for losing the war on drugs, failing to stop the criminal organizations that are literally killing one another for the privilege of satisfying our demand, while our citizens continue to pay to have drugs delivered to them. And when the drugs pollute our neighborhoods and kill our children, they complain that law enforcers haven't done enough.

But, the problem begins with the drug abuser. Police can reduce supply and make it riskier to deal in drugs. And while an overabundant supply can create its own demand, it can't account for the totality of the mess we've created for ourselves. It's a problem of supply and demand. And demand reduction isn't in the law enforcement toolbox.

So, some say legalization is the answer. However, surrendering to drug abuse is not a viable option. Not only will it make these stupefying drugs more readily available to demean even more of us, but bloat the welfare state with more addicts, and create a turned-on / tuned-out workforce. That doesn't bode well for an industrialized nation relying increasingly on technologically savvy workers. But our increasing tolerance for drug abuse is moving us in that direction. Marijuana is a good example.

Medical marijuana does have its benefits. There are medicines being produced from cannabis sativa L that reduce nausea and increase appetite for chemotherapy patients and treat MS-caused spasticity and certain forms of childhood epilepsy, and more are on the way. However, none of them are smoked. Smoking marijuana is not medicine.

Nevertheless, smoking pot is now legal for medicinal purposes in a majority of States, and some even allow it to be used recreationally. However, politicians and voters shouldn't be the ones deciding which substances constitute medicine; only the Food and Drug Administration should do that. And the FDA has said for years now that smoking marijuana has no medical use and a high potential for abuse.

TERRORISM

We didn't ask for the war with radical Islamic terrorists. It was bequeathed to us by generations past. We have reacted to our share of it with good intentions, a worthy cause to protect the life and limb of our citizens, the duty of every government. And we've won our share of battles. The strategy we adopted to fight terrorists abroad in their breeding grounds rather than have to confront them at home makes good sense. However, putting that plan into practice has been a classic example of "Do as I say, not as I do."

In the western world, nations have put its law enforcers in charge of combating domestic terrorism; in the developing world, militaries have been put in charge. Granted, it takes a military force to counter terrorists armed with military-style weapons, which is the case in many developing countries. However, terrorist organizations that cannot be destroyed on the battlefield must be dismantled in courts of law. And by putting most of our bullets down military barrels, the unintended consequence has been to empower and embolden institutions that have historically been the greatest threat to civilian control of governments in the third world.

This disparity between our support to soldiers and cops abroad should come as no surprise. We have a standing, active-duty military that can be deployed at the drop of a green beret, but no equivalent organization to aid foreign police. Those jobs are largely outsourced to a mish-mash of companies contracted

☆ ☆

by the Departments of State and Justice, who in turn hire mostly retired law enforcement officers to do the job. In Afghanistan we even turned police training over to the U.S. Army for a while, a dangerous precedent since they operate under quite different rules of engagement.

The long-term internal security of the citizens in the developing world rests with their police, not their militaries. A better balance needs to be struck.

☆ ☆ ☆ ☆ ☆ ☆

In common with elders of past generations, I too have worried about the next generation. However, having worked over the years with criminology undergraduate students and Army ROTC cadets at the Pennsylvania State University, and having been told of the caliber of special agents being graduated from the DEA's Basic Agent Training course, I am confident they will win their share of battles. But it will take enlightened leadership to win the broader political and social wars.

There are hundreds of books like this one with stories of the successes and failures of previous government undertakings. The study of these "lessons learned" can enable the next generation of leaders to pursue necessary and well-intended causes to protect our citizens and national interests and succeed with a minimum of unintended consequences — whether the causes are popular or not.

☆ ☆

ACKNOWLEDGEMENTS

I owe a debt of gratitude to my dear wife Joy Raye Lutz, née Cherwinski, who followed me to the far corners of the earth, giving up any thought of a career of her own in order to support me and to raise our two daughters. And thanks to daughters Amy Lyn Hallacher and Cindy Anne Quigley-Beauchamp who I dragged around the world until they went off to college, never quite knowing where to call home. They suffered through much disruption in their lives but seldom complained, and later in life eased my mind by saying those experiences had made them better persons. Joy, Amy and Cindy allowed me to pursue my dreams. I can only hope they have fulfilled a few of their own, and that many more will follow.

This book wasn't intended to be an autobiography, so short shrift was given to my upbringing. However, I haven't forgotten where I came from. Musicians both — my father, George Christian Lutz, a professional singer and church soloist who gave up any thought of fame and fortune to marry my mother Ruth Edith Lutz, née Quillen, a piano teacher, church organist and choir director — they raised my brother George Jr. and me in Southwest Philadelphia, first in a tiny two-bedroom apartment on Sansom Street, and then a small row home on Webster Street. We were poor, but they were rich in faith, role models for life. They also made me realize that musical talent often skips generations.

My father died while I was a freshman in college. He gave me my start in life, but didn't live long enough to see what kind of person I turned out to be. My mother lived to a ripe old age and rooted her entire life for George Jr. and me, even helping to pay for my college education with money she received in survivor benefit funds after my father's passing. A lovely person who adored her daughter-in-law and granddaughters, she played the organ at church and the piano at evening concerts for invalids at her assisted care living facility up until almost the day she died.

As for my writing, after a career of "just the facts, ma'am," it was Ruth Story who introduced me to creative writing in an Osher Lifelong Learning Institute memoir-writing course she called "True lies and Real Fiction." And thanks to my friends in Writers Ink, a creative writing club in the community of Keowee Key, for allowing me to bounce my stories off them — in particular the late Parky Dodge who encouraged me to write them, Ellen Mims who edited each one, and Dave Axelson for his critiques. Much appreciation to my sons-in-law Winston Beauchamp for many helpful suggestions and Craig Hallacher for his advice. And kudos to my professional editor, Frank Sabina, for his endless patience while polishing off the manuscript. Any errors are due to my stubbornness or faulty memory.

I am grateful for those who inspired me, taught me how to do my job, and helped shape my career, among them Peter Bensinger, Tom Cash, Fred Dick, Dick Johnson, Jack Lawn and Doug Wankel. And I thank colleagues Frank Balazs, Paul Brown, Walter Brown, Tom Byrne, Bob Cope, Dodge Galanos, Gary Fouse, Bill Glanz, Steve Greene, Dave Lodge, Mike Nerney, Cheryl and Al Nugent, Rick Scovel, Tim Steen, Doug Vance, Enrico Verdolin, Dave Westrate, and Penn State Professors John Kramer and John McWilliams for helping me with various aspects of the book.

And a special thanks to the long ago departed Lionel G. Stewart, without whom my career would have been much less productive and far less interesting!

☆ ☆

ABOUT CHARLES LUTZ

A Pennsylvanian by birth, Charles Lutz earned a B.A. in Political Science at the Pennsylvania State University in 1967, and in 2009 was named a Liberal Arts Centennial Fellow. He also undertook graduate studies in Criminal Justice at the Florida International University.

Although this is his first book, he has written articles published in the Weider History Group's *Vietnam* magazine and in his local newspaper. He ended full-time employment fifteen years ago and retired with wife, Joy, to the Golden Corner of western South Carolina where he carried out international consulting, private investigations, and State Department-contracted background investigations.

Now he mostly writes and plays at golf.

UNPOPULAR CAUSES

☆ ☆

UNPOPULAR CAUSES

☆ ☆

Made in the USA
Middletown, DE
06 July 2022

68628224R00201

CHAPTER 1

A NEW BEGINNING

Lyric

I sat in my room, staring out of the window. It was summer, and I spent most of it in my bedroom. After Daniel's funeral, I couldn't force myself to leave. Talking to Michael helped, but it wasn't enough. I felt so lost.

Tonight Lex planned to surprise Piper with a promise ring. The occasion should have been joyous, but it wasn't. I didn't want to leave, let alone celebrate. Uncle Noah and Dad couldn't persuade me to go. I wanted to stay at home.

Then I heard a knock on my door.

"Leave me alone, Dad! I'm not going!" I said, but the knocking continued. Finally, I answered my door. "Michael?"

"I heard someone wanted to be a hermit." He leaned against my door frame. I looked at him. He entered my room. "It's a pleasant room for a girl's room."

"What are you doing here?" I furrowed my eyebrows.

"I could ask you the same thing."

I sighed as I walked away from him. "I want to be alone."

"Why?"

I glance at him.

He walked towards me. "Why? Give me one excellent reason."

I stood there as he hammered at me with question after question until I snapped. "Because if I leave, then he's gone!" I looked at him as he looked at me, then I broke. "He left. Why did he leave? Why Michael? What did I do? Please tell me what I can do to bring him back?" I cried.

He wrapped his arms around me as I sobbed.

"You can't. Death is the end. I wish we could, but you can't. All you can do is keep going."

"But how? It's like I'm drowning." My body heaved with sobs.

"With help."

It was the first time I cried since Daniel died. I couldn't cry.

He held me and stroked my hair as I cried. Ma and Dad came to the door and watched us.

"Lyric, it'll get better. Take it minute by minute, hour by hour, and day by day. Some days will be good, and some will be bad. The good will outweigh the bad. It's grief, and it sucks."

I buried my head into his chest, wanting this pain to leave

We stayed there for a while. Having Michael here helped.

I stopped crying, and we sat on the floor with our backs against the bed.

"Do you feel better?" Michael asked me.

"That's the one hundred thousand dollar question."

"Lyric, it will get better. If you let me help you through this, I promise it will get better. Deal?"

He held out his hand. I sighed, placing mine in it. Then something weird happened. I felt a warmth I hadn't felt in a while. After Daniel, coldness surrounded me. It felt strange.

He released my hand and stood up. I followed suit.

"Now, why don't you get ready, and I'll meet you downstairs."

I nodded, and he left so I could change.

*****

"Well?" Maverick asked.

"She's changing. I can't guarantee she'll be happy," Michael said.

"It's a start," Dad said.

My door opened, and everyone watched as I came down the stairs in a summer dress. I wanted to get tonight over with and go back to my room.

We left and went to a place where Lex is giving Piper a promise ring. When we arrived, I sat alone. I didn't want to dampen the mood, but I also didn't want to bother.

Piper arrived, and Lex told her these beautiful romantic things. I wanted to gag. I sat there with a sour puss on my face as romance filled the air.

Then when Lex opened the box, revealing the ring, that was it for me. I got up and walked away. I know I should be happy, but I was anything but happy.

The restaurant was by water, so I watched the ripples. I took a seat, looking into the distance. The waves crashed upon the shore, calming me.

I sat there when I heard someone ask, "Beautiful, isn't it?"

"Are you following me?" I asked Michael.

"Nope. I thought I would go for a walk." He shrugged.

"Don't worry. I won't drown myself."

"Now, what would make me think that? You're a depressed individual dealing with a hell amount of grief."

I glanced at him as he smiled.

"You're strange."

"And you're exquisite for a sour puss." He made a face. "Look, I'm Lyric, who's a giant crab."

"Shut up!" I gave him a playful shove.

"Then lighten up. Yes, someone died, but you didn't. You're still alive. So, start living." Michael gave me a soft smile.

"You won't stop until I agree, will you?"

"Nope."

"Good luck because you'll need it."

"Hmm. I accept your challenge."

I stared at him as he stood up and walked away.

What the hell did that fool have planned? My guess is nothing good. What did I get myself into with Michael?

*****

Michael

I walked up.

"Well?" Major asked.

"Lyric thinks she crawled into that grave with Daniel, but I won't let her. She deserves to live, love, and laugh again," I said.

"What do you have planned?" Maverick asked me.

"I'll show her how to live again because she isn't living. She exists. She should enjoy her life, not let life pass her by. Daniel may have had problems, but she doesn't deserve to deal with them." I walked away.

Major looked at Maverick. "That isn't good."

"Nope," Maverick said as he looked back at him. "Michael doesn't like when someone else gets dragged down by another. Now excuse me. I have a temperamental person to deal with in the form of Larkin."

"Good luck, brother." Major chuckled.

Maverick went to find Larkin. No one understood what was going on with those two.

CHAPTER 2

CHALLENGE ACCEPTED

Lyric

I awoke to someone staring at me.

"Ack!" I fell out of bed.

"Aww, that's so sweet you fell for me. Although, it's way too soon." Michael leaned over the bed.

I glared at him and got up in a huff. "Why are you here?"

"Well, it's your bedroom."

"I know, you dolt! Why are you standing in my bedroom?" I stomped my foot.

"Because you need to get up, although you look cute when you drool and your face is all contorted, but I digress. Get dressed."

"What if I don't want to get dressed?"

"Oh, it's not a request. Either you dress, or I'll dress you." Michael smirked, crossing his arms.

"You wouldn't?"

"Do you want to find out?" He arched an eyebrow.

"Nope

"Excellent choice." He turned and left my room, closing the door behind him. What is wrong with this guy?

I got dressed and walked out of my bedroom. Then I made my way downstairs. He was waiting for me as Ma and Dad watched us. I walked over to him with my arms crossed. "Okay, I got dressed now. Can I go back to my room?"

"Why? So, you can mope all day? I don't think so." He grabbed my hand and dragged me out of the house. We started arguing as he closed the door.

"Why do I have a feeling I'll have to talk to him?" Dad asked Ma.

"Because you will." She giggled.

"Isn't he too old for her?"

"Nash, there is no age limit with love." She shrugged, walking away.

*****

I got into Michael's car. I didn't want to be here and tried to stay locked away, not wanting to go out. I wanted people to leave me alone.

He got in and pulled out as I crossed my arms and sat there. I didn't know where we were going and didn't care. I didn't want to be here.

Michael drove until he pulled into a parking spot.

"Where are we?" I looked around.

"You'll see. Come on." He got out of the car and started walking up a path. Great. He left me here to die. Fine, so be it. I sat there and stewed until I heard a noise. Screw that. I refuse to have a bear eat me. Not today, Yogi, not today.

I ran up the path until I found Michael. He was sitting on a rock, looking out over the city. I took a seat next to him.

"I came here after my parents died, and Uncle Mike came and got us. I couldn't stand the hovering, but I also knew I had to take care of my sister and cousins. I couldn't let them go to foster care. My parents would have hated it, and so would have my aunt and uncle."

"Didn't you grieve?"

"When I was alone, I grieved. I couldn't do it in front of my family while they were grieving. Mia would cry herself to sleep every night. Major and Maverick were on a downward spiral. None of us managed our grief well, so I remembered what my dad said."

"What was that? Live."

"No, grieve." Michael looked at me. "Grieve, cry, get angry, but grieve. Allow yourself to feel pain, then when you do, remember that you still have to live."

I stared at him.

"Lyric, get angry, cry, let it all out, but don't jump into that grave with him."

"I can't."

"Why not?"

"Because I can't! Then it means he is dead! He's never coming back! I hate him so much! Why did he leave? Why Michael? What did I do to make him leave? Why?" I started sobbing. I was so angry, yet so lost.

He pulled me to him. "You did nothing. It wasn't your fault."

"But he said he loved me. If he loved me, then why did he leave me?" I sobbed.

"Because he was sick. Daniel had problems no one could stop. Even if you tried, it would still have happened. Lyric, you're suffering from a broken heart. It's okay. We all deal with a broken heart in our lives." He stroked my hair as I cried.

That's all I could do.

Michael was right. I needed to grieve, and that's what I did. I grieved.

*****

Over the next few weeks, I cried. Michael sat with me as I cried. He offered comfort in a way I never expected. When you suffer a loss like us, it bonds you together.

I hope one day, I'll stop crying.

*****

I woke up, rubbed my eyes, and sighed. I rolled over and hugged my pillow as my door opened, and in walked Michael. He walked over and took a seat on the bed next to me.

"Good morning, sunshine," Michael said.

"You are way too chipper in the morning. Do you know that?"

"Well, someone has to be since you're a gloomy Gus." He grinned.

I laughed at his ridiculous grin.

"Ha! I got you to laugh!"

I buried my head into my pillow and groaned. "I don't want to laugh."

"It's too late. You already did." Michael smirked. Ugh, I wanted to kill him for making me laugh, but I accepted defeat. I rolled onto my back.

"Fine, you win. What do you have planned for today?"

"The beach. Get dressed." He got off the bed. "Oh, and wear a nice bikini." He closed the door.

Okay, so Michael's a perve. Fantastic.

I threw off the covers and crawled out of bed. I changed and realized I had lost weight. I ate a little because I hadn't been hungry. I secured my bathing suit so it didn't fall off, then I put on a top and shorts.

I grabbed my bag and walked out of my room. I didn't know why my family felt the need to go to the beach. The last time I was at the beach was with Daniel. I refused to go back. It was too hard. I didn't even know why I was going today.

*****

We pulled into the parking lot and got out of the car. My siblings and cousins were already there, along with Michael's family.

He looked at me. "Ready?"

"No, but I don't have a choice." I didn't want to be here.

"Nope." He smiled, walking towards them.

We walked up, and everyone was having fun.

"It looks fun," he said.

I stood there.

"But then again, if you prefer not to have fun, I can't make you." He shrugged.

I furrowed my brows at him.

"But you're more fun out of your siblings, or was that Lakin. Eh, I can't keep you, girls, straight." He walked away.

"Wait. What?" I ran after him. "Hold up!" I ran over and grabbed his arm, stopping him. "I am way more fun than Lakin or the others."

"Oh, yeah?"

"Yeah!"

"Then prove it." He walked away.

Ugh, I will prove to him I am way more fun than my siblings.

"What is he doing?" Larkin asked Maverick.

"What Michael does best. Proving someone wrong." He smirked.

I ran and jumped on Michael's back. He stumbled forward before regaining his balance.

"Excuse me, but I didn't order a monkey on my back."

"Too bad, now give me a piggyback ride."

"Well, if you insist." He shrugged.

Ha! Take that!

Then he hooked my legs with his arms and took off running. He ran into the water and jumped in with me still on his back. While we were in the water, he let go of me.

He popped his head, as did I.

"Michael!"

"You said piggyback ride. You didn't specify where." Michael smiled. Damn it.

Then he started splashing me.

"Stop it!"

"Nope." He swam over to me and picked me up, tossing me into the water.

"Michael!"

That was it. I got tired of Michael's shit, so I swam after him. We played in the water as the others watched us. Then they heard laughter.

"It's good to hear her laugh again," Marshall said.

"Yeah, it is," Lex said.

I couldn't help but laugh as we tried to outdo each other. It felt good to laugh again.

*****

I sat on the beach, watching the sunset, when Michael took a seat next to me.

"Thank you," I said, glancing at him.

"For what?"

"For this, it felt good to laugh." I moved my hand through the sand.

"I'm glad." He smiled. We sat there in silence for a few minutes before he said, "You have a beautiful smile. You should show it more often." He stood up and walked away.

My eyes widened as my jaw dropped, watching him walk away. Oh, boy.

CHAPTER 3

LEARNING TO GO ON

Lyric

After the day at the beach, I started feeling like myself a little more. I even went for a run.

I ran down the street, letting the sun warm my skin, and the fresh air filled my lungs. The feeling was incredible. The birds chirped, and sprinklers turned on. As I kept stride, someone ran next to me. I knew who it was.

As we ran, keeping an even stride, we spoke nothing. We didn't need to. Having Michael here was enough for me.

We ran until we stopped to catch our breaths.

"If you wanted to take a run, all you had to do was ask. All this chasing you is tiresome." Michael grinned, causing me to snicker.

We started walking. "It's funny." My breathing calmed.

"What is?"

"It's the first time I've wanted to go running. Everything seems like it's new." I looked ahead.

"Because it is. When you suffer a loss, it changes you. You aren't that same person as you were, but don't allow it to consume you."

"I see that. I felt so lost. How do you go on when you're grieving?"

"You do."

We walked. With Michael around, I felt more like myself. There was something about him.

We stopped and got breakfast. We ordered our food.

"When's the last time you ate?" Michael asked.

"I don't know. Why?"

"Lyric, you've lost weight."

"I know. I haven't been hungry."

"But you need to eat. When you're grieving, everything feels like an effort. Trust me. You need to take care of yourself."

The server returned with our food, and we started eating. I couldn't believe how hungry I was. I devoured everything on my plate as Michael glanced at me.

When we finished, he paid the bill. I protested, but he wouldn't hear of it. He was happy I was eating.

We got up and walked out of the diner, making our way back to my house. We said bye and parted, but a part of me didn't want him to leave. I furrowed my brows.

I entered the house. What was happening to me? Why does it feel like a part of me left when Michael wasn't here? I brushed off the thought. It was dumb.

*****

That night I awoke with a nightmare. I needed to get out of here. I climbed out of my window and walked in the darkness.

My bare feet moved along the cold cement until I found myself in front of a house. I knocked on the door.

There wasn't an answer. I kept knocking until someone answered. "Lyric?"

I stood there as Michael rubbed his eyes. Once he focused, he saw me standing there in my bare feet and pajamas.

"Another nightmare?"

I nodded.

"Come on." He ushered me inside, closing the door and leading me to his room. Once inside, he closed the door. I climbed into his bed. He followed suit, crawling in next to me.

I laid down, and he laid down behind me as he wrapped his arm around me. I snuggled into him as I drifted off to sleep.

I had told no one about the nightmares except for Michael. Most nights, I found myself at his door, needing comfort. He offered without hesitation.

It was the only way I could sleep. My parents didn't know until they found me gone one morning. Michael told them what was happening. They left me alone.

I awoke the following day as Michael was still sleeping. His door opened, and Maverick gave us a look and shook his head as he chuckled.

"You know, at some point, you both need to admit you like each other," Maverick said.

"Maverick?"

"Yeah?"

"Go away."

Maverick laughed, closing the door.

"He's right," someone said.

I saw Michael awake.

"What?" I asked.

He rubbed his face. "Not that I don't enjoy our late-night cuddle sessions and all. Is there a reason you keep showing up at my door all hours of the night?"

"I couldn't sleep." I got out of bed.

He propped himself up. "Lyric?"

I started pacing. "I don't know! It's like I have these feelings that I shouldn't have! I shouldn't be feeling these things for you! But I do! And I don't know what to do! I don't want to feel things!" I paced.

Michael got out of bed and walked over to me. I paced, trying to avoid him, but it was no use. He pulled me to him as I squirmed. "Look at me, Lyric."

I moved in his arms as his hand caressed the side of my face. I turned my head into his palm. His warmth was terrific as he tried to capture my eyes with his.

Then he leaned in, and I closed my eyes as he pressed his lips against mine. I fought but finally gave in to him. He wrapped his arms around me as I wrapped my arms around his neck.

The kiss was sweet, like him. I melted into it as our lips moved in sync with each other. I never wanted it to end.

Then he pulled back and looked into my eyes.

"You have to stop fighting this," Michael said.

"I'm scared."

"I know, but I promise not to hurt you. Lyric, I like you, and I want to be with you. We can take it as slow as you like."

"What about school?"

"What about it?"

"I'm leaving in a few weeks."

"So?"

"So, you aren't coming." I furrowed my brows.

"Who says?"

"What?"

"I'm going to school, along with everyone else. I spoke to my uncle. My parents and Major and Maverick's parents left him in charge of our trust fund. He told me to go."

I had no words. All I could do was smile at Michael. He smiled back before leaning in and kissing me again. Slow was good. I could manage slowly.

*****

We sat on the bed while I played with my fingers. It was something I did when I was nervous, and Michael was making me nervous right now.

"Lyric?"

"Huh?"

"What's wrong?"

"Nothing."

"I've spent enough time with you to know when something is bothering you."

"Nothing is bothering me."

He placed his hand on mine. "Lyric?"

I hated how he could see right through me.

"Okay, I think you're much older than me, and it feels weird. Does it feel weird to you?"

"No."

"Oh."

"Look, I know I'm six years older. Trust me. Age is a number. I'm still that same guy who sat with you at the funeral, staying with you when you didn't want to go out and letting you cry."

Michael's hair fell onto his forehead. He had the prettiest blue eyes with a close-cropped beard defining his jawline. He could look at you with an intensity that could make you squirm yet soft to make you comfortable.

Compared to when he was sixteen, he had grown into a man with more sophisticated features. He was stunning, and he terrified me.

"I like you, Lyric. I've always had. When I first met you, I thought nothing of it, but getting to know you this past summer made me like you more. It's scary to let yourself feel again, but trust me, it's worth it."

"Can I ask you a question?"

"Anything."

"Did you have a girlfriend?"

"I did. I had a couple. But after my parents died, the one I was seeing couldn't manage my grief. Plus, she didn't like the fact I had to take care of three other people. In her words, I wasn't serious about us."

"I'm sorry to hear that."

"Don't be. I don't need someone in my life who wants to be selfish. I know it sounds harsh, but that's my family. They had lost someone, too."

He slid his hand into mine, intertwining our fingers.

"I can't tell you, it'll be easy, but I'll tell you, it'll be worth it. Take it day by day."

"Okay."

What did I have to lose? I already sunk to the depths of despair. There was only one to go, and that was up.

CHAPTER 4

TAKING IT SLOW

Lyric

I wasn't sure how to feel. Was it too soon? Is it too intense? Is Michael too old for me? Ugh, I hated this. I felt like I was betraying Daniel.

I threw myself onto my bed. I was so confused. I'm having feelings for Michael that I shouldn't have. I know he said we would take it slow, but I didn't know what to do.

My door opened, and someone laid down next to me.

"No offense, but if you smother yourself, you're doing it wrong," Larkin said.

I turned to face her.

"I'm just saying."

I placed my face back into the pillow. "Lark, I'm so confused."

"About what?"

"Michael kissed me."

"Excuse me. Repeat what you said."

I sighed, lifting my head. "He kissed me. Twice."

"Isn't there some rule about locking lips with another guy when your boyfriend dies? Like a waiting period?"

"That's the dumbest thing I ever heard."

"Well, excuse me, it's not like I know a lot about these things."

"Know what?" Lakin asked.

She and Luna walked into the room.

"Lyric is sucking face with Michael as her dead boyfriend is resting in peace. Well, at least, I hope it's in peace. Can you go to heaven for being selfish?" Larkin asked.

"Who cares about the philosophical aspect? I want to know more about this kiss," Luna said, jumping onto my bed.

Lakin stood there.

"I can't talk about this," I said, standing up.

"Why not?" Luna asked.

"Because it's wrong," I told her.

"How is it wrong?" Lakin asked me.

"I don't know. It is," I said.

Everything was confusing me.

"Lyric, Daniel died. He's not coming back. Do you want to stop from being happy because of your feelings for a dead person?" Larkin asked me.

I sighed.

"Look, no one says you have to rush into anything, but at least, give him a chance," Lakin said.

It's easier said than done.

＊＊＊＊＊

I heard Dad say, "Lyric! Michael's here!"

I looked at my sisters wide-eyed. Uh-oh.

I couldn't talk to him, so I did the only thing possible. I climbed out of my window and made my way to the tree next to it. Thank God that tree was there.

I shimmied my butt down as my door opened.

"Maverick?" Larkin asked.

"Did she leave through the window?" He asked.

"Nope, she disappeared into thin air."

Maverick gave her a look as she smirked.

I made my way down the tree. As soon as my feet hit the ground, I turned and screamed. Michael stood there.

"Don't do that!" I grabbed my chest.

The guy almost gave me a freaking heart attack.

"Then don't leave through the window." He shrugged.

I gave him a look.

"Is there a reason you needed to exit through your window and not the door?"

"I'm practicing my lumberjack skills. You never know when you'll need to climb a tree and chop it down."

"Everyone knows lumberjacks are in outrageous demand." He shrugged.

"Exactly." I tried to walk by him, only for him to catch my wrist and pull me to him. My heart thumped. He held me close to him. Damn, he smelled nice.

He moved a strand of hair from my face as he looked into my eyes. Being this close to him was making me feel so many things.

"Kiss him already!" I heard Luna say.

My sisters had their heads sticking out of my window, along with Maverick.

"Yeah, kiss me already," he said.

I tried to resist, but the more he looked at me, I leaned into him until our lips met. Our kiss started slowly. Then he deepened it. I wrapped my arms around his neck as he wrapped his arms around my back.

Michael did something to me. Being here with him felt so right.

As we kissed on my front lawn, Lex and Piper stopped and watched. My parents opened the front door and saw us.

We stood there, kissing as our lips moved in sync against each other. Not even Daniel kissed me like that.

Dad shook his head as he turned and went back into the house. Ma giggled as she followed him.

Lex and Piper walked by laughing. My sisters and Maverick smiled as Michael kissed me, and I kissed him back. At that moment, nothing mattered except for us in front of my house.

He pulled back. "So, about taking it slow."

I smiled.

*****

Over the next few weeks, that's what Michael and I did. We took it slow. Michael showed me things that amazed me.

We would go for runs and breakfast. We would take walks as Michael held my hand and talked. When I had a nightmare, I would show up at his house and crawl into bed with him, snuggling up. He never turned me away but held me.

We would see movies and have dinner, but we spent time together. Michael showed me how to live and not exist. For that, it made me grateful. I was so glad he came into my life when he did because I needed someone and that someone was Michael.

"You're quiet," I said as we walked along the riverbank, hand in hand.

"I'm thinking."

"About?"

He stopped and turned to me. "Us."

"What about us?"

Please don't tell me this is over. I looked at Michael with hope.

He squinted his eyes, licked his lips as he thought about it. "I want to make us official."

"What?"

"I want you to be my girlfriend." He leaned into me.

"Are you sure?"

"Yes, unless you have other plans." He shrugged as he walked away.

Wait. Did Michael leave me hanging?

I ran after him and jumped on his back. I wrapped my arms around his neck as he stopped.

He turned to me. "Is that a, yes?"

"What do you think?"

He lifted my legs as he started walking, giving me a piggyback ride. I nuzzled into his neck as I held on tight. With Michael, he would show me a whole another way of life, and it excited me for once in my life.

CHAPTER 5

ONWARD AND UPWARD

Lyric

Today we headed to school. Our parents, along with our aunts and uncles, were helping us get situated. Starting over felt weird. So much has happened since we graduated. I didn't think I would ever feel like myself again. Then Michael came. I was still cautious about us.

I had been so enamored and in love with Daniel. His death left a big void in my life. How do you allow yourself to love someone? In the back of your mind, there's a chance it could end at any moment. That question lurked in my mind.

We drove to the college, which was three hours from our home. When we pulled into the town, it was different. Dad drove us by the college, and I looked at Saintwood College. That was an unusual name.

We made our way to our prospective houses. The Bobbsey twins were staying with us. Wasn't that special?

The others had their own house while the Harper family had theirs. Daniel would be staying with Uncle Nathan and Uncle Noah's kids. Sigh.

"Lyric? Are you okay?" Dad looked in the rear-view mirror.

"Yep, I'm peachy," I said.

The others looked at me as I stared out of the van's window. It will be a long year.

＊＊＊＊＊

We pulled into the driveway and got out. I stood in front of the house, looking at it. Then two hands rubbed my shoulders.

"I'm sure the house isn't going anywhere," Michael said.

"You're right. Houses rarely move." I faced Michael as he placed his hands on my shoulders.

"It's okay. I know."

"You're not mad."

"Nope, I'm as cool as a cucumber."

"Michael."

"Lyric, it's okay. I know you're thinking about him. But give yourself time. I'm not going anywhere." He leaned into me, smiling.

"Come on, love birds, these boxes won't move," Nixon said, walking by us.

Thanks, Uncle Nixon, for that inspiring moment.

We grabbed a box, taking them inside. I cannot wait for the parental units to leave.

I walked into a room and set a box down, as did Michael. I checked out everything.

"I'm sure you won't find treasure if that's what you're seeking."

"Don't hate. I like to check out my surroundings when I'm in a new place." I checked the closet.

It was a standard room with a bed and a dresser. I closed the door and stood there while two hands rubbed my shoulders.

"It seems overwhelming. When you get into the swing of things, you will be fine."

I let out a sigh as he moved his hands from my shoulders to around my waist as he slid them around to the front. He rested his chin on the top of my head.

"I know it'll be fine, and things will get better. I'm…"

"You're what?"

"I don't know. I don't even know how to explain it."

I knew what I wanted to say, but I didn't know how to get the words out. It terrified me. It scared me being away from home, and of these feelings, I was having for Michael.

I needed him to tell me it would be okay. I needed him to say it was okay to feel this way. I needed to know it's okay to feel this way because I was drowning.

"Look at me, Lyric." He made eye contact with me. "It will be okay."

"Will it? Because it feels like I am drowning."

"Yes."

I wasn't so sure until he took my hand and led me out of the room. We walked past everyone as they watched us, and he didn't say a word. I couldn't even say anything.

We walked down the stairs. As we passed my parents, along with Nixon and Kat, he said, "Lyric and I are going for a walk. We'll be back in a little while."

With that, we left.

Dad watched us. "As much as I would like to set him straight, I'm more worried about her."

"Nash, it'll be okay. He's the best person for this situation," Ma said.

"I'm worried, Mags."

"Brother, we're all worried about her, but I don't think he'll hurt her," Nixon said.

"Why do you say that?" Dad asked.

"Because I'm sure Noah will get to him first before you do." He said, walking past them.

Ma giggled.

Dad rolled his eyes. "Come on. Let's bring the rest of this stuff in."

*****

Michael

As we walked, Lyric didn't say much. I understand the place she was in because I had been in it myself after losing our parents. Even though she seemed like she was back to her old self, she wasn't, and I knew it. That would take time.

Death is an interesting concept. You become stronger or sink deeper than you should. Lyric was stronger than she realized. She needed to understand that.

We walked, hand in hand, not saying anything. Lyric needed time to breathe, so why not take a walk and check things out. What could it hurt?

We made it to town and came across a bakery. Perfect.

We entered. An older woman greeted us.

"Welcome to Kate's Bakery. What can I do for you?" The woman asked.

"Can we get two coffees and two muffins? I'll have the apple, and she'll have the blueberry," I told the woman.

"Sure. Have a seat, and I'll bring out your order." The woman walked to the counter.

We found a table and sat down. It was a quaint bakery, and the woman was warm and friendly.

As we sat there, she brought our stuff, then took a seat. Lyric stared at her.

"So, are you doing better?" The woman asked Lyric.

Lyric knitted her brows.

"Oh, forgive me. I'm Kate. I'm the one who helped your parents open their bakery. I heard it had burned down, but they're rebuilding," Kate said. Lyric's face softened, then the woman turned to me. "Michael, why haven't you called me?"

"I've been busy." I picked up my cup, taking a sip.

Kate looked at me, then at Lyric. "Yeah, I know."

I shrugged.

She turned to Lyric. "Sweetheart, what you're going through right now is normal, but don't let it consume you. Grieve if you must, but at some point, move on."

"You sound like you understand," she said.

"I do. I lost someone I loved very much. I didn't think I would ever feel better or myself, but I got back to my old self with love and support. Well, not exactly my old self, but I could move on."

"Did you ever meet anyone after everything that happened?"

She gave Lyric a soft smile. "No, but that doesn't mean you shouldn't. Give it time. The right person will understand." She glanced at me while I sipped my coffee.

*****

Lyric

Michael sipped his coffee and smiled. I narrowed my eyes at him as Kate got up and made her way to the back. Why does it feel like this was a setup? Because it was.

That little sneak. I knew what Michael was trying to do. Hmm, two can play that game.

"I see what you're doing," I told him.

"I don't know what you mean."

"You do, too."

"Nope, not a clue."

"You do so. You're trying to get me to open up more and let you in." I wiggled my finger at Michael.

"For one to open up, one must be open, which, my dear, you aren't." He picked up his muffin and took a bite.

"I am so."

"Nope."

"Yes."

"No."

"Yes."

"Nope, I don't believe you. Try again."

He was making me angry.

"I do so!"

He put his muffin down, leaned forward. "Prove it."

Something ignited inside of me. Without thinking, I grabbed Michael's shirt and yanked him to me as I crashed my lips into his. At that moment, I realized what he had been doing. He was challenging me to give in to my feelings I had thought only existed for Daniel. What I felt for Michael was different.

A desire and passion unlocked and ignited inside me, which wasn't there with Daniel. Yes, I loved Daniel, but it was different. But with Michael, the unknown scared me.

Do I embrace the unknown or not? I wasn't so sure.

CHAPTER 6

JUMPING INTO THE DEEP END, FEET FIRST

Lyric

After our great kiss, we broke free and sat down in our seats. As we ate, we couldn't stop smiling. Once we finished, we tossed our stuff into the garbage can and left.

We walked back to the house, and this time, I slid my hand into Michael's as we walked. I tried to act nonchalant about it, but deep inside, I was bouncing around.

After we returned, Michael kissed me and left. I didn't want him to leave.

I walked inside, to a bunch of grinning twits, except for Dad. Dad doesn't smile, not with boys.

"What?" I asked.

"Did you have an enjoyable time?" Luna asked me.

"It was okay." I shrugged, walking past them and running upstairs to my room. I didn't want to deal with a million questions. I wanted to unpack and think about today.

It didn't take long before I set up my room. It was doable.

I opened the door to have my sisters and Piper fall into my room.

"Can I help you?" I asked everyone.

"We came to see if you needed help," Lakin said.

"No, I'm all set," I said with a look.

They got up, and Larkin asked, "Then do you mind telling us why you have a goofy-looking grin on your face?"

"I don't have a goofy-looking grin on my face," I said.

"Because you look like someone who got a puppy."

"A puppy?"

"I'm having an off day, okay?" Larkin rolled her eyes at me.

I shook my head.

"So, what's going on with you and Michael?" Luna asked.

"I don't know." I shrugged.

"What do you mean, you don't know? You do, or you don't," Larkin told me.

"Michael stirs something inside of me I've never experienced. It's like he understands me better than I understand myself." I sat on my bed. "And it scares the hell out of me."

"Lyric, do you like Michael, or are you afraid to allow yourself to like him because of Daniel?" Piper asked me.

"A little of both." I sighed.

"Look, I know you're scared. But trust me. My cousin only has the best intentions. He won't hurt you. When he cares, he cares deeply. It's the same when he loves someone," Piper said.

That's when it happened. I made a break for it.

They ran after me, calling my name as Dad followed suit. I whipped open the door, only to smack right into someone and fall backward. I looked up.

"We need to have a conversation about you falling for me," Michael said, leaning over me.

I glanced at him and laid back down.

＊＊＊＊＊

Michael

I sat on the couch in the living room while everyone hung out in the kitchen as Lyric paced, rambling. I learned with her that when something confuses her, she rambles a lot.

I sat there as she kept rambling. I saw the others poking their heads out of the door. With this family, you can't hide anything.

I looked back at her as she took a deep breath.

"Are you done?" I asked.

"I guess."

I stood in front of her. "Okay, now that you had your turn, now it's mine. I don't care what reason you think this won't work because I know it will. How do I know? Because I know you."

"No, you don't."

"Okay, let me give it a shot."

She crossed her arms. "Fine."

"You like rock music, but when you're feeling romantic, you like love songs. Your favorite color is purple. The color of your eyes is like the color of the sky. You like stupid comedies, which most people don't understand. You enjoy writing and have journals upon journals of it. You don't have the patience for frivolous things or people. How am I doing?"

"Okay, fine. So, you know basic stuff about me. You still don't know me."

"Oh? You bite your bottom lip when you're nervous. When you're confused, you pace and ramble. You shut down when you're sad and get super excited when you're happy. I know your siblings, along with your family, are everything to you. I also know you're close to your Uncle Noah because you're like him. How about now?"

"Um, well, uh." She bit her bottom lip.

I stepped closer to her and pulled her close to me. I took my hand and pulled her chin so she was looking at me. "You can find every reason this won't work, but I'll find every reason it will."

Her mouth opened, but no words escaped.

"Lyric, I know you're scared, but you don't have to be. When someone cares about you, they'll do everything they can to be with you. No matter what you say or how hard you push me away, I'll push back that much harder. I'll wait until you give in and realize I'm not going anywhere." I leaned down and kissed her. She resisted at first before wrapping her arms around my neck, kissing me back.

I threw everything into that kiss like I have every time. I wanted Lyric to know how I felt. They say actions speak louder than words. I'm sure my efforts were speaking loud and clear.

We broke from our kiss as I leaned in. "You're mine, and I'll take excellent care of you." Then I leaned back, watching her face turn pink.

"And what if I don't want to be yours?"

"Oh, you do because I'm the only one that has ever made you blush." I smirked.

She looked at me, wide-eyed.

Michael 1 Lyric 0.

*****

Lyric

I stood in stunned silence. I've never dealt with someone so sure of themselves. Michael had this unexplained confidence in himself that left me in awe.

No matter how hard I pushed him away, he pushed back harder to prove to me he wasn't going anywhere. Do I allow myself to give in and see the possibilities? Do I keep pushing until he finally gives up and leaves?

The thought of him leaving and never seeing him again tore me apart, and I couldn't help but cry. He pulled me closer as I buried my head into him and cried. That's when I realized I didn't want to lose him.

Ever since the funeral, he has always been there. When I have nightmares, he lets me sleep with him, making me feel like everything is okay. He listened to me cry and never once turned me away. He comforted me in a way I never thought possible. I didn't want to lose him. He meant way too much to me.

"Don't leave me."

"Leave you? Yeah, that won't happen."

I looked at him with tear-streaked cheeks. "Huh?"

"Sorry, sweet cheeks, but you're stuck with me." He smirked as I stared at him. "That means I'm not going anywhere, except down the aisle to an altar when I marry you."

My eyes widened as he smiled. Did he say marry me? Ah, hell. Here we go.

"But don't worry, we have plenty of time until that happens. We need to start with our first date, don't you think?"

All I could do was nod.

Then Dad came out of the kitchen and into the living room. "Did you say what I think you said?"

We looked at Dad as the others followed him.

"Let me get this straight. You're planning on marrying Lyric?" Dad asked Michael.

"We'll go on a date so I can work my magic on her." He smiled.

Dad's eyes narrowed as his jaw and his fists clenched. That was so not good.

Maverick walked over. "I would suggest you duck right now."

"What?" Michael turned and looked at Maverick. Before he knew it, he turned and got met with Dad's fist. He fell onto the floor.

"Dad!" I spoke.

"I told you to duck," Maverick said.

"Nash!" Ma said.

"Where's popcorn when you need it?" Nixon smirked.

My siblings and cousins rolled their eyes.

I helped Michael up as he rubbed his jaw. "Dad, you can't keep hitting guys I care about!"

"Lyric, you're my daughter. It's my job to protect you, your sisters, and your brother," he said.

"And you're doing a bang-up job at it," Larkin said.

"Not now, Larkin!" Dad said.

"Excuse me, but the last time I checked, we're Grays. Even though we're girls and Lex acts like a girl," I told Dad.

"Hey!" Lex said.

I looked at Lex. "Oh, give it up. You act worse than when Lakin's on her period."

He glared at me, and I rolled my eyes.

"As I was saying, you taught us to take care of ourselves." I had no issue standing up to Dad, and he knew it.

"Nash, she's right," Ma said.

"Mags, they're our babies," he said, turning to her.

"They can manage themselves. Considering the kids have the Gray genes, they're a force of nature. Look, I know you want to protect them, but they can manage things. Plus, Michael doesn't strike me as the type who has any ill will towards her. He's a genuine guy who cares about Lyric."

He looked at Ma and sighed.

"Fine." He turned to Michael. "Break her heart, and I'll break your neck."

"No worries there," Michael said.

"How come you aren't that protective with us?" Kain asked Nixon.

"I don't have to worry about girls with you both. I figure if you mess with the wrong girl and break their heart, their daddies will take care of you." He smirked.

"Thanks for the vote of confidence, Daddy-O," Kaiden said.

"Well, don't screw up, and you'll be fine." Nixon shrugged.

I looked at Michael. "Let's get some ice for your jaw."

We walked to the kitchen as he said, "Your dad has a mean left hook."

"Yeah, Maverick already found out. That's why he told you to duck. All he did was kiss Larkin." I laughed.

"So, about that date."

We walked into the kitchen.

I didn't know what would happen between Michael and me, but I wanted to find out. It was time to see the possibilities out there. Michael would show me things I would never imagine.

CHAPTER 7

JEALOUSY IS A BITCH

Lyric

After our parents left for home, we got settled into the rental house. I could do this. I could be with Michael.

Ugh, I wish things were more straightforward than this. Why was I so scared? Why did I have doubts?

The girls and I headed to town to have lunch and check out the area. Then I saw Michael talking to another girl by a storefront. What the hell?

I stopped as the other girls were walking. They stopped when they realized I stopped walking. They walked back to me.

"Is there a reason your feet aren't moving?" Larkin asked.

I said nothing but stood there, watching Michael with a chick. My blood began to boil.

"That's the reason," Lakin said, pointing at Michael and the girl.

"It's not what it seems," Piper said.

The girl leaned over and kissed his cheek.

"Or not," Piper said.

"My brother is an idiot." Mia facepalmed herself.

I went to find out what the hell was happening and punch out the chick. I wasn't sure which one would happen first. My guess was the second part.

"Ooh, someone's getting their ass beat," Luna said as they followed me.

I balled my fists as I stormed towards them. The girl put her hand on Michael. Yep, it would be the second part. Screw the first.

As soon as I reached them, they turned to me.

"Hey," Michael said.

"Hey," I said, faking a smile.

"Lyric, this is......"

He didn't even get to finish her name before I hauled off and punched her, causing her to fall onto the ground.

"Lyric!" Michael said.

He leaned over and helped the girl up as she held her nose.

"What the hell?" He checked the girl.

I stood there, seething.

"I'll go, Michael," she said while holding her nose and walking away.

He turned to me. "What was that about?"

"I'm yours, but hey, let's flirt with some other chick."

"I wasn't flirting! We were talking!"

I stood there, fuming. "And the girl kissing you on the cheek and touching you isn't flirting?"

"Yes, did you see me return those affections to her?"

"I didn't have to. What I should have seen was you pushing the girl away, but you didn't." I turned and started walking away.

"Lyric!"

I turned around. "Forget it, Michael! I knew this was a mistake!" With that, I walked away. I was so done. At least with Daniel, his death was the reason I had a broken heart. That was bullshit.

Mia walked up to him. "Well, that went well."

He gave her a look.

"Michael, what were you thinking? Lyric already feels like people will leave her because of Daniel. Now you made her feel like she doesn't even matter."

"Mia, if you and everyone else would give me a chance to explain. You would realize that Mara, the girl who Lyric punched, is gay. I helped her with an issue she was having with her girlfriend."

"What?"

"I met her when I was getting my stuff for school. We talked, then she told me about her girl. I told her about Lyric."

"So, what was with the kiss on the cheek and the touching of the arm?"

"She was thanking me for the advice. That is all."

Mia sighed.

"I wish she would have asked."

"It's Lyric Gray. The Grays usually fight, then ask questions later. Plus, I believe she was jealous. I also believe you'll have to kiss much ass, brother dear."

"Thanks a lot. You're an immense help."

"What are little sisters for?" She smiled.

He gave her a look.

I'm beyond pissed and went for a walk. My sisters left me alone. They knew I was furious and did this often when I needed to cool off.

I'm usually the calmer and more rational of us. Larkin is sarcastic, while Lakin has a temper. Luna is the most insecure one, while Lex is the shyest out of us.

I found a park and walked over to a railing. There was water which always calmed me, like home.

I called the one person who would know what to do.

Hello?

"Hey, Uncle Noah." My voice cracked.

Lyric? What's wrong?

"He lied to me, Uncle Noah."

Who? Michael?

"Yes, I saw him with some girl, and she kissed him and touched him."

Shh, it's okay. It's not what it looked like with Michael and this girl.

"I'm done, Uncle Noah. I can't do this anymore. I'm tired of getting my heart broken. I knew this was a mistake."

Listen to me, Lyric. I don't think Michael is like that. He's a moral guy. You need to cool off and think with a clear head.

I sniffled as he talked to me. We talked for a while until I stopped crying, then I hung up.

"You know, it's not all bad," someone said.

I saw a guy with auburn hair look at me.

"Who are you?" I sniffled while wiping my eyes.

"My name is Drew."

"Well, Drew, do you always listen in on personal conversations?"

"It's hard when you're in public blubbering like a chick."

"I am a chick."

"Yeah, well, I guess then, blubbering suits you." He smirked.

I gave him a look.

"Look, no offense. But it sounds like you're jealous."

"I am not jealous."

"Oh, you're jealous, all right. Jealousy seeps off you like the rain. Let me guess. You saw some dude you like, talking to another girl." He arched his brow.

"You don't know what you're talking about."

"Oh, I know more than you realize because I have a girl. Let me tell you. She has shown jealousy like there is no tomorrow. You should get your facts straight before jumping to conclusions. Someone should buy you a trampoline."

That's when we started going back and forth until we started laughing.

*****

Michael

I searched for Lyric. Asking her sisters was a terrible idea after Lakin hauled off and hit me, not once but twice. I swear they get their left hook from their dad.

I walked until I came to a park by the water and saw her. She was talking to a guy and laughing. What the hell?

My blood boiled as I watched them. Oh, hell no. That girl was mine.

I walked over to them as they stopped laughing, then looked at me. I hauled off and threw a punch at the guy as he caught my fist. Then he applied pressure, causing me to drop to the ground on my knees.

"I'll go out on a limb and say this is the guy you have been blubbering about," he said, releasing my hand.

I stayed on my knees, rubbing my hand and wrist when I saw a girl walk up.

"Matt and the others are waiting for us, Drew," she told him.

"Sorry, I got caught up a bit," he said.

"Seems like it," she said, looking at me. "Hi, I'm Liz."

"I'm Lyric, and this big twit on the ground is Michael."

"I see. It was nice meeting you, but we have to go." Liz grabbed the guy's hand and dragged him away.

I can't win today. I finally got up.

"Was that necessary?" Lyric asked.

I turned around and looked at her.

"What the hell happened to you?"

"Lakin happened. I made the mistake of asking your sisters where you were and got answered with a fist. Your family has anger issues."

"Nope, it's Lakin and Uncle Nathan." She smirked.

I sighed and walked over to the railing. I leaned on it, and Lyric stood next to me. "I wasn't flirting. I was helping someone with their girlfriend problem."

"Oh."

"I would never do that to someone who I care about." I ran my hand through my hair.

"Yeah, Uncle Noah said I was jumping to conclusions."

"Uncle Noah?" I looked at her.

"Well, it's not like I'll call my dad. He already wants a reason to bury you." She giggled.

I faced her. "Lyric, I'm crazy about you. Seeing you with another guy made me realize I don't want to see you with anyone else except for me."

"Was someone jealous?" She said with a sly look.

"Maybe." I shrugged.

"Then I guess we're even." She shrugged.

"Wait. You were jealous."

"No."

"You were jealous." I smirked.

"Nope."

I pulled her to me. "Jealousy is a bitch, but it also tells me one thing."

"What's that?"

"That you love me."

"Psh, what? You're crazy."

I leaned into her ear. "Deny it all you want, but you're in love with me. That's okay because I'm in love with you."

I pulled back, and she looked at me wide-eyed. I'm going to let that sink in for a minute.

It was true. I didn't like Lyric but was in love with her. Now to get her to admit the same to me. That would take work.

CHAPTER 8

FIRST OFFICIAL FIRST DATE

Lyric

After what Michael told me, it shocked me. He is in love with me. Oh, my God, I thought.

I tried to avoid the subject like the plague. Sure, I like Michael. But was I in love with him? I didn't know.

Tonight, he was taking me on a date. Our first official date, and I was nervous. I hadn't been on one since Daniel. Trying to get ready was iffy. Everything I tried on wasn't working, and my sisters weren't any help.

Piper came over to see Lex and ended up helping me. Thus, we're best friends. She gets me. I swear if Lex screws this up with her, I'll beat his ass.

As I got ready, there was a knock at the door.

"Lyric, lover boy is here!" Kain said.

"Thanks, Frack!" I spoke.

He looked at Michael. "Break her heart, and I'll break your neck."

"That is violent. Don't you think?" Michael asked him.

"I'm a Gray. What do you expect?" He shrugged.

Kaiden walked over to them.

"This is true. We don't appreciate it when one messes with one of our own. Plus, we watched Lyric fall apart after Daniel," Kaiden said.

"I know. I was there," Michael said.

"No, dude. We saw what happened that night. She was hysterical when they brought her home," Kain told him.

"I know. Maverick was with her, and so was Lex. He told me when he got home what happened," he said.

They looked at him.

"Trust me. I've been there," Michael said.

"Hey, yin and yang, leave him alone," Lex said, walking over to him. He looked at Michael. "Lyric is finishing getting ready with Piper's help. She'll be down in a minute."

A couple of minutes later, I came out of my room and saw him. He was wearing a button-up, short-sleeve shirt, and jeans. He had styled his hair. Whoa, he looked hot. I can't do this.

I turned, only met by my sisters and Piper, who shook their heads and pointed to go. Traitors.

I sighed and turned, making my way downstairs. Michael smiled at me.

"You look amazing," Michael said.

"Thanks," I said.

He leaned over and gave me a sweet kiss on the cheek, then took my hand and led me out of the door. We walked to the car and got in, then he pulled out and drove to our next destination.

As we drove, we sat in comfortable silence. I didn't know where we were going. For all I know, Michael could drive me to my death. Remind me to hurt Larkin for watching that horror film last night.

He pulled into a parking lot. I saw the lights, rides, and people walking around with music playing.

I turned to him. "A carnival?"

"I figure we could have some fun and talk. You can't talk while watching a movie, and restaurants seem stuffy."

He got out, and so did I. We walked around for a bit, checking out everything.

"I haven't been to a carnival in years," he said.

"Are you serious?"

"Not since my parents died. I wasn't inclined to visit one. Plus, I was busy being a grownup." He sighed.

"You had to grow up fast, didn't you?"

"Yep, but I don't regret it. It kept us together. My parents, aunt, and uncle would have hated for the others to go into foster care. When you must care for others younger than you, you need to act older and more responsible. I saw the boys falling into the trap of being cavalier with girls and stopped it. Mia was fighting more. I know it was because they were angry. Hell, I was angry, but you can't let anger win."

I listened to what Michael said. It seemed like he didn't get didn't have time to focus on himself and what he wanted. He was too busy taking care of others. I lost Daniel, but at least I didn't lose four people at once. I couldn't imagine whether something happened to my parents or my uncles, especially Noah.

"What?" He asked.

"Nothing. It's stupid." I shook my head.

He stopped and looked at me. "Tell me."

"I was thinking, here you lost four people and took care of others while trying to deal with your grief. Here I'm wallowing because I lost one." I shook my head.

"Lyric, it doesn't matter how many people you lose, whether it's one or four. A loss is a loss. You grieve the same. Never think losing someone you have loved and cared about is stupid because it's not."

At that moment, I understood Michael better than anyone. I realized why he said nothing about how I was acting or pushed me to get over it. He knew grief was grief, and there was no time limit. Because of that, I understood everything now.

He looked at me. "What?"

"You're right."

"About?"

"It's how I feel. If I allowed myself to open to the possibilities of loving someone, I'm betraying Daniel. But I'm not because each love is different." I shrugged.

"Why, Lyric Gray, are you saying what I think you're saying?"

I gave him a look.

"Admit it." He leaned forward with a smile.

"I admit nothing."

"I dare you."

"Nope."

"I double-dog dare you."

"Nada."

"I triple dog dare you." He grinned at me, enjoying this way too much.

"Oh, look, a Ferris wheel." I walked away from him.

Ha—Lyric 1, Michael 0.

I walked over to the Ferris wheel as Michael followed me and waited in line. As the line moved, we handed the guy a ticket and got on. We sat in a cart, and the guy secured the bar.

Then, as the wheel moved, we went around twice before it came to a stop at the top.

"Lyric, why is it so hard to admit you love me?"

"Because if I admit it, then it becomes real. When it becomes real, then something happens, and I'm left alone once again."

"That's why you're afraid because you think I'll leave." His blue eyes met mine.

"Yes."

"Lyric, I'm not Daniel. Daniel had problems that went deeper than anyone realized. I won't make you fall in love with me, then abandon you. When a woman gives their heart to someone, they do it with the intention that they're giving it, so you take care of it. No man should ever destroy something that special. Let me take care of your heart, please."

I stared into his eyes. It's all he had been doing. Why else would he do the things he has been doing? Michael was trying to love me, and I didn't even realize it, but I do now. That's when it hit me. That was the moment I fell in love with Michael Harper.

"Okay, you can take care of my heart." I took a deep breath and found the words to tell him. "I'm in love with you."

A smile curled upon his lips, as did mine. He placed a hand on the side of my face and kissed me. I at once kissed him back.

The Ferris wheel started moving as we kissed until it was time to exit the cart. Then the operator cleared his throat. We broke from our kiss and got up, exiting the seat. Once we walked off the platform, Michael slid his hand in mine, and we went to get food. I'm hungry.

"It's good to see you eat. It worries me you aren't eating."

"So was everyone else. It's hard because when you don't want to eat, you can't force yourself."

"Lyric, you've lost more weight."

"I know. Trust me. I know." I sighed.

He looked at me with concern.

"Michael, I promise I don't have an eating disorder. I do like food. I'm not hungry."

It was true. I figured it was from grief, but I hadn't been hungry. I don't even know why. I know it started last year but told no one.

"Have you seen a doctor?"

"No."

"You should go. Lyric, not eating isn't healthy and damages your body."

"Larkin has a metabolic disorder, but hers is where she eats but never gains weight. Considering we came from the same egg, it's possible to have a similar disorder."

"So, explain how that works with the five of you?"

"My ma went through a health issue back in college, and something about medicine. She lost a chunk of her memory, trying to rectify the damage the other doctor did. She ended up ovulating several eggs. Larkin and I came from one. Lakin and Luna came from another. While Lex came from a third egg."

"So, it wasn't from fertility treatments?"

"Nope, it's a fluke." I shrugged.

"Interesting."

"What's interesting is that your family has a thing for my family." I smirked.

"Yes, I know. Trust me. I hear all about it." Michael rolled his eyes as I giggled. "First, you have Mia, who can't keep it under control. I heard about the Thanksgiving incident."

"Oh, I know. I thought Dad would kill Lakin, especially when Nixon caught them."

"Then you have Major who's trying to keep your sister at arm's length, so your dad doesn't throttle him. Then there's Maverick, who, God bless his heart, is the biggest twit to walk the face of the earth."

"Harsh, don't you think?" I asked him.

"Considering Maverick is always messing things up, that's a gracious way of putting things. He tries, he does, but his execution is a bit off."

"Then I'll have Nixon pray for him because Larkin isn't the type to give in."

"I heard what happened. Is Larkin okay?"

"Somewhat. Larkin had a troublesome time opening before everything, but she wouldn't talk about it after that day. We didn't even know until it came out. She guards herself more so than the rest of us. It takes a lot for her to let anyone in."

"Makes sense."

We continued eating and talking before riding more rides. After a few hours, Michael took me home. He walked me to the door and kissed me goodnight before turning to leave. I watched him go as I leaned with my back to the door. Yep, I'm completely in love with Michael. I was so screwed.

Then the door opened, causing me to fall backward. I hit the floor with a thud and looked up as everyone looked at me, grinning like fools.

"It's official. Our crazy sister has fallen in love with Michael," Larkin said.

"Excuse me. I'm not crazy," I said.

"Yeah, you are," Kaiden said.

"I'm guessing the date went well," Luna said to everyone.

"Seems like it," Lakin said.

"Still here," I said, lying on the floor.

"Well, if he hurts her, we'll hurt him," Kain said, cracking his knuckles.

"He won't hurt her, you twit! He already got a taste from lefty," Lakin said, holding up her fist.

"Excuse me, I'm still here," I said.

"Do you think he'll propose?" Luna asked.

"Oh, then Dad will kill him," Larkin said.

"Again, still here and still on the floor," I said.

Lex walked over and helped me up. "Lyric, this is no time to lie around."

"My family is a bunch of tools." I sighed.

"So, how did the date go?" Luna asked.

I smiled as they smiled back. Everything would be beautiful.

CHAPTER 9

AWW, YOU'RE ALL SOAKED

Lyric

The next day, water woke me up, getting tossed onto me. I awoke startled to see Michael holding a bucket, along with Maverick. Both had stupid-looking grins on their faces.

"Aww, you're all soaked," Maverick said.

I glared at him.

"It's nice to see that I can make you wet, sugar lips." Michael grinned.

"I'll throttle you both." I scrambled out of bed and chased them. When I get my hands on them, they are so dead.

"It looks like your boy toy is at it again," Lakin told Larkin.

"He isn't my boy toy. He is a twit." She rolled her eyes.

"But a hot twit." Luna smirked.

"And I'm telling Major," Larkin said.

"Oh, come on! That isn't fair."

"Then keep your eyes off, Maverick."

Both Lakin and Luna clamped their mouths shut.

I couldn't catch Maverick but caught Michael as I tackled him to the ground. Then he flipped me onto my back and pinned me down.

"We need to have a conversation about you falling for me." He smirked.

I gave him a look and rolled my eyes before he crashed his lips into mine. Our lips moved in sync as we kissed. As we continued to kiss, Major walked up. "I see you finally got it together."

We stopped and looked at him as he chuckled and walked into the house.

"Your family is something else."

"Yep, but I love them anyway."

Then we heard someone say, "You said what!"

"I'm guessing Larkin ratted out Luna," I said.

"Come on. I need to beat some sense into Major before he screws things up again." Michael helped me up.

We walked in and saw Major yelling at Luna. "What the hell is wrong with you? My damn brother!"

"Major, it was a comment!" Luna said.

"I don't care! You don't even make comments about other guys, including my damn brother!"

"Whoa, back off, buddy," I told him.

"Piss off, Lyric!"

That's all it took until Michael grabbed hold of him and took him down. He held him down and placed his knee into his back. Wow.

"Get off me!" Major said.

"No, not until you calm the fuck down!" Michael said.

We stood there, shocked. Usually, Michael showed a calm side, but this was a whole new side to him.

Then he hauled off and smacked Major hard. "You never talk to Luna that way. I warned you about this, Major. I won't hesitate to beat the shit out of you."

Maverick walked in and stopped dead in his tracks.

Michael turned to him. "Don't even think about interfering, or you're next."

Maverick stood there, not saying a word.

"Whoa, what's this all about?" Kain asked, walking in with Kaiden.

Michael turned to Major. "You'll never disrespect them or anyone else. I won't tolerate your bullshit. Do you hear me?"

"Yes."

"Now, you fucking apologize."

"I'm sorry, Luna and Lyric." Major's voice cracked.

Mia walked in and over to Michael. "Michael?"

"What?"

"He's had enough, don't you think?"

He looked at her, then released Major, who got up.

"Was that necessary?" Mia asked Michael.

"I don't know, was it?"

She looked at him.

"Mia, I told you, the minute you fuck up, I would deal with you. I won't stand by and allow you three to act like assholes to anyone. You're all the better than that."

That was a whole different side to Michael that I had never seen.

He looked at Luna. "Get your shit together. You want him to act like a dutiful woman. Don't make him feel like he has to be insecure because you are." Then he turned to Larkin. "And you stop giving my cousin the runaround. He deserves better than that, not a stupid game you or anyone else feels the need to play with him. You might have loyalty to your family, but so do I. I won't watch anyone toying with them, including you." With that, he walked away.

I stood there, shocked. I had never seen Michael so angry. Piper walked in with Lex and saw everyone standing there. "Why is Michael mad?"

"He doesn't like how everyone is acting," Kaiden said.

Lex sighed. "Is there one day when someone isn't causing issues?"

"Nope." Kain shrugged.

Then he pulled out his phone and made a call. Great. That only means one thing. Yep, we were getting a visit.

*****

Michael

I sat in my living room, stewing. What is wrong with everyone? They lost their damn minds. I needed to cool off. Lyric tried calling me, but I didn't answer it. I needed to calm down. It was a side I didn't want her to see.

There was a knock at my door. I got up and answered it.

"Can I help you?" I asked Nash.

"No, but we can help you," Nash said, standing there with four other guys. "Can we come in?"

Before I answered, another said, "Sure we can." They walked inside as I looked at them, then followed the five of them.

The Gray brothers stood in front of me. I had heard a lot about them from my uncle, Mike. They were something else while growing up from the stories he heard about them.

"It seems you have an issue with our nieces," one brother said.

"And you are?" I asked.

"Noah," the brother said.

"I'm Nixon," another brother said.

"Nathan," a third brother said.

"Nolan," the last one said.

I pointed to each one. "Nash, Nixon, Nathan, Noah, and Nolan?"

"Yep," they said.

"Okay," I said.

"So, would you care to explain what happened? Lex couldn't tell me much when he called because he walked in after you left," Nash said.

I sighed, then explained what happened to them. I knew it was better to be straight with the brothers than bullshit them. That would never fly.

"Sounds familiar," Nixon said, looking at Nash.

Nash gave him a look and rolled his eyes. "You'll never let me live that down, will you?"

"Nope," Nixon said.

"That is great. Our tool of brothers is reminiscing about Nash's stupid mistakes with Maggie," Nathan said.

"Yep," Noah said.

"Can we move along? You both arguing is like watching two cats screw," Nolan said, making a cat noise.

"Listen here, tool, don't make me take you outside and beat your ass," Nixon said. "I'm still pissed about that time we ended up in jail together."

"I already told you I was sorry," he said.

Then they bickered, and it all made sense. The quints were like them. Oh, shit.

"I don't mind watching you argue with each other, but how does this help me?" I asked.

They stopped and looked at me.

"I'm glad you ask," Nixon said.

It wouldn't end well.

After a discussion, including their bickering, we went back to the house. We walked inside, and I thought the quints would piss themselves.

"Sit," Nash told them.

All five of them sat down.

Then the brothers ripped into them except for Lex. He didn't say much. I stood there as it happened. Let's say it wasn't pretty. Every time their cousins tried to add their two cents, Nixon told them to shut up.

After they finished, I stood in awe. Major, Maverick, Mia, and Piper stood in the corner, not saying a word. I don't think they knew what to make of it.

Then the door opened, and I saw four guys walk in and turn to leave when Nathan and Noah stopped them. "Oh, don't leave so fast, boys. We have a bone to pick with you."

"Why is it every time the quints do stupid shit, we get our asses nailed?" Marshall asked Murphy.

"Because we're related to them," Murphy said.

"Care to explain why you four got caught by campus security?" Nathan asked them.

"Shit," Noel said.

"Yeah, shit is right, and you're in deep," Noah told him.

They walked over, grabbed the guys by their shirt, and shoved them out of the house.

"Should we help?" Nolan asked Nash and Nixon.

"God, no. We have enough to deal with without dealing with those twits, too," Nixon said.

"Get your shit together. You must get through four years of school together. Next time, I get a phone call. I'm sending Grammy," Nash told them.

"Ah, no, no, that's okay," Lakin said.

As they talked to everyone, I walked over to my sister and cousins. "Are we good?"

"Yeah, don't sweat it," Major said.

"Michael, we would never disrespect you," Maverick said.

"Yeah, I know, but I want to make sure you do well. I want our parents proud of you," I said.

"They are." Mia smiled.

"You should talk to someone else," Piper said, pointing at Lyric. I nodded and walked over to her. I took her hand and led her into the kitchen.

"Look," I said.

She crashed her lips into mine. I didn't hesitate to kiss her back. She pulled back. "You were saying."

"Never mind." I pulled Lyric back to me and kissed her again.

That was the thing about Lyric. I didn't need to explain it to her. She got it. For that, it made me grateful. Most people wouldn't understand, but she did because she dealt with her family issues like I did.

That made me love her even more. One day, I would make her my wife.

CHAPTER 10

FIRST-DAY PROBLEMS

Lyric

Today was the first day of college with different schedules. After leaving high school, you wouldn't have to deal with the same stuff because you're older. Yeah, that wasn't the case. There's always one person who makes your life a living hell.

I got lucky when a chick zeroed in on me. I attended my first class, which was fine. My second class proved to be different.

I sat there, listening to the teacher as he called on me. "Miss Gray, what are your thoughts?"

Everyone looked at me, and a girl said, "Oh, I don't think she knows how to speak. She would prefer to grunt and use her fist like the Hulk. Hulk smashes." The girl slammed her fists onto the desk as everyone laughed. I gave her a look and rolled my eyes.

"I'm glad you like the Hulk, but my favorite Marvel character is Iron Man. Do you mind if I answer the question now, you twit?"

She shot me a glare.

"The antagonist is trying to separate the couple because they're jealous. They don't like to see them happy, but they still won't be happy if they succeed. They need the misery to survive. It's a bit cliche," I said.

"Do you think the antagonist could change?" The professor asked.

"Only if they're willing to, but otherwise, no."

"Thank you."

I noticed the girl still staring at me. What the hell was her deal?

After class, I walked out of the classroom. The girl and her little trolls cornered me.

"Listen, bitch. I don't know who the hell you think you are, but you better watch your back," the girl said.

"Does your tactic work? It's so high school mentality," I said.

"I'm warning you." She glared at me.

"And I'm warning you to back off."

"Oh, what are you going to do, cry? Cry for me, crybaby." She taunted me as the other girls laughed. Then I did what Grays do best. I hit her. Then her trolls jumped me. Fantastic.

They pinned me as the other girl laid into me, going full throttle. I tried to break free. After that, I remember little.

*****

"Get off of her," a muffled voice said. "Lyric? Lyric? Can you hear me?"

"Michael, we need to get her help," another muffled voice said.

Someone lifted and carried me. I'm guessing it's Michael. I didn't have the strength to open my eyes or respond. I knew I hurt and felt tired.

＊＊＊＊

I opened my eyes, but the light was too bright.

"Lyric?" Someone asked.

"Can someone turn off the light?" I asked.

The light disappeared.

"Baby girl?" I heard Dad say.

"Dad?"

"I'm here, and so is your ma."

"Dad, I swear they started it."

"They said you threw the first punch."

"Yeah, but."

"The school doesn't tolerate fighting. They're putting you on probation."

"But they jumped me!"

"I know, but those girls made it seem like it was your fault."

I couldn't help but cry. I defended myself, and these girls made me look like the bad guy. It made me angry.

"Lyric, there's another problem," Ma said.

"What now?" I sighed, wiping my bruised face.

"Michael says you haven't been eating. When the doctor ran tests, he found out you have a metabolic disorder like Larkin. Why didn't you tell us?"

I sighed.

"I didn't want you to worry. You had worried about me while I was dealing with Daniel's death. I didn't want to add more worry to the situation."

"Well, they're putting you on medication. It'll help you feel hungry and gain weight." Ma explained.

At least, it solved that problem. That still didn't solve my other issue with school.

It also set me back with any progress I was making with Daniel. I was finally starting to move on and be happy. All it takes is one person to come along and ruin it. FML.

The following day, the doctor released me. I attended school while the other girls taunted me into fighting. When I wasn't at school, I stayed in my room. My family tried to help, but it didn't matter—the less contact I had with people, the better.

I also wouldn't eat. My anxiety was through the roof. I had no appetite because I would forget to take my medication. Yep, I was a mess.

*****

Michael

"Where is Lyric?" I asked, entering the house.

"She's in her room and refuses to come out except for class," Lex said.

Maverick and I made our way upstairs. Lyric was becoming more and more withdrawn, like when Daniel died. Every day when I wasn't at school, I would sit by her door in the hallway and talk to her. She was refusing to unlock her door. She said she wanted no more trouble.

I'm done with waiting. So, I had Maverick pick her lock. Yeah, don't ask.

I opened the door to see her facing her window.

"Why are you here?" She didn't look at me.

"Because I love you, and I refuse to let you sink into that hole you were in after Daniel died."

"It doesn't matter. No matter what I do, everything turns bad. I couldn't save Daniel, and I can't save myself."

"No, but I can." I walked over and wrapped my arms around her as she broke down.

"Please, Michael, leave me alone. You're better without me dragging you down." Lyric crumpled to the floor, pulling me with her.

"Lyric, I'm better with you in my life than without you. I'm not letting you go or leaving you. I told you I would never leave you, so don't leave me." I stroked her hair as she cried. God, she was so thin.

I figure she would have fought me, but she didn't. She cried until I didn't hear her cry anymore. That's when I noticed she fell asleep.

"She's exhausted," Larkin said. "She hasn't been eating and refuses to sleep. Every time she does, the nightmares come back."

"Michael, we don't want to lose her. She's a part of us. Please keep us from losing her," Lakin said.

I looked at Lyric's siblings. I had never seen the quints so upset. I also knew they had one hell of a bond between them, so you can imagine how they felt.

I nodded as I looked at Maverick. "Call him."

Maverick nodded and left the room. Lyric needed serious help. More than what I could give her. That's when I had Maverick make a call. If she hated me, I didn't care. This situation had gone on way too long.

Later that night, Jordan showed up, along with two guys, taking Lyric.

"Why? Why? Would you do this?" She asked as they dragged her out of the house, and I followed. "I hate you! I hate you all!" She kicked and screamed as they loaded her into the ambulance.

We watched as they closed the doors after restraining her.

Jordan looked at me. "She doesn't hate you, but she needs serious help."

"Why does it feel like I betrayed her?" I asked him.

"Everyone feels that way, but Michael, she gets help, or everyone will lose her. I have to do her paperwork." Jordan left.

I stood there. It would be another battle for Lyric, but I wouldn't leave. I made a promise and intended to keep it.

*****

Lyric

I laid in bed, wanting to hurt every single one of them. How could everyone do this? I was fine. I stayed to myself, trying not to fight, and now I'm locked up in a nuthouse. I hated them all.

I laid there, and they brought me food, but I refused to eat. What I couldn't resist were the injections they gave me when they held me down. That sucked.

I'm stuck. So much for enjoying college. All I got was trouble. FML.

I didn't care what anyone said. Everyone was enemy number one, especially Michael. I was so furious with him. Then Jordan would try to talk to me, but I refused to speak to him. I didn't want to be here. It was complete and utter bullshit.

It's now my life. Fantastic.

"Lyric, how are we doing today?" Jordan asked.

I sighed, looking out of the window. It had been a few weeks since I arrived here. If I didn't try, I wouldn't be leaving. I even tried to fake it. Yep, that doesn't work.

I turned and looked at Jordan as he sat in a chair. "Like I want to cry all the time."

"Did you sleep last night?" Jordan asked.

"A little, then the nightmares came."

"Have a seat, and I'll explain what's happening." He pointed to a chair.

I took a seat.

"You're suffering from depression which accompanies grief. You also developed anxiety from recent events. Along with these factors, your metabolic disorder is causing you not to eat. Our goal is to get you better and home, but I need you to work with me."

I thought about it. "So, if I do what you want, then I can leave?"

"Yes."

"What about visitors?"

"First, we focus on your the treatment, then the visitors. Baby steps."

I didn't have a choice. I'll try, or I'll stay here. Great.

"What do I have to do?"

He smiled.

*****

Michael

Not seeing Lyric killed me, but she needed help. The situation frustrated her family. It didn't help that those girls jumped her, helping to create this mess. They started talking about her, calling her a nut job. The quints took exception and took matters into their own hands.

I walked out of school to find the girls tied to a flagpole in their underwear with the word bully written on them.

"You've got to love the quints." Major chuckled.

"This isn't funny!" The head girl said.

"It's damn funny considering what you did to our sister!" Lex said.

"You're going to pay for this!"

"Nope, because now everyone knows the person you are, along with your trolls. You bullied our sister that she needed treatment for help! Do you think it's cool or funny to jump someone? Three against one doesn't sound fair!" Larkin said.

"I love it when she's fired up," Maverick said.

I looked at him as he grinned.

"We want everyone to see who you are," Lakin told them. "Look, everyone! These people are the reason kind people commit suicide."

Luna stepped towards her and smacked her across the face.

"Damn," Major said.

"That is for my sister. Stay the hell away from her," Luna said.

I stood there and watched it all happen. As much as I don't condone this behavior, I know those girls deserved it.

People left. I walked over to the girls and leaned into them. "Stay away from Lyric, or I won't hesitate to end you."

Their eyes widened as I smiled.

"Are you threatening me?" The head girl asked.

"No, sweetheart, I'm promising." I put the fear of God into her. Then I heard it. I glanced and saw the puddle. I walked over to Major and Maverick.

"What did you say to her?" Maverick asked.

"I gave her a piece of advice." I shrugged before walking away. With the people I loved and cared about, I would do everything to protect them. People I love had been taken from me. I refused to let it happen again. Not now or ever.

CHAPTER 11

GETTING BETTER

Lyric

My family brought my schoolwork to the hospital, so I didn't fail. It sucked. I should attend school, not be locked away.

I started my therapy sessions to deal with my grief about Daniel's death and other issues. It included nightmares. They also started me on medication for anxiety and depression. They added them with the current medicines for my metabolic disorder. Jordan said it was temporary until I felt better, then he would wean me off the meds depending on my need.

They finally allowed me visitors. People took turns coming to see me, and I waited for one person. I figure everyone else came to see me. He would come, too. At least, I hope he did. He said he loved me, right? When you love someone, you show them. So, why did it feel like it wasn't true?

The door opened, and a nurse entered. "Are you ready for your visit, Lyric?"

"Yeah." I sighed. It's one of my siblings or cousins or someone else. No one gave me a straight answer about Michael and figured he finally had enough. They all leave at one point.

The nurse led me through double doors to a room with tables, and I stopped. He waved to me and smiled. I made my way over to him and took a seat.

"I didn't think you would come." I looked at the table.

"Why?"

"Because everyone else had come. You didn't."

"Because I was taking care of something. But I'm here now."

I couldn't look at him. I didn't want his pity, and I couldn't bear it if he told me bye. He moved to a seat closer to me.

"Lyric, look at me."

I lifted my eyes and met his eyes.

"I wanted you to focus on getting better. I figured while you did that, I could take care of something important. When the doctor releases you, you won't deal with any issue that hinders your progress."

"So, you don't want to call it quits?"

"What? No, where did you get that idea?"

"I thought."

He held my hand. "You thought wrong. I meant what I said. I'm not going anywhere. I would never do that to you."

"So, what were you doing that kept you from visiting?"

"Do you want to know?"

"I don't think so."

"Trust me. It's for the best."

We sat there, talking as a news report played on the TV.

Local college student Courtney Thames is missing. Police are looking for any leads or connections to her disappearance. If anyone has any information, please contact the local police department.

My jaw dropped open when I saw who it was. Then I looked at Michael. "You didn't."

"What? No, Lyric. I'm a lot of things, but a serial killer isn't one."

My eyes widened.

"It was a joke."

I facepalmed myself. That's great, I thought to myself.

*****

Michael

Great, that's all I need is people suspecting me of that troll's disappearance. I'll hurt Frazier when I see him. That is the last time I listened to Kate.

I stayed with Lyric until visiting hours ended. They took her back to her room, but not before I kissed her. Damn, I missed her lips. I missed holding her. I missed her, but I knew this is what she needed.

I walked out of the hospital and over to Maverick.

"How is she?" Maverick asked.

"Much better. I wish I would have come sooner." I sighed.

"Don't beat yourself up, Michael. You were busy with something."

"Maverick, at no point should anything take precedence over someone you love. You should have seen her face. She thought I was ending things. The last thing I want to do is have her feel like she isn't important when she is."

"But you were making it so she could return without any issues."

"But not at the expense of her thinking I don't care about her or love her. That isn't right."

"Why does it seem this relationship isn't a random thing?"

"Because it's not. I meant what I said. Lyric is mine, and I'll make her my wife one day."

He dropped the subject and got into the car. I followed suit. I know what people thought, but I fell in love with Lyric Gray the day of that damn funeral. Since then, I have had this need to protect her. To see someone so broken had broken my heart.

*****

After that day, I saw Lyric every day. She seemed happier and was doing much better. Every time she came into that room, her face lit up. She had a glow that hadn't been there. I couldn't wait for her release.

That day finally came, and I picked her up after fighting with her siblings. I swear they're a rough bunch. I'm sorry, but I wanted to hold her forever and never let her go.

I walked into the hospital, and they led me to her room. I knocked on the door as she was finishing her packing.

"Ready?" I asked.

"Almost." She zipped her bag. I walked over and grabbed one as she flung her other bag over her shoulder. Then I leaned in and kissed her.

Damn, I missed those lips. Lyric had soft, plump lips. When you kissed them, it was pressing your lips against a cloud. As much as I wanted to fantasize about Lyric's lips and their lusciousness, I needed to take her home. I'll work on them later.

After getting her discharge papers, we left the hospital. I hope this is the last time she will come back, until later, when she has our child. I need to stop getting ahead of myself.

I drove her home, and the minute we walked into the door, she got tackled by four thrilled siblings. The quints had a unique bond. Even if they were at odds with each other, the other four were always there when one of them needed something.

"It's so good to have you back, sister," Larkin said.

"It's good to be back," Lyric said.

"Are things good?" Lakin asked.

"Yeah, they are." She smiled.

"You look better," Luna said.

"I'm feeling better. I could get sleep and eat. I even gained a little weight," Lyric replied.

"Yeah, but you still look too thin," Lex said.

"The doctor said it would take a while to put on weight. If I take my medication, it will happen. Then they will adjust it," she said.

"It's good to have you back," Larkin said, smiling.

That was the first time I ever saw Larkin smile. Usually, she has a sour puss on her face or a real serious expression. Hmm, I knew how to help Maverick with his dilemma.

I gave them time together and told Lyric I would be back later. Then it was my turn.

*****

Lyric

It was good to be home. You never realize how much you take home for granted when you don't have it. I missed my siblings, along with Frick and Frack. I missed being with Michael.

I also missed my bed, my room, my clothes, my home. Trust me. You would, too, when you sleep on a mattress that isn't a five-star hotel.

I took my bags to my room with Lex's help. The minute I set them down, I crawled into bed and groaned.

"That's kind of disturbing when you do that," he said.

"Brother, when you are without your bed for three weeks, you enjoy every moment you can when you return." I buried my face into my pillow. I didn't care if I sounded ridiculous. I missed my bed.

As I laid there enjoying my bed's comfiness, I heard Lex say, "Our sister is weird."

"Yeah, and so are you, but you don't see us complaining," Lark said as I giggled.

I missed Lark, my other half.

As I groaned from the luxuriousness of my bed, I didn't hear anyone else come to the doorway. I got lost in my euphoric state of heaven.

Michael came up and saw me, then shushed my siblings as he made his way over to me. Something significant settled on my back.

"Lex, you better not be doing some freaky shit!" I spoke.

"Ew! Gross! No offense, but that's disturbing," Lex said, leaving

Then someone whispered into my ear. "I could think of so many things I could do to you."

My head snapped up, smacking someone's face with the back of my head.

"Damn it, Lyric! That freaking hurt!"

I turned my head to see Michael rubbing his nose. Oops.

"So much for being seductive." He contorted his face.

I couldn't help but giggle, even though I tried to stifle it. It didn't work. Michael flipped me onto my back, then sat on me, keeping me pinned to the bed.

"Thanks for the head butt. I wasn't exactly looking for a nose job." Michael leaned forward.

"Well, never startle someone." I shrugged.

He gave me a peck on the lips then climbed off me, lying down next to me on the bed. He took my hand in his as he played with my fingers. "It's good to see you are smiling and happy."

"It feels good to be happy. Although going to a mental hospital wasn't my ideal choice."

"I know, but sometimes, you need professional help others can't offer. I was afraid I would lose you when I found you." Michael played with my fingers but wouldn't look at me. I didn't understand why.

"But you didn't, and I'm still here." I smiled.

He glanced at me, then diverted his eyes back to my hand. That's when it hit me. Michael was on the verge of crying. That's why he wouldn't look at me.

I lifted his face to face with me, even though he tried not to until we made eye contact. That's when I saw the tears fall. I placed my hand on his cheek while pressing my forehead against his.

"Michael, I'm not going anywhere. I promise. As much as I hated being in there, I finally understood more about myself than I ever did. I also learned that what you did for me was what I needed."

He nodded as I wiped my thumb under his eyes. He pulled me to him and kissed me in a way no one had ever kissed me. He poured such emotion into that kiss. Then it got heated, but I stopped. "Michael."

"I know. Sorry, it's that I want to be with you completely, and I know you're not ready."

"At least, not yet." I arched an eyebrow as a smirk played upon my lips.

He gave me a look and rolled his eyes. "Yeah, don't tease me. That isn't fair when you do."

I laughed, and he did too. It was so good to laugh again. For once, I finally felt like myself for the first time in months. Michael had an enormous hand in making it happen.

CHAPTER 12

THIS SHOULD BE FUN: A HOMECOMING CHAPTER

Lyric

Homecoming was coming up, and we all went shopping. I wanted to find something beautiful to wear. During our excursion, I found an ice blue knee-length dress to wear, along with matching shoes. I also had to wear a smaller size because I still wasn't back to my healthy weight. Jordan said it would take time.

I stood in front of the mirror and sighed.

"What's wrong?" Larkin asked.

"I'm afraid Michael will find me unattractive because I lost so much weight."

"Lyric, Michael doesn't care about your appearance. He cares about you. If he didn't, he wouldn't have had Maverick call Jordan about you."

"I know, but I wanted him to be proud of me."

"He is," Mia said.

I turned to her.

"Michael is so proud of you, Lyric. He doesn't care about your appearance. Michael cares about you. When you were in the hospital, all he thought about was you," Mia said.

"I guess I don't want to let him down," I told everyone.

"Trust me. You won't. Michael adores you," Mia said.

I gave her a soft smile. I bought the dress anyway. I wanted to look and feel exceptional for Michael.

The other girls each bought a dress and shoes to match. Afterward, we grabbed food. It was nice to sit down and eat with my sisters, along with my friends. I had missed it. That was until two girls wanted to cause trouble.

"Oh, look, it's the nut job," they said.

"Oh, look, it's someone who doesn't want their cheap-ass hair extensions," Lakin said.

"Aww, the mental case needs someone to protect her," the other one said.

"I don't," I said. "See, I can manage myself, but I chose not to stoop to your level. Now run along, little doggies." I motioned at them.

"That's because you're chicken. Bawk, bawk, bawk."

We gave her a look. Was this chick twelve?

"Did anyone ever tell you that you look ridiculous?" Kain said, standing behind her.

"When did we move to a farm?" Kaiden asked him.

"Around the time, they brought in the sows,"

The girls turned to face them.

"Who are you?" One asked.

"Who we are is not important. Well, it is, but that's beside the point. You're nothing but a bunch of cackling hens," Kain told them.

"You're nothing," one said.

"Ew, say it, don't spray it," Kaiden said, wiping off his face.

"Now we need a rabies shot. Thanks," Kain said.

I tried not to laugh, but it was so hard.

"I'm sure Daddy-O will love to hear that a rabid dog attacked his poor defenseless sons. In fact, why don't we call him?" Kain dialed Nixon and put him on speaker.

What did you do this time?

"Well, rabid dogs infected us with rabies. We might die," Kain said.

Are you sure? Damn. Why do all the good things happen when I'm not there?

"I'm hurt. How could you not feel bad for your flesh and blood?"

It's hard to feel bad for the spawn of the devil himself. But I guess I can throw you a bone.

I was dying at their exchange, as were the others.

"Cute!" Kain said.

Your mother thinks so. Anyway, I'm guessing two twits like to run their mouths.

"Yeah, they're giving Lyric a tough time."

Oh? That's a damn shame for them because we all know what happens when someone takes on the Grays.

"Yep."

After a minute, I stopped laughing and decided enough was enough. While Nixon was still on the phone, I got out of my seat and stood in front of the girls.

"You can call me names. You can judge me all you want, but you don't know me. You know nothing about me. You assume things, but you don't know what I've been through in my life. How dare you stand there and judge me when you're not perfect? No one is. That is the problem with people. They judge. They assume the wrong things without seeing the entire picture. Yes, I went to a mental hospital to get help, but I also walked in on my boyfriend, who shot himself in the head. I've been dealing with that every day since then. It's okay because I'm a nut job. I don't need people to fight my battles because I can fight them myself," I told them.

Everyone stood there as I walked past them. The girls stood there, shocked, while everyone looked at them. It's easy to judge someone until you walk a mile in their shoes. You don't know their story or what happened to them. Go ahead if that makes you feel better to make them feel worse than they already do.

I wouldn't let this set me back. I had come too far to let those awful girls' words make me feel worthless. I was better than that.

I took a walk to clear my mind. I needed to decompress after that exchange. I'll admit, those girls' words hurt. It hurts more than anything, but people will think what they want. But here's the thing: opinions are like assholes. Everyone has one.

I leaned against a railing when two arms slid around me.

"Hi," I said.

"Hi."

"I'm not even going to ask how you found me."

Michael nuzzled into my neck as I leaned my head back. I loved this feeling. Michael had a calming effect on me, which was nice.

"Did you eat?"

"A little."

Then Michael pulled his arms away and took my hand, yanking me forward.

"Ack!"

He pulled me behind him.

"Where are we going?"

"We're returning so you can finish eating!"

I laughed, then jumped on his back. He gave me a piggyback ride.

We got back to the restaurant and walked in. I saw the girls, and so did Michael. He gave them a look, and they scampered away. Then we walked over to the table. He grabbed a chair as I sat down.

I started eating. Once I finished, we paid the check and left. Michael took me home and dropped me off so I could get ready. I couldn't wait.

*****

Michael

We got ready for homecoming. I could tell that Lyric had a rough day. But she didn't let it defeat her, which made me proud. The past four months had been rough for her. Even being there wasn't enough when someone hits their breaking point.

Seeing her eat was vital. I worry about her constantly. She had put on weight, but she still had a way to go. That was fine. We would continue to work on it.

Once we were ready, we left to go pick up the others.

I knocked on the door, and Kain answered it. He and Kaiden were on their way out to pick up their dates. Everyone came down except for Lyric, which worried me. Then I heard a door open, followed by heels clicking against the hardwood floors.

She appeared in an ice blue, knee-length dress with matching shoes. She was breath-taking.

She walked up to me. "You look handsome."

"Well, you look stunning." I pulled her to me and kissed her. She giggled against my lips before pulling back. A smile formed upon her face, which I loved seeing.

I slid my hand into hers, intertwining our fingers as we walked out of the house. Tonight, we'll have fun.

We arrived at the dance and music was playing. People were dancing and talking. I led Lyric onto the dance floor and started dancing with her. Having her in my arms was incredible. As we danced and enjoyed ourselves, some people had to ruin it.

"Hey, asshole! I hear you're giving my girl a troublesome time!" I heard someone say

I stopped and sighed. There it is—that one person who ruins your night.

I turned and ducked as a fist came flying, only to nail the person in the chest, dropping them.

"Shit!" The guy said.

I leaned over, with my foot on his back, while holding his arm. "Did you think I would let you hit me?"

"You're hurting me!"

I applied pressure. "Good, now let me make myself clear. Leave my girl, me, my family, and my friends alone before I break your damn arm."

His eyes widened as people watched. I wasn't playing with him or anyone. I gave his arm another slight twist with enough pressure that caused him pain but didn't break it.

"Okay! Fine! You win!"

I released his arm and stepped back. The troll helped him up as another guy took a step. Major, Maverick, Frick, and Frack, along with Lex, stood there, shaking their heads.

Then I saw four more guys walk over and look at them. Those must be the other cousins.

The trolls and their dates backed off and walked away. Everyone went back to dancing. I turned around as Lyric grabbed me and crashed her lips into mine. I wrapped my arms around her as I kissed her back.

We stood there, making out for a bit before dancing. I wasn't much for school dances, but Lyric made them better.

We stayed for a while before heading out. We ended up back at my house and chilled out. I gave her a tee-shirt and a pair of sweats to wear since she only had her dress.

We both changed and laid on my bed.

"Tonight was fun," I said, smiling.

"It was, and you were so hot when you took a big dolt down." She giggled.

I arched an eyebrow. I had to keep from jumping on Lyric because she made it hard, in more ways than one.

"You know, there are so many things I would love to do with you, but I'm a gentleman and am refraining myself." I shrugged.

She smiled. "Good, because when the time is right, it'll be worth it."

"Yep."

She looked at me.

"Is the time right, now?"

She gave me a look.

I laid there. "How about now?"

She rolled her eyes.

"Now?"

"No, Michael. Damn, you're impatient." She sighed.

"I can't help it if my girl is hot." I shrugged.

Then a pillow hit my face as she giggled. I grabbed the pillow from her then pulled her to me, kissing her. I'm good at waiting for her. I would wait for her forever.

CHAPTER 13

TAKING IT EASY

Lyric

The night of homecoming, I ended up staying the night at Michael's place. The evening exhausted me, and he wanted to make sure I ate something. The day had taken an emotional toll on me. It usually does when people set out to make your life harder than needed. Do you allow them?

After eating, I laid in his bed, trying not to overthink. I had a habit of doing that. No matter what you do, there will always be that one person who thinks less of you. There still is.

Being a Gray comes with the territory of people judging you. The difference was that we rarely cared about what people thought. That's what bothered them the most is the fact of who we are. We didn't have to prove anything to anyone.

As I laid there in my thoughts, Michael laid down next to me. "What are you thinking?"

"How callous people can be."

"There will always be those insensitive people out there. They're so miserable that they would rather try to make other people miserable. Instead of fixing what's wrong with them, they would rather focus on other people's faults."

"It's a shame, isn't it?"

"Nope, because most people who are miserable end up alone and miserable. I prefer to be happy." He smiled, which made me laugh. Michael had an interesting perspective.

He pulled me to him and kissed me as he deepened it. I wrapped my arms around his neck as I kissed him back, but we stopped before it went further. I wasn't ready yet.

The last person I had been intimate with on that level was Daniel. It's a little hard to shift gears to another person once you have been with someone in that way. For me, it was at least.

I rubbed his cheek with my thumb as I held it in my hand. We stared into each other's eyes, holding the gaze between us.

"I'm sorry, Michael. I'm not ready yet."

"Don't be sorry, Lyric. When you're ready, you'll let me know. What kind of guy would I be if I forced you before you were ready?"

"A foolish one?" I shrugged as he rolled his eyes. I couldn't help but laugh as he pulled me to him.

I cuddled into him and drifted off to sleep. I needed the rest. Within minutes, I was out.

*****

I stirred and opened my eyes to find Michael gone. I glanced at the clock, and my eyes widened. One in the afternoon! What the hell?

I grabbed my phone and had thirty-seven missed phone calls and fifty text messages. I had a couple of unsavory voicemails from all my siblings, Frick, and Frack.

Who do I call first? Let's see. Who won't give me a challenging time? Nope, nope, nope, nope, I thought as I scrolled through my phone. It screwed me on who to call except for one person who doesn't say much. Yep, I'm calling that person.

I dialed a number. The person picked up after the first ring.

Hello?

"It's me. When we returned, I spent the night at Michael's house. I woke up a few minutes ago."

Did anything happen?

"What? No! Come on! What kind of girl do you think I am?"

Do you want me to answer that?

"Thanks for the vote of confidence."

No problem, Lyric.

"You're a real twit. Do you know that?"

I can't be a bigger twit than you. Beggars can't be choosers.

I sat there, thinking to myself, why did I call this tool? Oh, that is right. He's my freaking brother.

Don't worry. I'll beat off the dogs so they don't jump on you when you come home.

"Have I told you how annoying you are?"

No, but you do it, anyway. So, what else is new? Are you okay?

"Yeah, Michael made sure I ate and got some sleep. Although I need to take my medication."

Good. We'll see you later.

I told Lex bye and hung up. I crawled out of bed and looked for my purse. I found it, digging through it to find the pill bottle. Popping the lid, I shook one out onto my hand and walked into the bathroom, closing the door behind me.

*****

Michael

I came up to check on Lyric to see if she was awake. Yesterday was a rough day for her. I didn't understand how people can be so cold and callous towards someone because they can.

No one has a right to be nasty because they think they have the right. Everyone has a battle they're fighting. Sometimes, a little compassion goes a long way. I learned that from my dad.

I remember he told me, even if someone allows you to hurt someone, don't. It makes you no better than them. People will always attack someone they feel is weaker also if they aren't. Healthy people don't hurt others because they can. They help others because that's who they are.

I always kept that advice in the back of my mind.

When I came into my room, I found Lyric gone. I don't think she went far, considering her stuff was still here. I noticed the bathroom door cracked.

I checked it and was about to open it. Lyric screamed, causing me to yell.

Once we collected ourselves, she hauled off and smacked me on the arm. "Don't do that! You almost gave me a freaking heart attack!"

"Well, don't run off without telling someone."

"I went to the bathroom to take my medication." She held up the pill bottle to me.

"Oh."

"Yeah, and I made everyone upset when I didn't come home. My family hasn't heard from me, and my brother was no help." She sat on the bed.

"That is my fault. I should have called your family."

"It's no one's fault. I'm eighteen, not five. I'm with you. Where does my family think I am?"

I sat down next to her. "Lyric, people will still worry no matter what age you are. I know I still worry about my family."

"I know, but they also have to understand I'm doing well. Although, I'm not sure about sleeping until one in the afternoon."

"Last night drained you. I figured you needed the sleep."

"I also need to take my medication, so I can eat."

"Point made."

"Now, I need food." She grinned, which made me smile. Hearing her say that made me happy. I couldn't stand girls who starve themselves because they think a guy likes them that way. I prefer girls with good appetites who enjoy food.

We got off the bed and went downstairs. Maverick was making lunch. I gave him a hand while Lyric took a seat at the table.

"I figure you would be with Larkin," I said, grabbing food.

"Well, since she's a tough nut to crack, which is a no." He sighed.

"I take it she still hasn't let her wall down."

"Not after that one time. I'm making headway. Then I screw it up." Maverick stirred the pot.

"You know, if you want to get Larkin's attention, why not make her food?" Lyric asked.

"I tried that. Larkin took the food and walked away. I mean, what does a guy have to do to make a little headway with someone?" Maverick asked.

"Get someone to help you, who Larkin won't say no to," I said, looking at Lyric while Maverick did the same.

"What? Why are you looking at me like that?" She gave us a weird look.

We walked towards her as she looked at us.

"Lyric, one thing makes Larkin happier than food," I told her.

"Like what?" Lyric asked.

Maverick and I smiled.

"Oh, come on," she said.

"Give the poor boy a bone, Lyric," I said. "For me?"

She narrowed her eyes on me. "That's a dirty trick, Michael."

I smiled.

"Fine, but if this goes south, it's on you," she said.

"But it won't. Give Larkin a little nudge," I said, getting a look from Lyric.

"Okay, fine. What do you two tools suggest?" Lyric asked us.

"I'm glad you asked," I said.

"I didn't mean it like that, but go on," she said.

That's when I decided how we should do it. Maverick needed a foot in the door to help him on his way. Whether it progressed is on him. That should be fun.

CHAPTER 14

SURPRISE!

Lyric

How did I get roped into this situation? Oh, that is right. Michael has a weird charm that makes you want to help him. I swear he was getting it later.

I came home and got tackled by everyone. After the million questions and yelling, I found my footing. Now to figure out how to get Larkin to agree to Michael and Maverick's plan. That would take finesse and a lot of tact.

I took a relaxed approach with my tactic.

I strolled into Larkin's room as she was reading through a notebook. "Hey, Lark?"

"Yeah?" Larkin looked at her notebook.

"I'm wondering if you wanted to hang out tonight?"

"Yeah, sure." She didn't bother to look up from the notebook.

"How about we grab some dinner and see a movie?"

She stopped to look at me, and I knew that look. Larkin was astute to things.

She closed her notebook, tossing it onto the desk. "Okay, what's up?"

"What do you mean?"

"Lyric, you're terrible at acting casual. What gives?"

"Okay, fine. Michael and Maverick want to have dinner tonight with us."

She arched an eyebrow and narrowed her lips. "Why?"

I sighed. "Because Maverick wants to get to know you better."

"I'm fine with me over here, and he's way over there." She pointed with her finger.

"Lark, give the guy a break. He's trying."

"Yeah, well, when he ignored me, that spoke volumes, didn't it?"

I pursed my lips. Plan A ended as an epic failure. Time for Plan B.

"Fine, you leave me no choice." I shrugged.

I walked to the door, opened it, and my six cousins entered.

"She's all yours, boys," I said.

They walked over as I left the room. Thank you, Uncle Noah, for giving me the suggestion with what you did to Ma.

*****

"Was it necessary to bound and gag her?" Michael asked me in the front seat.

I turned to see Larkin glaring at me. Maverick sat behind Michael, wishing he was anywhere but here.

"Hey, I tried Plan A. That didn't work. So, I resorted to Plan B." I shrugged, and he sighed. Let's hope Larkin doesn't kill Maverick.

*****

We got to the diner, and they brought Larkin out of the car. As they untied her, I said, "Don't even think about doing what you're going to do. I don't want to call Dad and Ma and tell them why we're in jail again."

Michael and Maverick looked at me.

"Don't ask." I shook my head.

They finished untying her, and she crossed her arms. They took a step back while I rolled my eyes. Cowards.

I walked over to her. "Now we'll eat, then see some lame-ass movie because that's what you do when you go out with someone you like."

"I dislike him," she said, pointing at Maverick.

"Oh?"

"Yes."

"Then why do you get jealous when another girl even looks his way?"

"I do not!"

"Uh, huh, sure, you don't." I rolled my eyes.

"I don't know what you're talking about." She shrugged.

I gave her a look. Okay, she wants to play, let's play. I turned around and walked over to Maverick, and touched his arm.

Michael leaned over to me. "What are you doing?"

"Give it a minute. I'm proving a point."

It took less than a minute before Larkin stormed over and yanked me away from Maverick. "Don't touch him!"

"But why? You don't like him. You said it yourself." I feigned innocence.

"Because, because, ugh."

Maverick stood there with his hands in his pockets while Michael watched.

"Okay! Fine! I like him!" She spoke.

Maverick's head snapped in her direction. "You do?"

"Yes, but don't overthink it." She turned and walked away.

"That is good enough for me." Maverick smiled as he followed her.

I couldn't help but laugh at the way they were acting. Larkin always had a more tough exterior to her. Luna was boy crazy, and Lakin was more into chicks. I was low-key about everything. The problem was my sister never even mentioned any guy she liked while growing up.

Michael stopped me from following them into the diner. "So, what's Larkin's deal?"

"To be honest, Larkin has always been more guarded about things, even with boys. She has never spoken about liking someone, ever. At least, not to me." I shrugged.

With that, I went into the diner.

*****

Michael

As I watched Lyric go into the diner, I had to wonder if there was more to Larkin's reasons than anyone realized. It was time to find out.

We ate and talked. Lyric is right. Larkin guarded herself, and Maverick was dying, trying to make conversation. It was time to put my theory to the test.

"Tell me a little about yourself, Larkin," I said.

She shrugged. "There's not much to tell."

"I'm sure there is. So, why don't we cut the bullshit and get to the point?"

She frowned at me.

"Lyric tells me you have never liked a boy before Maverick."

"Michael," Lyric said.

I looked at her. "It's fine." Then I turned back to Larkin. "So, I'll guess there was a boy, and it didn't end well for you."

"I-I don't know what you mean," she said.

"Oh, you do."

"N-no." Larkin gave me a look, which I've seen before with Mia.

"Larkin, he hurt you, didn't he?"

She opened her mouth, then shut it. That's all I needed to know. I knew who it was. It doesn't take a genius to figure it out.

"What's going on?" Lyric asked me.

"Larkin should be the one to tell you, and I don't think you'll like it," I told her.

Lyric looked at me, then at Larkin. "What's he talking about?"

"No one," she said.

"Lark?"

"Drop it, Lyric."

"No, I won't drop it. What is Michael talking about, Larkin? Was there something going on between you two?"

"No."

"Then what?"

She stared at Lyric, not knowing what to say.

Then I finally said, "It was Roger."

"What?" Lyric and Maverick asked, shocked.

Larkin shifted her eyes down as she looked at her hands.

"Roger was a guy she liked until he ruined it for her when he did what he did," I said.

"Oh, my God," Lyric said.

"Larkin? Why didn't you tell me?" Maverick asked her.

"Would it matter?" She asked.

"Only to help you."

She turned to him. "I had a crush on Roger, but he was dating Piper. I didn't know he was that kind of guy. I thought he was this grand guy until he wasn't. Afterward, thinking of liking another guy terrified me. If someone I liked could do that to me, who's to say another one wouldn't?"

Maverick sighed. "It doesn't."

I knew what he thought because it's easy to figure out. Maverick figured he didn't stand a chance now. Sometimes, we need perspective.

"Then why not take your time and get to know each other as friends," I said.

They both looked at me.

"I mean, what could it hurt? Who knows, you may find out you both like each other." I shrugged.

They looked at me and each other.

"I guess that would work." Larkin shrugged.

"Yeah, sure," Maverick said.

"Good, now let's finish dinner, then see a movie before we miss it." I finished my food, as did everyone else. Once we finished eating, I paid, and we left for the movie theater within walking distance. Maverick and Larkin were ahead of us.

Lyric looked at me. "How did you know about Larkin?"

"It's easy to figure out. Think about it. You like someone. The person hurt you as Roger did with Larkin. It'll make you distrust any guy, let alone yourself."

"I guess so. I never thought about it."

I stopped her. "Don't overthink it, Lyric. Something tells Maverick will win her over one day."

Then we heard an "Ow!"

"Or not," I said as we hurried over to them.

"What was that for?" Maverick asked, rubbing his face.

"You tried to hold my hand," she said.

"I was trying to hold open the door for you." He rolled his eyes.

"Oh."

Yep, they weren't getting off to a brilliant start, even as friends. That would take a lot of work. I grabbed the door and opened it, motioning for them to walk through, which they did. I shook my head. Yep, this would take a lot of time.

CHAPTER 15

BOO! A HALLOWEEN CHAPTER

Lyric

Today is Halloween, and everyone was in full scary mode. Halloween is our thing. We enjoy everything about it. However, my mind lingered with the day.

I couldn't help it. I thought about Daniel until Michael scared the shit out of me.

"That's not funny," I said, smacking him.

"It was a little funny." He chuckled.

I rolled my eyes at him.

"You're a twit." I sighed.

"Yeah, but I'm your twit." He placed his hands on my waist and pulled me close to him. Then he crashed his lips onto mine. I wrapped my arms around him as I kissed him back.

With Michael, even if my mind lingered, it didn't stay there for long. He knew how to bring it back to the forefront.

"If you two keep making out like that, we'll never finish," Kaiden said.

"Oh, we'll finish in like twenty years, or Grammy may outlive us," Kain said.

"She will. What does Grampa feed her? Because that woman won't die."

"Some weird-ass shit. Who knows?" Kain shrugged.

"I beg your pardon, but I don't eat weird-ass shit even though Nathaniel tries to feed it to me," we heard a voice say. Oh, no.

We turned to see Grammy, along with Grampa and Nana, walked up.

"What are you doing here? Not that we aren't ecstatic to see you and all. But why?" Kain asked.

Grammy whacked Kain with her cane. "I know sarcasm when I hear it, you twit. Remind me to talk to your twit father."

"Oh, please do," Kaiden said.

She hauled off and whacked him.

"Sonofabitch!" He grabbed his leg.

We watched as she walked up to us. She sized up Michael.

"So, you're dating my granddaughter," Grammy said.

"Yes, ma'am," Michael said.

"Are you high or something?"

"Excuse me?"

"High? You know, like toke the Ganga, Maryjane, the herb special. Weed, deary."

"No."

"Well, what good are you?" She sighed, walking into the house.

Michael gave me a look.

"Ignore her. She doesn't do that," Grampa said.

"No, but I would like to start, Nathaniel!" She spoke.

"I swear I'll hurt Jonas and Cayson when I see them," he told Nana.

"Yep."

They walked inside.

"Well, Grammy is interesting," Michael said.

"You haven't seen anything yet."

We walked into the house. Grammy was sitting on a couch and patted a seat next to her when she saw us. Oh, man.

We walked over and sat down on each side of her. She looked at us, then at Michael. "You remind me of my Nathaniel, who I love, but he's a king-size twit."

Michael knitted his brows, and I facepalmed myself.

"At least, you didn't waste time getting together with Lyric as he did with Patty. I swear that boy couldn't get it together to save his life."

"Well, I love Lyric. Why wouldn't I want to be with her?"

"Because most people stop themselves from wanting happiness. Life is too short to be miserable all the damn time. Well, in my case, too long." She smirked.

Michael chuckled. I had to wonder if there was something wrong with him.

"That is true. People worry too much about others to enjoy their lives and the people in them. They would rather be miserable and wallow in past events than move forward."

I turned and looked at him.

"You sound like you've been there," she said.

"Yes, ma'am, I have. But the past doesn't define you. It helps shape you into the person you are."

"That is good. Never wallow. It does nothing for anyone. You live and love like each day is your last because one day it might be." She grinned.

There was truth to those words.

"Now, have you two done the hippity-dippity yet?" Grammy asked.

"Excuse me?" Michael asked.

I facepalmed myself.

"You know the freaky, coitus, mating, nooky?"

He cocked his head and squinted his eyes.

"Sex, dear." She patted the side of his face.

"Oh."

I buried my head in my hands.

"No, we haven't. Lyric isn't ready, and I won't push her."

She turned to me. "Slow on the uptake, are we?"

I gave her a look.

"You're young and viral. You know your grandfather, and I went at it until the day he died. We were having some fun, and the minute he exploded, so did his heart. There's nothing such as giving a whole new meaning to the big O." She gave us a devilish grin.

"Oh, God," I said.

"Yeah, that's what he said too, dear. Keep up," Grammy told me. "Hey, if you go, then go in a blaze of glory."

I couldn't sit there anymore. This entire conversation was unnatural. So, I got up and left.

*****

Michael

Grammy was quite an interesting character, but she was realistic. I listened to her, and she made sense. Yeah, she may appear bold and brassy, but she told it like it was. Her brassiness could turn off some people, but she made sense if they listened.

There is a time and place for everything. There was also a point where people must understand words can hurt. Grammy didn't say what she said to be hurtful, but sometimes, people took it that way. Life isn't always fair and happy. Sometimes, it's harsh. People can be insensitive and not realize their words hurt others. That's not being truthful. It's ignorant.

I enjoyed listening to the old bird. Grammy was insightful about life where others weren't. She knew who was decent and who wasn't.

I went to find Lyric after Grammy caught wind of the others. I figure I'd let her have time with her family.

I found Lyric in the kitchen, pouring a cup of coffee. I walked over and slid my hands around her waist.

"I'm sorry about Grammy. Sometimes, she can be crazy." She sighed.

"I found her delightful."

"What?"

She turned to face me. I placed my hands on the counter. "Your grandmother is a wise woman. Yes, she may say things people find insulting, but that's because people are way too uptight. Let me ask you something. When Daniel died, did she ever make you feel worse than you already did?"

She thought about it, and her brows furrowed. "No, she didn't."

"Exactly because she's a wise woman and lived a long time. She knows the difference. It's making someone realize they are being a twit and knowing when they already feel bad as it is. There's a difference."

"I guess I never looked at it that way."

"Few people do. Come on. I'll show you." I took her hand and led her out of the kitchen. We listened to what her Grammy was saying. Never once did I hear her say something hurtful or judgmental.

We snuck away and went outside as I saw Lyric's grandparents on the back deck. They hugged her.

"How are you doing, kiddo?" Her Grampa asked her.

"Much better," Lyric said.

"That's good to hear."

"Can I ask you both something?"

"Sure," they said.

"Has Grammy said anything hurtful when she is honest?"

Nate thought about it. "No. Sure, Ma can say things people will take the wrong way. With the important things, she never attacks someone. It's not who she is."

"What do you mean?"

He sighed. "When someone attacked your nana one night, she helped take care of her, but she also told her parents. It's what you do. The last thing you do is kick a dog when they're down."

I listen to the three of them talk. Lyric was getting a better understanding of Grammy than she realized. Sometimes, a little perspective helps.

*****

Lyric

As everyone was getting ready, I talked to Grammy. She was sitting at the table drinking a cup of coffee while wearing a pair of devil horns. That was an exciting look.

I took a seat at the table with her.

"Nice costume," I said.

"It's simple and easy. That is my motto." Grammy smirked.

"Can I ask you something?"

"I suppose. What's on your mind?"

"Do you ever feel people judge you because of your behavior?"

"Ask me if I care what people think? That would be a big fat no. I don't give a flaming shit about what people think about me. People are too rash to judge others based on a few things. They don't see the entire picture, but what they want to see."

"I never thought of it like that."

"Few do. Most people have a stick up their ass, anyway. If they pull the stick out long enough, they'll see more and not be so stiff in their way of thinking. Those people are boring. They don't live life. When you love, you don't have time to judge others."

Wow, Michael was right. People didn't listen to her enough. I know we didn't, but she made perfect sense.

The others came down in costumes as I sat there, and they looked at us. Then they bolted. Grammy chuckled as I laughed.

I got changed and left. It was Halloween.

*****

I left the house to find Michael waiting for me. I ran over and threw my arms around his neck as I crashed my lips into his.

We pulled apart.

"Not that I'm complaining, but what was that for?"

"Because sometimes, living is better than existing." I smiled as he smiled back. He kissed me, and we made our way to a party.

We had fun but left to head back and watch horror films. It's our tradition.

It didn't help with a running commentary from Grammy.

"Don't go in there, you twit!" Grammy said.

Scream!

"I told ya, but hey, don't listen to me." She shrugged.

We looked at her as we watched the movie. Every time something happened, Grammy yelled at the screen. Yep, she was one of those people.

She went to bed, thank God. It's not that I don't enjoy my family, but sometimes, things they do can annoy the piss out of me.

We fell asleep watching movies. As I slept, someone held me. While half asleep, I opened my eyes to see Daniel. What the hell?

"Daniel?"

"I thought you loved me."

"I do."

"Then why are you with him?"

"Daniel."

"It's all your fault." He got up.

"Daniel! Wait!"

I found myself standing in his bedroom. Then it happened.

Bang!

I stood in horror as he pulled the trigger and collapsed onto the floor. Then I screamed.

CHAPTER 16

OUR PAST CAN HAUNT US IF WE LET IT

Lyric

"Lyric!"

Arms held me as I screamed and babbled. Oh, my God! That was a hellish nightmare.

"Lyric! It's me, Michael. Open your eyes."

I opened my eyes, glancing around the room. Everyone was staring at me as Grampa and Nana came downstairs.

I buried my head into Michael and clung to him. The nightmare terrified me, and I felt horrible. His words sliced through my brain and heart. It was all my fault.

Michael held me as I repeated the words over and over. Then what I said next shocked everyone. "I can't do this."

I pushed him away as I got up and ran. He ran after me.

"Lyric!" Michael chased after me until he reached me, then stopped me.

"I can't do this! Because I fell in love with you, I betrayed Daniel! I can't betray him! It's all my fault! Because of me, he killed himself!"

"Lyric, you didn't cause his death! He was sick! Your mind is working overtime! Your survivor's guilt is eating at you! It's not your fault, baby."

I cried. "So, why does it feel like it is?"

"He was your first love. Because he didn't break up with you when he left, he died. How do you hate a ghost? You don't."

I cried as he pulled me to him. It was another setback for me.

* * * * *

Maverick called Jordan, and he drove to meet me. Since it was late, he came to the house. We sat and talked. He helped me understand what Michael was saying.

Then he gave me something to relax my mind a bit. I was emotionally and mentally exhausted. The nightmare was horrible.

As we finished up, my door opened. "Lyric?" A familiar voice asked.

"Dad?"

He broke the gap between us as he wrapped his arms around me and held me. Next, other arms wrapped around me as someone said, "We got you." Uncle Noah held me, along with Dad.

Then I heard Ma ask, "Where's my baby?" She pushed them away as she hugged me. Yeah, never get in between our ma and us. She pulled back. "Are you okay?"

"Now I am," I told her.

"God, I was yelling at your father to drive faster to get here," Ma told me.

"Yeah, thanks for that. It's not like it was fun explaining you were going into labor to get out of a ticket," Dad said.

"But you can't have kids," I said.

"No, but who will question someone who looks like they will." Noah smirked.

"Hey, a mother has to do what a mother has to do! I pushed five kids out of a small hole. I deserve to reach them," she said with Dad giving her a look.

"Who called you?" I asked them.

"We did," Grampa said.

"Sometimes, a child needs their parents," Nana said.

"And sometimes, people need sleep!" We heard Grammy say.

Yeah, this would be a fun night.

*****

Michael

After everyone got settled, I laid in Lyric's bed, waiting on her. No way was I leaving her alone. She came into the room and walked over to the bed.

"Excuse me, what do you think you're doing?" Lyric asked me.

"Waiting on my beautiful girlfriend to join me." I smirked.

She rolled her eyes as she climbed into bed. She crawled under the covers, and I snuggled up to her.

"I didn't mean what I said earlier." She sighed.

"I know. It's a minor setback. We'll get through this."

She nodded as she held onto me. I could tell the nightmare terrified her.

I wanted her to know she could hold on tight, and I would never let her fall.

Once she relaxed, she fell asleep. I stayed up and kept watched. Her eyelids fluttered, and she snores. She looked so small as she laid there. Daniel's death had taken a toll on her in so many ways. How could he do that to her?

Daniel had no right to make her feel like this, even if he was sick. I know people say that's wrong. People don't understand how someone's sickness affects the surrounding people. It's rough because they're on the outside looking in with no way to help.

Lyric beat herself up, mourning him and losing herself. She didn't deserve it.

People think suicide isn't selfish, but it is. It leaves people without answers and too many questions. It leaves people behind, wondering if they did something wrong like Lyric is doing now. I hate seeing her like that.

I laid next to her and held her. As much as I wanted to stay up, I couldn't and fell asleep. Let's hope Lyric doesn't have any nightmares.

*****

I awoke the next day to find three guys staring at me. That is great.

"Dad! Grampa! Uncle Noah! Will you stop staring at Michael like he's your next target!" Lyric said.

I sat up in bed as she walked over to us.

"I'm making sure no hanky panky happened in here last night," Nash said, glaring at me.

"I'll assume you mean sex, and you'll realize when that happens, Lyric and I will be alone," I said, then smiled.

Nate facepalmed himself. Nash's vein popped out of his head. Noah rolled his eyes.

"I swear I'll beat your ass!" Nash said, lunging at me

"Nashville Nathaniel Gray!"

He stopped and cursed to himself.

"Don't you even dare do what you're going to do!"

Damn, I've never seen someone put Nash in his place.

"It looks like someone is still afraid of Mommy." I grinned.

Yeah, that was not the right thing to say. Nash yanked me out of bed and raised his arm while the others tried to stop him, only for someone to say, "Nash! Drop him!"

He let go of me as Maggie walked over.

"Mags, give me a break," Nash told her.

"No, stop hitting people."

"That is my baby girl. I don't need some guy deflowering her."

Lyric looked around the room. Interesting.

"Nash, she is eighteen. When it happens, it'll happen. Need I remind you I was eighteen."

"You remembered?"

"Well, no, your brothers told me." She shrugged.

"Of course, they did." He sighed.

"What? Did you think we would let her wonder about you two? No, she had a right to know what a tool you can be," Noah said.

"Noah, you're not helping," Pat said.

"All right, settle down. This arguing is getting us nowhere. I'm sure Michael wasn't doing anything Lyric didn't want him to," Nate said.

I sat on the floor as they went back and forth.

"Can I get up now?" I asked.

"No," they said.

I sighed as Lyric helped me up. She turned to them. "Look, can you discuss things out there?" She pointed at the door. "I have things to discuss with Michael if you don't mind."

They looked at her and said, "Fine."

They walked out, and she closed the door. I sat down at the bedside. She joined me.

"I'll take a wild guess that you and Daniel did the hippity-dippity," I said, which made me smile.

"Last Thanksgiving. He's the only one I've been intimate with."

Now I understand everything. Lyric had an emotional connection with Daniel. That's why she felt the way she did. The minute you become intimate with someone is the minute you develop a bond.

"That's why you're feeling the way you are. When you're intimate with someone, you develop a bond with the person. It's so intense you still hang on to them even long after it ends."

"Makes sense." She sighed. "What about you?"

"I won't lie. Yes, I have been intimate with women. The first one was around the time my parents died. She couldn't deal with the grief we were going through, or I took care of my sister and cousins. So, she left."

"What about the others?"

"They didn't last long because I refused to bring them around my family. I didn't need my family to get attached to someone if it wouldn't last. The women couldn't understand, and I didn't care. My family came first."

"And me? Where do I fit into this?"

"You, you're special. You made me fall in love with you the first time we talked."

"When we were kids?"

"No."

"Oh."

"The day of Daniel's funeral."

"What?"

"I saw you sitting in this chair alone, broken. How you mourned for someone you loved yet didn't know what to do. How, when you cried, you cried for your broken heart. Then when I walked over, sat down, and looked at you. The minute you turned your head and looked at me, I saw it. That twinkle you had in your eyes. The same one you had the very first time we met."

She smiled. It was something about Lyric's eyes that drew me to her. The first time was a chance. The second time was love.

Then we heard yelling.

"That sounds like Larkin."

We got up and left the room. That can't be good.

*****

Lyric

We came out of my room and saw Larkin throwing things at Maverick, as did the others.

"Oh, come on! We were kids!" Maverick said.

"Kids? You shoved my head into the mud!" Larkin said.

I looked at Michael, who looked at me, confused.

"I was joking!"

"It wasn't funny!"

"Larkin, I was thirteen!"

"And a tool!"

"I don't remember meeting Maverick when we were ten," I told Michael.

"I didn't think you guys did."

"That's because you weren't home," Dad said. "You had gone on a trip with Noah and Marcy, along with the boys."

"Oh, right. We went to Cedar Point. Larkin didn't go, but Luna did," I said.

"I couldn't figure out why I didn't like you until you mentioned you and Major went mudding. Then I realized you were a tool to me." She glared at him.

"Okay, yeah. I was an inconsiderate prick. I was thirteen."

"Well, now you can go get bent." Larkin entered her room and slammed her door shut.

We stood there as Maverick looked at Michael. "You know how you always tell us our past can haunt us?"

"Yeah?" Michael asked.

"Well, mine blew up in my face." Maverick sighed and walked away.

"See, what I mean? Maverick means well. His execution is a bit off," Michael said.

I looked at him, then got an idea.

"I have an idea." I motioned with my finger.

They looked at me.

"It's time to do things the Gray way." I grinned.

They knew what that meant.

CHAPTER 17

CONSPIRING AT ITS BEST

Lyric

You know how, when you have these genes running through your body, you ignore thoughts. Yeah, we didn't. Only because we're Grays, and Larkin is a being twit.

I love my sister, but she's a twit. Yes, Maverick shoved her head in the mud because she said something sarcastic to him. From what Lex told us, he explained what happened. Let me backtrack to what he told us.

Flashback: eight years ago
Larkin

Lyric and Luna went to Cedar Point while the three of us stayed home. Lex wasn't big on roller coasters, and Lakin and I didn't want to go.

We hung out with Piper to find out her cousins were visiting, who is Major and Maverick. Piper said Major is fourteen, and Maverick is thirteen. Okay, no big deal. I didn't come to see them, but Piper.

We were outside playing when we heard voices yell. I turned to see a boy come out of the back patio door. He was adorable.

Then I saw another boy come out. Whoa. He was even cuter.

"I told you they wouldn't like it," the first boy said.

"Who cares? They need a sense of humor." He shrugged.

"Hey Piper," the first one said.

"Hey, Major."

While they talked, I stared at the other boy. He had spiky dark hair and was adorable. I couldn't help but stare at him.

"What are you looking at?" The boy asked.

"Who, me?" I asked.

"No, your shadow. Yeah, you."

"Uh, nothing." My brows furrowed.

"Good, because it's creepy."

Okay, he's mean.

I kept playing and stuck with Lakin. If Lyric were here, she would beat him up. I wish Lyric were here.

Every time I turned around, he kept saying things to me until I snapped.

"Yeah, well, who names their kid Maverick? Sadly, you got your stupid name from a movie!"

"What did you say?"

"Are deaf now? Because I'm sure you're stupid too, Martin, Maury, or whatever the heck your name is!"

"That's it!"

He chased me until he tackled me and shoved my head into the mud, along with my clothes. He got off me. I stood up as my bottom lip quivered, and tears formed.

"Oh, is the whittle baby going to cry!"

"I hate you! I hate you so much. I turned and walked away, leaving him shocked, along with the others.

"Mav, that was harsh," Major said.

"I didn't mean it. The girl made me mad," Maverick said.

"Yeah, well, you did," Lakin said.

Maverick looked at them as they shook their heads. He turned and walked away.

"What is wrong with him?" Lakin asked.

"Maverick hates people teasing him about his name. People at school tease him all the time," Major said.

"Good luck, because when Larkin doesn't like someone, it stays that way." Lakin shrugged.

I walked into the house, and my parents looked at me covered in mud. I shook my head and walked past them. I wouldn't let them see me cry, not today or ever. I knew people didn't like me. They made it clear to me as Lyric protected me, along with the others. They were the only ones I needed.

End of flashback

Lyric

"I remember that day. Mav was pretty mean to her." Major sighed.

"Larkin doesn't open up to anyone. She doesn't want to get hurt," I said.

"So, how do we fix this?" Luna asked.

"I say we lock them in a room and let them beat the hell out of each other," Lakin said.

"Lake, violence is not the answer, but a locked room is," I said, giving them a look. Then we planned.

My sister is stubborn, but she had feelings for Maverick when he wasn't a twit. We needed to get them together alone in a locked room and let them figure it out.

Michael and his family took care of Maverick while we took care of Larkin. They needed to work their shit out.

We made our way to a haunted house since it was still up for the rest of the week. We also paid the people to do us a favor. They agreed. We needed to make sure they didn't know about the other being there.

We went first, followed by the others. The minute Larkin went into a room, they waited until Maverick did too. Then they locked them in as the rest of us escaped. Yeah, we're shits for doing it, but they needed to get it together.

*****

Larkin

The minute I heard the door lock, my eyes widened. Then I heard someone in the room with me. I started pounding on the door.

"Open up! Let me out!"

I heard nothing.

"Please! Let me out!" I cried. I couldn't stand to be here, especially with someone I don't know. That reminded me of what Roger did, and I panicked.

"Let me out! Let me out!" I scratched and pounded on the door.

Then someone wrapped their arms around me, which sent me into a full-blown panic mode.

"Get off me! Don't touch me! Please!" I sobbed as they tightened their arms around me.

"Larkin, it's me, Maverick. It's okay."

I started crying as he held me.

"I got you. Relax. Nothing will happen to you."

"But you're mean!"

"No, I'm not. I was wrong for what I did to you, and I'm sorry."

"But why? Why did you do it?"

"Because I was angry and hurt. I was thirteen and took it out on you when you did nothing wrong. You didn't deserve it."

I broke down and cried in his arms. I wanted people to like me. Every guy I came across did the opposite. It makes a girl feel like she doesn't deserve love, and she's worthless—first Maverick, then Roger. I couldn't win.

"I was stupid. I was stupid for what I did. I was stupid for not realizing what an amazing person you are. I'm a stupid boy." He sighed, which made me laugh a little.

He turned me around, and I looked at him through glassy eyes. I could see the moon shining through the window, hitting his face, showing his remorse.

"Larkin, I'm sorry I hurt you. I regret that day every day. After that, I promised myself I would never hurt another girl.

That and after Michael beat the shit out of me when he found out." He sighed.

I couldn't help but giggle.

"But walking into that bakery, and seeing you again, told me I had one chance to make things right. You weren't that ten-year-old girl anymore. You were older and more guarded. I hated myself knowing I started it all."

"Then be truthful with me. Did you know I was the girl Jordan sent you to help?"

"No, he didn't give me a name. He said what town you lived in, and you worked in a bakery. I didn't know it was you until I saw you, then my heart sank."

He let go of me, walked over to an empty desk, and leaned against it.

"I talked to Michael and explained everything, then I cried. I didn't know what I would do because you already hated me. Then add what happened, and there's no way you would open up to me."

I stood there, not knowing what to say. Yes, Maverick was mean to me, but hearing him tell me those things and mean it, was a different story.

"How do I trust what you're saying is the truth?"

"You don't, and I don't expect you to trust me. All I can do is prove it."

"Then prove it."

"You want me to prove it."

"Yes."

"Fine." He closed the gap between us as he grabbed my face, crushing his lips onto mine. I stood there as he pressed his lips into mine, then moved my hands to his back. He threw so much into that kiss. I gave in and kissed him back.

*****

Maverick

As I held Larkin's face and our lips connected, so did our emotions. It was a long time coming. I never wanted my lips to leave hers. We had shared kisses, but this one was different. It wasn't one-sided.

Then it hit me. All Larkin wanted is truth and trust. She wanted to know I wouldn't let her falter in tough times. She wanted someone to catch her.

When I pulled that stunt, ignoring Larkin, which proved her right. I didn't blame her, but I had to show it to her because I wanted her.

My heart started beating fast as we continued our kiss. I realized I didn't like Larkin, but I fell in love with her. She was the other half I needed in my life. If this kiss is necessary to prove it, then I would show her.

I licked her lips, and she parted them. I slid my tongue into her mouth, letting our tongues dance around each other.

I walked her until her back hit a wall as our kiss grew hungrier. I placed a hand on the wall to support myself as I held her waist with the other. She grasped my hoodie as we continued our passion-induced kiss.

Then the door opened. "Well, that's one way to get them to talk," Kain said.

We stopped, turning to look at them.

"I don't think they meant that way, although that is an interesting technique if I say so myself," Kaiden said.

"Will you twits leave?" Larkin asked.

"Yeah, sure. Don't get yourself knocked up," Kain said as they walked away.

She shook her head as I smiled. I pressed my forehead against hers. "If I must prove to you every day that you can trust me, I will. I can't be without you, Larkin. Please give me a chance." I caressed her cheek.

She looked at me with her bright blue eyes. "Okay."

At that moment, she was giving me a chance. A chance to prove myself. An opportunity I couldn't take for granted. It's my only chance. I leaned in and gave her a soft kiss.

They say the eyes are the window to the soul. They convey so many emotions, and no matter how much you hide, your eyes reveal all. Hers said it scared her, but she had hope.

Larkin hopes that someone will catch her. I made a promise to myself. If I had to, I would always be there to find her. Why? Because I fell in love with Larkin Gray, and one day, I would make her mine.

CHAPTER 18

ASSUMING MAKES AN ASS OUT OF YOU AND ME

Lyric

As the days flew, it wouldn't be long until finals were upon us and Christmas break. Maverick and Larkin were taking things slowly and getting to know each other. Slow was good for them.

Lex and Piper were still going strong, and I was happy for them. They deserved happiness. Lakin and Mia were on a sound footing. Major and Luna? Well, they were still trying to figure it out. Even Frick and Frack found two girls who tolerated them.

Michael and I had an unconventional relationship. Things were heating between us, but I slammed on the breaks every time it got to that point. I knew he would get tired of waiting for me.

I mean, even the most patient guy would get tired of a girl riling him up, only to stop it.

Then the inevitable happened. I saw Michael with another girl on campus. They talked and laughed, but instead of letting my jealousy get the best of me, I called it a day. I couldn't fault him for finding interest in someone else. Daniel damaged me.

*****

Michael

I was talking to Trisha when her boyfriend Henry walked up. He snaked his arm around her waist.

"Hey, Michael," Henry said.

"Hey, Henry."

"I was telling Michael that the four of us should have dinner together," Trisha said to him.

"Sounds good. Let me know when and where. But we need to get going, or we'll be late meeting the wedding coordinator," he said.

"Oh, right. See you later, Michael."

They parted ways with me. Now, to meet up with my girl.

*****

Lyric

I walked to the house and ran to my room, slamming the door shut and locking it. That caused Lakin to come out of her room.

She knocked on my door. "Lyric?"

"Yeah?"

"Are you okay?"

"I'm fine."

"Are you sure? You don't sound fine." She furrowed her brows.

"I'm fine. If Michael comes over, tell him I'm not home."

"Why?"

"Because he found someone new. I hope they're happy together."

I cried.

"Are you sure?"

"Y-yes." I sniffled.

She turned and walked away.

*****

Lakin

I am going to kill him. I want to rip off his head and beat him with it—all this lovey-dovey shit. You're mine. I want to be with you, blah, blah, blah. I'm so glad I'm with a chick.

I left the house with one thing on my mind. I would find Michael and beat the hell out of him. No one messes with my big sister.

I found Michael with Maverick and Larkin.

"Hey, Lake," Larkin said.

I slammed into Michael.

"What the hell?" Michael asked.

"What the hell is right! How dare you dump our sister? You couldn't even find the courage to do it to her face! You had to show her! What the hell is wrong with you?"

"Me? I don't even know what the hell you're talking about, Lakin! I haven't even seen Lyric yet, and I didn't break up with her."

"Funny because you with another girl says otherwise! Get your head out your ass!" I turned and walked away.

Larkin looked at him. "I might be slow to the party, but if this is what it is, you have a lot of explaining to do to Lyric."

"I was talking to Trisha, and her fiancé walked up. We were making plans for the four of us to have dinner together. Trisha is an ex-girlfriend. We ran into each other and were catching up!"

"Yeah, but with everything that is happening with Lyric. She already feels you're tired of her because she hasn't slept with you yet."

"Great." He sighed.

"No offense, cuz, but straightened this out pronto before her dad and uncle caught wind of it. Neither one plays with her," Maverick told him.

While they were figuring out things, I went home. I can't believe that tool. Michael's lucky I didn't beat his ass. I found Mia waiting for me.

"That's not a cheerful look," she said.

"Your brother is a tool."

"What else is new?" She shrugged. "What did he do this time?"

"He got tired of Lyric and dumped her by hooking up with another chick."

We went inside.

"That doesn't sound like Michael."

"Are you defending him?"

"Are you sure you want to go there?" Mia gave me a look that I knew well.

"I don't want to see her hurt." I threw my hands up in the air.

"Lake, Lyric has to realize that not everyone will set out to hurt her."

"I know, but seeing her the night she found Daniel, I had never seen someone so broken. It was like each of us felt her pain. A pain so great you can't breathe." I took a seat on the couch.

Mia joined me.

"Lyric is the strongest one out of us. She keeps us together and in line when we're out of control. But when she's falling apart, so are we. I hated to see her like that."

Mia wrapped her arms around me and comforted me.

*****

Michael

Enough was enough. I'll show Lyric how serious I am about her. I stormed over to her house with Maverick and Larkin behind me.

I whipped open the door and startled Lakin and Mia, giving them a look, and cracked my neck. The situation pissed me off. Someone accuses me of shit I didn't even do.

I ran up the stairs, and knowing she locked the damn door, I picked the lock. Oh, yeah, I knew a lot more than she gave me credit for knowing. I flung open the door, startling her.

"Michael?" Her brows furrowed.

I marched over to her. "Let's make things clear. I'm not freaking cheating on you! I don't do that shit!"

Her eyes widened.

Maverick closed the door to give us privacy.

"I fucking love you! Yes, you frustrate me! But what else is new? But if I must prove it, then so be it." I grabbed her face and crashed my lips into hers, taking her by surprise.

She fought at first until she finally gave in. Things got heated as passion overtook us. We tore at each other's clothes, tossing them aside. I picked her up as she wrapped her legs around my waist. I carried her to the bed and laid her down.

I pinned her wrists down above her head as I positioned myself between her legs. Once I lined myself up, I slid inside of her, all the while never breaking our kiss.

I slid in and out as I thrust inside of her. I released her wrist and moved my hand to her leg, gripping her thigh as I made love to her. She placed her hands on my head, running her hands through my hair.

I left her lips as I moved to her neck as she wrapped her arms around my neck. At that moment, it was only the two of us.

I flipped her on top of me as I held her as we continued to make love. It was something both of us had waited for, and the moment was perfect.

Then I flipped her onto her back as we continued until her muscles tightened. I knew she was close. I leaned in. "It's okay, baby. I got you." She gave in and moaned as she released, causing me to let go with her. I laid there, gazing into her eyes as she gazed into mine. "I love you, Lyric Gray."

"I love you, Michael Harper."

I kissed her as I laid down and pulled her to me while covering us. As we laid there, I ran my fingers up and down on her arm.

"What are you thinking?" I asked her.

She turned and looked at me. "Did you wear protection?"

My eyes widened. Well, shit, so much for the afterglow. We hurried out of bed and dressed. I whipped open the door. We ran downstairs, almost knocking over Lex.

"Sorry, Lex!" I said as we bolted out of the house. Yeah, we were on a mission, not for Nash to kill me. If Lyric gets pregnant, I'm a dead man.

We went to the pharmacy and bought the morning-after pill, along with a box of protection.

Once we returned, she took the pill, and we collapsed onto the bed. She started laughing.

"What?" I glanced at her.

"I was thinking, we better hope my dad never finds out you 'deflowered' me." She giggled.

"Oh, yeah. We know what a scoundrel I am for 'deflowering' someone deflowered." I smirked.

She laughed more. I pulled her to me, kissing her. "I'm sorry."

"I know, but I still love you anyway." I pulled her to me, giving her another kiss. It didn't matter the situation because Lyric was it for me. She has my heart forever, even if she acts like a twit from time to time. It's all about balance.

CHAPTER 19

THE INVITATION

Lyric

After that day, Michael and I grew closer and more in love. I could finally move forward from Daniel. Being with Michael was everything I had hoped for and more. Michael was so different from anyone I had ever met. He was enough for me.

We hung out at his house on the couch when Maverick walked in and handed him an envelope.

"What's this?" He took it from Maverick.

"It looks like a wedding invitation," Maverick said.

He opened it, and sure enough, it was. He read through it and noticed there was a spot for a plus one. "Do you want to be my plus one?" He asked me.

"On one condition."

"What's that?"

"If the wedding sucks, we can leave."

He chuckled. "Yes, we can leave if the wedding sucks."

"Then yes, I'll be your plus one." I shrugged.

Michael filled out the card and placed the response card in the envelope. This wedding gave me a bizarre feeling. Do you know the kind that will end in heartbreak? That would be the one.

✳✳✳✳✳

A week before we headed home for Christmas break, Michael and I attended his ex's wedding. The wedding was beautiful, and so was the bride.

I didn't know why she and Michael broke up. She was stunning. Looking at her made me feel like I didn't measure up. Stupid, I know, but when you see someone like her, you can't help but wonder.

Michael gave my hand a gentle squeeze, and I looked at him. He smiled. Then I realized it didn't matter. The way Michael looked at me made me feel loved.

Once the wedding was over, we made our way to the reception. We found our seats and sat down with other people who we didn't know. That is the problem with most weddings. You get stuck with people, and you get forced to act polite even when you don't know them. It was always tricky.

We sat there and conversed with the people at our table out of politeness. Then they served dinner. After eating, I got up to use the bathroom.

While in the bathroom, I couldn't help but overhear a conversation.

"Oh, my God, Trisha. Did you see the girl Michael brought with him?" Someone asked.

"Yeah, I heard she has issues, and Michael kisses her ass," Trisha said.

"I don't know why," another said.

"Because Michael feels sorry for people. Do you know when we were together, he was so busy with his family I got pushed aside?" Trisha asked the other girls.

"I still can't believe he did that. What was he thinking?" One girl asked.

"He wasn't, but it didn't matter. Henry kept me warm many nights if you know what I mean," Trisha said

"Ooh, girl. Michael sure didn't know what he was missing." One laughed.

I waited until they left to exit the stall. Wow, that blew my mind. How can someone be so cold?

I furrowed my brows and went to check if Michael wanted to leave. If we stayed any longer, things would get worse.

I found Michael, who was talking to the bride and groom. Great.

"Lyric, I want you to meet Trisha and Henry," Michael said, introducing us.

"Yeah, hi. Michael, can we go?" I asked Michael.

"What?"

"I'm not feeling very well."

"Oh, did you catch something?" Trisha asked.

"Something like that," I said to her with a look.

"Lyric," Michael said.

"Michael? Please?"

"Excuse me, but you're acting rude," Trisha said.

I looked at her.

"Lyric?" Michael asked.

I looked at her, then at Michael. "Fine, since I'm acting rude, the bride has a big ass mouth."

"Lyric!" Michael said.

"I would appreciate it if you left," she said.

Michael furrowed his brows at me. Then I figured, okay, if he would act like this, I might as well drop the hammer.

"Okay, I'll leave. But you should know Trisha said, you're only with me because you feel sorry for me. So, I'm guessing bedding me was part of it. She also cheated on you while you were taking care of your family. When your parents died, she hooked up with her now-husband. But I'm rude." I turned and walked away, leaving them stunned.

I walked out of the reception and grabbed my coat. Then I called Lex to pick me up. I heard noises and yelling coming from the place but didn't bother to go back inside.

Lex pulled up, and I got into the car. We pulled away as Michael ran out of the reception to find me, but I was long gone.

*****

In the car, I sat there, staring out of the car window, deep in thought.

"Want to talk about it?" Lex asked.

"Nope, I want to go home and take a bath." I continued to look out of the car window. I should have listened to my gut. Once again, I look like the twit.

When we got home, I faked a smile as I walked in. It's easy to do, considering I had done it for months.

"How was the wedding?" Larkin asked.

"Um, it was okay," I said.

"Where's Michael?" Lakin asked.

"Oh, he stayed. I got tired, so I called Lex to come to get me," I said. I didn't want to get into it tonight. I walked up the stairs as tears fell down my cheeks.

Once I was upstairs, I drew a hot bath and climbed inside. I laid back and soaked. All those words played through my mind. Was I that bad? All I wanted to be was happy. People couldn't let me stay happy.

$$*****$$

Michael

After punching out Henry and shoving cake into Trisha's face, I ran out of the reception to find Lyric, but she left. Shit!

I ran to my car and got in. I can't believe what a twit I was to think she was rude. Lyric wanted to help me, and all I did was treat her like she was causing problems.

I drove over to her house and knocked on the door. Larkin answered. "Do I want to know why you're bloody and covered in a cake?"

"Nope," I said.

Lakin saw me. "Oh, this is priceless." She laughed.

I gave her a look. "Is Lyric here?"

Luna stepped into view. "She's upstairs taking a bath. Although I would take a shower and wash the cake out of your hair."

Larkin grabbed a chunk of cake from me, popping it into her mouth. "Mm, chocolate."

I rolled my eyes, walking past them. I ran up the stairs and down the hallway until I found the bathroom. I opened the door and stepped inside, closing it behind me.

"Michael?" Lyric sat up and stared at me.

I walked over to her. "Lyric, I'm a twit. I should have listened to you, but I didn't. I know you were trying to protect me, and all I could do was treat you like you were rude."

She stared at me.

I paced back and forth. "I mean, you have every right to be mad. Who wouldn't be mad? I'm supposed to love and protect you, and I didn't. Now, I lost you forever, which sucks because you're the best damn thing that has ever happened to me. But you know, that's what I get for being a king-size tool."

Lyric tried to get my attention until she said, "Michael!"

"What?" I stopped my ramble.

"Why do you have a busted lip, a cut over your eye, and are covered in a cake?"

"Funny story. I beat the shit out of the groom and shoved cake into the bride's face. Then all hell broke loose."

"You didn't?"

"Yep, I did. That reminds me, the owners barred me from that place. I have a restraining order against me."

She laughed.

"This isn't funny!"

"It's a little funny." She laughed.

I gave her a blank expression as she laughed, then joined her. I stripped off my suit and climbed into the bathtub.

"Michael!"

"Well, I need a bath. Pass the soap." I held out my hand.

She rolled her eyes and handed me the soap. I grabbed her wrist and pulled her to me, pulling her into a kiss. We pulled back.

"I'm sorry. I should have listened to you."

"Yeah, but as you said, you're a king-size tool."

"Gee, thanks."

"But I still love you, Michael Harper." She pressed her lips to mine. I didn't hesitate to kiss her back.

We finished up in the tub and ended up in her room. After having makeup time, we both laid in her bed, looking at each other.

"I've learned a valuable lesson tonight," she said.

"What's that?"

"I'll never go to another ex's wedding again." She giggled, which made me chuckle.

"Well, I learned something myself."

"What's that?"

"You're the best damn thing that has ever happened to me, and I never want to lose you. I love you, Lyric."

She placed her hand on my cheek. I pulled her into a kiss. Yep, I would never make the same mistake I made tonight. It almost cost me someone significant, and her name is Lyric Gray.

CHAPTER 20

HOLLY: A CHRISTMAS CHAPTER

Lyric

Finals were over, and we headed home for the holidays. It made me happy to know I wouldn't be alone for a holiday, thinking about Daniel. Sure, Michael and I might have our difficulties, but we work things out. Neither of us is perfect, which is fine by me.

Once we got home, our parents tackled us. They missed us. It didn't matter because we missed them, too.

After getting settled, I heard a knock on my door. Dad was leaning against it.

"Hey," I said.

"Hey, baby girl. Are you good?"

"Yeah, I'm good." I smiled as he strolled over to me.

He wrapped his arms around me, giving me an enormous hug. I didn't hesitate to hug him back. "It's good to see you are smiling again."

"It's good to be smiling again."

"Does this have something to do with a certain Harper boy?"

"He makes me happy."

"I know," He sighed, dropping his arms.

He took a seat on my bed. I joined him.

"It's hard to see you and your siblings grow up. I remember when you were little. I wanted to keep you little forever."

"All parents do, but we grow up at some point."

"Yes, I know. Trust me. I know." He took my hand and held it. "I want you all happy. A father doesn't want to see his babies hurt."

"Trust me. I am, even when Michael's a complete tool."

I explained what recently happened. Dad laughed and explained what happened to him. I couldn't help but smile when he told me what Ma did. If things had turned out differently, I would have done the same deal. We got our crazy genes from her.

Then the fighting started, and Dad checked to see what was happening. Ah, it's good to be home.

After getting settled, Larkin walked into my room.

"So, I have a question. Let's say there's this boy who can be a twit but can also be sweet. Do you think it would be wrong for me to feel something for him? You know, with everything that happened?" She bit the tip of her thumb.

"If you like this boy, it shouldn't matter. Are you afraid to like Maverick, Lark?"

She sighed. "Lyric, I'm afraid if I get close to him or anyone, that I'll get hurt. I mean, look at what Roger did."

"Roger is a dick, and he made a dick move." Hearing Roger's name pissed me off.

"I know, I'm afraid it'll happen again," her voice cracked.

I furrowed my brows. Larkin can say things that seem offensive, but it's how she protects herself.

I walked over and hugged her.

"Listen to me. If Maverick's worth anything, he'll wait. He'll be gentle and kind. He'll take excellent care of you and won't make you do anything you're not ready for."

"And what if he doesn't wait? Then what?"

"Then Maverick isn't the one."

She nodded as I smiled at her.

I hated Roger for what he did to my sister. He made it so she couldn't trust anyone. My gut told me that Maverick wasn't anyone. There was something about the Harper family that made them different. As much as you wanted to get mad at them, you couldn't.

We left my room, only to get told that our parents had a surprise for us. What now?

*****

We pulled up into a parking lot and got out of the cars.

"You rebuilt the bakery?" Larkin screamed in surprise.

"Yep, it's ready to go," Dad told us.

We cheered. The bakery was an enormous part of our lives, and it was good to see it working again.

The bakery was different but better. Then we heard a bell chime.

"Is anyone home?" Someone asked.

We turned to see our uncles, which we ran to them. We all talked at once as they listened and laughed. We missed them so much.

Noah pulled me aside. "So?"

"I'm happy." I grinned.

"I'm glad. I worry about you."

"I know. The past few months have been rough. I didn't think I would ever get through it or be myself again."

The others looked on at us.

"Lyric, losing someone is devastating. No one expected you to bounce back right away, but it worried us."

"I know, but it took someone special to show me death is not the end. Sometimes, we keep going even when we want to give up. I realize now that even when I wanted to give up, no one would let me."

Everyone looked at me.

"Lyric, we want you to be happy," Nixon said. "We want each of you to be happy." He looked at Larkin, who looked around. "Lark?"

"What?" Lark asked.

"You've been acting like a squirrel."

"I don't know what you mean."

Nixon gave her a look as she walked away.

"Okay, fine. There's this boy that I sort of like. But here's the thing, what if things progress and I can't stop them? What if what happened with Roger happens with him? What if?"

We watched as she broke down.

"What if Roger damaged me beyond repair?"

"What if I said that would never happen?" Someone asked.

We turned to see Maverick, along with the others.

"You don't know that. No one does."

Maverick walked towards her. "But what if I do? What if you're not damaged because what happened wasn't your fault?" He reached her and placed his hands on her face. "What if I said you are the most amazing person I have ever met? That your face lights up at the thought of food. You have a bond with your siblings that is indescribable. You hide your hurt with sarcasm. That all you want is people to be your friend. What would you say when I tell you I'm not in a rush and will follow your lead?"

"Then I would say I'm scared to death."

"It's okay to feel scared. It's the unknown, but I can tell you I like you."

She nodded as she hugged him, catching him off guard, but he hugged her back.

As we stood there, Michael leaned in. "Maverick doesn't like Larkin."

"What?" I gave him a look.

"He's in love with her." He gave me a knowing look as my eyes widened.

Well, shit. I turned and looked at Maverick and Larkin. Houston, we have a problem.

*****

Michael

I knew once I told Lyric that it would shock her. But that was the truth. Maverick was in love with Larkin Gray.

We hung out for a while. Then I wanted to take Lyric somewhere. I had something planned for her.

I drove her to this place and pulled into a parking lot. We got out and walked into the building. I took her hand as we walked to a room. Then once inside, I turned on a light. She stopped, frozen in her tracks.

"Oh, my God." She walked around and looked at all the different paintings on the wall. I stood there with my hands in my pockets, feeling nervous.

"These are amazing."

I stayed quiet until she came to a painting of her.

She stood there in awe as I stood there, waiting for her to speak. I didn't know what she would say.

She turned to me. "Who did this?"

"That would be me."

"What?"

I looked at the floor.

"Wait. Did you do all these?" She pointed at all the paintings.

"Yeah,"

"These are amazing. I didn't know you were an artist."

"It was something I dabbled with when I was younger. It helped me relax when I lost my parents."

She walked over to me. "They're amazing. You have genuine talent, Michael."

"I wanted to show them to you before the art museum opened the exhibit."

"You're showcasing them?"

"Yes, the money will help with my family's schooling."

"I thought your parents left you and your family life insurance money."

"They did, but it will only last for so long. We have three and a half years of schooling to do. Mia is starting. Maverick will intern, which means he doesn't get paid. Major will be an apprentice, which means he doesn't get paid either."

She looked at me.

"Unlike most people, we aren't rich. We don't have people to pay for our way. That's why I worked three jobs to support them. I made sure they stayed out of trouble and did well in school." My voice raised as my blood boiled. "But you wouldn't know that, would you?"

She stared at me as I regretted my words which slipped past my lips.

"Lyric, I didn't mean it."

"No, you meant it. Now I know you think I'm a spoiled rich kid whose parents gave her whatever she wants. It's fine. I thought you were different." She walked away.

Damn it! That was not how I wanted this evening to go.

*****

Lyric

I walked out of the gallery as tears fell down my cheeks. I didn't think Michael saw me like that. My parents had money, but they never flaunted it and did something they loved. They never taught us to consider money more important than people.

I called and had someone pick me up after walking a while. The person pulled up, and I got into the car.

"Thanks, Uncle Noah." I turned and looked out of the window.

"Do you want to talk about it?"

"What's there to talk about, Uncle Noah? I'm a spoiled rich kid who doesn't understand struggling." I sniffled.

"Okay, let's get ice cream and talk." He pulled out.

*****

We entered an ice cream parlor and got some ice cream before taking a seat. I sat there, jabbing my ice cream with my spoon.

"Lyric, relationships aren't easy. They're hard. But people work at them."

"I know. But every time I turn around, it seems like we're falling apart more and more. When does it get to the point when you finally call it a day?"

"You don't."

I glanced at him.

"When you love someone with so much intensity, you never give up on them. Even your parents crashed and burned at one point." He made a crashing sound.

"What?"

"Yeah, your dad could be a royal tool. He couldn't decide if he wanted to be with your mom, so she dumped his ass." He chuckled.

"Oh?"

"Yep, then he saw her with other guys. Yeah, my brother let jealousy get the best of him. They got back together only for her to lose her memory of them. But he never gave up on them. If he did, I'm sure Nixon and Nathan would have beat the shit out of him."

I laughed. "What about you?"

"I would have laughed." He smirked, causing me to laugh even more.

As we talked, I felt better. Then I noticed someone standing there. We saw Michael.

"I will give you two a minute." Noah got up and gave Michael his spot.

Michael looked like he had been crying.

"I'm sorry. I hate that I said those things because I know that's not you. Since my parents died, I have struggled to take care of my family. When people assume things, it makes it harder. I don't want you to give up on us. I can't handle it if you're not in my life. Please don't leave me, Lyric." Tears fell down his cheeks.

I sat there. That was the first time I saw Michael broken. He was usually so happy and cheerful, but now he was hurting. So, I did the one thing I could think of at that moment. I got out of my seat and slid next to him in the booth. I wrapped my arms around him, comforting him, then I let him cry.

He held on tight as he buried his face into me, crying. Sometimes, we don't need to say anything but let people know we care by showing it. A simple hug will do.

After a few minutes, I said, "As much as I get mad at you, I could never leave you, you twit. I love you way too much."

He chuckled before lifting his head to look at me.

"Michael, we'll fight. It's inevitable. But we'll still be together. The heart wants what the heart wants."

He nodded before pulling me into a kiss. We pressed our foreheads together and looked at each other. Thanks to Uncle Noah and our talk, now I understand things better. Relationships aren't perfect. People fight, but love gets you through it all.

*****

The rest of the Christmas break was better. Michael and I had our fights, but we always made up afterward. Dad kept trying to keep us at a safe distance, only to earn a slap from Ma.

My siblings were crazier than ever, but nothing new there. When aren't they crazy?

An enormous thing happened at Christmas. Since everyone was coming to our house because it was our turn to host, our home was crazy.

We got everything ready, albeit with arguing. Every Christmas, someone fights, and Dad has to referee. It's a typical day at our house.

Everyone arrived, and Christmas was in full swing. It was nice to see everyone.

Then came the time for the gift exchange. As we exchanged gifts, Michael had a special gift for me. With everyone gathered around, admiring what they had received, he took my hand and led me to the tree.

"Michael? What's going on?"

"Look in the tree, and you'll see something special to you from me." He stood with his hands behind his back.

I looked through the tree and found a bulb with my name on it. I pulled it out and studied it, then realized there was a button. I pressed the button, and the top popped open. My eyes widened.

Then Michael got down on one knee.

"Lyric Gray, when I met you at sixteen, I didn't know I would fall in love with you. But the day I took a seat next to you was the day you captured my heart. We'll have our differences and difficulties. A wise person told me when you love someone as deep as the ocean. You hold on to it. It's a once-in-a-lifetime of love."

I stared at him in stunned silence.

"That person was your dad when I asked his permission to ask you the next question. Lyric, will you marry me?"

My mouth dropped open as Dad smiled.

My heart was beating out of my chest as I cleared my throat. "Yes, Michael Harper, I'll marry you."

He stood and picked me up, swinging me around. He crashed his lips into mine while everyone cheered and clapped.

Ma looked at Dad. "Why, Nash, have you become soft?"

"No, Mags, seeing her happy is what matters the most, and he makes her happy." He smiled as she kissed him.

Michael set me down and took the ring out of the bulb, sliding it onto my finger. For once in my life, I knew with Michael, life would be beautiful. I loved Daniel. But he led me to the person meant for me. Daniel's death led me to someone new. For that, it will forever make me grateful.

They say we weather the storm to see the rainbow. That is true.

CHAPTER 21

GETTING BACK TO IT

MICHAEL

We returned to school after Nash had a long talk with me about Lyric. They didn't mind if we got married but wanted us to finish school. I agreed.

When we returned, we also continued living in separate houses until we got married. It didn't mean there wouldn't be sleepovers.

Major came inside, walked into the living room, and took a seat as we were hanging out at my house.

"I'll take a random guess and say you don't seem thrilled at the moment," I said.

"I would if Luna would understand I'm taking things slow instead of her trying to get into my pants."

"And how is that a problem?"

He gave me a look but didn't answer the question. I knew why because Lyric was here.

"It's not important. I should keep my distance for a while." Major sighed.

"Do you want to do that?"

"No, but Michael, you know how much this means to me."

"Wait, I'm confused," Lyric said.

I gave Major a look, and he rolled his eyes while motioning his hand.

I turned to Lyric. "Major is traditional with relationships."

She cocked her head, then glanced at Major, who diverted eye contact, then her brows lifted. "Oh."

"Yeah, so, there's a slight issue with Luna not putting on the brakes." I didn't need to go into detail. Lyric could figure it out.

"I can talk to Luna and have her cool her jets a bit," Lyric said.

"Something because I like her, but I don't need to complicate things. Thanks, Lyric," Major said, getting up and hugging her.

He left the room.

"And that's why I love you."

"And here I thought it was for my body." She smirked.

I rolled my eyes, making her laugh.

Next was Maverick. He plopped down in the chair.

"Okay, what's up?" I asked.

"That girl is driving me crazy," he said.

"I thought you were taking it slow."

"I would if she would move slow. She doesn't move at all." Maverick sighed.

Lyric rolled her eyes.

"Okay, first, Larkin doesn't enjoy hovering, but she doesn't like it when you become disinterested. She likes to feel like she's in control and loves food," Lyric told him.

"So, what you're saying is I should buy food, throw it at her, and walk away?" Maverick asked.

"Yep."

"Thanks, Lyric." Maverick got up, walked over, and hugged her.

As we continued hanging out, Mia walked in. She walked over and fell into the chair, face first.

"Is there a reason you face planted in the chair?" I asked.

She groaned.

"Lakin?" I asked.

"Yep."

"Okay, what happened?" It didn't matter the answer since I knew.

She pushed herself up and turned to face us. "Okay, so, we went to see a movie. Lakin wanted to see an action flick, but I wanted to see a rom-com. She pouted, and I teased her. Then we argued, she stormed off, and here we are."

"I see,"

"Why does it always have to be her way?"

I glanced at Lyric, and she gave me a look, rolling her eyes.

"I'll save a lot of breath and call my uncles," she said.

"Oh?" Mia asked.

"Yep, they enjoy dealing with the quints," I said.

"Thank you, Lyric." Mia got up and hugged Lyric.

"Are they always like this?" Lyric asked.

"This is a good day for them." I smiled.

Then the door opened, and in walked Piper.

"Please tell me you aren't having issues, too," I said.

She gave me a look. "No, I came to grab something. Lex and I are going to the movies." Piper ran up the stairs, and Lyric giggled.

"Remind me when we get married to buy a lock and a chain for our house," I said as she nodded.

*****

Maverick

After talking to Lyric and Michael, I left to talk to Larkin. All I needed to do was sneak out without them knowing. I looked around my bedroom. I guess it is the window.

I opened the window. Damn, it was so cold my nipples could cut glass. They were so hard. *Oh, right, coat,* I thought, snapping my fingers. I threw on a jacket and then climbed out of the window.

It wasn't the most brilliant move since it's January, and there was snow and ice on the shingles. I climbed out and slipped, sliding off the shingles and onto the ground, hitting it with a thud.

While groaning, I saw movement in the house. Shit. I got up and stumbled away as the door opened. Note to self, the next time I sneak out, use a door at least.

I hobbled over to Larkin's and knocked. Lakin answered. "I thought you left?"

"I did. Now I'm back." Acting aloof, I limped past her and earned a look. I might be a twit, but at least I have my dignity.

I made my way upstairs and knocked on Larkin's door. She answered it. "Why are you here?"

"Because I'm sure I broke something." I winced.

"Like what?"

"My dignity." I cringed, hobbling into her room. She closed the door. I laid on her bed on my stomach because, well, my ass was hurting a bit.

She walked over to me. "Maverick? Are you okay?"

"I'm fine." The bed muffled my voice.

"Are you sure?"

"Yep."

"So, if I do this, you won't get mad?"

"Do what?"

She hauled off and smacked my ass.

"Jesus Christ, Larkin!"

"Thought so." She sighed and walked over to me. She leaned over me. "Take off your pants."

"Shouldn't you buy me dinner first?"

"Oh? Do you want to go there?"

"Well, it's the thought that counts?"

"Undo your pants."

"Fine." I undid my pants, and in one fell swoop, Larkin yanked them off. Damn, she doesn't waste any time.

Then she pulled down my boxer briefs to reveal my ass. I was feeling quite exposed.

She sighed. "You have an enormous ass bruise on your tushy."

"Did you say tushy?" I gave her a look.

"Yeah, so?"

"That is kind of cute."

"And you're a twit."

I sighed.

"Hold on. I'll get you an ice pack."

She left the room, and I laid there. That's not what I had in mind when I came to see her tonight.

She returned with an ice pack and placed it gently on my tushy. That is a change for Larkin.

"What?"

"I thought you would slam the ice pack on my ass."

"You have a lot to learn about me." She rolled her eyes.

"Okay, then explain it because I'm dying. Everything I do backfires on me. How about a little leeway?"

She looked at me with her blue eyes. "Have you ever thought you're trying too hard?"

"Huh?"

"You're so busy chasing me you haven't realized you don't have to."

I looked at her, bewildered.

"You don't get it, do you?"

"Nope enlighten me."

"Maverick, of all people, I figure you would have figured it out by now."

I stared at her.

"Okay, fine. Sometimes, when you stop chasing, you realize the person isn't running."

I thought about it. Well, shit. I threw my head onto her bed. "I'm a twit, aren't I?"

"Nope, you're slow on the uptake." She smirked.

"So, all this time, I had to stop chasing?"

"Yep." She nodded.

We looked at each other. Then I did the one thing I've wanted to do since that night. I pulled her to me as I kissed her. She didn't fight me but kissed me back.

Things were about to get interesting between us.

CHAPTER 22

HAPPY HAPPY BIRTHDAY, AND VALENTINE'S DAY CHAPTER

Larkin

Did you ever question the universe and all its nuttiness? Yeah, I have been asking that every single day since I met Maverick.

Things between us have been hot and cold, but lately, they have been hotter than freezing.

Knock! Knock!

"Lark! Are you up?" Lakin asked.

Maverick and I stopped making out and looked at the door.

"Uh, yeah!" I spoke.

"Well, Ma and Dad called. They are coming in for our birthday, along with our uncles."

"That is super." After realizing what I had said, mine and Maverick's eyes widened.

"Super," he mouthed.

I shrugged.

"What?" Lakin asked through the door.

"Uh, nothing."

"Larkin! What's going on?"

The door handle turned, and I shoved Maverick off the bed, not realizing his shirt was still on the bed.

She opened the door and walked in as I noticed his shirt. Shit.

I grabbed it and whipped it at Maverick, lying on the floor on the other side of the bed.

"What's that noise?" Lakin asked me.

"What noise? I heard no noise that you mentioned."

"It sounded like someone moaning."

I clamped my mouth shut. I'll hurt Maverick because I told him to be quiet.

She gave me a look as I gave her one back, then she shrugged and left, closing the door behind her.

I leaned over the side of the bed and gave Maverick a look.

"What? Is it my fault you have scrumptious lips? No, plus, we're to take this slow, remember?"

"What they don't know won't hurt you." I shrugged.

"That makes me feel so much better." He sighed.

"Good, now get back up here and finish what you started." I smirked.

Maverick popped up and crawled onto the bed as he crashed his lips against mine.

Did we go further? That would be a big fat no. I wasn't ready or even prepared to go public with us.

For now, what we're doing will suffice.

*****

As our birthday neared, our parents, aunts, and uncles arrived to celebrate our birthday. This thing with Maverick would be harder to hide.

All Maverick and I had to do was play it cool. Easier said than done. I mean, what was I thinking? Oh, that's right. I wasn't. I was doing so well, not letting anyone get near me or our lips touching. Yet here I was, finding myself in these inappropriate situations with Maverick.

I was in trouble with a capital T. Even when I tried to resist him, I couldn't. It wasn't all the making out we were doing, but I was falling for him. FML.

*****

Our birthdays arrived, and so did everyone, including my favorite uncle, Nixon.

They all came to see us. After hugging my parents, I gave Nixon one.

"Hey, kiddo," he said, squeezing me.

"Hey, Uncle Nix." I hugged him back.

He let go of me and gave me a look. "You look different."

"I don't know why."

"You look happy."

"Who, me? Meh." I shrugged.

He gave me a look. It's Nixon that we're talking about here, who can see right through anything. It's freaky.

Nixon saw Maverick and made a beeline towards him. Well, shit.

"So, let me get this straight because we already know Lakin and Mia aren't, so we're good there. You like my niece?" Nixon asked Maverick.

I facepalmed myself.

"Well," Maverick said with a look.

"There isn't a well about it. You like each other or don't. Stop dancing around like two tools and get to it," Nixon told us.

Maverick and I glanced at each other, a bit confused.

"That means give it up already. Everyone knows you've been sneaking around with each other. No one says anything," Nixon said with a look.

It was disturbing how Nixon understood things. I talked to other people before shit went south.

*****

Maverick

Larkin talked to her other uncles while I got stuck with Nixon.

"Let me give you some helpful advice about my niece," he said. "Larkin is a tough nut to crack. Even when you crack the shell, you still must crack the nut inside it. It's a given."

"I don't know how to take that."

"Are you a twit or something? I told you. Crack her damn shell."

Whoa, this dude has some anger issues.

"You're a bright kid. Well, at least, I hope you are because I would hate to have twits for nieces and nephews."

This guy was something else.

"All I'm saying is if you want her, then prove it. Show her she's amazing and unstoppable. When she's down, lift her. When she falls, pick her up. When she wants to give up, fight for her. Prove to her that you're the man that backs her one hundred percent."

Nixon might be sarcastic, but he made sense. Larkin was a tough cookie, but that's because she hasn't had it easy with people. People judge her. Even as I did, but I was also young and stupid.

Nixon was right. I had to show Larkin that she's special to me. I needed to be that person who stood with her and supported her no matter what. I wanted to be that person.

I stood there as she talked to her dad and uncle and decided it was time to prove how much she meant to me. I walked towards her as people watched me, and I said, "Excuse me." I twirled Larkin and crashed my lips into hers.

I wrapped my arms around her and gave her a mind-blowing kiss in front of everyone.

We pulled away from each other, and I looked at her. "I don't want to hide anymore. I want everyone to know how I feel about you. I want you to know how I feel about you." I took a deep breath. "I'm in love with you."

Her bottom jaw dropped open.

"I don't care what anyone says."

"Excuse me?" Nash said.

I looked at him as did she and took a step behind her. "Well, except you." I shrugged as Nash took a step towards us.

Larkin put up her hands. "Stop."

We all looked at her, as did Nash.

"I get you to want to protect us, but Maverick won't hurt me," Larkin said.

"How do you know?" Nash asked her.

"Because I love him," she said without hesitation, causing everyone to gasp.

I stood there in shock. Then I fell backward and passed out.

✶✶✶✶✶

Larkin

Leave it to Maverick to make a dramatic move. I rolled my eyes as I tried to wake him, except he wasn't waking.

"Maverick?" I asked.

I shook him and nothing. What the hell?

As everyone gathered around, I was freaking out. Oh, God.

Then it happened. Maverick grabbed me and pulled me into a kiss. I pushed him away and smacked him.

"Ow! What was that for?" He propped himself up.

"That's for being a twit and scaring the shit out of me."

"Considering the hassle you've been giving me, you deserve a little payback." He smirked.

"Oh?"

"Yes."

He gave me a look, and I got even. Hey, I'm a Gray. I stood up and walked over, grabbed a plate with cake, and brought it over to him.

"I brought you some cake." I smiled as he smiled, then smashed it into his face, making everyone "ooh."

The plate dropped as cake covered his face. He pulled me to him, crashing his lips into mine. He got cake all over me, that tool.

He pulled back, and I rolled my eyes as he chuckled, making me laugh.

"So, you love me?" Maverick asked.

"Unfortunately, I do."

"Good." He pulled me into a kiss.

As we kissed on the floor, Nixon walked over to Dad. "Look at this way, brother. The way your girls are going, it looks like I may perform a wedding ceremony at some point."

Dad looked at him. "Why does this not surprise me?"

Nixon chuckled.

It turned out to be a wonderful birthday and Valentine's Day. Maverick and I declared our love for each other and had cake to boot. It doesn't get any better than that.

CHAPTER 23

SPRING BREAK, HERE WE COME

Lyric

Now the cat was out of the bag with Maverick and Larkin. Things returned to normal. They still had their issues, but they were their issues.

Major was still dealing with Luna. It was getting to the point things weren't good between them. They say love does not run smoothly. In their case, it was rocky.

Mia and Lakin were still going at it like cats and dogs and not in the arguing sense. I swear those two get unholier every day.

Lex and Piper were the only ones out of us who knew what they wanted. Lex always did. He let his shyness stop him.

As for Michael and me, things were fantastic. We understood many things, like the fact I hated he had grown a beard.

"Shave it," I said, holding out a razor.

"Why?"

"Because I don't like it."

"That isn't a reason, Lyric. It would help if you had a valid argument about getting what you want. That is not a valid argument."

"It's almost summer. What do you need a beard for, anyway?"

"Because it makes me look rugged." He smirked.

"And your enormous ass arms don't?" I pointed to his muscular arms.

His smile faded.

"Hey, you said to improve my argument, so I did. Now shave the damn animal off your face!"

"No."

I glared at him as he turned and walked away. I followed him.

"Where are you going?"

"Home."

"Why? We have a date."

"Not anymore."

"What?"

"When you stop acting like a toddler, then we'll have a date." He walked out of the door, leaving me dumbfounded.

Lakin and Mia walked in. "Why's Michael leaving, and why does he look hella pissed?" Mia asked.

"We got into an argument over his beard, and he told me there would be no date until I grow up. I think he broke up with me."

"What was the argument about?"

"I demanded he shaves his beard. Why?"

"Because Michael doesn't like demands. He never has. The minute that happens is the minute Michael stops. He hates it because he feels people are acting like children trying to get their way." She shrugged.

"Fine, I'll talk to him since we're all leaving for spring break in a few days," I told Lakin and Mia.

It was ridiculous.

*****

Over the next few days, I tried to talk to Michael, but he shut me out. It got to the point I gave up and had enough.

I knocked on his door. He answered.

"Since you won't talk to me like a civilized adult, then it's time to call it a day," I said.

"What do you mean?"

"You may have things you don't like, but so do I. I don't enjoy someone shutting me out. Take your stupid ring and shove it where the sun doesn't shine." I removed my ring and threw it at him. Then I turned and walked away.

"Lyric!"

I flipped him off. Screw this shit. I'm a Gray.

When I got home, I slammed into the house, alerting everyone I was home. They all looked at me.

"Michael and I are no more. The wedding is off. I'm now alone." I tried not to crack even though my heart was shattering into a million pieces.

I walked past them up to my room. I closed the door, leaning with my back against it and sliding down to the floor. The tears came fast and furious.

I know I broke up with him but icing me out wasn't mature either. I would be alone. Daniel left, and now I pushed Michael away. FML.

*****

I rode with Frick and Frack to Myrtle beach since we were going there for spring break. Everyone was coming. I didn't say two words since Michael and his family were joining us. Fantastic.

When we arrived, I grabbed my bag, made my way into the house, and walked past Michael, not saying anything to him.

"How long are you two going to keep this up?" Maverick asked him.

"I don't know." Michael shook his head.

"I would fix it."

"Yeah." Michael sighed.

I found a room and set my stuff down. I didn't feel like being happy. All I wanted to do was cry, and that's what I did.

I heard a knock on the door, and it opened. "Lyric?"

I wiped my eyes. "Yeah?"

"Can we talk?"

"About?" I continued to wipe my eyes.

"Us."

I stood there, not knowing what to say until I finally said something.

"It's okay. I mean, I acted like a toddler, and you had every right to be mad. And because you took a stand, I figure, I'll let you off the hook. I mean, it's fine. That way, you don't have to worry about me." I turned to him. "I'm fine." My voice cracked. "I'm fine." Then I cried.

He walked towards me and wrapped his arms around me. "You're not fine." He held me.

I buried my head into his chest and cried.

"Why did you give me back my ring?"

"I figured you didn't want to marry me. You weren't talking to me."

"Because I was angry. I still want to marry your twit ass."

I chuckled.

"I didn't want to say something rash. That's why I said nothing. If I took time to cool down, I would talk to you with more level-headedness. But I never expected it to escalate this far. I am sorry."

"I am too." I sniffled.

I lifted my head and noticed he didn't have his beard.

"You shaved?"

"Yes."

"Why?"

"Because I realized some things aren't worth losing the one you love. It doesn't mean I'll cave every time you threaten divorce when we're married."

"Fair enough." I smiled.

He leaned down and gave me a kiss which I returned. Before I knew it, things got heated. After two rounds. What? It's been a while. We got dressed and made our way to the beach.

Everyone was already there when we walked hand in hand on it. Michael stopped me.

"You forgot something."

"I did?"

He reached into his pocket and pulled out the ring. Then he took my hand and slid the ring onto my finger.

"There, much better. The next time you remove that ring will be when I place a wedding band on your hand. Capeesh

"Capeesh."

He pulled me to him, crashing his lips into mine. Then he hauled off and picked me up, tossing me over his shoulder, running towards the water as I screamed.

The minute we hit the water, he threw me in. I played a little joke on him and didn't surface right away. It helps when you can hold your breath for extended periods underwater.

He searched and yelled for me until I grabbed ahold of his leg and yanked him underwater. He realized what I did and grabbed hold of me. We appeared from the water and started splashing water at each other until he dunked me, and I dunked him back.

Michael was right. Sometimes, people fight over the dumbest things, and it doesn't matter. When you get past hurts and realize the fight wasn't worth it, you understand better. Then you can move on and be happy.

It wouldn't be our only time of fighting. We're human and far from perfect. People will fight. It's whether you let it consume you. Plus, there's always makeup time. That's the best part.

CHAPTER 24

HEADING INTO THE HOMESTRETCH

Lyric

Spring break ended. Things returned to normal. We had finals to contend with before going home. That meant our parents would arrive to bring us home.

It had been one heck of a year with everything I had been through with Daniel and school. But I came out of it stronger. With a bit of guidance from Michael and help from my family, I could move on.

Finals came, and so did our parents to collect us. I wasn't sad it was over. It relieved me. I was ready to go forward instead of living in the past.

*****

Our parents arrived, along with our aunts and uncles, to collect us. I was finishing up when I heard a knock at my door. I saw Dad standing there.

"About ready?" Dad asked.

"Yes." I shoved the last item into a box.

I went to pick it up, and he walked over to help me.

"Thanks, Dad."

"I'm proud of you, Lyric."

"You are?"

"You've come a long way from last year."

"I guess we need the right people to be there for us." I smiled as he leaned over and kissed my cheek. With that, we walked out of the house to our cars. He loaded up my box, and we all got into vehicles.

We pulled out and onto the road. I sat next to Michael as he drove, and he held my hand. It had been one hell of a year, but things would be fine.

*****

It took three hours to get home. Once we arrived, Michael dropped me off, and we brought our stuff into the house.

Ma and Dad guided us. Once we got settled, we all gathered into the living room. I sat on the couch, as did Larkin, Lakin, and Luna. Lex tried to join us, but we shoved him off while laughing.

Then he jumped on us.

Dad looked at Ma. "I'm so glad to have our babies home."

"Me too." She smiled.

"It's good to see them back to their old selves."

"It took a long time to get here, but they're happy, Nash. Isn't that what we wanted for them?"

He sighed. "Yeah, but Mags, I can't help but worry about them."

"It's our job as parents to worry. Now help me make dinner or no dessert for you later." She smirked.

"Well, in that case." He grinned as she rolled her eyes as they entered the kitchen.

"I can't believe we survived the first year," Lakin said.

"I can't believe you didn't put someone in the hospital," Larkin said to her.

"Meh, it was a slow year. Give it time." Lakin smirked.

I laughed.

"Well, I decided that it's time Major and I took a break." Luna sighed.

We all looked at her.

"Dare I ask why?" Larkin asked.

"I don't think he's into me. I like him and all, but I'm tired of getting rejected." Luna sighed.

"Major has other reasons for what he's doing," I told her.

"Whatever it is, I'm over it," Luna said.

"What about you, Lark?" I asked her.

"What about me?" Larkin asked.

"Now you and Maverick seem like you're getting closer. When are you finally going to cave?" I asked Larkin.

"One, I am not, nor will I ever cave to that twit. Two, I'm not sure," Larkin said.

"Not sure about what?" Lakin asked.

"This, him and me," she said.

"Wait. You declare your love for him and make out with him, and you're not sure. Are you some twit?" Lakin asked her.

"No, it feels like a terrible idea," she said.

Larkin made no sense. Here she had a guy crazy about her, and she still wasn't sure about things between them.

It was the beginning for them.

*****

Larkin

At dinner, I didn't say much. I had too much on my mind. What I didn't tell everyone was the reason I was against Maverick and me. I was freaking scared to death.

Any time I felt even something, Roger's face appeared. A few times, things got intense between Maverick and me, where I lashed out at him.

Sex scared me to death. Roger made sure it did.

After dinner, I went up to my room and sat by the window. I didn't want to talk to anyone. I wanted peace and the images to go away.

I closed my eyes, and they all came flooding back.

Flashback

"Lark! Hurry!" Lyric said.

"Hold your ass, will ya?"

The school had cleared out as I finished up, then made my way to the parking lot. As I walked down the hallway, I heard a noise. I stopped, and the minute I turned, a fist hit my face, knocking me off my feet.

I tried to get to my feet, but someone grabbed me by the hair. I struggled as they pulled me into a room.

"You dirty slut," I heard them say as they tore at my skirt and panties. I tried to fight as they hit me over and over until I couldn't fight anymore. Then it happened, pain, unbelievable pain. I felt like Roger was ripping me into two. I screamed, and they pressed their hand over my mouth.

I realized it was Roger. Oh, God. He held me down as he continued until he finished. He got off me. Before I moved, he hauled off and gave me two swift kicks into the stomach, then one to the head.

He walked away, and I tried to stand, but only to fall. I finally crawled and stumbled home.

I didn't realize I was screaming until I heard someone say, "Larkin!"

"Oh, God! Make it stop!" I grabbed ahold of them.

"I got you," they said as they engulfed me with their body. I clenched the person's shirt and sobbed. "I got you, baby."

I realized who it was. I looked up and saw Maverick's blue eyes.

I buried my head into his chest as he held me. Then Dad walked over and rubbed my back as I heard a familiar voice, "Lark."

I peeked out to see Nixon. At that moment, I felt safe.

It will be a long summer. Thank you, Roger, you douche. I freaking hate you and hope you rot in jail.

As I sat there while the three most important men in my life stood by me, I knew I would be okay. I hope so.

CHAPTER 25

YOU, SIR, ARE A TWIT

Larkin

I awoke to see Maverick smiling at me. "That is kind of creepy."

"I don't think so. It's nice to wake up to a smile." Maverick shrugged.

I furrowed my brows at him, then looked at my clock. It was eight in the morning, so I did what any college kid on summer break does. I rolled back over and went back to sleep.

"Oh, no, you don't." He laid on top of me.

I groaned. "You're a twit."

"Yes, but I am a hot twit who loves you." He gave me a sloppy kiss on the cheek.

I sighed.

"Lark?"

"Yes."

"Are you okay? You didn't have another nightmare again, did you?"

I didn't look at him, and he knew. Yeah, the nightmares have been more frequent lately. I didn't understand why.

I was doing fine. Then boom, the nightmares started all over again. Why do I have to be the one to deal with this? Why does life hate me so much?

He pulled me to him. "Lark, it's okay."

"Mav, it's not okay. I can't even function like most people. A relationship terrifies me."

He looked down at me as I looked at him, emotionless. I refuse to cry.

"I know someone who can help."

I gave him a look.

We drove about an hour until we pulled up to an enormous house. He got out and motioned for me to follow him. "Come on."

I got out and followed him as we walked up to the front door. He knocked twice, and it opened to a guy. "If you're selling anything, we aren't buying." Then he slammed the door on us. Okay, this twit was annoying.

The next thing we heard was yelling. "Liam, who's at the damn door?"

"It's some freaking solicitors!"

We stood there as the door opened to reveal Jordan. "Forgive my idiot son." He sighed.

"No worries. It's always a delight to see Liam," Maverick said, earning a look from Jordan.

"Yes, I know. Thanks for the reminder."

I found the Maverick's sarcastic side hot. Who knew?

Jordan stepped aside as we walked inside, and he closed the door.

"Jordan, you idiot! I'll beat your ass," a petite woman said, walking into the room.

"What did I do?" Jordan asked the woman.

"You gave the double troubles half of your DNA."

"It's not my fault they're idiots. I blame Frazier."

"And I blame you, so we're all even." She smirked.

He gave her a look as we stood there.

"Elena, this is Maverick and Larkin, who I mentioned to you."

She looked at us. "Oh, hello."

I stood there, not sure what to do. I only knew Jordan because of him helping Lyric. I didn't know the rest of them.

"Maverick, I need to go over some things with you."

Maverick nodded, leaving me alone with Elena, who was beautiful. Well, I wasn't.

"Do you drink coffee?" She asked me.

"Uh, yeah, sure." I shrugged.

"Follow me." She turned and walked away. I followed her to the kitchen. "Take a seat." She pointed to a chair at a counter. I walked over and sat down as she poured coffee into two mugs. Then she placed a cup in front of me.

"So, Jordan tells me you're having a troublesome time."

"I thought doctors couldn't discuss patients. You know, with all that confidentiality crap."

"He's not your doctor. Maverick is a counselor and intern for Jordan."

She was intelligent.

"Now, you're wondering why you're here."

"The thought crossed my mind." I shrugged.

"Jordan thought it would be best to talk to someone who had been through it." She took a sip. My head snapped in her direction, stunning me. How could someone like her have been through what I went through? She seems so at ease and happy.

"You're wondering how I became the person I am now."

I won't lie. This chick is smart.

"When I was sixteen, I was innocent and naïve. I met a guy, and my brother didn't like him. I didn't understand why. He was everything a girl could want in a guy. He was charming, nice, hot, and thought I was the girl. But he became controlling and abusive. I ended things."

I sat and listened to Elena.

"The day I went to his house to end things was the day he changed my life. He hit me, but he took my innocence from me."

"Did he rape you?"

"Yes."

"What did you do?"

"I called Jordan. Ryan would flip, but Jordan wouldn't. I felt safe when he came and got me. Jordan called my brother and Frazier, even though I begged him not to tell them. He said they needed to know. Then he would stay with me at night so that I could sleep. Our friendship turned into love. I wish my first time would have been with Jordan because he made it special." She gave me a soft smile.

"So, I won't feel this way forever?"

"I know it's scary, but trust someone will catch you when you fall." She winked at me.

As I sat there, we talked. Elena listened. It helped to know I wasn't the only one who had been through it.

We finished, and Jordan and Maverick walked into the kitchen. I watched Jordan wrap his arm around her waist and kiss her forehead. It gave me hope.

We hung out and met the rest of his family. Elijah was goofy with his corny jokes. Liam seemed like a prick but could eat like there was no tomorrow, and J.J. was quiet. It's unnerving. All had jet black hair like their father, but Liam was the only one with ice-blue eyes.

After a while, Maverick and I left. He pulled out of the driveway and started for my house when I stopped him. He slammed on the breaks causing us to jerk in our seats.

"What?"

"Can we go somewhere other than my house?"

"I guess." He shrugged, placing his foot on the accelerator. We drove, and he pulled off into a parking lot. I got out and ran. He ran after me until I stopped at the railing, along the water.

"Lark?"

"I don't want to be angry anymore. I don't want to be afraid. I don't want to push away someone because I'm terrified."

He walked towards me. "What are you saying?"

I turned to him. "I'm saying I want someone to catch me if I fall. I want to know I can trust that you'll never hurt me. I want to know that if I fall in love completely, that you will, too. I want to know that I can say, through it all, you love me for all my scars. I want to know."

He walked over to me and placed his hand on my face. "I can do all that. For you, Larkin, I'll do anything even if I have to move mountains."

"Do you promise?" I furrowed my brows.

"I promise." He smiled, then leaned in and gave me a soft kiss.

I wrapped my arms around his neck. He placed his hands on my waist as he kissed me. Then we pulled back and put our foreheads against each other.

"The reason I can promise is I'm completely in love with you."

"Yeah, but you already told me on my eighteenth birthday, you twit."

"Yes, I know, but I didn't add a part to it."

"What's that?"

"To be mine."

My brows raised.

"What do you say, Lark? Will you be my girlfriend?"

CHAPTER 26

WHAT DO YOU SAY?

Larkin

My heart was beating out of my chest. Maverick asked me to be his girlfriend. I remembered what Elena said, "The right one will catch you. They will protect you. They will be the one who loves you when you're damaged."

Maverick loved me even when I didn't love myself or also like myself. What did I have to lose?

"Well?" Maverick asked.

"Yes," I said in a whisper, "on one condition."

"What's that?"

"That you never give up on me."

"Oh, baby, I'll never give up on you." He placed his hands on my face and pulled my lips to his. His kiss was loving. I have never felt this way with anyone.

I placed my hands on him as he kissed me. Then he pulled back and put his forehead against mine. "I'll take such wonderful care of you."

"I know." I smiled, surprising him.

"You have a beautiful smile."

"Oh?"

"Yep, Larkin, you are beyond beautiful."

I couldn't help but smile. I had never felt this way about someone. Yeah, I had crushes, but I always got crushed.

He lowered his hands, and I wrinkled my forehead until he slid his hand into mine.

"It's a perfect fit." He smiled.

I was bursting at the seams as we turned to walk, only to have three stop us.

"Well, look what we have here, boys, if it isn't Maverick Harper. Don't think I didn't forget about you breaking my nose, dickhead," one guy said.

"It didn't help your face," Maverick said.

I stood there as the guy turned and saw me. He eyed me up and down. "Well, well, well, if it isn't Larkin Gray."

Maverick's grip tightened around my hand.

"Roger told me what a sweet piece of ass you are." He snickered.

That's when Maverick released my hand and hauled off, punching him. I stood there, shocked as he jumped on the guy as the other two guys tried to pull him off.

"Don't you ever talk about her like that! Or look at her! Or think about it!" Maverick said. He threw punch after punch as people stopped and stared.

I grabbed his arm, stopping him mid-punch. "Maverick! Stop! You're scaring me!"

He looked at me as I stood there. Tears started forming. I couldn't stand violence, not after what happened with Roger. It scared the shit out of me.

He dropped the guy. "Stay away from her."

I was shaking as he walked over and pulled me to him. I buried my head into his chest as he held me.

"Come on. Let's get you home," Maverick said.

I nodded as he led me to the car. The car ride home was silent as I stared out of the window.

When we got to my house, he led me out of the car and into the house. Dad and Ma met us as we came into the house.

"Oh, my God. What happened?" Ma asked us.

"There was an incident at the park. Do you mind if I help Larkin?" he asked.

"No, go ahead," Dad said as Maverick helped me upstairs. He looked at Ma. "Mags, something major happened at that park."

"I know, Nash. Did you see his hand?"

"Yeah." He sighed.

"Should it worry us?"

"I don't know, but if he lays one hand on her, I'm laying one hand on him or two."

*****

Maverick

My hand hurt like a bitch. It was swelling, and I'm sure I broke it.

I hated Clay Walker. He was a dick in high school and still a dick to this day. He and his goons had no issue going after people weaker than him. It was his M.O.

I sat Lyric on her bed as I looked at her. My hand was bloody and bruised, but I didn't care. She needed me.

"Oh, God. Your hand," Larkin said.

"It's fine."

"No, I need to get something for it." She got up, but I grabbed her arm to stop her.

"They hurt your hand." Larkin wouldn't look at me.

"Larkin."

"You need to clean it so it doesn't become infected."

"Larkin."

"Then we have to bandage it and ice it."

"Larkin!"

Her head snapped in my direction as she cried. "Maverick."

"It's okay. I won't hurt you."

She started crying as I pulled her to me. It was all starting to make sense now. Larkin had PTSD. The attack started it, but any time something violent happened, she shut down.

I should have seen the classic signs. All rape victims deal with it. The nightmares, the flashbacks, they're all triggers.

"Please don't leave me." She sobbed as I held her.

"Never, you're stuck with me."

She let out a slight laugh.

"Baby, you need the help I can't provide. I'm too close now," I reasoned.

She looked up at me. "What?"

"Larkin, you have post-traumatic stress disorder. Anyone that has been through what you've been through develops it. It's time we have someone help you a little better."

"You won't leave me, will you?"

"No, I'm not going anywhere."

She laid her head into my chest. "Okay."

It was time to get Larkin the help she needed. I didn't want to lose her, but she would lose herself if I didn't help her.

After her mom cleaned and bandaged my hand, I explained to them about Larkin. They both agreed she needed help. So, I made a call.

Within the hour, Jordan arrived and helped lead Larkin out. She didn't fight. She went as her parents and siblings looked on as she got into a vehicle.

I followed them. I didn't want Larkin to deal with this alone. She needed to know, no matter what, we wanted her to feel better.

Jordan explained that with enough help, she would be back to her old self. To me, it didn't matter. I would take her any way I could.

Once Jordan checked Larkin into the hospital, I helped get her settled. She took a seat on the bed. "I guess you never expected to ask a nut job to be your girlfriend, did you?"

"You're not crazy. You need help, and this is the best place for you." I took a seat next to Larkin.

"Even years later, Roger is making my life hell." She sighed.

"Not anymore. Now it's time for you to fight back. The first thing you do is get yourself better. Show Roger that he didn't win."

She nodded as I wrapped my arm around her, pulling her to me.

"You promise you won't leave me?"

"I promise."

She gripped me. Now it was time for her to fight. To show Roger that he didn't win and to fight for herself. I would be with her every step of the way. She wouldn't fight alone, not anymore.

CHAPTER 27

HELP IS ON THE WAY!

Larkin

Spending time in this place wasn't bad. It's not my first choice. What can you do? It took me a few days to open. I wasn't like the others and didn't need to tell them my life story.

Ma, Dad, my siblings, grandparents, and the others visited me every day. Maverick came to see me every day, too. We would talk about everything.

Uncle Nix came to see me a lot too. I loved it when he came to see me.

"How are things going? They aren't making you nuttier than you already are, are they?" Nix asked.

"Nope, I'm the sanest one here."

"Are you sure about that? You realize who your parents are, don't you? Wishy-washy and forgetful."

I giggled.

He smiled. "It's good to hear you laugh."

"It feels good to laugh. It's been a long time." I sighed.

"I wish you would have come to us sooner. Lark, we worry about you. We were there when your mom had you. We helped bring you all into the world."

"I know. The attack humiliated me. How do you tell people not only did someone beat the hell out of you but also took your innocence?" I wiped tears away.

"But it wasn't your fault. Roger had no right. He's a coward and a tool for doing that."

"Uncle Nix, I was fifteen and had a crush on him. I never thought that would happen. He was dating Piper. How do you tell people this without them looking at you differently?"

It was true. Roger was dating Piper, and I had this crush on him. I was fifteen and never even had my first kiss. Even during the assault, I wouldn't let him kiss me.

My first kiss happened with Maverick. Thank God for that.

"What are you thinking about?" Nixon asked me.

"My first kiss."

"Oh?"

"Maverick was my first kiss. At least, Roger didn't take that from me."

"Oh?" Someone asked.

We saw Maverick standing there. Busted.

"I'll leave you two to talk," Nixon said, getting up.

He left, and Maverick took his place.

"So, I was your first kiss."

"Yes."

"Interesting."

"Was it bad? Did I do a poor job? Because I hope I've gotten better. I mean, I can work on it unless you're bored with me. You're not bored with me, are you? But then again, you might be tired of dealing with me. You're not tired of dealing with me, are you?" My dam broke because of my therapy sessions.

I wasn't as closed off, and my mind was racing. So many thoughts were exploding in my brain.

"Lark!" He said, getting my attention.

I stopped. "Oh, right. I'm rambling. Sorry, I'll stop."

"No, you're fine. I love to hear what's going on in that head of yours. You used to be such a closed book. Now I can tell what you're thinking."

I looked at him.

"Lark, I'm glad I was your first kiss. I know how important a first kiss is to a girl."

I smiled as he smiled back.

Maverick was amazing. We had a rough start as kids, but it changed as we got older. He turned out to be this goofy, charming, thoughtful person who never gave up on me. I couldn't have asked for a better boyfriend.

*****

After a few weeks, they released me. The nightmares had stopped, and they gave me ways to deal with the triggers. My only fear was that they would release Roger, and he would come looking for me.

When I got home, my parents gave me the news that changed my life.

I walked in, and everyone greeted me with hugs. Dad handed me a letter.

"This came for you," Dad said.

He handed me an envelope with the return address, Jackson Prison. I took it from him and opened it.

Larkin

No matter what I say, you'll never forgive me. I was a bastard for what I did to you. I took something that didn't belong to me.

The reason I'm saying this is the same thing happened to me in prison. I screamed and cried, only to hear my screams for help go unheard. Every night is the same. I deserve it, though.

You never realize how horrible you are until you come face to face with the same situation when you're on the receiving end.

I took so much from you, and for that, I am sorry. I know I don't have a right to ask for forgiveness because I don't deserve it. But I hope you can forgive yourself and not carry the blame. You did nothing wrong.

You deserve to be happy with someone who will cherish you in a way you deserve. Once again, I am sorry.

I promise to never contact you after this. You deserve freedom from the past.

Roger

I looked up from the letter, shocked. Everyone looked at me.

"Baby girl, that letter came four days ago. The next day we received a call from the prison," Dad said.

"What did they say?" I asked.

"The prisoners beat, raped, then killed Roger. They slit his throat from ear to ear."

My blood drained, and the room spun as Maverick caught me and helped me to the couch. My torment was over, and it was all surreal.

Nixon walked over and crouched in front of me. "It's over, Lark."

I looked at him and the others as they all nodded. It was finally over. Now I could move on with my life.

I cried as Maverick held me. Relief washed over me, and the dam finally burst. It had been a long time coming. For once in my life, I could look towards the future without issues.

*****

I awoke the next day to see Maverick sleeping next to me. I brushed his hair from his forehead. He looked so peaceful.

My door opened, and I looked at Dad, who looked at me as I put my finger to my lips, silencing him. He gave me a look as I rolled my eyes. Then he closed the door.

Maverick stirred before waking up.

"Morning," he said.

"Morning."

He rubbed his face as I laid there.

"Your dad will kill me if I keep staying here."

"We were watching a movie, and you fell asleep."

"It was a boring movie." He shrugged.

"I thought you said you liked those kinds of movies." I looked at him as if he was crazy.

"No, I said I liked whatever you liked. It's my way to spend time with you." He smirked.

I whacked him with my pillow. Then he pinned me to the bed.

"Not cool," Maverick said.

"Well, we already know you aren't, where I'm fabulous." I grinned.

He rolled his eyes, then leaned in and kissed me. I pushed him off me, causing him to fall back onto the bed.

"Breakfast?"

"You've read my mind." I climbed over him, kneeing him in the stomach. Oops, my bad. He chased me out of the room and down the stairs. We ran into the kitchen only to stop. He crashed into me, causing us both to fall on the floor.

"Nice that you two could join us," Dad said, cooking.

"Well, twit here needed his beauty sleep," I said, getting up, along with Maverick.

My siblings snickered.

Dad handed us a plate, and I looked at mine. He rolled his eyes, took it back, and piled more food on it, then gave it back to me.

"Thanks, Daddy-O," I said.

"I liked it when she sulked. She didn't talk."

Ma smacked him as we laughed.

We sat down and ate as we talked about our plans for today. Then there was a knock on the door, and in walked the others. Dad handed them all a plate of food.

It was nice to be around everyone, talking and laughing. I finally felt like myself. But people would throw a monkey wrench into things.

CHAPTER 28

BEACH PARTY

Larkin

We gathered our stuff for a beach party. I didn't want to wear a swimsuit, so I dressed in an airy dress. All I wanted to do was have fun. It had been a while since I could enjoy myself.

We made our way to the beach, where more people had gathered. Maverick and I got out of the car and walked towards people, stopping to talk to a few.

"Well, well, well, look who showed up to the party," Clay said.

"Do you want to go another round with Maverick?" Glen asked.

"Do you think I care? He attacked me, and now I'll return the favor." He smirked.

"You realize his family along with the Grays are here, don't you?" Rob asked him.

"I'm not afraid of them. What is everyone going to do, anyway?" He shrugged.

"Beat the hell out of you," Glen said.

"Look, all I need is to separate the two of them. Then I can do what I need to do and give Maverick the payback he deserves," Clay told them.

"Man, you're not thinking of doing what I think you'll do, will you?" Rob asked.

"Nope, I'll use her to lure him alone. Then it's payback." He rubbed his hands together.

They looked at him as he told them what to do.

After talking to many people, I needed to find a bathroom. As I went looking, someone grabbed me.

*****

Maverick

Larkin disappeared for a while. How long does it take to use the bathroom? I searched for her until I found her tied up. I ran over to untie her, and her eyes widened.

As I removed the duct tape from her mouth, she said, "Maverick, watch out!"

Before I reacted, a chunk of wood came flying at me, hitting me and knocking me off my feet. I tried to get up, but then I got smacked again, knocking me out.

*****

Larkin

I yelled and screamed as Clay beat the hell out of Maverick while his cronies watched. I cried until I was hoarse when I heard voices.

Clay and his tool friends took off as everyone showed up. Lex and my cousins untied me as Michael took care of Maverick while Major called 911.

I broke free and pushed Michael out of the way. I grabbed Maverick. "Wake up. Please, Mav. Wake up." My voice cracked.

"Larkin, let me take care of him. Please," Michael said.

I released Maverick as Michael tended to him.

The ambulance arrived, and the paramedics helped Maverick. The paramedics loaded him onto the gurney and took him. I cried as Lex held me.

All I wanted was to make sure he was okay. We left, heading to the hospital. As soon as we arrived, I got out and ran into the hospital.

I ran to the desk, but they wouldn't allow me to see him. Michael could see Maverick since he was his legal guardian. I started screaming at them, while the others had to restrain me before they kicked me out of the hospital.

I wanted to see him.

Dad, Ma, and the others showed up.

"Dad! Tell them to let me see him!" I spoke.

"Lark, calm down," he said.

"No! They won't let me see him! Please, Dad!"

Dad wrapped his arms around me as I broke down. I wanted to see Maverick. Why doesn't anyone understand?

We waited until Michael came out. I ran over to him. "Michael?"

"Larkin, they beat him pretty badly. He has swelling in the brain, and they're trying to get it under control. He also has a broken nose, cheekbone, three fractured ribs, and a broken arm."

I stood there, shocked.

Michael put his hands on my arms. "Breathe. As soon as they get him stabilized and moved to a room, you can see him."

"Is he going to need surgery?" Major asked.

"It looks like it," Michael said.

The doctor came out to talk to Michael, along with Major.

I stood there, lost. It can't happen to Maverick because he is a good guy. Why him of all people?

The doctor finished and went back through the double doors. Michael and Major walked over.

"Well?" Dad asked.

"They can't get the swelling down and are taking him into surgery," Michael said.

The room spun. Before I knew it, I fell with Dad catching me. Everything caved in on me at once.

I woke up startled by someone who said, "Shh."

The room was dark, which was my room. I came face to face with Maverick.

I touched his face as he shined a light. My eyes widened as I screamed.

*****

I awoke startled while yelling.

"Lark?" Someone asked.

I glanced around at the beach and Maverick sitting next to me. People were talking and having fun. So, I did the next best thing. I pinched him.

"Ow, what was that for?" He rubbed his arm.

"Making sure this wasn't a dream."

"What dreams do you have?"

"The kind where you get beaten up. That reminds me. I thought you could fight."

"Uh, I can, but only when needed." He gave me a look.

"Well, the next time, I yell, Maverick duck. You duck."

"Okay." Maverick rolled his eyes. Then we heard someone ask, "Maverick Harper?"

We noticed two cops standing there.

"Yeah?" He asked.

"Stand, please," the officer told Maverick.

We stood. The cops turned him around and cuffed him, arresting him for assaulting Clay Walker.

"You can't do this!" I spoke.

"Ma'am, we don't have a choice," they said, turning him around and walking him to the car.

Michael ran over to me. I told him what was going on, along with Major. They took off and went to the police station.

It's a mess — time to call in some reinforcements.

*****

Someone cleared their throat.

The desk Sergeant looked up from his form. "Can I help you?"

"Why yes, you can, Sergeant Taggert," Nixon said.

"With what?" The Sargent asked.

"By telling us why you arrested someone for assault," Dad said.

"Because it's assault," he said with a look.

"Was it assault or self-defense?" Nathan asked.

"Huh?" The cop asked.

"Well, think about it. You got one side of the story, but you didn't get the other side," Noah said.

"Oh, this ought to be good," he said, setting down his pen.

"Keep up, donut chaser," Nixon said. "You arrested someone for assault yet bother to ask him if the other tool struck him first. Am I right?"

"What does that have to do with anything?" The cop asked.

"Everything, you twit. Damn, you're slow. Lay off the donuts, and your brain can function," Nixon said.

Nixon's comment didn't sit well with the cop. Nixon ended up in the jail cell, along with Maverick.

"Don't ask. It isn't my first go-around with jail."

While they locked up Nixon and Maverick, Nolan called Grampa.

He did what!

"It's Nixon, Dad. What can we say? It's the Gray way."

That's not funny, Nolan!

"No, what's not funny is he better hope he doesn't get stuck in a cell with bubba and drops the soap."

The others snickered.

Even as adults, you boys can't stay out of jail. You're like Cayson in that aspect.

Nathaniel Mark! You get that twit out of jail, along with that other twit! Grammy said in the background.

Ma! Stay out of it!

Whack!

Ow! Stop hitting me with your damn cane!

Then stop acting like a twit and get your boy and that other yahoo out! Grammy told Grampa.

Fine. Give me a few minutes.

He hung up, and Nolan looked at the others. "Well, Dad's on his way."

They rolled their eyes.

CHAPTER 29

SUCK IT UP, BUTTERCUP!

Maverick

"So, I take it you've been to jail a few times?" I asked Nixon.

"A few? Pft, try about a dozen." He laughed.

I did a double-take.

"Let me give you a piece of advice. When you get involved with a Gray, two things happen. One, you end up in jail. Two, there's always an issue with your significant other and yourself. Three, you deal with Grammy."

"That is reassuring."

"Well, we're Grays. What do you expect?" Nixon shrugged.

Then we saw a cop walk into the back, along with a guy.

"Hey, Dad." Nixon waved.

"Don't hi Dad me," he said.

"Would Daddy-O be better?"

"No."

"Tough crowd." He shrugged.

The officer opened the cell door. We sat there as Nate walked into the cell.

"Now explain to me how you two ended up together here," Nate said.

"Well, he hit some tool, and I got mouthy with another," Nixon said, pointing at me.

"Why does this not surprise me?" He sighed and waved at the door.

"Did you fart?" Nixon asked.

"Out!" He pointed at the opening.

"Damn, you don't have a sense of humor, do you?" He asked Nate as we walked to the door.

"Considering I had you five, I have an immense sense of humor." He rolled his eyes.

We walked out of the cell and towards the front, as Nate and Nixon argued. We walked into the police station's central part, and an older woman stood there.

I turned to walk back, and they grabbed me. "Yeah, I don't think so," Nixon said. They turned me around and shoved me forward until I came face to face with her.

"Do you think that's an excellent idea?" Nash asked them.

"Eh, Grammy needs to christen him." Nixon shrugged.

I stood in front of Larkin's grandmother, who eyed me up and down. I didn't know whether it should worry or scare me.

Then she took a few steps closer. Then it happened, *whack*! Christ on a bike. The older woman whacked my leg with her cane. I hopped around as the others snickered.

"Oh, suck it up, buttercup! Now pull up your big boy panties and stop being a twit! If you want to be a man, then be one and take care of my granddaughter. She doesn't need some dumbass boy fighting. How are you supposed to take care of her if you're sharing a cell with that other twit?" She waved her cane at Nixon, who shrugged. "Now, get it together." She turned and shuffled away. "Nathaniel, you better help me before I electrocute your ass again!"

Nate sighed and ran after her. Well, that was interesting. Nash took me back to his house, where a thrilled Larkin met me.

When I walked in through the door, she ran and tackled me, knocking me onto the floor. Everyone laughed.

Then she crashed her lips onto mine.

"Someone missed you." Michael smirked.

"No shame." She shrugged.

"Not that I don't appreciate this interesting homecoming, but can I get up?" I asked.

Nash walked over and picked her off me as I got up. Then he set her down.

I dusted myself off as someone jumped on my back. I sighed. "Lark?"

"Yes?"

"Do you mind?"

"Nope, you go about your business while I hang around." She giggled.

I couldn't help but chuckle.

"Well, in that case." I left the house with Larkin on my back. I looped my arms under her legs and gave her a piggyback ride until we came to a local park.

I set her down and slid my hand into hers, interlacing our fingers. We walked hand in hand with each other.

"Your grandmother is interesting."

"Yeah, Grammy Gray has a way about her."

"She whacked me with her cane and told me to get together."

"That is her way of welcoming you to the family."

I stopped and pulled her to me. "Then it's okay with me." I pulled her into a kiss as she wrapped her arms around my neck. I picked her up and swung her around.

Music started playing, and I set her down. I stepped back and bowed — she curtesy. I took her in my arms and danced with her.

We moved together, and I twirled her. As we danced, people stopped and watched us. I didn't care. I was enjoying my girl.

I turned her around until her back was against my chest. I wrapped my arms around her. We swayed together as I nestled my head into her neck.

Then I turned her out and pulled her back. We danced more with the music playing until I dipped her. People clapped and whistled as we laughed.

I loved her smile. Besides her eyes, it was the best feature she had because it was beautiful. I never wanted her smile to disappear. If I had to do everything in my power to keep her smiling, I would do it.

I took her hand, and we walked away until we came across some swings. We both sat down and started pumping our legs until we started swinging.

We swung to see who could go the highest, then jumped, landing on the ground. We both laughed like two kids. I rolled over and crashed my lips onto hers.

Larkin was my heart. She had been through so much, and I wanted to protect her. She needed someone to be that guy.

We stuck around, watching the sunset, then headed back to her house. We walked inside, and her parents were on the couch.

"How was your evening?" Her dad asked.

"It was amazing." She smiled, going to the kitchen.

"Maverick," Nash said.

"Yeah?" I asked.

"Thank you."

"For what?"

"For making her smile again."

Her mom nodded in agreement.

"I want her to be happy," I said.

"We know," her mom said. "You have to understand the Gray family is a tough bunch. They love deeply and fiercely. Even when they act like a tool." She glanced at Nash.

"Hey! I've apologized countless times," Nash told her.

"Best thing, I can't remember that part." She giggled.

"You are so going to get it." He tickled her.

I hope one day that's me and Larkin giving some poor guy a tough time.

Larkin walked out, eating a sandwich.

"Where is mine?"

"In the kitchen." She thumbed at the kitchen.

"Oh?"

"Yes." She shrugged.

Then I made the dumbest move ever. I took Larkin's sandwich, trying to be funny. That's the worst mistake ever. She hauled off and punched me in the gut, knocking the wind out of me, then yanked the sandwich out of my hand.

I coughed. "I thought you loved me."

"I do, but not when you take my food." She shrugged.

"Are you saying you love food more than me?"

"Yes." She walked away as her parents laughed. Pft, women.

Note to self, never touch Larkin's food. Not if I want to stand upright and breathe.

CHAPTER 30

BACK TO SCHOOL, WE GO

Larkin

We returned to school and got settled. As soon as we did, I took off to see Maverick. I knocked on the door, and the minute he answered it, I jumped on him, knocking him to the ground.

Michael walked by. "It's nice to see you two falling for each other."

Maverick rolled his eyes as I giggled.

"Not that I'm not happy to see you, but I thought we were meeting later?"

"I couldn't wait." I grinned.

"Well, in that case," he said, pulling me into a kiss.

"Can you two make out somewhere else, so we don't trip and break our necks?" Major asked.

We stopped kissing. "Who pissed in Major's Cheerios?" I asked.

"Major and Luna are taking a brief break," Maverick said. "Okay, a big break."

"That bad?"

"There's a difference of opinion." He sighed.

"Just because you and Luna broke up doesn't mean you have to be a tool!" We heard Mia say.

I sighed. We got up, and Mia came downstairs. "Michael, I swear to god, if you don't do something about our cousin, I'll call Lakin!"

Well, shit.

"What did he do this time?" Michael asked her.

"He took all my stuff and threw it out of my room!"

Then we heard Piper say, "What the hell, Major? That is my head!"

"This can't be good," Michael said.

We all went upstairs to see Major throwing stuff. Piper was rubbing her head.

"That is it. I'm staying with Lex until he gets his act together." She stormed off.

"Make that two of us." Mia left, too.

"Great," Michael said. He went into the room and subdued Major as he broke down. He waved at us to leave, which we did.

We left the house and went to get something to eat. We entered a local diner and sat down.

After ordering our food, we talked.

"Not that I'm happy about this change in attitude, but what gives?" Maverick asked.

"What do you mean?"

"Before, you wouldn't give me the time of day. Now you're tackling me. Why?"

"I guess, knowing Roger's dead and never able to hurt me gave me a sense of relief. Like I can finally breathe. I couldn't before."

"That bad?"

"It was horrible. It's like I'm a prisoner in my mind. Fear consumed me. I don't want to feel that way anymore. I want to be happy."

The server brought our food as we talked, ate, and shared laughs. It was a glorious feeling. For once, I could be myself. Maverick laughed as we spoke to each other. Then trouble happened.

"Oh, look, who it is?"

We saw Clay standing there. What did he want?

*****

Maverick

Is there one day I don't have to deal with this tool?

"So, aren't you going to tell your naive girlfriend the truth?" He asked me with a smirk.

I glared at him.

"Then I guess I'll tell you. Your boyfriend here has a thing for boys and girls," Clay told Larkin.

I stood up. "That's a damn lie!"

"Oh? So those nights we spent together meant nothing?"

I glared at him. "You're a liar!"

"Yeah, keep telling yourself that. Bye now." Clay stalked off as I clenched my fists. I ran my hand through my hair in frustration.

"Mav? Is there something you want to tell me?"

I took a seat and took a deep breath. "Clay and I used to be friends until he put a move on me one day. I told him I wasn't interested, but he wouldn't let it go until we got into it. Since then, he has set out to wreck my life."

"You're not gay, though?"

"No." I shook my head.

"I don't understand. Why would Clay make a move knowing that?"

"I don't know."

I didn't know. Clay knew I was into girls, but he would make up some outlandish story every time he saw them with one. The minute he tried to kiss me was the minute I hit him. I needed to talk to Michael.

We left the diner, and I took Larkin home, then went home. When I came inside, Michael and Major were in the kitchen. Major seemed like he had calmed down a bit.

"How was lunch?" Michael asked.

"Fine, until Clay told Larkin we had steamy nights together." I shrugged.

They both looked at me as I gave them a look.

"Is that douche still claiming things happened between you two?" Major asked.

"Yep, and I don't know what to do. The last time I hit Clay, I landed in jail with Nixon." I sighed.

"It's time to get a PPO against him," Michael said.

"I can handle myself, and jail doesn't bother me. I don't want Clay going after Larkin," I said.

"Well, you in jail bothers me. Get the damn PPO, Maverick."

Michael wasn't the type to mess with walking the straight and narrow. If we got detention, we got our asses beat. If we got into a fight, we got our asses whipped.

"Okay, okay. I'll get one." I sighed.

"Good."

"So, what happened to you and Luna?" I asked Major.

"She broke up with me. That's what happened."

"Why?"

"Not having sex means I don't love her. What does sex have to do with anything?"

"Because she's insecure." I shrugged.

"I get that, but you know my feelings about premarital sex."

"It's still mind-boggling to me."

"That isn't funny, Mav."

"It was a little funny." I snickered.

Yeah, I shouldn't have said that because Major and I were on the ground fighting. Michael had to break it up.

"Knock it off, you two!" He yanked us apart. He looked at Major. "You get your shit together." He turned to me. "And you stop giving this twit a tough time for his beliefs." He looked at both of us. "There is nothing wrong with waiting."

"Oh, and you and Lyric waited?" Major asked.

We both looked at him.

"Yes, we did until she was ready." Michael looked at me. "What about Larkin? Have you and Larkin had sex? Since you shouldn't wait to have sex."

"That is different. Larkin went through a horrible experience," I said.

"No, it's not, you tool. If Larkin went through it, you respect her enough to wait. Your logic escapes me, cuz. Sex isn't a game or a joke, but private and personal. If Luna can't understand that, then she needs to grow up," Michael told me.

"You're a hypocrite," I told Michael.

Then he hauled off and punched me. I stood and wiped my mouth, glaring at him as he glared back. I was over it. I turned and left.

"Maverick!" Michael said.

"Fuck off, Michael!"

I needed some air, only to meet more trouble. What the hell? Why must my day get better and better?

I stood there surrounded by Clay and his goons. I knew I wasn't going down without one hell of a fight, not now or ever. Bring it on, boys.

*****

I woke up two hours later, bruised, bloody, and sore. There was a lot of blood, and they tore my clothes. I searched for my phone and dialed a number.

The person answered on the first ring.

"It's me. I need help. Come alone and don't tell anyone." I hung up and tried to get up, only to collapse.

A few minutes later, the person showed up. "Jesus! What the hell happened?"

"I don't want to talk about it. I need help." I coughed.

"Maverick."

"*Please*, Kain. Don't tell anyone."

"Larkin?"

"No! She can't know!" I was on the verge of crying.

"Your family?"

I shook my head. I needed to go somewhere until I was better. No one could know what happened.

"Okay, I know a place I can take you."

Kain helped me to the car. We drove over to a house, and he helped me to the door, then knocked. It opened.

"Kain? Maverick? Christ, what the hell happened?" Marshall asked.

"Marshall, he needs help. He doesn't want his family or Larkin to know. He won't tell me what happened," Kain told him.

"Bring him in," he said as we entered the house. They took me upstairs, and he called Murphy into his room.

I laid there as Murphy walked in, and they talked to him, then they left. Murphy walked over. "Okay, I'll clean you up and check you out. Stay right there."

He returned with a first aid kit, a pan of water, and a washcloth. As he cleaned me up and bandaged me, he checked me over and sighed.

He crouched in front of me. "Maverick."

"No," I said.

"We need to call the police."

"No."

"Why not?"

"I don't want anyone to know."

"Then tell me who did this."

"Clay Walker and his goons."

I looked away. I didn't want to talk anymore.

He left the room and closed the door.

"Well?" Marshall asked.

"What they did to him wasn't normal." He sighed.

"Now what?" Asked Kain.

"I don't know, but he doesn't want his family or Larkin to know." He sighed, rubbing his forehead.

The three of them looked at each other as Kain pulled out his phone.

"Who are you calling?" Marshall asked.

"Well, he said he didn't want his family or Larkin to know. He said nothing about my dad," he said as the phone rang.

What frack?

"We have a problem."

What did you do?

"It's not me. It's Maverick."

What happened?

"You need to come and see for yourself. Dad, it's bad."

Kain, it's okay. I'm on my way. I'll be there in a few hours, and I'm bringing company.

Nixon hung up, and Kain looked at Marshall and Murphy.

"What did he say?" Marshall asked.

"He's bringing company," Kain told them.

They sighed. That meant the brothers were on their way, and the shit was about to hit the fan.

CHAPTER 31

FALLOUT

Maverick

I laid there on Marshall's bed, feeling numb. I know this because I'm learning it. I also know what to do when things like this happen, yet I did the opposite.

I didn't want to see anyone but knew I needed someone. I couldn't right now. While I laid there, staring at the wall, I heard voices. I didn't get up to see who it was.

Nixon and the others walked in. "Where is he?" Nixon asked.

"Upstairs," Kain said, pointing to the second floor.

"Stay here." He came upstairs, knocked, but I didn't answer. Then he opened the door, entered, and closed the door.

"Maverick?"

"What?"

"Talk to me."

"What's there to say? I deserve this." I stared at the wall.

Nixon furrowed his brows. "Why on earth would you think you deserve this?"

I faced him. "Because I do."

He walked over to me as I sat up. I was so sore. He wrapped his arms around me, and that's when I broke. I cried as I held tight onto him. I missed my dad.

"Shh, I got you."

"Why? Why me?"

"Because they're animals. It's not your fault. You didn't deserve this."

I couldn't help but feel like it was my fault. If I hadn't gotten into that fight with Michael and left, I wouldn't have put myself in that position.

"Maverick, I know you blame yourself. Trust me. You did nothing wrong. They were targeting you."

I buried my head into him.

"Does your family know?"

"No."

"They need to know."

My head snapped up. "No!"

"Maverick, look, I know you don't want them to know, but they need to know. If you don't tell them, I will."

"You can't, not if you're a minister."

"Oh, no! You're not using my job against me! Not this time."

"I thought it was fair." I shrugged.

"And you need serious help. Look, I get it. But I can't in good conscience allow this to happen. Now take it easy. I'll be back." Nixon released me, getting up. He left the room and closed the door.

He came downstairs to the others.

"Well?" Nash asked.

"This is a freaking mess, but we need to talk to Michael." He sighed.

Nash and Nixon left while Nathan, Noah, and Nolan stayed.

"How bad is it?" Nathan asked his boys.

"It's bad, Dad. We don't know what they did, but they used an object on him. I found traces," Murphy told him.

"All right, get him. He needs a hospital. You're premed, but he needs a professional," Nathan said.

Murphy nodded as Noah said to Nolan, "Let's go."

"Where are we going?" Nolan asked.

"To talk to Larkin," he said, walking out of the house as Nolan trailed him.

*****

Nixon and Nash showed up at my house and knocked on the door. Michael answered. "What are you guys doing here?"

"You have a problem, and we're here to solve it," Nixon said, walking past him, along with Nash.

Once inside, they told Michael and Major everything. Both were fuming.

"Sonofabitch! I'm going to fucking kill him!" Michael said.

"I'm taking it these two have a history," Nixon said.

"Yeah, they were friends until Clay became obsessed with him." Michael sighed.

"How bad was the obsession?" Nash asked.

"Bad, I had to switch Maverick schools, along with the others. We had to move. Then we heard nothing until recently. That's why Maverick ended up in jail," Michael told them.

"Well, it sounds like this is the beginning, and you have a vast problem on your hands," Nixon told him.

"Yeah, I know. I told Maverick to get a PPO," Michael said.

"Oh, to hell with the PPO, we are doing this the Gray way," Nixon said.

Nixon and Nash cracked their knuckles.

*****

Larkin

There was a knock at the door. "I'll get it!" Lyric said. Good, because I'm enjoying my sandwich. Then I heard two familiar voices.

"Uncle Noah? Uncle Nolan?" Lyric asked.

"Hey, sweetheart," Noah said, hugging Lyric as the others came out. I walked out of the kitchen. What are they doing here? Better yet, where are Dad and Nixon?

They saw me. "Lark, there's a problem," Noah said.

Everyone looked at me when I was mid-bite.

*****

"Are you freaking kidding me?" I threw my plate against the wall.

"Well, that's one way to handle things," Nolan said.

"How could they do that?" I was ranting and raving, pacing back and forth.

"Because they're animals," Noah said.

"Animals that we need to beat to death," Lakin said. "Let me do the honors." She cracked her knuckles.

"Where is Maverick?" I asked.

"On his way to the hospital if we know Nathan," Nolan said.

"I'll go and see him," I said, running out of the house. They ran after me as I got into the car. They stopped and looked at me. "Less staring, more driving, you tools!"

They all got into the cars, and we headed to the hospital. As soon as we got out, I ran inside. A nurse tried to stop me. I knocked her out of the way.

"That's one way to get your point across," Nolan said.

"Yeah, I don't think Nash would appreciate it if we allowed his kid to get arrested," Noah said.

"Why? It's not like this is their first go-around with the law."

"Call big brother, you tool." Noah ran after me.

I ran into the back, getting yelled at by the staff. I didn't care. No one was stopping me from seeing my guy.

I found Maverick with Nathan. He was on a stretcher in a hospital gown and a sheet. He looked at me as I walked over to him. I wrapped my arms around him, and he did the same. Then he cried.

"I'm sorry," Maverick said.

"It's not your fault." I stroked his hair.

He held me tighter as I held him. At that moment, I knew how everyone else felt with my experience, helpless. But I also knew how important it is to be there for someone.

Nathan left us alone to talk.

I wiped his tears.

"Don't hate me, Lark."

"I could never hate you. I love you too much." I smiled as Maverick nodded. "But you need to talk to me. Remember, we need to trust each other."

He nodded again.

"So, talk."

He told me everything. I stood there, listened, and couldn't believe it. My heart ached for Maverick, who was a respectful guy and didn't deserve what happened.

A few minutes later, Michael and Major showed up. Maverick looked at them, and they walked over, throwing their arms around him.

"I'm sorry, Michael," Maverick said.

"It's okay. It wasn't your fault," Michael told Maverick.

"But if I wouldn't have run off at the mouth, it wouldn't have happened."

"Look at me, Maverick. No matter what, this isn't okay. No one, and I mean, no one has a right to do this."

Maverick nodded.

"So, what now?" I asked them.

"Well, Clay is a dead man," Michael told me.

"And so are his goons," Major said.

I didn't blame them. Michael and Major were angry. I know because I've been there.

The police arrived and talked to Maverick. Hearing him recount what happened made my stomach turn. I also knew I had to be there for him. He needed me.

Once they finished, they talked to the staff and gathered evidence. I pulled up a chair next to the bed and sat down. I laid my head on the bed, and Maverick rubbed it. He did it when I was feeling stressed.

"Lark?"

"Hmm?"

"I don't want this to set you back. You've come too far."

I lifted my head. "Mav, it won't set me back. I'm tired of people trying to wreck things. It doesn't change things between us."

He reached for my hand and interlaced our fingers. Maverick was my heart. When he was hurting, so was I. I wish I would have let him get closer sooner. I couldn't imagine my life without him now.

While we were dealing with this situation, Dad and the others searched for Clay and his goons but found them long gone.

"Now what?" Noah asked.

"Now we wait," Nixon said, picking up a piece of paper.

"What's that?" Dad asked.

Nixon sighed. "Trouble."

He handed the paper to Dad, who looked at it. Then he looked at Nixon. "Someone better tell me why the hell this tool has information on my daughter before I lose my shit."

"Because there's more to this than anyone realizes," Nathan said, handing Dad another piece of paper.

They all looked through the papers. They realized Clay had gathered not only pictures but information on everyone. We had now become human targets, and we didn't know why.

It had become more than an obsession with Maverick. This situation became more significant than any of us knew. Would they be able to find him before he found us?

CHAPTER 32

DAY BY DAY

Larkin

The hospital released Maverick, and our dad and uncles headed home. They said they had to take care of something at home.

I helped Maverick into his house and got him settled into bed. Once he was all situated, I sat with him.

"It'll be okay," I told Maverick.

"You won't look at me differently, will you?"

"No, why?"

"I don't want you to see me differently."

I furrowed my brows.

"Mav, Clay and his goons beat and assaulted you. Three guys jumped you and did horrible things to you. None of it was your fault." I crawled over to him as he looked down. I lifted his face. "Look at me. What have you always told me?"

"It wasn't your fault, and you didn't deserve it. You're a kind, decent person who deserves kindness."

"Exactly, and the same goes for you." I wrapped my arms around him. He wrapped his arms around me as we held each other.

Maverick needed someone to comfort him and understand how he felt. I could give him both. I hope one day he understands.

He fell asleep, and I went downstairs to get something to eat.

"How is he?" Michael asked me.

"Lost, confused, angry, hurt, and so many more emotions. Maverick doesn't want me to think less of him, which I don't." I sighed.

"We know."

"Do you mind if I make something to eat?"

"Not at all. The kitchen is through there." Michael pointed to the kitchen, and I went to make a sandwich. I searched through the cabinets and found a plate, then got some silverware, along with food. I made a sandwich and ate it.

Major came in a few minutes later. "Hey, I wanted to say thanks."

"For what?"

"For taking care of my brother."

"It's what you do when you love someone." I shrugged.

"It's great."

I ate and looked at Major. He wanted to ask me about Luna.

"Luna is miserable."

"What?"

"Luna is your reason for coming in here." I ate.

He knitted his brows and narrowed his eyes.

"Look, Major, I get your reasons for waiting, but I know my sister. Luna has always been more insecure than the rest of us. She feels if guys aren't ogling her, then she's not attractive. A little stupid if you ask me, but that's me." I shrugged.

"I tried to talk to her, but she won't listen." He shook his head.

"Because she's a Gray. None of us listen. It's inevitable. Plus, she has Ma's insecurity genes and Dad's stupidity."

He lifted his brows.

"Did you think I would say what a swell person my sister is? Excuse me, but no. My siblings are twits. You have Lyric, who finally got her head out of her ass about Michael. Lakin would rather use her fists instead of her brain. Then sweet Lex, who's a brilliant tool."

"That is an interesting way of viewing your siblings." Major gave me a strange look.

"You have your ideas, and I have mine. But if you want Luna, then show her why your beliefs are so important. Then she might get a clue." I finished my sandwich and put my plate in the sink.

"Excuse me. I have to care for my guy." I walked by him.

I went upstairs and checked on Maverick. He was awake.

"That was a quick nap," I said.

"Yeah."

I crawled into bed with him and wrapped my arms around him. We didn't talk. I could tell he didn't want to talk. I was the same way. So, I laid there with him.

Maverick

I laid with Larkin. We didn't talk about what happened, which was okay. I didn't want to talk. So many emotions were running through my mind. I had to see Jordan, which I hated to do.

I know I'm going to school to become a therapist, but sometimes, you must see one, yourself. I hated the thought of it.

The next day, Larkin came with me to see Jordan. She waited in the waiting room while I saw him.

"Take a seat, Maverick," Jordan said, motioning to a chair.

I sat down. Jordan took a seat in front of me.

"You know how this works. You can talk, or you don't have to, but to work through it, you need to talk."

I took a deep breath. "Why me? Why did this happen to me? I don't understand."

As information started pouring out of me like a dam breaking, Jordan sat there and took notes. He asked questions here and there, but he listened.

Our session ended.

"Maverick, here is my advice, keep with the sessions and take it day by day. That's all you can do. You suffered a sexual assault."

Hearing those words broke me. I was a guy. How does this happen?

I thanked Jordan, and we scheduled another session so I could continue them. I walked out to the waiting room, and Larkin stood.

"Ready?" I asked.

"Yes."

I took her hand and led her out. I didn't want to talk or think about what happened but wanted the experience to disappear.

We returned home, and I went straight to my room. I didn't want to talk.

"How did it go?" Michael asked Larkin.

"It went." She shrugged. "It'll take time. All I can tell you is be patient."

With that, she came up to my bedroom. I stood at the window, and she wrapped her arms around me. I placed my palms on her arms.

Larkin was the only one I would allow to touch me. She was the only one I trusted. When Larkin touches me, I feel like myself. When she didn't, I felt empty and disgusting. Her touch comforted me.

"What a way to start the school year, huh?" I asked.

"It'll get better, Mav. But it'll take time."

"I know." I sighed.

We stood there for hours. I needed Larking to keep holding me. She's my heart.

CHAPTER 33

STARTING SCHOOL AND DEALING WITH ISSUES

Larkin

Beep! Beep! Beep! Beep! Crash!

I stirred as someone else rolled over, then popped up. I checked my phone, and my eyes widened.

"Shit!" I said, running out of bed.

Maverick sat up and rubbed his eyes.

"What's going on?"

"We're late!"

He glanced at his phone. His eyes widened as he scrambled out of bed. We raced around, getting dressed before flying out of my room and almost crashing into Lex.

"Sorry, Lex!"

We took off for class.

There's nothing like being late on the first day of class. Our professors didn't find it funny or cute when we interrupted our classes. It's excellent that we only had two classes today. Note to self, never let Maverick sleep next to the alarm clock.

After my second class, I met Maverick. He came walking out, and I kissed him as he took my hand.

"How was the class?" He asked.

"Boring." I shrugged. "I mean, how the heck am I supposed to know the answer to x? It's not like y has been so forthcoming."

He laughed.

"Ha! I made you laugh with algebra humor!"

He pulled me into a kiss while chuckling against my lips. "Yeah, you did. Thanks." Maverick placed his forehead against mine.

Then some guys walked by and started spewing homophobic names at Maverick. It shocked us until someone hauled off and dropped them.

We stood there to see Kain and Kaiden standing over them.

"What was that? I didn't quite get that. Care to repeat it," Kain said, staring the guy down.

"They need another beat down to get the point across. We don't tolerate that shit," Kaiden told him.

Frick and Frack hauled off and kicked the guys as other guys fought with them. Maverick and I jumped in and joined them. The fight turned into a full-fledged brawl until Michael, Marshall, and Murphy broke it up.

"That's enough!" Michael told everyone.

Maverick looked like he was ready to break.

"Larkin, take Maverick home," Michael said.

"Come on, babe," I said, leading Maverick away.

There would be more significant problems to come. Those guys that said that spewed those names detested gay people. But there will always be homophobic people.

I brought Maverick home. As soon as we got inside, Major and Mia met us. Maverick walked by them and ran to his room, slamming the door behind him.

"What happened?" Major asked.

"After class, a group of guys started calling Mav fag, queer, dicklicker. Kain and Kaiden came by and dropped them. Then others joined, along with us before Michael, Marshall, and Murphy broke it up," I said.

"I know what guys you're talking about on campus. They're tools," Mia said.

"Mav was afraid people would think he's gay because of the assault," I said.

"But Maverick isn't gay," Mia said.

"I know, but when someone assaults you, you have all these thoughts and emotions running through you. It's not logical. All you can do is work through them," I said.

"How were you able to move on?" Major asked me.

"I didn't exactly move on. What helped was knowing Roger wouldn't hurt me anymore. It was fear," I said.

"Well, until they locate Clay, I doubt Maverick will move on." Major sighed.

I checked on Maverick. I heard items breaking. When I opened the door, a chair came flying at my head. I ducked as Maverick unleashed his rage.

Major ran upstairs and saw the destruction. He tackled Maverick. "Maverick!"

"Get off me! Don't touch me!" Maverick said.

I ran over and pushed Major away. "It's me! Maverick, it's me!" I got him to focus on me. He grabbed hold of me and cried.

"It's okay, baby. No one will touch you except for me."

He held me tight.

"Call Jordan," I told Major.

He pulled out his phone and dialed Jordan. Then he handed the phone to Maverick. Maverick talked to Jordan and calmed down. He told Maverick he would be in town this week and would meet him.

They hung up, and we sat there.

"Sorry, Major," he said, wiping his face.

"No, I'm sorry, brother," Major said. "I wasn't thinking."

"Let me talk to your brother for a minute. I'll be back."

He nodded as I got up and left the room with Major. We went downstairs.

"Larkin," Major said.

"Major, there are things you need to understand. When someone attacks a person, the last thing you do is touch them. Your touch makes their skin crawl. When you do it, and they're unleashing their rage, it triggers memories. For the longest time, I wouldn't allow my dad, brother, uncles, or cousins to come near me or touch me."

"I didn't realize it was that bad." Major sighed.

"You have an innate fear. Even though you know someone you love would never do that, you can't help but feel that way. Trust is an enormous factor. Maverick was the first guy I even felt comfortable enough to touch me. There was something about him. I couldn't explain it."

"So, how were you able to let your dad hug you?"

"Maverick told me my dad would never hurt me. He said he wasn't the type to hurt me. He loved me too much and said it was an unconditional love, which is true. My dad has always been there for us. I had to trust him." I shrugged.

"I trust you," someone said.

I turned to see Maverick on the stairs.

"That's why you're the only one I will allow to touch me. I know you would never hurt me."

I walked over to him and stepped until I reached eye level. "And neither will they." We turned and looked at Major and Mia. Then we turned back to each other. "Maverick, what happened to you was horrible, but your family loves you. They would never hurt you."

Major and Mia nodded.

He said, "It will take time. Be patient."

"We can do that," Major said.

I took Maverick's hand in mine. Time was our friend at this point.

*****

3rd Person

There was a knock on the door, and Nash answered it. Nathan walked in with a file and handed it to him. Nash opened the folder and looked through it.

"Any luck?" Nash asked.

"We're getting closer," Nathan said.

Then Nixon, Noah, and Nolan entered.

"I want this tool found and taken care of now. I won't allow this asshole to harm my kids!" Nash said.

"Yeah, but your kids aren't the only ones he has information on," Nolan said.

"Nash, we're as pissed as you are. If he has this information, why? If his beef is with Maverick Harper, then why collect information on our kids?" Noah asked.

"Good question," Nash said.

"Unless this is a smokescreen," Nixon said.

"What do you mean?" Nash asked.

"Think about it. Clay Walker's father is Quinton Walker," Nixon said.

"Who the hell is Quinton Walker?" Nolan asked.

"Beats the hell out of me," Noah said.

"Quinton Walker had a thing for our dear brother's girlfriend, Sarah. Nash got her, and he got pissed," Nixon said.

"I didn't even know Quinton Walker," Nash said.

"No, but he knew you." Nixon shrugged.

"People are tools," Nathan said.

"That and they freaking hate us because, well, we're the Gray brothers who are hot," Nixon said.

They all looked at him, and he smirked.

"Stop being a tool," Nash said.

"After you, brother," he said.

"Look, I don't give a flying fig who this tool Quinton is or his stupid beef. I want his kid's ass on a silver platter. He wants to hunt our kids. We'll hunt his ass," Nash said.

He left the room as the others looked at Nixon. "Now what? Because Nash has Dad's temper, and it's way worse than Nathan's," Noah said.

"Find Clay Walker and his goons." Nixon shrugged.

"Does Maggie know?" Nolan asked.

"Do I know what?" Maggie said, walking into the house. The boys looked at each other. Maggie didn't know, and they weren't about to tell her until one let it slip.

*****

The brothers heard a crashing sound, and Maggie said, "I don't give a shit, Nashville! You find him because if something happens to our kids, I'll cut off your balls!"

Nash left the room and walked down the stairs. He walked over to his brothers. "Which one of you tools told her?"

His brothers pointed at Nixon, who gave them a look. Nash hauled off and hit him.

"I deserve that." Nixon rubbed his jaw.

"Now, let's go. I want to keep my balls, thank you very much," Nash said.

As Nathan left the house, he said, "Nash will have blue balls for a while."

"When this is over, we'll get him a cake," Nolan said as they follow him.

CHAPTER 34

A CARNIVAL AND SWEET ROMANCE

Larkin

A carnival was in town, and I thought Maverick could use some fun. He's had a lot on his mind with everything that happened, so I enlisted everyone to help me get him there.

We walked up to the carnival, and he stood there. Everyone went off in different directions. I turned to him. "Come on."

"I don't know about this, Larkin." He sighed.

I took his hands. "Do you trust me?"

"Yeah."

"Then trust me with what I have planned." I smiled at him.

"Okay."

I dragged him to the first ride. After riding a few rides, we made our way to the moonwalk. We seem old for it, but I explained what I wanted to do to the operator. He agreed to let Maverick and I go in alone.

We kicked off our shoes and climbed in. Then we walked around. Finally, I started bouncing around while Maverick stood there.

"Come on, Mav! Join me!" I bounced around.

"Lark, this is ridiculous."

"Suit yourself." I shrugged and bounced around. Maverick watched me until I knocked him down, causing him to bounce around. I moved away from him.

"Do you find that funny?"

"A little." I motioned with my finger and thumb while smirking.

"Oh, you'll get it."

He chased me as I laughed. Then he tackled me, causing us to fall and laugh.

I got away from him as we bounced around, laughing, to the point we fell.

Finally, our time was up. We crawled out of the moonwalk and grabbed our shoes. We walked over to a picnic table and sat down, putting on our shoes.

"See, you can laugh." I gave him a slight shove.

"Yeah, guess I needed that." He chuckled.

"Mav, I know what you're going through, but trust me, it's not always going to be that way. We can let them win or fight to get our life back." I looked into his ocean blue eyes with my sky-blue ones.

He slid his hand into mine. "I love you. Thank you."

"That's what you do when you love someone unconditionally." I smiled.

Maverick leaned in and kissed me, then stood and pulled me along with him. We walked around and got some cotton candy. We ended up with more on our faces than eating it. He grabbed me and gave me a big ole kiss. We laughed against each other's lips.

Michael and Lyric saw us.

"It's good to see him smile and laugh. He hasn't smiled lately," Michael said.

"If anyone can get him to smile, it's Larkin."

"What do you mean?"

"Before Roger attacked Lark, she was the one who could get anyone to laugh. She is like Uncle Nixon in that aspect. After he attacked her, she didn't smile until Maverick came along."

"Do you think people come into our lives and make a difference?"

"Yep, considering you came into mine." She smiled as he kissed her before heading off to the next ride.

Maverick and I got cleaned up, then walked around until we saw people dancing.

"Want to dance?" I asked him.

"I would love to dance." He smiled and led me to the dance floor. We started dancing.

Maverick spun me around and pulled me to him. We started dancing, moving to the song. Then he twirled me out and brought me back as we danced. Then he turned me around until my back was against his chest. He held me in his arms as we swayed back and forth.

Then he released me as he held my hand, and we danced in step with each other. As we danced, people cleared, and the others walked up and watched us.

It didn't matter if people were watching. Our eyes were on each other. We stepped with each other as we danced. Then he pulled me into his arms and spun us around. Everyone smiled while watching us.

Then he and my family joined us on the dance floor. We all got into step and danced. We kept in sync with each other. Talk about a mob flash. It was so amazing.

As the song ended, he dipped me. Then things got interesting as Will Smith's Switch came on the loudspeaker.

We all started swaying our hips. We clapped and stepped as we all danced. The one thing about us Grays is we all knew how to dance.

Before I knew it, Michael, Major, Lex, and Maverick picked up Lyric, Luna, Piper, and me, flipping us. Then they reached between their legs and pulled us through them.

As we all danced in step, people danced from the sidelines. It was beyond fun.

We walked off the dance floor and went to get some food. As we ate, we heard arguing. We turned to see Major and Luna fighting. Then Major stormed off, and Luna was crying.

We walked over, and she was sniffling.

"Luna?" I asked.

"Oh, hey Lark," she said, wiping her face.

"What's going on?"

"It's nothing. Don't worry." Luna walked away.

Maverick shook his head. "For once, I'm not getting caught up in anyone's drama, and neither are you. Let's have a good night." He took my hand and led me to get something to eat.

After eating and riding a few more rides, we left. We walked hand in hand back to Maverick's house. I yawned.

"Tired?" Maverick asked.

"Yeah."

We went inside and up to his room. He gave me a pair of sweats and a tee shirt to wear. I went into the bathroom and changed. Then I came out to see him lounging in bed.

I crawled next to him and laid my head on his shoulder. Then we heard the door slam.

"Major must be home." He sighed.

I giggled as the door opened.

"Yes?" Maverick asked.

Major entered the bedroom. "Do you think I'm difficult?"

We looked at each other, then said, "No."

"Do you think it's unrealistic that I want to treat someone with love and respect?"

"No, not at all," we said.

"But then again, I can be stubborn."

We nodded.

"But I also don't have to go against my beliefs."

We shook our heads.

"I need to think about this more." He left the room and closed the door.

"If those two don't see how perfect they are for each other, they're bigger tools than we thought."

Maverick laughed.

He pulled me to him and kissed me on top of the head. That's what was great about us. Neither of us was rushing anything. We were taking our time, which was worth it for both of us.

Maverick was my heart, and I was his. Together we were complete.

CHAPTER 35

STEP BY STEP

Larkin

Each day, Maverick started handling his situation better. He continued with his sessions. Any time he had a setback, I helped get him back on track.

We were taking it step by step, day by day. We also spent time together. If I wasn't at his house, he was at mine.

While we dealt with our situation, we got pulled in the middle of Major and Luna. I wish those two would get it together.

While we dealt with that issue, we weren't aware of someone watching us from afar. The person kept their distance and kept their head down.

It would get interesting for us.

*****

3rd person

"Well?" Clay asked as they walked into a house.

"They don't know what's coming," they said to him.

"Good, I want them to pay for everything."

"What's our next move?" One guy asked.

"We keep our heads down and stay out of sight. When the time is right, it's payback." Clay smirked.

While Clay is planning his moves, Nash and his brothers are hunting for him and his goons.

*****

"Is this tool some ninja?" Nixon asked.

"Something, but he'll wish he never messed with us," Nash said.

"Every time we have a lead, they wipe all traces of him," Nathan said.

"Yeah, but even if he wiped every trace, people leave carbon footprints," Noah said.

"Let a pro at this," Nolan said, pushing Nathan out of the way.

"You know, I can still beat your ass, baby brother," Nathan said.

"Bite me, you tool. I'm not that skinny kid you can beat up anymore," Nolan said.

"No, but you're still a pain in the ass," Nixon said.

"Do you want to go, old man?" Nolan asked.

"Sure, bring it on, you twit," Nixon said, egging him on.

Nash smacked them both in the head. "Knock it off, you tools! Or you can deal with my wife!"

"Pft, she doesn't scare me." Nixon laughed.

"Oh, yeah? Did you forget our wives are best friends?" He looked at Nixon.

"Way to ruin my fun time, brother," Nixon said.

Nolan typed in some commands and up popped a black screen with a lot of lettering. He kept typing as they watched.

"What the hell?" Nathan asked.

Then a screen popped up.

"Whoa," they all said.

"Please tell me you did not hack some security system," Nash said.

"Nope," Nolan said.

They all breathed a sigh of relief.

"I hacked a satellite." He grinned.

They all did a double-take.

"Great, we'll go to jail," Noah said.

"Screw jail. We're going to federal prison," Nixon said.

"Relax, dumb and dumber. I didn't hack a government satellite. This one transmits from campus," Nolan said, rolling his eyes.

Nixon and Noah smacked Nolan upside the head. Nolan glared at them.

"Oh, stop your glaring, you pansy," Nathan told him.

"Can you focus for a minute? We're getting off track," Nash told them.

"See this?" Nolan pointed at the screen.

"Why no, George, we don't see that because it's the size of an ant," Nixon said.

Nolan pressed a button, zooming in. "Now, do you see it, Grampa?"

Nixon glared at him.

"Isn't that Clay?" Noah asked.

"Why, yes, George, it is. Wow, you're a bright one." Nolan rolled his eyes, earning a smack from all his brothers. "Christ! Was that necessary?"

"Yes!" They said.

"I'm in my late thirties, and you all still pounce on me like I'm a teen," he said.

"Oh, suck it up, buttercup. No one has time for your whiny diatribe," Nixon said.

"I thought you didn't care," Nathan said.

"I care when the big mouth tells my old lady, I'll have blue balls for years to come. No way in hell will I let you tools buy me a cake," he said.

"When's the last time you got laid?" Nathan asked him.

"What kind of question is that?" Nixon asked.

"An honest one," Nathan said, shrugging.

Dad shook his head. "Can we stop discussing Nix's sex life or lack thereof and get back to the task? Clay Walker, the tool who knows everything about us."

"Well, it seems our little tool has been sticking close to campus. Someone is helping Clay," Nolan said, pointing at another picture of someone.

Nolan zoomed in on the person.

"Do me a favor and send that picture to everyone. I have to get home," Nash told Nolan, who nodded.

He left Nathan's house and made his way home. He walked in, and Maggie came out of the kitchen.

"Well?" Maggie asked.

"We have them."

She ran and jumped on him.

He wrapped his arms around her. "Mags, we'll find them. I promise."

"I want our babies safe."

"So do I."

*****

Larkin

As we all hung out, our phones beeped with a new message. We all opened it, and our eyes widened.

"No way," we all said.

We called each other and our parents to get answers.

*****

Luna

I was coming home from the library when someone grabbed me.

They dragged me behind a building. I struggled and fought when the person hit me. I tried to defend myself when they beat the shit out of me, breaking my nose and arm.

A shrill scream escaped my lips as someone pulled them off me. They hauled off and let it rip, beating the hell out of the person until they took off.

I was screaming as they leaned over me. "Luna."

"Ahh!"

"Shh, it's me." Major pulled out his phone.

I held my arm and laid my head on the ground while crying.

An ambulance arrived fifteen minutes later. The paramedics gave me something for pain and put me on the stretcher, loading me into the ambulance's back. Major climbed in after and rode with me as I laid there, sniffling.

"I'm here, baby."

"Don't leave me."

"Never." He stroked my cheek with his thumb.

*****

Larkin

Maverick's phone rang, and he answered it. "What? Calm down, Major. What do you mean you're at the hospital?" We all looked at him, then his eyes widened. "We'll be right there."

I looked at Maverick.

"Luna is at the hospital. Someone attacked her."

That's all it took. We ran out of the house and raced to the hospital.

Lyric called Dad to let him know. He was beyond pissed, as was Ma. Dad said he would be there as soon as he could, and he was bringing company.

We ran into the hospital to find Major. The four of us were talking at once until Major finally got a word in edgewise.

"They took her into surgery! That's all I know!" Major said.

We didn't need to say anything. We all thought the same thing. The situation pissed us off. Those assholes hurt one of us, and someone would pay.

Then our phones lit up with the same message.

That is the beginning. Tell your family to back off, or someone else is next. - Blocked number.

"Now, what do we do?" Lakin asked.

"Well, they want to mess with one. They mess with all," Lyric said.

"They think our dad and uncles are crazy. They haven't seen anything yet," I said.

"Sucks to be them," Lex said.

Frick and Frack agreed. Mess with a Gray, and you have trouble. Hell has no fury than attacking one of us. God have mercy on their soul because we won't.

CHAPTER 36

OUTCOME

Larkin

Luna was recuperating from her attack. Maverick was attending his counseling sessions with Jordan. Lakin was fuming, and the rest were ready to pounce. I was enjoying this delicious sandwich.

"What are you doing?" Lakin asked.

"I'm eating. What does it look like I'm doing?" I ate my sandwich.

"We're trying to find out who is doing this."

"Correction, you found out who is doing this. Dad and our uncles already know who is doing this, so let them deal with it." I shrugged.

"What is wrong with you? Don't you care about our sister?"

Lakin was grinding on my last nerve. I set my sandwich down and brushed off my hands.

"Listen, Lake. I care about Luna and the rest of you twits. I'm sick and tired of you thinking you can use fear and intimidation with me."

She glared at me as I glared back.

"What's going on here?" Mia asked, walking into the kitchen.

"I'm explaining to my dear sister that I'm sick of her shit," I said.

"Lake?" Mia looked at her.

"It's fine, Mia. Larkin is a self-centered bitch when the attention isn't on her," Lakin said.

"That isn't fair, Lakin," I said.

"Oh, boo-hoo. Life isn't fair, Larkin. Get over it, you enormous baby!"

I walked away and left the house.

"Don't go away mad! Go away!" Lakin said.

What is wrong with her? Lakin has never attacked one of us. She protected us. None of it made sense.

I walked to clear my head until someone grabbed me. The person's fist flew, hitting me and triggering Roger's attack. I went into full panic mode, kicking and punching.

I scrambled to get away when they grabbed my leg. As the person pulled me to them, I grabbed the most significant rock I could find and slammed it against their head. They stumbled back and fell. I got to my feet and bolted.

I reached Maverick's house and pounded on the door.

"Open up! Please!" I saw the person stumble towards me. No one was coming, and I ran. I darted, finding a house.

If this is a nightmare, I need to wake up. As I ran, I crashed into someone.

"Christ, Lark!" The person said.

I glanced around, not seeing anyone.

"Lark?"

"They hit me. I kicked, punched, and hit the person with a rock," I said, scanning my surroundings.

"Who?"

"Roger is trying to get me. Please don't let him get me." I squirmed in the person's hands as I cried. "Please, make him go away!"

"Lark, shh, it's okay." The person pulled me to them.

"Let's get her back to the house," Michael said as Maverick nodded. They walked me back to their house.

Once inside, I sat on the couch. I had a bloody lip, which Maverick cleaned. Michael brought me a glass of water since I was shaking.

Maverick finished cleaning me up. "Lark, why were you alone?"

"Lakin and I got into a fight. I left. I wanted to clear my head," I said, taking a sip of water.

"What did she say?" Michael asked.

I told them what Lakin said. Michael nor Maverick was happy. Michael called Lyric and told her, and she was beyond pissed. We could hear screaming on the other end.

Michael hung up. "Yeah, Lyric said she would take care of Lakin."

"I don't understand. Lakin has never been this insensitive to us. I don't know why she attacked me like that," I said as tears fell. I couldn't help it. Everything was hitting me all at once. Maverick pulled me to him as I cried.

*****

Lyric

I got off the phone with Michael and hunted for Lakin. Once I found her, I jumped on her, slapping the shit out of her.

"What the hell, Lyric?" Lakin pushed me off her.

"What the hell is wrong with you, Lakin? Why would you say those things to Larkin?"

"Say what?" Lex asked, walking in with Piper.

"Our dear sister here called Larkin a self-centered bitch! She said not everything revolves around her!" I spoke.

"Why would you say that?" Lex asked Lakin.

"I was angry, okay? We're trying to find this twit who attacked Luna. She's eating a sandwich!" Lakin said.

"Larkin is always eating. Why should that matter now?" Lex asked.

"Because she needs to know our sister is in the hospital! And, and, and," Lakin said, not able to finish her sentence.

"And what, Lake? You don't think Lark cares?" I asked.

She stood there as her fist clenched, and tears fell down her cheeks.

The door opened, and Luna hobbled in. "I'm home." She saw us and became confused. "What's going on?"

"Do you want to tell Luna, or should we?" I asked Lakin.

"Tell me what?" Luna asked.

"Oh, big mouth here called Larkin a selfish bitch. She decided Larkin wasn't concerned enough about you," I told Luna.

"What?" Luna asked.

"Go ahead, Lake. Tell Luna how you attacked our sister, then drove her out of the house only for her to get attacked again," I said.

"What?" The three of them asked.

"Oh, that's right, you don't know. Larkin got attacked but was lucky to get away. It triggered memories of Roger!" I spoke.

"Oh, my God," Lakin said.

"You don't get it. Larkin has finally gotten back to her old self. You threw her under the bus because you can't control your temper," I told Lakin. "Get it together."

With that, I walked away.

"I didn't know! I didn't know she would get attacked," Lakin said while crying.

"Lake, you need to talk to Larkin." Luna hopped over to the couch with Major helping her.

*****

Larkin

Lakin walked out of the house, making her way over to Maverick's house, and knocked on the door. While trying to keep her composure, Maverick answered the door.

"Can I talk to Larkin?" Lakin asked.

"Yeah, sure." He shrugged, stepping aside.

She entered. The minute she saw me with a busted lip, she broke. "Oh God, Lark." She started crying. I got up and walked over to her, closing the gap between us. She grabbed hold of me.

"I'm so sorry." Lakin hugged me.

I held her as she cried. Yeah, we have our issues, but we're still sisters. Lakin lets her anger get the best of her, but she has our back.

Once she stopped crying, I looked at her. "Now, who's the big baby?" I asked.

Lakin laughed. "Real cute." She wiped her eyes.

"You deserve it." I shrugged.

Lakin took my hands in hers. "Lark, Roger is dead. He'll never hurt you. Whoever did this isn't him."

"I know. Maverick talked to me." I sighed.

"I need to control my temper better."

"Yeah, you do, but I get it. What would we do if we met these people? Lakin, they're dangerous. They hate anyone who doesn't fit into their mold."

"I know, but I can't stand by and let them keep attacking people. They went after Luna thinking she was me."

At that moment, I knew why. "Oh, God."

"What?" Lake asked.

"I know why."

"Okay, why?"

"If these people are helping Clay, they're doing it for their reasons. If they're as bad as we think, it's only a matter of time before Clay won't be any use to them."

"What do you mean?" Maverick asked.

"Clay is gay, right?" I asked.

"Yeah, so?"

"So are Lakin and Mia. They hate homosexuals in any sense, but they hate others too. They will stop at nothing until they rid every one of them from campus."

It was a matter of time before this hit closer to home. How do we stop it before it happens?

CHAPTER 37

LYING LOW

3rd person

"What do you mean, you're finished now?" Clay asked them, raising his voice.

"I'm saying we're done with you, fag. How I ever agreed to help your kind is beyond me," the person said.

"My kind?"

"The wrong kind and your behavior are despicable. Nowhere in the Bible does it say man lay with man. You sicken me. Every single one is sinful traitors."

"We're not friends, but I want them destroyed!"

"You have that right. We aren't friends and never will be friends. You're lucky you're still breathing. Let's go, boys."

Three guys walked out of the house where Clay was hiding.

Rob looked at Clay. "Dude, that guy is the biggest homophobe on campus. He hates all gays. Why would you want to work with him?"

"Because he hates the Grays and Harpers as much as I do," Clay said.

"Why? Because Maverick turned you down. Come on, Clay. You and everyone else knows Maverick doesn't swing that way," Glen said.

"It doesn't matter. The minute Maverick hit me, our friendship was over," Clay said, storming out of the house.

Rob looked at Glen. "Why will this end badly?"

"Because it will. That dude's beef is with Lakin and Mia. That's why he hates those families. He can't stand gay people. It has nothing to do with Clay's little tiff with Maverick."

Clay made a mistake forming allegiances with the biggest homophobe on campus. Derek Crandall hated anyone who was homosexual and felt it was unnatural. He also hated that we all accepted it.

The worst part is, he had a significant run-in with Lakin in high school while she and Mia were on a date. He tried to attack them with his cronies, only to get his ass handed to him by a girl. Well, never mess with a Gray.

*****

Larkin

I was lying on my bed reading when someone's lips touched my neck.

"Can I help you?" I asked.

"Nope, I'm showing my girl some attention." Maverick kissed me even more until his lips found mine. He had the softest lips ever, and his kisses were gentle.

While we made out, I heard Luna coming up the stairs. We stopped and got off the bed.

We walked out to find her struggling.

"Do you need some help?" I asked.

"Nope, I got it. I'm an independent woman who doesn't need anyone or anyone's help." She struggled, trying to get up the stairs while holding her crutches.

Then we saw Major come in and walk up the stairs. "Luna," Major said.

"I got it. I do," Luna said while struggling.

"You have a broken arm and leg. Plus, you're trying to go upstairs with crutches. That makes no sense."

"People aren't always going to be around to help me, so I have to learn to do things for myself. You know, like the night Derek Crandall broke my arm and leg. I didn't have help, so I don't need help now." She finally got to the top of the stairs and made her way to her room, hopping into it.

"She hates me," Major said.

"She doesn't hate you, Major. She's angry and hurt. Give her time. Be her friend," I said.

He sighed and walked up the stairs, going into Luna's room.

"Now, where were we?" Maverick asked, picking me up and carrying me back into my room while his lips connected with mine.

After making out for a bit, the subject of sex reared its ugly little head. We needed to talk about it at some point. With what both of us went through, it needed discussing.

We sat on the bed.

"I don't know, Lark. I mean, before, it would have been something I would jump on, but now, it scares me."

"It scares me, too. How do you let yourself be that intimate with someone? Do you act romantic? Do you lie there? What do you do?"

"I guess you let it happen."

"How?"

Sex scares me to death.

He reached over and pulled me into a kiss. I kissed him back. Before I knew it, we were removing clothes. I didn't think or worry. It was about trust, which was huge for us.

Then Maverick entered me, and I gasped. He took his time. When he nestled himself inside of me, he waited until I relaxed, then he started moving inside of me.

He held me as his kisses lingered as he thrust inside of me. I couldn't believe the pleasure I was feeling. It was gentle and loving. Maverick took his time as he made love to me.

Then I released and screamed out. "Maverick!"

"Larkin," Maverick breathed.

After it was over, both of us cried. Sex was so emotional for both of us, knowing what we had been through prior. We ended up holding and comforting each other.

He looked at me. "I'm sorry."

"For what?"

"It was too soon." He wiped his face.

I touched his face. "No, it was perfect."

He pulled me to him as I held him. It wasn't romantic with hearts and flowers, but it was idealistic and perfect for us.

As we laid there, basking in the afterglow of being together, problems were arising.

*****

3rd person

"What now?" A guy asked Derek.

"First, we take care of that fag, Clay. His filth is lingering, and the world needs purification of those deviant souls. Then we end those other ungodly people."

The guy took a seat as Clay started.

"My fellow godly brothers and sisters, we are among an abomination that roams this campus. In the Bible, a man will lie with a woman, and a woman will lie with a man. God struck down those that did not adhere to his ways. We will follow his ways and rid this earth of that unholiness that abounds." He waved a Bible in the air.

"Amen, brother Derek!" A man said.

"Now, I want you all to lie low. We must keep the attention off us. When the time is right, Judgment Day will be upon us. We will judge, convict, and end them to return this campus to its godly ways. Can I get an amen from everyone?"

"Amen!"

"That's right, my brothers and sisters, let's show them they aren't welcome." He smiled.

CHAPTER 38

ANOTHER HOMECOMING AND MORE PROBLEMS

Larkin

After that day, Maverick and I trusted each other. He was the only one I trusted with my body, and I was the only one he trusted with his. It was a significant step for us. So was sex.

When you engage in it the right way, you want it all the damn time.

We collapsed onto his bed after the third round. Our breaths became ragged, and I brushed my hair away from my face.

"You are such a horn dog," I told him.

"Me? Excuse me, missy, but you're the one who jumped on me when I opened my door."

"But only because you have a weird evil attraction to you."

"Oh, right, because I'm hot." He smirked.

"If you say so." I shrugged.

"Oh, I say so." He pulled me to him.

I couldn't help but laugh as he started tickling me.

"Can the two unholy people get dressed and come out? We have problems," Michael said through the door.

We sighed, getting up and throwing on some clothes. We came out of the room and came downstairs to see everyone. That wasn't good.

"What's up?" I asked.

"Besides, your moaning, not much," Kain said.

"I wasn't moaning," I said through gritted teeth.

"Oh, Mav! Right there! Harder! Faster! Oh God, Mav!" Kain said, mocking me.

"Don't let Uncle Nash hear you say that, or Mav is a dead man," Kaiden said.

"Keep your trap shut, and you won't have to worry about having no teeth," I said.

"Then buy stock in the raincoat factory. I'm sure if you girls get knocked up, he'll flip," Marshall said.

"Oh, he'll flip all right. It was nice knowing you, Maverick." Murphy grinned.

"I doubt everyone is here to discuss my dad stopping Maverick from producing. What's up?" I asked as Maverick gave me a look. "Sorry, babe, but the minute he finds out, I would wear a cup."

Then, like clockwork, Maverick fell backward on the floor, startling everyone.

"He's fine. Now, what's going on?" I asked, rolling my eyes.

"Homecoming is coming up, and we need to keep an eye out. If Derek Crandall has plans, he will execute them at a big function," Michael told everyone.

Maverick finally got up. "Thanks for the concern, baby." He rubbed his head.

"Don't be a twit. You're fine," I said.

"Look, we know he has targets, undesirables as he calls gay people," Michael said. "I don't want to take any chances. So, at homecoming, stick close to each other. Pay attention to your surroundings."

I sighed. Why does a tool have to get his panties in a bunch? Why does he need to attack people because of their sexual orientation? That never made sense to me. We love who we love. What does it matter who it is?

I mean, think about it. I love a twit.

Michael lectured us. Boy, he likes to lecture. How do the Harpers put up with him all the time? But then again, I have Maverick as a boyfriend.

We went back up to Maverick's bedroom and laid on his bed, well, after being unholy again.

"This is getting out of hand," I said.

He pulled me to him. "Do you want to stop?"

"Well, let's be reasonable, shall we?"

He pulled me into a kiss. Okay, so I enjoy sex. That's a first.

*****

We all got ready for homecoming, and the guys came to pick us up, except for Luna. She sat this one out because of her leg and arm. I didn't blame her. We all left and headed to the dance.

*****

Luna

There was a knock at the door. I hopped over and opened it to find Major standing there.

"Shouldn't you be at the dance?" I asked.

"Well, I figure we could hang out." Major shrugged.

"Why?"

"Why not?"

"Because we broke up."

"It doesn't mean friends can't hang out together."

"I guess, but that's all it is." I hopped back to the couch.

He followed suit and sat in a chair.

"I guess you couldn't find a date."

"Nah, dances are boring."

"Uh-huh."

"What about you?"

"I have a broken leg and arm. Who the hell wants to go with a disabled person? Plus, it's not like guys want me anyway." A tear fell down my cheek and brushed it away.

"I'm sure there's a guy that wants you."

"Nope, I resigned myself to the fact, I will never be like my sisters. I mean, you don't even want me, so why should anyone else?" I returned to my movie, leaving Major to furrow his brows.

✶✶✶✶✶

Larkin

We arrived at the dance and hit the dance floor. As we all danced, I noticed Derek Crandall in the corner with two people watching us.

"What?" Maverick asked me.

I sighed. "I have an unpleasant feeling about this dance."

I nodded, and Maverick glanced at what I noticed. We watched as they turned and walked away.

"Yeah, I do too." Maverick led me over to Michael and Lyric.

"Is there a reason you two look ridiculous dancing that way?" Michael asked us.

"Well, I could answer that in so many ways, but I'll save it for later," Maverick said.

I rolled my eyes. "Look, you twit, we need to leave, like now."

"Did you call me a twit?" Michael asked.

"Yes, would tool be better?" I asked.

Lyric snickered.

Then it happened. Doors slammed shut and locked. The lights turned off, and people panicked. Then something busted through the windows as a fire started.

"Oh no, not again," I said as the place caught fire.

Maverick grabbed my hand as Michael grabbed Lyric's while the others followed suit. We needed to get the hell out of here.

Smoke engulfed the place, and we started coughing. Michael, Maverick, and the guys grabbed whatever they could. They threw it at the windows until the glass shattered.

They helped us out, along with anyone else. Once we were at a safe distance, we coughed, trying to expel the smoke out of our lungs. The place exploded as we flew backward.

We sat up, and I said, "Well, there's nothing like having an explosive homecoming."

They all looked at me as I shrugged.

*****

Paramedics arrived, as did the police, along with firefighters. They checked us out, and I had a sharp pain in my side. I looked down to see my dress covered in blood. What the hell?

A paramedic cut open my dress to reveal a gash. I didn't even know I had gotten cut. They gave me a local and stitched me before placing a gauze pad on it. It looks like I'm heading to the hospital. Fantastic.

*****

I removed my dress at the hospital as they checked me out and gave me a pair of scrubs to wear. Maverick stayed with me.

The others got checked out, too.

I sat there as Maverick held my hand. "Luna had the right idea." I sighed.

"We can't stop living because a maniac has an issue with people."

"Mav, he tried to kill us tonight."

"Well, there's that." He shrugged.

"You're such a twit." I sighed.

He moved in front of me and placed his hands on my face. "But I'm your twit."

"Yes, unfortunately, I'm in love with a twit." I smirked.

He leaned forward and kissed me.

Then we heard a commotion. Well, shit.

We turned to see Dad barge in, along with my crazy uncles.

"Is there a reason you're acting like lunatics?" I asked them.

"Is there a reason you're trying to get yourselves blown up?" Nixon asked.

"Touché," I said.

Dad walked over to me and hugged me. "Are you okay?"

"Yeah, I'm fine. It's not the first fire I've been in."

"That isn't funny, Lark."

"Who's laughing?"

He rolled his eyes, then looked at Maverick. "Why do you look guilty?"

"Who, me? I'm not guilty," Mav said.

Nixon walked over to him. He took a whiff and turned to Dad. "Oh, he's guilty, all right. You can smell it on him."

That's all it took. I got between Dad and Mav. "Dad, I'm nineteen."

"And I'll break his legs."

"Are you serious?"

"Lark, you're killing me. Can't you let me have my moment?"

"What moment? Acting as a tool?"

"She's got you there, brother," Nixon said as the others snickered.

"Will you tools act like fathers and go check on your kids?" Dad asked.

"Sure, why not, tool?" Nixon shrugged as they left the room, laughing.

I winced in pain. Maverick helped me.

"Now, if you don't mind, I would like to feel misery without you trying to kill my boyfriend," I told Dad.

"That's reassuring," Maverick said as Dad gave him a look. You know the look that says I'll rip off your head and beat you with it. Yep, that would be the look. Maverick stood close to me. Chicken.

"I'll check on your sisters and brother, then check on Luna. I'm watching you." he pointed at Maverick. He kissed me on the forehead, then left.

"Your dad is. How should I say this?" Maverick asked.

"Interesting?"

"Scary." He raised a finger.

I couldn't help but laugh, then winced in pain. Poor Maverick.

This situation was far from over, and things were getting started with Derek.

CHAPTER 39

ADVICE FROM THE BROTHERS

Larkin

After what happened at homecoming, we didn't see much of Derek. It wasn't to say he wasn't lurking in the bushes like the tool he is, and he's a big one.

I don't understand how someone can hate people based on certain things. I hate many people because they're plain assholes. But you don't see me blowing up any building, now do you?

That was the thing about us. Out of the five of us, I didn't hesitate to let a person know I detested them. I know, shocking, right? But if you're a twit, then forgive me for treating you like one.

Take Luna, for example. She is the biggest twit out there. Well, a close second to Lex. Lex is still a twit. Anyway, I'm getting off-topic. My sister has some idiotic way about her. Let me explain.

Maverick and I were hanging out as usual. Okay, we were making out. A girl has needs, and well, so does her hot boyfriend. Never tell him I said that.

We heard arguing. Can't a girl get some peace as her boyfriend is doing unholy things to her? During our enjoyment, we heard arguing, causing Maverick to stop.

I lifted my head. "Why did you stop?"

"It's hard to focus on dessert when people are arguing." He sighed.

"Who cares about them? Keep going."

"Lark." He gave me a look as I sat up and took my hand, pushing his head down. "Get back to being unholy, you twit."

He gave me a look as I sighed. Fanfuckingtastic. My twit sister's arguing distracted my boyfriend. That was it. I moved off the bed, but not before smacking him with my leg. Hey, he deserved it for letting some tools distract him.

I walked out of my room as Luna and Major argued. I walked down the stairs. "Is there a reason you two are bickering like an old married couple?"

"There's no reason. Major was leaving," Luna said with her arms crossed.

"Okay, not that I want to play Doctor Phil and all because he's not all that attractive, but can't you two twits get it together?"

They both look at me.

"Look, no offense, but you need to stop running around with the poor me attitude," I told Luna. Then I looked at Major. "And you, I get the entire celibate thing, but did you think this through when you got together with my sister?"

They both stared at me.

"Okay, new tactic. You like Major. He likes you. Now kiss each other, you twits! It isn't freaking Barney, and I don't enjoy having to explain things to you."

Major left. Well, that didn't go as planned. How the hell did Uncle Nixon do this with my parents? It was time to ask him.

I FaceTime Nixon because this always goes over so much better than texting.

It rang, making that weird musical beeping noise. Then Nixon appeared on the screen. "Hey, Larky," Uncle Nixon said.

"I will ignore that."

"Okay, hi, twit. Better?"

"Larky isn't so bad." I rolled my eyes.

"Do you have a point? It's not that I don't enjoy hearing from my favorite niece."

"Okay, I'll get to the point. How did you get Ma and Dad together?"

He rubbed his chin. "Good question because I'm still trying to figure out how the hell that happened. Oh, that's right, your nana decided we needed to get them together."

"Okay, I don't know how that helps my situation."

"I thought you and that twit already did the ring around the dipstick?"

"It's not Maverick and me."

"Well, it can't be Lyric because I'm sure Michael already popped her weasel. Lex already had his cherry popped. Forget Lakin. That girl popped her and the others' jack in the box a long time ago. That is a sight I will never unsee."

"Focus, Uncle Nix."

"Oh, right, continued."

"Thanks? Anyway, it's Luna."

"Heh? You called me about that lunatic?"

I didn't know how to respond to his question.

"Larkin, you know Luna is Uncle Nolan's territory. Both were in a rush to get their cherry popped. I swear, he is the only fifteen-year-old that has ever gotten me and him arrested for being in a whorehouse."

That was a new development. I don't even think I want to know.

"Um, okay, I'll ask Uncle Nolan." I ended the call before saying bye. Yeah, I expected a tongue lashing later. Nixon hated it when people hung up on him.

I called Uncle Nolan. He answered. "Yo, baby Nash."

I gave him a look. What the hell was wrong with my uncles?

"Uncle Nolan, I need your help with Luna and Major."

"Let me think." He rubbed his chin. "Yeah, I got nothing."

"You're an enormous help." I sighed.

"I got arrested in high school and almost got the family killed in Hawaii for my antics."

My jaw dropped open.

"Bye now." He hung up.

I was batting zero for zero. Okay, I called Noah next and got two for the price of one with Nathan included.

"Hey, little Maggie," they said.

My right eye started twitching. "I need advice."

"Which one is it?" Nathan asked.

"Luna," I said.

"We're out," they said, hanging up. Nathan and Noah were no help.

Finally, I went to the last person I wanted to ask. I made the call and sighed.

"Hey, baby girl," Dad said.

"Hey, Dad."

"What's up?"

"It's Luna."

"What's wrong with Luna?"

"Major and her like each other, but all they do is argue. I'm worried about her, Dad."

"Lark, sometimes, couples have to figure it out."

"I hate seeing her so miserable. I know she feels alone, and it's not like my uncles are an enormous help." I sighed.

"Because sometimes, two people have to find their way back to each other."

"How did you and Ma work it out?"

"We let our hearts lead us. Sure, everyone gave us a push, but it was up to us to make it work. All you can do is give them a push, but it's up to them to work it out. It's time to call in reinforcements."

I thought about it and knew what I needed to do. "Thanks, Dad. I figured it out."

"Anytime, baby girl." He smiled.

Then Lakin came into the house. "Is that Dad?"

"Yep," I said.

"Hey, Daddy-O."

"Lake, never call me that," he told her.

Then Lyric came downstairs. "Hey, Daddy-O," Lyric said.

"Are you kidding me?" Dad asked.

She shrugged.

Then Luna hopped in, and Lex walked over to us. "Hey, Daddy-O," they both said.

"Mags! Our kids are comedians!" He spoke.

"What else is new?" Ma asked, walking over to the screen. "My babies!"

"Hey, Ma," the five of us said.

"I miss you, crazy kids!" She was bouncing around.

"Woman! Settle down!" Dad told her.

She stopped. "I will not. These are my babies, which I will remind you, you haven't been doing a superb job protecting them. Nashville, I didn't go through hell and back to have your brothers see things they shouldn't see and deliver our babies. And Lex, thanks for taking your sweet time getting here," she said.

Lex rolled his eyes as we teased him.

The five of us sat around, talking to our parents for a while. They missed us, but we missed them, too. Between the two of them, they brought us into the world and loved us. We couldn't have asked for better parents.

After we hung up, Luna got up, and I stopped her. "Luna?"

She looked at me.

"I know it may not seem like it, but the reason you fight with Major is you're afraid he won't love you enough to stay," I said.

Our siblings got up and walked over to us.

"It's not that. I'm tired of feeling disappointed and unwanted," Luna said.

We stood there. Luna was insecure, and nothing we could say or do would change that. Only one person could help, and he wasn't here.

"Thanks for helping, but I'll be fine." She sighed, turned, and went upstairs.

We needed more help, a lot more help. The only way Grays know best, the Gray way with a bit of Harper thrown into the mix. A smile curled upon my lips.

CHAPTER 40

THE GRAY/HARPER'S WAY

Larkin

If you want to get things done, then sometimes, you need some finesse. Unfortunately, we weren't those people. Have you met us?

We took a page out of Dad's and our uncle's book and thought kidnapping is the best way. It wasn't too hard with Luna since her leg made her an easy target.

Major was a little more challenging as a target. Michael, Kaiden, and Kain got him pinned down as Maverick stuck him with a needle.

"This is for your good, brother," Maverick, administering pharmaceuticals to Major.

When Major calmed down, he stood up only to fall right on his face.

"What the hell did you give him?" Michael asked Maverick.

"It's a liquid tranquilizer." Maverick shrugged.

"How much did you give him because he looks dead?" Kain asked.

"Well, I had to calculate his weight by height to figure out the dosage. I'm sure I gave him the right amount," Maverick said.

"Are you sure? I'm sure he's comatose." Kaiden smacked Major twice.

"I could have been off a tad," Maverick said, moving his fingers.

"Great, people will think we're trying to kill him." Michael sighed.

"Yeah, about that, I haven't had my training in pharmaceuticals yet," Maverick told Michael.

"That is even better, tool," Kain said.

I opened the door and walked into the house. "Dare I ask why Major is on the floor out cold?" I asked.

"Your twit of a boyfriend knocked out Luna's potential boyfriend or husband. We still haven't decided how this will go down yet," Kain said.

I rolled my eyes. You ask them to do one thing, and they can't even do that right.

Lyric walked in a few minutes later. "What's taking so long?"

I pointed at Major, who was lying on the floor, enjoying his coma nap.

"What did you do to him?" Lyric asked the others.

"Oh, numbnuts here gave him a tranquilizer. We're deciding whether we'll go to jail or not." Kaiden gestured at Maverick.

Lyric looked at me. "Your boyfriend is a tool."

"Well, so is yours," I said.

"Get him up and to the car. You know the minute Dad finds out, he'll kill us," she said.

"It doesn't matter because I'm sure Dad will hurt us," I told her.

"Your dad? Oh, no, no, no, try our dad, especially when he finds out we didn't even ask him to help us," Kain said.

"Well, by doing this, they'll understand why," I said.

Michael bound and gagged Major.

"But then again, the shit will hit the fan."

Michael picked up Major. "Damn, he needs to drop a few pounds."

"Who cares? You need to work out more and build bigger muscles," I said as they all looked at me. "Move along, people. We're on a mission."

We left and got into our cars. Yep, Dad would kill us for this stunt.

*****

Major

I woke up with a nasty headache. I found myself on a bed in a hotel room. As I raised my hand to rub my eyes, that's when I saw it. I did a double-take.

"It's about time you woke up," Lakin said.

"What's happening, and why am I wearing a wedding ring?" I asked everyone.

"Major, say hi to your wife," Larkin said, stepping aside.

My jaw dropped as I saw Luna sitting there. "Wife?" I asked everyone.

"Wife, love muffin, ball, and chain. Whatever you chose to refer to her as," Larkin said.

I sat there, stunned. Luna sat there, not knowing what to say.

"See, we heard you have this hang-up with premarital sex, so we helped you both out with your dilemma. We figured if you two got married, then you both would do the deed, and we can all move on," Kain said.

I put my head in my hand.

"That isn't what I want," I said.

"Then what do you want?" Maverick asked.

Before I answered, Luna said, "See, even married, he doesn't want me. No one wants me." She stood as I lifted my head. "Can we go home so I can call Dad and ask him to help me annul this?" She hobbled to the door as I stood up.

"Can I have a few minutes alone with Luna?" I asked everyone.

"Better make them good because the minute Dad finds out, we're in deep shit," Larkin said.

They left Luna and me alone. I walked over to her.

"It wasn't my idea. I didn't know my family would do this," Luna said, trying not to cry.

"I know, but it's time we talk."

She furrowed her brows.

"Look, I have met no one like you in my life. You drive me crazy, but if it were anyone else, it wouldn't be the same."

"Then why don't you want to be with me?"

"Who says I don't want to be with you?"

"You keep pushing me away. I get affectionate, and you put on the breaks. It's like no matter what I do, you find me repulsive."

"Is that what you think?"

"Well, don't you?"

That's when I decided enough was enough. "Ah, hell." I broke the gap between us as I crashed my lips into hers. Things got heated as we started removing clothes. When we were down to our underwear, I picked her up and carried her over to the bed.

Then it hit me. Shit. I stopped.

"Now what?" She looked at me with furrowed brows.

"One a minute." I held up a finger, went to the door, opened it, and someone handed me a condom. I grabbed it and closed the door. Then I went to open it, and a line of them fell. Well, okay, then.

I walked back over to Luna and pulled her panties off, then pushed off my boxers. I opened one and rolled it on, then climbed between her legs and lined myself up at her entrance. I pushed inside of her as she gasped. I stopped as she groaned.

I captured her lips with mine as I started thrusting until I picked up the pace. Okay, this was freaking amazing. I had never experienced pleasure like this in my life. It was way better than my hand. I could get used to it.

Before I knew it, we both groaned against each other's lips.

*****

Larkin

"I can't believe you gave him six condoms," I told Maverick.

"Well, considering this is his first time, he'll need them."

Then Major said, "Holy shit, that was amazing!"

We all laughed.

"When are we going to tell them the truth?" Lakin asked.

"Soon, because knowing Luna, she'll call Dad," I said.

"Dad is so going to kill us," Lex told us.

"That's why you get to explain things to him," I said, tapping him on his cheek.

He gave me a look, and I smirked.

Yeah, I was a stinker, but as Grays, we have no issue throwing everyone under the bus. If anyone knows anything about us, Lex is the first to get tossed under the bus.

We figure we would let Major and Luna get acquainted and tell them the truth later.

CHAPTER 41

FREAKY FRIDAY: A HALLOWEEN CHAPTER

Larkin

Did you ever wake up to the sound of someone pounding on something? No, I mean, pounding on a door. Because we did and also yelling, don't forget the yelling.

We went downstairs, and Lyric opened the door, then slammed it shut. I rubbed my eyes as Lakin went into the kitchen. Lex sat down on the couch while Frick and Frack joined him.

"I know this might be a dumb question. Who's at the door?" I asked Lyric.

"No one." Lyric shrugged.

I gave her a strange look.

"No one, except for Dad, Ma, and our uncles." She shrugged.

That jolted us awake as we heard a crash in the kitchen.

"Don't mind me!" Lakin said from the kitchen.

Bam! Bam! Bam!

"Lyric Lucille Gray! Open this damn door!" Dad said.

"That would be a no!" Lyric said.

"Excuse me? I don't think I heard you!"

Lyric motioned for us to leave.

"No, Espanol!"

"That's no Spanish, you twit!" Nixon said.

"My bad! I shouldn't have taken French in school!" Lyric said.

Lyric needs to quit talking, like right now. We all tried to make the great escape only to have Dad and Nixon catch us. Well, shit.

"March," Dad told us, pointing to the living room. He forced us to sit down. Yeah, Dad was a tad angry.

Then the door opened. Michael, Maverick, Piper, and Mia walked in with Nathan and Noah. They took a seat across from us.

Okay, we were missing Nolan, which means he's with Major and Luna.

Dad and Ma stood in front of us, and they didn't look happy.

"Explain to me how my little Luna bell married a man who I wanted to rip off his arms and beat him with said arms." Dad had such calmness that it scared the dead.

"Well," I said.

"Larkin Patricia Gray, shut it!"

Well, okay, then.

"It was their idea," Lex said, throwing us under the bus.

"Lex Nathaniel Gray? Do you think you had nothing to do with this?" Ma asked him.

We looked at him, and he said under his breath, "No."

They stood there, and I'm sure they were drilling a hole in our heads with their glares.

"Oh, for Christ's sakes. Major and Luna didn't get married!" Lakin said.

"What?" They asked.

"We made them believe they got married so that Major would get laid, and Luna wouldn't feel like a loser," Lakin said.

Oh, Lakin, noooo.

"Let me get this straight, Lakin Margaret Gray. You and the rest of those tools convinced those other twits that someone would marry them so that they can have sex." Dad said.

"Well, when you put it like that, it sounds terrible," Lakin said.

"Uh, Lake?" Nixon asked.

"Yeah?" Lakin asked.

"I would shut up right now if I were you," Nixon said.

We all placed our faces in our palms. That was so not good.

Then the door opened, and in walked Nolan, Major, and Luna, not looking happy. Oh, shit.

Luna hobbled over to us. "So, you made us think we got married so that we could get it on."

"Well, we thought it was a superb idea." I shrugged.

"You're unbelievable! I can't believe you! How dare you think this was even okay?" Luna gave us a tongue lashing. Then the words flew. Whoa, our sister has some colorful language.

When she finished, Major laid into us. Fantastic. That's what I needed before I had my coffee.

Major got done voicing his opinion, and man, was it loud. We apologized until everyone's facial expression changed.

We stopped and looked at each other as they all started laughing. We sat there, confused.

"Wow, you're a bunch of tools. Do you know that?" Nixon chuckled.

"Say what?" Lakin asked him.

"Luna called us after her, uh, a special night with Major. She said she and Major got married. When we checked with Nixon, he said there wasn't a way someone could marry them without proper paperwork," Ma said.

"So, we know they aren't married," Dad said. "It doesn't mean I'm still not going to beat Major's ass for deflowering my baby."

Major kissed Luna. "I'm going to go."

With that, he bolted with Dad hot on his heels. Good luck, Major.

"Damn, look at big brother go," Nathan said.

"Run, Major, run!" Noah said as they both laughed.

Luna hobbled over and took a seat with us. "Look, I know you all want to help, but sometimes, you can't fix things. The people in the relationship have to fix it themselves."

"We know Lu, but we hate to see you unhappy," Lake said to her.

"I know, and I couldn't ask for better siblings. Sometimes, I need to figure things out on my own," Luna said.

Then Dad and Major walked into the house, and Major was holding his nose. "Major and I came to an understanding. He won't be a tool, and you'll be less insecure, so he doesn't become a major tool. Isn't that right, Major?" Dad smiled as Major nodded.

"Come on, Major, I'll get you something for your nose," Ma said, leading him into the kitchen.

If I didn't know better, it was freaky Friday here because things were so nutty.

*****

Since it was Halloween, we hung out and watched scary movies. Our parents and uncles stayed and watched them with us.

I got up and went into the kitchen to get something to drink when there was a knock at the door. Now, who was it? I opened the door, and one of Clay's goons stood there.

"What do you want?"

"I came to deliver a message," Glen said.

"What kind of message

"Watch your back."

Why would I want to listen to a guy when he is causing us issues?

"Is that it?"

"Larkin, I'm warning you. Derek Crandall has plans. I can't believe Clay was even helping him."

"Considering what you and those other tools did to Maverick, why should I believe you?"

"Because I'm telling you that stuff is going down. You don't have to trust me. But I'm telling you now. It's a matter of time before Derek strikes. Look, I have to go."

That was odd, but whatever.

Maverick walked into the kitchen. "Who was that?"

"Glen."

"What did he want?"

"We need to watch our backs."

As much as I didn't trust Glen, one thing was for sure. I didn't trust Derek even more. That guy was a loose cannon.

We went back into the living, and I took a seat. What Glen said bugged me. The conversation was making it hard to focus on the movie. Did you ever have a terrible feeling about something? Yeah, that was happening to me. Things would get bad soon enough.

CHAPTER 42

ARE YOU FREAKING KIDDING ME?

Larkin

With our little shenanigans behind us, okay, I wouldn't say little. We lied to Major and Luna, kidnapped them, and drug them, so they could finally get their freak on with each other. Yeah, we're little stinkers. Have you ever been in a house where all someone does is whine about the other person?

That was Luna and us. Sex doesn't fix things. It helps, but it doesn't fix things. Even after everything, Major acted like a tool. I thought Lakin would beat him to a pulp when she got her hands on him.

Why do you ask? I'll tell you and save a lot of time. Major, the tool he is, decided to explore his options, I.e., other girls. That didn't sit well with Luna, and we all had to deal with it. Because of it, the situation put us at odds with the Harpers. Thanks, Major, you twit.

Let's rephrase that. The situation put Maverick and me at odds since he's Major's brother. The others stayed out of it. Have you ever heard of my brother's keeper? Well, that didn't apply to Maverick. Then again, the same can be said with Lex and us.

I'm getting off track. Damn Lex.

"Tell me how this situation is my fault?" Maverick asked me.

"Because your tool brother popped Luna's cherry, then dropped her. Marriage, my ass."

"That's Major! It's not me!"

"Yeah, I don't care. Do you have any idea what it's like to listen to Luna cry herself to sleep?"

"That isn't fair, Larkin. I don't control what my twit brother does. He's an adult."

"How about, oh, hey, Major, you twit, we didn't set you up, so you can nail anything that walks?"

"Are you freaking kidding me? Do you know how ridiculous you sound?"

"Not any more than you do." I crossed my arms.

"You know what, when you grow up and learn that not everything is your problem, then we'll talk."

"Are you breaking up with me?".

"What do you think?"

I stood there, shocked. I knew the minute I opened myself up and things were good, it would crash on me.

I said nothing but turned and walked away, leaving Maverick's room and house. I'm done.

I headed home. As soon as I entered, everyone looked at me. "Lark?" Lyric asked.

"Maverick broke up with me," I said.

They all stared at me.

Then, I saw Luna. My anger boiled. "And it's all her fault!"

"What did I do?" Luna asked.

"I tried to help you. Because of helping you, I got dumped. I should have stayed out of it." I glared at Luna.

"I didn't ask you to involve yourself. You did that all on your own!"

"Whatever. Poor Luna gets whatever she wants. Big crybaby."

"Lark, that's enough," Lyric said.

"Shut up, Lyric! You're as bad. How you get guys to fall at your feet is beyond me," I said.

"Enough, Larkin," Lakin said.

"Bite me," I said.

Lakin smacked me across the face, shocking me and everyone else. "Lark."

"Don't touch me!" I turned and ran up to my room. That slap triggered what happened with Roger. I slammed my door shut and locked it. I needed to hide, finding a safe place, and get away from Roger.

Then I heard pounding.

"Lark! Open up!" Someone said.

No, I wouldn't let him get me. The minute I opened that door, it was over.

"Larkin! Open up!" Someone said.

"Go away, Roger!" My tears fell.

"Roger is dead, Lark!" Someone said.

"No, he's standing there with you!"

"No, he isn't."

"Yes, he is." I started crying.

Then someone slammed themselves against the door, causing me to go into a full-blown panic mode. I wouldn't let Roger get me.

I ran to the window and opened it. I climbed out of the window when the door busted open. "Lark!" Someone said, but I didn't care.

I jumped.

*****

"Ahhh!" I spoke.

"Larkin!"

I was screaming.

"Larkin! Wake up!"

I opened my eyes and glanced around the dark room. Someone's hands touched me, and I panicked.

"Lark! It's me, Maverick!"

"Maverick?"

"Yes." He reached over, turning on the light.

I found myself in his bed.

The door opened. Michael and Lyric stood there.

"Lark?" Lyric asked.

"Luna and Major. Tool. Roger. Jump. We broke up. Maverick." I couldn't even form a proper sentence.

"Larkin, you're not making any sense," Maverick said.

Then I told him everything, and the three of them looked at me.

"I'm not crazy!" I spoke.

"Baby, you're not crazy. It was a frightful dream," Maverick said.

The dream seemed natural. I clenched Maverick's tee shirt as he pulled me to him.

Lyric called Luna and put her on the speaker. "Do you know what time it is?" Luna asked Lyric.

"Where's Major?" Lyric asked.

"He's next to me. Why?"

"Well, Larkin thinks he's out, catting around on you."

Then we heard Luna say, "Major, you tool! Are you freaking kidding me?"

"What are you babbling about?" Major asked.

"You better not be out chasing skirt on me!"

"And deal with Lakin? No, thank you."

"Satisfied now?" Luna asked us.

"Yeah, go back to sleep, crabby," Lyric said, hanging up.

Maverick held me in his arms, trying to calm me, but the stress was getting to me. I was having nightmares, which meant one thing, no sleep. With the whole Derek and Clay situation, it was getting to me.

Out of the five of us, I stressed out the most. Lyric dealt with problems while Lakin used anger. Luna showed her insecurities. Lex took things as they came. I bottled up everything until I landed back in the hospital. That was never a good thing.

It would prove to be a significant hurdle for me when everything caved in on me at once. Something would send me over the edge and shock everyone.

CHAPTER 43

ALL HELL BREAKS LOOSE

Larkin

After that night, I wasn't sleeping. I would use any means to stay awake. It also affected my eating. I can eat like there is no tomorrow and have a tough time gaining weight. Lyric and I have a metabolic disorder.

Between pills and coffee, I fought to stay awake, which resulted in me not eating. Every time I closed my eyes, a nightmare would happen. It was always Maverick and me breaking up, and it terrified me.

That was until my worst fear and nightmare came true. Because of the lack of sleep, pills, and not eating, I kept snapping at Maverick. Finally, he had enough, ending things with me.

I was a mess. My grades were dropping, and all I could do was cry. My siblings tried to help, but it didn't matter. No one could help me. That's when they called for help.

I shuffled through papers when I heard a knock at my door. I didn't bother to answer it and kept busy. The door opened.

"Lark," Dad said.

"Oh, hey." I smiled.

Dad and Nix stood there.

"I'm looking for an assignment. I know I put it here somewhere." I searched through my things.

"Larkin," Dad said.

"Oh, here it is." I pulled out a piece of paper. "Can you look at it and tell me if it's good?"

They took the paper and looked at it. It was nothing but scribbles. Nixon and Dad looked at it, then at me.

"Is it good?" I waited for their approval.

"Lark," Nix said.

I took the paper from them. "Yeah, it's terrible. I knew it was bad. It's another thing to add to everything I'm terrible at." I tried to keep my composure.

"Larkin, when's the last time you slept?" Dad asked me.

"Oh, no. I can't sleep. See, if I sleep, then it comes," I said in a whisper.

"What comes, sweetie?" Nix asked.

"The evil. It comes and takes Maverick away, but then again, it did." I shrugged.

They stood there with furrowed brows.

"See, I knew Maverick would get tired of me. I was right. So, ha! I told Lyric, but she kept saying to give him a chance. I did, and it still blew up in my face. Well, now everyone can leave me alone," I said.

They moved towards me. I backed away as Dad and Nix got closer.

"You can't make me love anyone. I refuse!"

Dad grabbed me as I fought him, but he held me tight. I struggled in his arms until I quit fighting.

"Why won't he love me? Is it because I'm damaged?" I asked.

"Oh, baby girl, he still loves you, but you need help," Dad said as I cried.

Nixon rubbed my back, offering me comfort.

After many tears and talking, they persuaded me to go home. I would finish out the semester with an incomplete in my classes. FML.

They helped me pack. Once I had two bags packed, they took the bags out of the room. I walked out of the room and saw everyone downstairs. I walked down the stairs with Dad and Nixon following me.

My siblings and cousins, along with the Harpers, stood there. Maverick wasn't there. They watched as I walked out of the house behind Dad and Nixon and got into Dad's car.

I looked out of the car window as they watched us pull away. I placed my hand on the window as they all waved. I saw my sisters and Lex look at me, heartbroken.

"Baby girl, it'll be okay," Dad told me.

I sat back, wanting to believe that, but I wasn't so sure.

*****

We pulled up to a hospital. I knew what this meant since I've been through it. We got out of the car and walked inside.

Dad filled out some forms. Once he finished, I gave him and Nixon a hug.

A nurse led me to a room as I set my stuff down. I was so tired. They brought me something to help me sleep. I took it and fell asleep in my clothes.

It didn't take long before I had a nightmare. The staff subdued me and ended up strapping me down. The staff gave me something to make me sleep. More and more horrors happened, but I needed sleep.

Then Jordan visited me. He took over my case and offered me compassion I wasn't receiving here.

He helped me work through the nightmares. We also talked about everything that was going on in my life. He ended up prescribing me anti-anxiety medicine. He said it should help calm me a bit.

His therapies helped me understand what sets off my triggers and how to cope with them.

Jordan also limited my visitors. He thought it would help my therapies better if we kept a small number of people visiting. I had to agree with the fewer distractions.

My parents and Nixon visited me. When I saw them enter the visitor's room, I hugged them. They filled me in with what was happening at home and school.

"How's Maverick?" I asked.

"He's good from what everyone tells me," Dad said.

"Oh." I didn't want to press for more information.

"Larkin."

"It's fine. I doubt Maverick's thinking about me. I mean, who wants to date a nut job." I shrugged, faking a smile.

"Hunny, I'm sure things will work out," Ma told me.

"I doubt it. It's time to move on. I was so much better off without dating anyone. It's fewer headaches. I mean, then Dad wouldn't have to worry," I said.

"Lark," Nixon said.

"It's fine. I mean, who wants to date a damaged person, right?" I asked.

They all looked at me with concern.

"I'll focus on getting better and trying to make up the classes I missed. I figure if I double up, then I can still graduate on time. Don't worry about me. I'll be fine," I said, trying to convince myself.

When you try to convince yourself that you're okay without someone, you aren't. I missed Maverick, but it didn't matter. I'm damaged and knew it. I focused on getting better, so I could go home for Christmas, at least.

*****

Over the next few weeks, I got better and went home. Thank God. I hated hospitals. Dad and Ma brought me home after they released me. Everyone was arriving in a few days.

I went to my room when I got home. I sat on my bed, fiddling with my thumbs. I didn't know what to do with myself. I glanced at my phone, tempted to call Maverick, but I didn't.

Screw it. I dialed Maverick's number. The minute I heard his voice, I hung up. Stupid, stupid, stupid. He doesn't want to talk to you. He broke up with you and has a girl now.

That thought burned me. My phone rang, and Maverick's name showed up on caller ID. I answered it.

"You're a freaking tool! I can't believe you moved on that fast! You suck monkey balls!" I hung up. Tool. I'm going to get some food.

*****

Maverick

"Well?" Michael asked.

"I'm in love with a nut." I sighed.

"Well, go get her, tool," Lakin said.

"Oh, I'll get her all right, but I have a plan." I grinned.

"Why will his plan blow up in our faces?" Michael asked Major.

"Because it's Maverick. Everything blows up in our faces," Major said.

I put my plan in motion and enlisted help. Considering it was me, I'll need luck.

CHAPTER 44

A CHRISTMAS FULL OF PROMISE

Larkin

I sat in my room, drawing in my sketchbook. Everyone was coming home for Christmas break, and I was single. Oh, yay!

The front door opened. I listened to everyone but stayed in my room. My door opened, and I glanced up from my sketchpad to see Dad standing there.

"Are you coming downstairs, Lark?"

"Nah, I'm good." I continued drawing.

Dad furrowed his brows.

It didn't matter because my sisters and brother ran him over to get to me. They jumped onto my bed, causing it to crash.

"Mags! It looks like Lark needs a bed!"

"Again?"

"Yep!"

I couldn't help but laugh with them as they hugged me. I missed my fellow quints. It was like a part of me was missing.

"You look good," Lyric said.

"I feel better. Jordan helped me a lot." I smiled.

"We're glad you're doing better," Lakin said.

I saw Luna's leg. "You got your cast off."

"Yes, I did, and Major loves that I'm not as hindered." She grinned.

"Oh," I said.

"Lark," Lex said.

"It's fine." I shook my head. "I have to get used to being single, right?" I got up. "I'm going to head to the bakery." I dashed out of my room, leaving them there. I didn't need a pity party or them to feel sorry for me. Maverick and I broke up, simple.

As I walked down the stairs and grabbed my coat, my parents stopped me. "Lark? Where are you going?" Dad asked.

"To check on the bakery, making sure we have everything stocked," I told them.

"Hunny, it's Christmas Eve," Ma said.

"It's fine. You all have a good Christmas. At least, without me, I won't ruin it for everyone else since that's what I'm good at." I zipped my coat.

"Baby girl," Dad said.

"It's okay, Dad. I'm used to it. I'll see you later." I left as my siblings came down to see the door close.

I made my way to the bakery. I pulled in and got out of the car. I walked up to the door and unlocked it. Then I clicked on the light and locked the door behind me. I walked to the back and removed my coat, getting to work.

I didn't mind staying busy because it kept my mind off things. I pulled down supplies, replenishing everything. I made sure it was ready for when Ma and Dad opened it.

As I stocked, I thought about things. How did it get this bad? Oh, I know, because that's my life. First, it's Roger, then Maverick, and everything else.

As I stocked, there was a knock at the door. I saw Uncle Nixon standing there.

"Lark! Unlock the door, or I'll end up with blue balls!"

I set the stuff down and walked over to the door, unlocking it.

Nixon entered, and I closed the door.

"Explain to me why you're a twit and not home with your family?"

I rolled my eyes and sighed. "I enjoy working."

"Who the frick are you talking to, Lark? No one enjoys working on Christmas Eve. Don't be a tool."

"I do."

"On what planet? Oh, that is right. It's Larkin's fantasy world."

"Did you come here to bust my chops?"

"Now, why would I do that? I came here for another reason."

"What's that?"

"That." He pointed behind me.

I turned, and my family stood there, along with the Harper family, including Maverick.

My mouth dropped open as Maverick walked towards me. "You make it very hard to surprise you, so I guess I'll have to do it here."

I stared at him as he got down on one knee. He pulled out a small velvet box and opened it.

"Larkin, before you fly off the handle because you do that often."

Everyone laughed. I had to agree with Maverick.

"This is a promise ring. I knew you needed help, so I had to break up with you for you to get it. I hated to do it, but there wasn't a choice. Now, I'm on a bent knee, promising never to let you go. To be there, through thick and thin, no matter what you say or do. I also promise to one day replace it with an engagement ring. Larkin Gray, will you accept my promise ring?"

I stood there in shock, not expecting that. There was only one thing I could say.

"I suppose, you twit." I sighed. He gave me a look, then I smiled.

He slid the ring onto my finger before crashing his lips onto mine.

I didn't realize how much I missed his lips. Things got a bit heated before Dad broke it up. Way to ruin a moment, Dad.

"No offense to anyone, but can we go back to Nash's and celebrate Christmas like normal people and not in a bakery?" Nixon asked us.

They all agreed and started to leave. I grabbed my coat only to have a person wrap their arms around me. Their head nestled into my neck. "I missed you."

"I missed you, too, but if you ever tell anyone, I said that I'd deny it."

"Meh, what else is new?" Maverick shrugged.

I couldn't help but laugh. I was in love with a twit, but at least, he was my twit.

After I got my coat on, he took my hand and led me out of the bakery as Dad locked up. It would be a good Christmas, and I couldn't be happier.

When we got back to school, the shit would hit the fan in the worst way, shocking everyone.

CHAPTER 45

IT'S GETTING HOT IN HERE

Larkin

We returned to school. Because of the incomplete, I took with my classes. It put me back a semester. That meant I wouldn't graduate with everyone else. It was that or take summer classes. I took summer classes. There was no way that I wasn't graduating with my siblings.

As for Maverick, he's still a twit, but he was my twit. When we got back to school, we wasted no time making up. We couldn't while I was home. I'm not Lakin, for crying out loud.

After our many, many rounds, I laid on his chest, circling my fingertip.

"I missed this." He stroked my arm with his fingertip.

I glimpsed him. "What? Sex?"

"No, you." He smiled.

I couldn't help but smile.

"It's crazy that you had to break up with me so I would get better," I said.

"Because you're so damn stubborn."

"And you're so dramatic." I rolled my eyes.

Mav tickled me until we fell out of bed, tangled in blankets. We hit the floor with a thud. Damn Maverick.

Then we heard a crash. We both looked at each other and scrambled to get out of the blanket with minor success. We kept tripping over each other until we got free and dressed.

We walked down the stairs, and I hid behind him as he grabbed a bat. We crept down the stairs, and he shushed me. You don't have to tell me twice. That's all I needed to do was announce to a crazy psycho killer I was here. I'm sure he won't ask me if I want a damn sandwich.

A sandwich sounds excellent now. Focus Larkin. You need to take care of a killer, not fill your stomach.

As we got closer, we saw a shadow, and Maverick swung. They ducked as he hit a lamp, breaking it.

"Jesus! Mav!" Someone said.

I ran over and turned on a light, stepping on a piece of glass. I screamed as I flicked the switch.

"Major?" Maverick asked.

"Yeah, what the hell is with the bat?"

"We thought there was an intruder, considering everyone left."

"Don't mind me while I'm freaking bleed to death." I hobbled over to the couch, leaving a blood trail along the way.

Maverick walked over and took a seat, lifting my foot. "Be right back." He dropped my foot, causing me to groan in pain. My boyfriend is a tool. Who the hell does that to someone who's injured? Oh, that is right. He does.

He returned with a first aid kit. He took a seat and lifted my foot so he could remove the broken glass from it.

"Explain to me why you broke the window, leaving the broken glass on the floor when you have a key," Maverick asked while working on my foot.

Is it wrong that he's turning me on? Focus Larkin.

"I forgot my key," Major said.

"So, you thought, breaking in would be a better alternative? What happened to picking up the phone and calling me." Maverick cleaned my foot.

That is still hot. Okay, Larkin. Settle down.

"I tried, but you don't answer when you're unholy." Major shrugged.

"Only because I haven't been unholy for the past few weeks." Maverick sighed. He finished my foot. Still hot. Down girl.

"I thought you were with Luna."

"Well, I was, then I wasn't."

"Explain."

"Her aunt is in town."

"And you left her?" I asked.

"Well, yeah, no guy wants to deal with that emotional wreck," Major said.

"If you don't get your ass over there, you won't have a girlfriend," Maverick told him.

That is so hot. What the hell was wrong with me?

"Turn around and go back. Make sure you take lots of chocolate. I'm sure you'll end up with blue balls after this episode."

Well, damn. I was ready to jump Maverick.

"Fine." Major left.

"I swear, sometimes, my brother is clueless."

"Is it bad that I want to jump you?"

His face snapped towards me as he got up and picked me up.

"Maverick!"

"Who would I be to deny someone their needs." Maverick carried me upstairs. Figures.

Note to self, never be around Maverick when he's making sense. More important note, never tell him I want to jump him.

I woke up the next day, aching. That damn Maverick. Okay, fine. I enjoyed myself a little too much. Sex was so much better when someone gives a shit about you. Not throw you into a room and beat the hell out of you. That thought made me frown.

"What's with the look?" Maverick asked.

"I'm thinking about how different sex can be." I shrugged.

"Lark, he'll never hurt you again."

"I know. It makes me angry."

Maverick caressed my face. "I know, and I wish it would have never happened to you, but we can't change the past. All we can do is move forward with people who love and care about us."

He's right, although I'll never tell him so. I know what Maverick would do if I did. He would get all excited and make an enormous deal out of it. Have you ever seen him make a tremendous deal out of something? I have, and it's not pretty.

"Lark, you have me now, and I made a promise which I intend to keep." He played with my fingers.

"So, you promise to keep being a twit? Good to know." I smirked.

He rolled his eyes. "I'll give you twit." He started tickling me as I squealed. Before I knew it, we became unholy. I don't think it matters what we did. The unholiness would abound between us.

Sometimes, you must go with it. I hate to say it, but Maverick proved me wrong in so many ways. It made me glad because sometimes, we need someone to prove us wrong to know what's right.

Roger showed me the wrong way a guy was with a woman. Maverick showed me the right way. Who would have thought a guy who shoved me in the mud would be someone I would fall in love with when I was older? I didn't.

CHAPTER 46

SPRING BREAK FIASCO

Larkin

We traveled to the beach house in Myrtle Beach for spring break. It's crowded with everyone having to bunk together. Imagine all the cousins, the Harpers, and us together in one house. It wasn't pretty, but it worked.

I needed space. I couldn't deal with a lot of people. I know there are many people at my house, but we also have our rooms. Maverick is lucky. I love him because I don't enjoy sharing my space with anyone.

After we arrived and got settled, I was getting anxious. It happened a lot while growing up. The one person who could calm me down wasn't here, Dad. The next best thing is Lex because he was a mini version of Dad.

I became overwhelmed while Maverick tried to calm me. It wasn't working. So, he left.

I paced back and forth, feeling my heart beat out of my chest when I heard a voice. "Lark?"

I turned and looked at Lex. "Make it stop. I can't do this."

He walked over and wrapped his arms around me.

"Deep breaths," he said.

I buried my head into his chest while he held me as the others watched us.

"What's going on with her?" Maverick asked Lyric.

"Larkin is having a panic attack. It happens where there are many people in the same house. Dad is the only one who can reassure her. If he isn't around, Lex is the next best thing. Our brother is a twit, but he's Dad all the way."

"Okay, it's us, the family, and the Harpers. Think of it as Dad, Ma, and our uncles being here. What would they say?" Lex asked me.

"That I'm fine, and everything is okay," I said in a whisper.

"Yes. Now, we're here to have an enjoyable time and some fun. Relax, Lark. No one will invade your personal space."

I nodded, taking a deep breath and letting go of Lex. He looked at me with those steel-grey eyes, like Dad's. That was reassuring to me.

I looked past him and noticed everyone was trying to break their neck to leave except for Maverick, who gave them a weird look. I couldn't help but giggle.

He walked into the room as Lex handed me to him, then Lex left.

"I'm guessing we'll need an enormous house when we get married."

"A little."

Maverick chuckled and wrapped his arms around me as I did the same. I know it's foolish to act this way, but it happens. My family got it, so they understood. I mean, they're crazy.

Once I was okay, we changed and made our way to the beach. I loved the sand between my toes and hearing the water. It was so relaxing, especially after everything that happened.

Maverick and I walked hand in hand on the beach. I got to thinking about everything, including the future, which was odd. I was never one to think about the future or anything. Not the way my life had been going.

I thought about what it would be like to be married with kids or at least one kid — watching Maverick chase a little boy. It was nice.

"What are you thinking?" Maverick asked me.

"Who, me? Oh, nothing." I shrugged.

"It isn't nothing. What is it?"

"Okay, fine. I was thinking about us married. You're chasing a little boy."

He stopped and looked at me. "You're not pregnant, are you?"

"No, you twit, I'm not pregnant." I rolled my eyes. "I thought what it would be like."

He moved a loose strand of hair away from my face. "Kids, hmm, I like that idea." A smile grew upon his face. "I would love to see a kid with ocean blue eyes running around calling you mom."

I couldn't help but smile. "Are you sure?"

"You would make an exceptional mother."

For that, I hugged him. I never thought I would be a wonderful mom, considering everything that happened. I couldn't even keep my life together.

"Larkin, I know you don't think you would be a good mom. Trust me. Kids change everything, including your perspective."

"I heard. From what my uncles and grandparents told us. My parents had their difficulties, but things worked out when we came along."

"All people have difficulties. No relationship is perfect, but if it's meant to be, it'll be."

I wrapped my arms around his neck, kissing him. Maverick, being Maverick, made it crazier as he lifted me off the ground, kissing me back. Then ran towards the water and tossed us both into the ocean.

"Maverick!"

We both stood up, soaking wet.

"Did you expect anything less?" He shrugged.

I gave him a look and pushed him into the water. He grabbed me in the process and took me with him. My boyfriend is a royal tool.

While Maverick and I were duking it out in the water, my siblings watched from the beach.

"It's good to see her smiling, finally," Lex said.

"We all have to go through something horrible to come out better," Lyric said.

"Yeah, but no one deserves to go through that. Not even us," Luna said.

"But it strengthens us. Life isn't fair. It's cruel. It's how we all deal with it that counts," Lakin told them.

"True, but it also helps to have people there to help you through those tough times," Michael said, walking up with the others.

"What do you mean?" Luna asked him.

"Maverick took it the hardest when we lost our parents. Out of the four of us, his anger got the best of him. He was angry for a long time. It took him time to come to terms with it. Then Larkin came along, and it was like something changed inside him," Major said.

They watched as we laughed and fought in the water. It took two people who had been through hell to understand why they needed each other. It might have taken a while to get here, but we did, and I couldn't be happier. Well, more content in my way.

Maverick might be a twit, but he was my twit, and I'd be lost without him. I knew one day I would marry that man, and we would have a little one with ocean blue eyes running around loose.

Maverick would need a lot of raincoats in the meantime.

CHAPTER 47

THINGS ARE GETTING OUT OF HAND

Larkin

After spring break, we returned to school and started our next semester. In two months, we would finish up our sophomore year. Well, my siblings would. I had to take summer courses, drat. Thank God for online classes.

We still had to deal with Derek Crandall and his tool ways. That dude needs to get laid or a whack upside the head. My choice would be the second way.

Who the hell cares who someone loves? The heart wants what the heart wants. My heart wanted Maverick. Does that make sense to you? Because it sure makes little sense to me.

Anyway, I'm getting off-topic. At the same time, we're trying to get through our finals to head home and deal with Ma and Dad's unholiness. Yes, they're still unholy. Derek put his plan in action with what he had in store for anyone who was gay, starting with Clay.

*****

3rd person

"Hold him still," Derek said.

Two guys held onto Clay while Derek beat him.

"Now, you know it's for your good. It's not natural that you lay with man. I'm cleansing you, along with others. Will you comply?"

"Fuck you," Clay said, coughing.

"Wrong answer." Derek delivered another blow until Clay wasn't breathing.

"Derek, he's not breathing," one guy said.

"He should have listened." He shrugged. "Take him and tie him up in the main area. I want everyone to know that we don't welcome homosexuals here. This school needs to be returned to its appropriate pure state and rid of this abomination."

"Yes, Derek," they said, dragging Clay away.

Derek stood there.

"Now what?" Another guy asked.

"Now, we take care of those two unrighteous people with the last name Gray and Harper. I can't believe those families allow such awful behavior."

"But Lakin Gray can hold her own. The last time you went after her, she kicked your ass," another guy said.

"That's because it didn't prepare me. Now, I will be, and you'll help me. Lakin Gray will see what happens when she takes on a man." He smiled.

*****

Larkin

The next day, I got ready for class. Lakin and I had a course together, so we made our way to campus. We talked on our way to class only to stop dead in our tracks.

Tied to a post was Clay bloodied and bruised.

"What the hell?" I asked.

Lakin walked over and checked for a pulse. "Shit, he's alive. Lark, call 911!" Lakin untied him.

I called 911, then helped her with Clay. As we helped remove his ties, I shook my head. As much as I hated Clay, I knew who did this and why.

The paramedics arrived, as did Michael and Maverick.

"Lark!" Maverick said. He ran over to me as I stood there and hugged me. "Are you okay?"

"I'm fine, but Clay isn't," I told him as his brows furrowed. "Mav, I know we hate him, but I also know things are getting out of hand."

"I don't care about the past." He shook his head. "I care about you."

I know the situation worried him, but I was more worried about my sister and Mia.

We watched as they took Clay away, as did others. That was a message to everyone, which meant things were about to get ugly between Derek and us. Like they weren't already unpleasant.

Since we knew Derek had it out for us, we took precautions. That also meant letting Dad know. There was a lot of cussing on the other end of the phone. Dad has some colorful vocabulary.

That also meant we would get a visit from Dad and our uncles. Yep, things were about to get interesting soon.

Now, we had to stick close to each other. If Derek wanted to go after us, he would. We couldn't let that happen.

*****

Kain and I had a class together. We came walking out after it finished to meet the others when Derek stopped us.

"Well, look what we have here, boys, if it isn't Lakin Gray." Derek smirked.

Is he for real? This tool is dumb.

Kain and I shrugged.

"Did you enjoy my message?" Derek asked with a stupid grin.

"You mean the one where you beat someone to death, but he didn't die?" I asked him.

His smile faded. I waited until he figured it out, then he said through gritted teeth, "Larkin."

"Ding, ding, ding, give the homophobe a cookie, you stupid tool." I gave him a look as Kain snickered.

He snapped his head towards Kain. "What are you laughing at, boy?"

"Well, first, that was funny. Second, I'm not your boy. Third, you're a backwoods tool that has no clue about shit. Must we keep going?" Kain asked.

Kain and Derek's interaction should be interesting.

Derek got in Kain's face. "You know nothing about me."

"That is incorrect. I know everything about you. Derek Crandall, age twenty, comes from Mary and Greg Crandall. Uses his religion to cover his homophobic ways when he's hiding the fact he loves men," Kain said.

I was trying not to laugh as Derek started fuming.

"Let me continue. You're crude and ignorant. People don't like you, and only the sheep follow you. Why? Well, I don't know why. Because all you do is bring people down. It's unfortunate because if you think about it, you're a delusional, selfish prick."

Did I mention Kain was studying psychology? Yeah, it surprised us, too.

"I would watch yourself," Derek told him.

"I would watch yourself, considering you have a lot of pissed off Grays and Harpers. That includes my dad, my uncles, and, oh, her father, which is Nash Gray. See, Uncle Nash has a nasty temper, worse than Uncle Nathan. Don't believe me. Go after one of his kids." Kain shrugged.

Derek looked at us. That was the thing about Dad. Nothing would stop him from protecting Ma and us, even if he were a tool when Ma and he were dating. According to our uncles, his love ran more profound than the oceans for the six of us. So did his protective nature.

As Kain and I walked away, he asked me, "Do you think it worked?"

"Oh, I know it worked. If it's people like him, they become sloppy. Roger became sloppy, and Derek will too, now that he's riled."

When you poke an animal, it'll attack. It will have devastating consequences. We would learn this soon.

CHAPTER 48

TROUBLE IS BREWING

Larkin

As the semester was ending, we worked to draw Derek out and take care of him. Dad and our uncles were arriving to bring us home from school. We didn't let sleeping dogs lie. We were causing more problems than we needed.

Have you ever poked at a vicious animal? You poke them enough. They finally attack. That's what happened between Derek and us. Except it came at someone else's expense, Mia.

Our dad and uncles showed up.

*****

Lakin

Mia and I were on our way to the house when that tool and his cronies' sheep grabbed us.

He knew I would beat his ass and pepper-sprayed me so they could take care of business. And business they took care of Mia and me.

"My eyes!" I said, trying to stop the burning.

"Lakin!" Mia said.

They grabbed, gagged, and bound Mia, doing the same with me.

Derek ordered them to load us in the car so they could finish the job.

*****

Larkin

We heard a knock at the door.

"I'll get it!" I said, opening the door. "Dad!"

"Hey, baby girl," Dad said.

I threw my arms around him. Damn, I missed him. He hugged me.

"What, no hug for me? What am I, chopped liver?" Nixon asked.

"Nope, a tool," Dad told him.

Nixon rolled his eyes.

I laughed as I let go of Dad and hugged Nixon.

"Hey, sweetie," Nixon said.

It was great to see them both. The others came in and saw them. My siblings crashed into Dad, almost taking him out while Kain and Kaiden greeted Nixon.

"Where's Lakin?" Dad asked as they let go of him.

"She should be back soon. She and Mia are on their way back," Lyric told him.

Dad looked at Nixon, who arched an eyebrow. "Why do I have a nasty feeling?"

"Because I do, too," Nixon said as they both left.

What the hell? We all looked at each other and followed them. Something tells me that Dad's feelings are correct.

*****

Lakin

The cars stopped, and Derek got out along with the others. "Grab them," he said, which they did.

They yanked both Mia and me out of the car. I tried to focus but was having difficulty because of the pepper spray. They held me as Derek looked at me.

"Not so tough now, are you? Now, you can enjoy the show." He clicked his teeth as they held up my head, making me watch.

He turned and walked over to Mia, who was struggling, bound, and gagged. Two guys held her as Derek looked at her. "You would be so pretty if you weren't so disgusting. But that's okay because I'm about to make this world beautiful again, starting with you."

He hauled off and hit Mia as I screamed against my gag, trying to break free. I watched in horror as Derek attacked Mia, hearing his fist connecting to her head and body.

It was a sight unseen as he carried out his punishment to the point Mia stopped moving. They dropped her as her body hit the ground. Then he turned and stalked over to me.

"One down, one to go," he spoke, hauling off and punching me.

As he brought his hand up again, someone caught him. "Bad move on your part."

He cocked his head to see Dad holding his hand as Nixon stood there. He saw his cronies on the ground with Nathan, Noah, and Nolan taking care of Mia.

His eyes widened in sheer terror. Dad yanked him away and beat the hell out of him. "You want to go after my kids and others? Let me show you what happens when you go after a Gray!" With that, he delivered blow after blow while Nixon helped me.

Once I was free, I ran to Mia, cradling her. "Come on, baby, wake up. Don't go to sleep." I rubbed Mia's face while Nolan and Nathan called 911.

Dad got off Derek and looked at him. "Enjoy prison, you piece of shit."

*****

Larkin

We all arrived, appearing from our cars as Michael bolted towards Mia. "Mia!" He ran over and pulled her from Lakin. "No, Mia! Don't leave me!"

Paramedics, police, and fire showed up afterward. It was a mess. They took Mia and loaded her into the ambulance as they worked on her. She was still breathing.

They tended to the others while police questioned Dad, Lakin, and our uncles. Michael went with Mia to the hospital.

We stood there in shock.

Once Dad finished with the police, he walked over to us, fuming.

"Why? Why would you do this?" Dad asked.

"We didn't do this," I said.

"Larkin! There are always consequences to your actions!"

"He has been attacking us! Don't you remember what happened to Luna or Larkin?" Lyric asked.

"You don't get it!"

"Then explain it to us, Dad, because no one was doing anything!" Lex said. Damn.

"People like Derek Crandall don't care! They will attack! Nathan has the evidence we needed to put him away, but because of this, he may get off!" Dad said.

We stared at him.

"Sometimes, you need to use your head. Sometimes, the Gray way isn't always best," Dad told us.

"Then sometimes, you have to fight, or they hurt you," Luna said.

We all looked at her.

"So, you know what it feels like to have your arm snapped or leg broken? The pain and fear you carry even after it heals? You might be mad at us, but what he did was ten times worse."

He looked at Luna with furrowed brows as Nolan walked up. "Nash?"

"What?" He asked Nolan.

"Someone said Clay Walker died," Nolan said.

Our eyes widened.

"They said the injuries he sustained in his attack were too much. The same could happen to Mia."

Oh, God, I thought to myself.

"I have to go," Lyric said, turning and walking away with us following her.

Lakin walked up to Dad. "Be angry but realize he started it. I'm going to the hospital and hope Mia will pull through this." She followed us.

Nixon looked at Nash. "Now, it is not the time to be a tool, brother."

"Shut it, Nix!" Dad said.

"No! How about you go be a dad to your kids who need one right now?" Nixon asked, then walked away.

They say, with every action, there is a reaction. With everyone's response, there is a consequence. It was a hard lesson to learn, and we needed to learn it.

What happened next would shock us all.

CHAPTER 49

REPERCUSSIONS

Larkin

After that night, there was a somber tone with everyone. Lakin was angry, which was understandable. None of us wanted to leave until we found out if Mia would wake up. Michael stayed with her every single day, as did Lakin.

The doctors said until she wakes up, we wouldn't know how much damage Derek inflicted. That's if she wakes up. God, let her wake up.

Anger has a funny way of doing more harm than good. It doesn't do anything for anyone. I know. After what Roger did, I let anger control me.

Nixon was right. We needed Dad and not his anger, but him. He knew that too but wouldn't admit Nixon was right.

Things were tense but didn't stay that way once Ma arrived, along with Nana, knocking some sense into him. Yeah, never piss off a Gray woman. It never ends well.

Mia woke up but had trouble. The attack damaged a part of her brain, affecting her speech and motor skills. She recognized us but understanding anything was rough. It would be a long uphill battle for her.

Michael stayed with her while we left to go home. He would bring her home after they released her. That didn't sit well with

Lakin, but Ma and Dad convinced her that Mia would be home. It didn't help that she snapped at everyone.

It would be a long summer if Mia didn't get better.

*****

Maverick

We were packing while Michael was at the hospital with Mia. Piper and I were trying to pack our stuff without Major.

"Maverick! Where is your twit brother?" Piper asked.

"How the hell should I know? I'm not his damn keeper."

"He's supposed to be helping since Michael is with Mia."

"Then hunt his ass down." I kept packing my stuff.

Piper called Lex to find out if Major was there but got met with a no, and Luna wasn't there either.

*****

Larkin

Luna's disappearance didn't sit well with our parents. I told them they were somewhere getting unholy.

Yeah, that comment earned an annoyed look from Dad.

What we didn't know was those two twits were doing while we were busy. When we found out, all hell would break loose. Hell, it wasn't a feeling. It would break loose.

I'm sure they made a stupid decision.

*****

We finished up, and Luna walked through the door, carrying a coffee. Dad gave her a look. "How long does it take to get a coffee?"

"Well, I went for a coffee, and so did Major. Then we got married. Now, I'm here," Luna said.

"Married!" We all said.

"You know when a man and woman say I do, and the judge pronounces them husband and wife. Married." Luna shrugged.

Well, the shit hit the fan.

Dad walked up to her. "Please tell me you're joking."

"Nope," Luna said.

Everyone runs because Dad will lose his shit.

"Hold up before you lose your shit. Excuse me." Nixon looked at Luna. "And what is wrong with me marrying you two twits?"

"Since my siblings faked a marriage for us and everything that happened, Major and I decided life is too short to waste any more time. So, we got married," Luna said.

I can't believe how calm Luna is acting.

Dad was ready to throttle her, and she irritated Nixon because he didn't marry them. It gets better and better.

Ma and Nana stepped in with Ma keeping Dad at bay, and Nana was a voice of reason.

"Nashville, you won't hurt this girl for making an adult decision," Nana told Dad. Whoa, I've never heard Nana call

Dad his full name. Shit got serious. Then she turned to Luna. "Okay, sweetheart, since you want to make an adult decision for whatever reason. Now you can be an adult, which means living with your husband."

"What?" Luna asked.

"Well, marriage is an enormous deal. I should know. I married your grandpa at eighteen. The minute we got married, I lived with him, as you will live with your husband."

Luna's face dropped.

"Marriage isn't a game. It's a commitment. You want this serious commitment. Now you can deal with it. Now, call your husband over here, so we can explain a few details."

Damn, Nana was serious.

Luna called Major, and he came over, along with Maverick and Piper. He told them about what they had done, and it didn't thrill them, either. Michael doesn't know yet. That should be fun.

Major and Luna sat on the couch while Nana, Dad, and Ma stood in front of them as Nana spoke.

"So, you both got married and want to be adults. When we marry in this family, we leave our family's home and live with our spouses, which you two will do. I hope you figured out a home and jobs, considering you'll need to pay for school. Don't forget essentials like utilities, rent, and food."

Luna's face dropped, and Major looked like he would hurl. Note to self, make sure you have things in place before getting married.

Luna glanced around, then at Major. "Our idea was dumb."

"You think? Michael will kill me," Major said.

"We rushed things."

"Or we rushed, period."

"What's that supposed to mean?"

"It means that we always rush things. Our relationship has never been normal." Major sighed.

"Then we should call it a day." Luna stood up and looked at our parents and Nana. "Is there a way to get an annulment?"

"Yeah," Dad said with furrowed brows.

"Good, because when we get home, we'll get an annulment. Major doesn't have to worry about me anymore." Luna turned and ran up the stairs.

Nana took a seat next to Major. "Do you love my granddaughter?"

"Unfortunately, yes. Luna drives me crazy, but I can't imagine not having her in my life," Major said.

"Rule one of marriage is you never give up."

"Huh?"

"She means you fight for her, you twit," Nixon said.

Major looked at Nana, then at Ma and Dad.

"I'm so confused," Major said.

Ma took a seat next to him. "Major, let me explain something to you about the Gray family. They mean well, but sometimes, their way is a lot different from people's understanding. It's not that we don't think you and Luna would make a wonderful couple," she said.

"Speak for yourself," Dad said, earning a look from Ma and Nana.

Ma rolled her eyes. "Prove it to Luna every day and stop being a tool like her dad."

"Hey!" Dad said.

"She has you there, brother," Nixon said.

Dad rolled his eyes. "Okay, I'll admit I had my toolish moments, but I made things right. Give me some credit."

"Oh, son, we know, and we know you're still a tool," Nana said.

We laughed.

"I won't win this, will I?" Dad asked.

"Nope," they both said.

"Fine, Major. I have one thing to say to you," Dad said.

He looked at Dad. "Welcome to the Gray family. Oh, and if you hurt my daughter, I'll hurt you." With that, he walked away.

He looked at Ma, and she said, "Welcome to the world of Grays, as we know it. Good luck, Major." She patted his shoulder and got up.

He looked at Nana. "Don't worry. It gets better." She smiled, then got up.

Then he had to face us. He looked at us as we looked at him. Oh, Major, you twit. Good luck. You'll need it.

CHAPTER 50

RETURNING TO HOME

Larkin

We returned home. It was nice to be home with everything that had happened, except I had to take online summer courses. Oh, yay!

I was busy signing up for my summer courses. Major had to tell Michael he got married, which Michael didn't take well. He also had to deal with Mia's care, who had to stay in a care facility to work on her motor skills and speech.

Thanks to Derek, she suffered a brain injury. The best part was he's rotting in jail. Yeah, the police had enough evidence on him to override all the shit we did. Plus, he murdered Clay Walker, which he calculated. The police charged Derek with first-degree murder.

I hope someone shanks his ass, and he rots in hell. He deserves to burn with all the other creeps living there.

Yeah, life was peachy at home.

*****

Lakin

I got up, showered, and dressed before heading to see Mia. As much as I wanted to be angry, I had other things to worry about now. Fucking Derek. I hope you have fun in prison, you bastard.

As I put on my shoes, Dad poked his head into my bedroom. "Do you want something to eat?"

"Nope, I'm on my way to see Mia."

He stepped inside my room. "Lake, you need to eat."

I stood up. "What I need is for my girlfriend to be okay and come home. Now excuse me, I'm going to see my Mia." I walked past him. I didn't mean to sound harsh, but all I cared about was Mia.

I went to the hospital to see Mia. They had her in a therapy room, working on her motor skills. I walked in and over to her. I crouched, and she looked at me. Then she smiled, which caused me to smile.

"Lak-in," she said.

"Hi, Mia, my baby."

"I m-iss y-ou."

"I'm here now."

Mia knew me, but her speech and motor skills were terrible. The doctor explained they would improve, but she would be different. How different? We didn't know. It was a wait-and-see process.

At least, she knew who I was. I stayed with her most of the day. Then Michael pulled me out into the hallway.

"How is she?" I asked Michael.

"The doctor said she would have a slow recovery, but there is more."

"What else?" I furrowed my brows.

"The part of the brain that Derek injured deals with maturity. Because he damaged it, Mia will have a childlike personality."

"What does that mean?"

"It means you'll need to be patient with her. She won't understand adult things like she did."

"Such as?"

"Such as relationships and sex. To Mia, it'll scare her."

"It's not about sex, Michael. To me, that doesn't matter. What matters is my heart is in that room." My voice broke as he pulled me into a hug. Mia was my heart. The other stuff didn't matter to me. She did.

Mia followed the therapist. I knew that we would get there. It was a matter of when it would happen.

To continue in The Gray Sisters: Expect The Unexpected.

Made in United States
Orlando, FL
04 March 2023

30694564R00193